D0073188

MAO'S MILITARY ROMANTICISM

MODERN WAR STUDIES

MAO'S MILITARY ROMANTICISM

China and the Korean War, 1950–1953

Shu Guang Zhang

UNIVERSITY PRESS OF KANSAS

Published by the University Press of Kansas (Lawrence, Kansas 66049), which was organized by the Kansas Board of Regents and is operated and funded by Emporia State University, Fort Hays State University, Kansas State University, Pittsburg State University, the University of Kansas, and Wichita State University

Library of Congress Cataloging-in-Publication Data

Zhang, Shu Guang.
Mao's military romanticism : China and the Korean War, 1950–1953 / Shu Guang Zhang.
p. cm. — (Modern war studies)
Includes bibliographical references and index.
ISBN 0-7006-0723-4 (cloth)
1. Korean War, 1950–1953—China. 2. China—Politics and government—1946–1974. 3. Mao, Tse-tung, 1893–1976—Military leadership. I. Title. II. Series.
DS919.5.Z45 1995
951.904'2—dc20 95-18532

British Library Cataloguing in Publication Data is available.

Printed in the United States of America

10 9 8 7 6 5 4 3 2 1

The paper used in this publication meets the minimum requirements of the American National Standard for Permanence of Paper for Printed Library Materials Z39.48-1984.

For my wife, Ni Chen

CONTENTS

MAPS AND TABLES

Maps

Tables

ACKNOWLEDGMENTS

The preparations for this book have taken much longer than I initially expected. However, there are several people whom I would like to thank. My mentor Professor John Lewis Gaddis urged me to work on a military history of Chinese intervention in Korea shortly after I had finished my dissertation under his supervision. My friends William Stueck, Chen Jian, and Xue Litai, all widely recognized and respected Korean War specialists, spent a great deal of time reading my manuscript. They not only shared their own materials with me but, more significantly, provided me with extensive written comments on drafts of the manuscript. Reviewing the manuscript for the University Press of Kansas, Roger Dingman challenged me to think more carefully about my conceptual framework. My colleage and friend Jon Tetsuro Sumida, a well-known military historian, generously gave me advice and moral support. Greg Hanna, a former student of mine, assisted with style revisions.

I also greatly benefited from a John M. Olin postdoctoral fellowship in the field of military and strategic history at Yale University (1990–1991). Offering the best training in military history, professors Paul Kennedy, Michael Howard, Jonathan Spence, Gaddis Smith, and George Andreopoulos all encouraged me to complete this project. An earlier version of chapter 2 was published in the *Journal of American–East Asian Relations* 1 (Spring 1992).

A word on the orthography. Attaching no political significance to it, I used *pinyin* for the names of all Chinese persons and places with the exception of Chiang Kai-shek and Kuomintang. The spelling of the Korean place names, both North and South, came from maps of Korea printed by the U.S. Army Corps of Engineers map service, which contain both Chinese characters and English transliterations. The spelling of Korean person-names followed the commonly accepted forms used in the English literature on Korea—for example, Kim Il-sung and Syngman Rhee.

Finally, to the many unnamed friends and colleagues who have contributed to my thinking about and writing of this book, I express my appreciation. Of course, I am responsible for any errors that it might contain.

ABBREVIATIONS

CCP	Chinese Communist Party
CMC	Central Military Commission
CPGC	Central People's Government Council
CPPCC	Chinese People's Political Consultative Conference
CPV	Chinese People's Volunteers
KMT	Kuomintang
NBDA	Northeast Border Defense Army
NKPA	North Korean People's Army
PLA	People's Liberation Army
PRC	People's Republic of China
ROK	Republic of Korea
UK	United Kingdom
US	United States
USSR	Union of Soviet Socialist Republics
US/UN	United States/United Nations

1. INTRODUCTION

The Chinese military intervention in the Korean War in late November 1950 greatly surprised the world. The surprise derived not only from the fact that the one-year-old Communist regime, the People's Republic of China (PRC), took the risk of engaging in a conflict with a superpower, but also from the fact that the Chinese peasant soldiers routed the best forces that the Americans could then gather. Twenty-eight hours after the Chinese People's Volunteers (CPV) had launched a massive offensive south of the Yalu River, General Douglas MacArthur "despondently" reported to Washington that the United Nations forces in Korea faced "an entirely new war." [1]

China's armed intervention was risky for the new regime. The country's war-waging capabilities seemed limited, for the nation's economy had yet to be reconstructed after the devastation of the bitter and costly civil war between the Communists and the Nationalists. Also, the new government's political rule had yet to be consolidated, since the Kuomintang (KMT) retained control of Taiwan and strategically important off-shore islands along the east China coast.

Moreover, the People's Liberation Army (PLA), a gigantic force of some 5 million, was an "anachronism": it lacked naval and air weaponry; its soldiers were irregulars; its command structure was rudimentary; its equipment was a hodgepodge and largely obsolete.[2] Unlike the wars fought against the Japanese and the Nationalists in the 1930s and 1940s, in this war Chinese Communist forces would fight on foreign and unfamiliar terrain. Moreover, they were to fight against the United States, the most advanced industrial nation in the world, and to combat an enemy force that enjoyed vastly superior air, naval, and ground firepower.[3]

It is undoubtedly central to students of the Korean War to analyze, from both military and strategic perspectives, *why* and *how* China intervened in order to fill a gap concerning the international background of the conflict.[4] More important, since the Korean War has been China's only prolonged conflict with a superpower, it would help to understand the basic factors that shaped Beijing's defense and foreign policy behavior.[5] Although not quantitatively or qualitatively comparable to the studies of the American intervention, scholarly accounts of the Chinese intervention are far from fruitless.[6] Indeed, previous English-language analyses have superbly assessed the origins of China's involvement, and it is interesting that Beijing's decision to intervene is "generally treated sympathetically."[7]

A predominant argument is that China was under threat. Allen S. Whiting,

Map of East Asia (Source: *Central Intelligence Agency. Reproduced courtesy of the University of Chicago Libraries)*

in his pioneering 1960 classic, *China Crosses the Yalu*, emphasizes the starkness of the political and military choices confronting Beijing in the second half of 1950. Primarily relying on the editorials of Chinese Communist Party (CCP) newspapers and journals and Beijing's radio broadcasts of the early 1950s, Whiting argues that the CCP leadership merely responded to what seemed an unambiguous, compelling threat to its security.[8] Using almost the same materials but discussing the relationship of different aspects of the war to China's military and foreign policy, J. H. Kalicki, Melvin Gurtov and Byong-Moo Hwang, and Gerald Segal have separately reinforced Whiting's thesis. They stress that, in the four months between the outbreak of the conflict and Chinese intervention, Beijing was preoccupied with national unity and therefore was initially concerned with pursuing the liberation of Taiwan. According to this analysis, problems of economic reconstruction also made China shy away from entanglement in military ventures in Korea. The CCP supported gains for the communist world, these authors argue, but not if it required China to abandon its primary objectives of national unity and reconstruction. Only after MacArthur's successful landing at Inchon in mid-September and his subsequent advance toward the Yalu in early October did the Chinese leaders begin to reconsider their priorities. Under the Whiting model, then, an imminent threat to China's border security compelled the PRC to intervene.[9]

In the 1980s, a new group of scholars emerged that, in most cases, relied on interviews with Chinese participants. Despite the variation in their sources, these scholars draw many of the same conclusions as the previous group did. For example, Anthony Farrar-Hockley interviewed former Chinese prisoners of war and reported that CCP Chairman Mao Zedong had redeployed tens of thousands of Chinese troops from the south to the northeast in the summer of 1950 just in case the United States expanded the conflict in Korea.[10] American diplomatic historian Warren I. Cohen talked to several former associates of PRC Premier Zhou Enlai during September and October 1986 in Beijing. The interviewees insisted that the Chinese were surprised by the outbreak of the war and that Beijing decided to intervene because the Americans were bombing Manchuria and U.S. ground forces were approaching the Yalu.[11] British writer Russell Spurr also conducted interviews, in China and elsewhere. In his book, *Enter the Dragon*, published in 1988, Spurr describes debates among the CCP leadership on the issue of intervention during August and September 1950. He depicts Mao as "more ready to contemplate intervention" than other top leaders because of his keen concern about national security.[12] Perhaps by far the most impressive study based on personal interviews is the article by Zhai Zhihai and Hao Yufan in *China Quarterly*. Citing information provided by "relevant people" in Beijing, Zhai and Hao claim that although the Chinese were unprepared for war in June 1950, by October Mao had come to see a direct conflict with the United States as inevitable. He believed that an American strike would probably originate in either Korea, Taiwan, or Indochina. Zhai and Hao contend that instead of waiting for the anticipated attack, Mao decided to move first and engage the Americans in Korea. The authors' most interesting insight centers on the relationships among Mao, Joseph Stalin, and North Korean leader Kim Il-sung. At the outbreak of the war, "only Stalin [not Mao] was informed of Kim's detailed plan and the possible date for action, since, in Kim's mind, the Soviet Union was the only patron capable of helping him to carry out his reunification plan." When Mao began to consider armed intervention in early October, he assumed he could count on Soviet air support. To his dismay, this turned out to be wishful thinking, for Stalin feared direct confrontation with the Americans. According to Zhai and Hao, when Mao concluded on October 13 that Chinese forces would have to enter Korea even without Soviet air cover, Stalin was "so moved by Mao's self-sacrifice . . . that he offered to increase Soviet aid on his own initiative."[13]

In the 1980s, primary documentation of Chinese involvement in Korea became accessible in China. First, selected works of top CCP leaders were published. *Mao Zedong Junshi Wenxuan—neibuban* [Selected military works of Mao Zedong—internal edition] printed in 1981, contained as many as sixty telegrams that had been drafted by Mao as instructions from the CCP Central Military Commission (CMC) from October 1950 to July 1953. Although some "security sensitive" information was sanitized, these documents provide remarkable new insight into Mao's thinking and subsequent decisions on Chinese intervention. An important addition to these telegrams is some twenty reports from CPV headquarters to Beijing; hidden in endnotes, the communiqués are often neglected by researchers. In the mid-1980s, Zhonggong Zhongyang Wenxian Yanjiu Shi [CCP Central Bureau of Archives and Manuscripts] began a lengthy project of compiling Mao's writings in *Jianguo Yilai Mao Zedong Wengao* [Mao Zedong's manuscripts since the foundation of the People's Republic of China]. The first four volumes, covering the period from September 1949 to December 1954 and coming out respectively in 1987, 1988, 1989, and 1990, contain several hundred telegrams written by Mao on behalf of the CCP Central Committee and CMC regarding the Korean conflict. Though still labeled as "internal edition," these reprints from the original Mao manuscripts, which remain classified, offer an unprecedented opportunity of probing into Mao's decision making during the war.[14] Meanwhile, the same bureau also compiled and published *Peng Dehuai Junshi Wenxuan* [Selected military writings of Peng Dehuai] in 1988 and *Nie Rongzhen Junshi Wenxuan* [Selected Military writings of Nie Rongzhen] in 1992. Since Peng was the CPV's commander in chief and Nie served as the PLA's acting chief of staff, they each played a crucial role in directing and organizing Chinese war operations. Their selected works, containing dozens of reports, memoranda, and speeches on Chinese intervention, are invaluable sources of information.

A number of reminiscences by senior Chinese generals and diplomats supplement these compilations. In memory of Marshall Peng Dehuai, who was ousted by Mao in 1959 and died during the Cultural Revolution, *Peng Dehuai Zishu* [Personal recollections of Peng Dehuai] was published in 1982. Peng's memoirs, originally written in the 1960s as an examination of his revolutionary experience, details his participation in the CCP Politburo's debate in early October on whether China should intervene and his command of the five consecutive offensives from October 1950 to May 1951. Peng candidly reflected on the difficulties of decision making and of conducting the subsequent military operations. In the early 1980s, Marshall Nie Rongzhen published his memoirs, in which he stressed how the prospect of direct Chinese intervention disquieted the highest level of the party and army; he also pointedly discussed the importance of logistics in modern warfare. More interestingly, Nie revealed that Kim Il-sung sent a special envoy to Beijing in January 1950 to arrange for the return of a large number of soldiers of Korean origin.

Three senior diplomats provide fresh insights into the often mysterious and complex relationships among Moscow, Beijing, and Pyongyang. Wu Xiuquan (the PRC's first deputy foreign minister in charge of Soviet and East European affairs), Shi Zhe (Russian language interpreter for Mao and Zhou) and Chai Chengwen (head of a Chinese intelligence group in North Korea in the early part of the war) published their memoirs, first in article form and then as books. Their commentaries document how Stalin, Mao, and Kim mistrusted and consequently manipulated one another. Adding to the current supply of sources is a series of memoirs on the Chinese conduct of the war written mainly by generals who participated in the fighting. Of particular interest are the recollections of former CPV deputy commanders Yang Dezhi, Hong Xuezhi, and Yang Chengwu; former directors of the CPV political department Du Ping and Li Zhimin; and former deputy commander of the 38th Army Jiang Yonghui. Each of these authors reflects on specific aspects of the war, such as combat operations, logistics, political control, field command, and communication. It is significant that, in writing their memoirs, most of those high-ranking officials relied not only on their personal papers but also on still-classified archives.[15]

New and primary material on Chinese intervention can also be found in the recently published official Chinese history of the war. Military historians at the Chinese Academy of Military Sciences, headed by Wang Hanbin, spent years writing an official account of the CPV war experience. A version for internal circulation was completed in 1985, and a revised edition of *Zhongguo Renmin Zhiyuanjun Kangmei Yuanchao Zhan Shi* [The war history of the Chinese People's Volunteers in the War to Resist U.S. Aggression and Aid Korea] became available to the public in 1988. Citing classified archives extensively, this volume is by far the most comprehensive assessment of the CPV war experience. Meanwhile, the China Today Editorial Committee, an official body organized to compile PRC history, completed another Korean War history book, *Kangmei Yuanchao Zhanzheng* [China today: The War to Resist U.S. Aggression and Aid Korea], in 1990, but its more important contributions are two volumes of *Dangdai Zhongguo Jundui de Junshi Gongzuo* [China today: The military affairs of the Chinese army] (1989), *Dangdai Zhongguo Haijun* [China today: The People's Navy] (1987), and *Dangdai Zhongguo Kongjun* [China today: The air force] (1989). These books contain useful details about the military conduct of Chinese infantry, artillery, tank, naval, and air forces on the Korean battlefield as well as discussions of equipment, rear services, and Soviet military aid. In addition, Beijing's military authorities produced four volumes of *Kangmei Yuanchao Zhanzheng Houqin Jingyan Zongjie* [A summary of the CPV rear service experiences in the War to Resist U.S. Aggression and Aid Korea] (1986–1987) and two volumes of *Zhongguo Renmin Zhiyuanjun Kangmei Yuanchao Zhanzheng Zhengzhi Gongzhuo Zongjie* [A summary of the CPV political work in the War to Resist U.S. Aggression and Aid Korea] (1985, 1989). Although such official accounts attempt to glorify the Chinese intervention, the information is generally insightful and cannot be found elsewhere.

Of the Chinese scholarly works on intervention, the most intriguing are Yao Xu's two articles and his book *Cong Yalujiang Dao Banmendian* [From the Yalu River to Panmonjum] (1985). Based on his own observations as a senior staff member at the CPV headquarters in the early 1950s and on some archival material, Yao emphasizes Mao's fear of a U.S. attack in the spring of 1950. Once the CCP chairman believed a confrontation with the United States was inevitable, Yao argues, Mao chose Korea as a more favorable battleground for China because its proximity to the Soviet Union would make it easier to obtain Soviet military aid. Yao also reveals that Stalin was reluctant to endorse China's entry because of the prospect of enlarging the conflict in East Asia.[16] Perhaps the best scholarly Chinese account is Xu Yan's *Diyici Jiaoliang* [The first encounter] (1990). Xu, a young military historian at the PLA National Defense University, concentrates on "reassessing the Korean lessons." While bestowing politically correct praise on Beijing's courage to engage the United States militarily in Korea, he casts serious doubt on Mao's "people's war" doctrine. The initial CPV offensive campaigns did suggest that the CPV troops had done well in mobile warfare. He points out, however, that optimism soon faded as Chinese soldiers were forced to fight a linear war along the 38th parallel with nonlinear experience and equipment. Superior U.S. firepower from land, sea, and air, along with superior communications and logistics, prevented the Chinese forces from achieving any substantial breakthrough. Believing that a nineteenth-century army cannot hope to win against a twentieth-century enemy, he calls for military modernization to be pursued at full speed.[17]

Two other studies worth mentioning are Ye Yumeng's *Heixue* [The black snow] (1989) and Qi Dexue's *Chaoxian Zhanzheng Juece Neimu* [Inside stories of decision making in the Korean War] (1991). Although historians have criticized his journalistic style, Ye presents important information based on his own access to the archives. For instance, he quotes in full a long telegram from Kim to Mao in early October in which Kim urged China to intervene.[18] Although rigidly following the official line, Qi is at his best when he examines how and why Beijing dismissed atomic weapons as not applicable to the limited war in Korea. More controversial is his insistence that U.S. forces deployed chemical and bacteriological weapons against the North Koreans and the Chinese during the war. Though the English-language literature has regarded the Chinese allegation as groundless, Qi challenges this verdict by documenting Chinese forays into antibacteriological warfare.[19]

Since the late 1980s, when these Chinese materials became accessible to Western scholars, more English-language studies of the Korean War have appeared. Jonathan Pollack's work is the first detailed treatment of newly published memoirs in China. Reconfirming the China-under-threat theme, however, Pollack argues that "Mao's paramount calculations concerned security." He contends that by the fall of 1950, the CCP chairman had already assessed the potential implications of intervention, including the prospect of a general war with the United States. In the end, Pollack concludes, Mao saw "little choice but to incur the costs and risks of war." As Pollack sees it, this decision to involve China led to "a risky but ultimately successful action."[20] Thomas Christensen and Michael Hunt are among the first to use Mao's telegrams printed in *Jianguo Yilai Mao Zedong Wengao*. Interpreting these cables, Christensen in particular argues that from October 1950 through January 1951, Mao demonstrated a considerable desire to expel all United Nation forces from Korea. Mao's aggressive strategy, Christensen believes, was founded not on his "overestimation" of China's military or economic strength but on his sense that "any other solution poses a greater threat to Communist

China's economic and political future." To Christensen, China and the United States were locked in "an unusual, long-term version of the security dilemma" and thus were mutually vulnerable to immediate attack.[21] Chen Jian, a Western-educated Chinese historian, has fleshed out this argument further but from a different perspective. Using the newly available Chinese materials, Chen examines the origins of PRC foreign policy and finds that Beijing's ambition was to restructure the existing international system in Asia. CCP leaders were overwhelmed by their "revolutionary diplomacy" as they weighed the pros and cons of intervention. Therefore, Chen asserts, they were deluded into thinking more about opportunity than danger in dealing with the Korean crisis.[22] A more recent book on Communist policymaking during the early period of the Korean War is *Uncertain Partners: Stalin, Mao, and the Korean War* by Sergei N. Goncharov, John W. Lewis, and Xue Litai. In light of the recently declassified Soviet documents and the spate of personal interviews, the authors contend that the North Korean invasion was planned, blessed, and assisted by Stalin and his generals and reluctantly backed by Mao at Stalin's insistence. The book shows how the interplay of Soviet and Chinese strategic preferences and the personalities of the Communist leadership shaped the Sino-Soviet alliance and China's participation. Given "the sloppy decision making, misperceptions, and perverted objectives," the authors conclude, China's intervention was reckless war making of the worst kind.[23]

Despite these new studies, the course of Chinese intervention remains obscure. There is no comprehensive assessment in the English-language literature of how China fought the war. Alexander L. George, in *The Chinese Communist Army in Action: The Korean War and Its Aftermath* (1967), summarizes the Chinese combat experience on the basis of what former Chinese POWs could recall years after the conflict was over.[24] Military historian Roy Edgar Appleman, in his remarkable studies of American combat in Korea, also sketches the Chinese performance on the battlefield. Yet because he compares the Chinese conduct of the war with a "classic military performance of antiquity" and sees China operating a "people's war" against a high-technology foe, Appleman's depiction is far from complete or accurate.[25] Although important in many respects, Mark A. Ryan's book, *Chinese Attitude Toward Nuclear Weapons: China and the United States During the Korean War* (1989), concentrates mainly on how the Chinese perceived and prepared for possible U.S. nuclear attack and how they organized countermeasures against the alleged U.S. chemical and biological warfare in Korea.[26] Since these scholars labored at a time when Chinese primary materials were inaccessible to the West, they hardly touched on Beijing's deliberations at the highest level during the course of the war.

Given the existing studies as well as the wide array of historical materials now available on Chinese intervention, the documentation exists to make a more comprehensive assessment of Beijing's decision making and military operations during the war. However, to advance our understanding of China's use of force behavior, a new conceptual framework is called for. According to Jonathan Pollack, the actual character of decision making is "rarely so rational or unambiguous," because leaders always have options, even if they do not always exploit them.[27] There is near-unanimity among Western scholars, as Rosemary Foot observes, that "Beijing's entry could have been averted and that the war could have been concluded in the autumn of 1950 if the United States had refrained from crossing [the 38th parallel]."[28] The same is true with the Chinese side. As the following pages will illustrate, different courses of action had been debated by the Chinese leaders, and each final decision was far from inevitable or unchangeable. There would have been a totally different result if Mao had given in to the nonintervention position strongly advocated by other top leaders at the Politburo meetings in early October 1950; if the well-known courageous commander Peng Dehuai had not agreed to replace the more cautious Lin Biao as head of the forces; if the leaders had hesitated to intervene when Moscow declined China's request for air support in mid-October 1950; if Mao and Peng had not abandoned the established strategy of overall defense in favor of an all-out offensive posture in November 1950; if Peng's later concern about the logistical difficulties had prevailed over Mao's desire to cross the 38th parallel and seize Seoul in late December 1950; if Mao had not forbidden the Chinese truce negotiators to compromise on the POW issue during the cease-fire talks in 1952.

There is reason to argue that, rather than merely responding to what was perceived as a compelling threat to their security, Beijing authorities chose to act aggressively, regardless of the calculated high risk and cost. To interpret why and how China resorted to force in Korea, this study will employ a *cultural* approach along the lines proposed by Akira Iriye: to see how aspirations, attitudes, beliefs, desires, idealism, sentimentality, and other "manifestation[s] of human consciousness" on the part of the CCP leadership shaped the Chinese intervention.[29]

History reveals that war is sometimes merely an idea that begins, and ends, in the minds of men. As John Mueller observes, over the centuries the opponents of war have counted its costs: in psychic terms, war is repulsive, immoral, and uncivilized, and in physical terms, it is bloody, destructive, and expensive. However, to statesmen, war can be an appealing option: "its psychic and physical costs may seem minor in comparison with political goals and objectives statesmen desire to accomplish."[30] Therefore, armed conflict has recurred in modern times because of war advocacy, because of enthusiasm for revolutionary violence, because of the belief that war will serve some cause of justice, or because of confidence in final victory. More important to this study, history reveals that this classic romanticism of war is especially attractive to militarily weak, economically underdeveloped nations that passionately hope to expand their power.

Mao, among other CCP leaders, seems to have accepted the conventional wisdom about the value of war. As a keen student of Chinese history, Mao came to grips with the violence of political struggle apparent in the nation's long history. As a self-conscious Communist, he accepted the teachings of Karl Marx, Friedrich Engels, and V. I. Lenin that violent revolution is the means by which the oppressed seize political rule. As a self-educated strategist, he perused the ancient Chinese art of war described by Sun Tzu and many others. He also read Carl von Clausewitz and saw the use of force as almost inevitable in politics. Based on his reading, Mao had formed a strong *belief* that "qiangganzi limian chu zhengquan [political power grows out of the barrel of a gun]." This conviction helped mold the basic elements of Chinese Communist revolutionary ardor and messiansim.

The Chinese Communist leaders learned from their experience that war and violence could settle disputes and, indeed, improve a situation. In the thirty years before the outbreak of the Korean War, the CCP had endured extremely difficult times, and armed struggle had always proved crucial as the party strengthened and grew. Eventually, the Communist triumph in the nation's three-year civil war (1946–1949) seems to have fostered their *enthusiasm* for the violence of war and revolution. The euphoria of victory, moreover, affected decision making. Buoyed by its enthusiastic public reception and bathed in martyrdom, the new regime desired to win at the international level after its national success. The Korean conflict appeared to be an opportunity for Beijing to show the Western world that China had finally stood up to foreign bullying and humiliation—and, to prove to the Eastern world that the Chinese Communists were not nationalists but reliable comrades within the socialist camp.

Yet Beijing's involvement in the war was the result of more than a moment's enthusiasm. It stemmed in part from the CCP's *confidence* in the people's war strategy. The man-over-weapon doctrine dictated that subjectivity, creativity, flexibility, and other human attributes were far more decisive in warfare than weaponry or technology. The Chinese Communists had little doubt about the validity of this doctrine since they believed it had been tested successfully in the anti-Japanese War (1937–1945) and the civil war. Following the precedent of these two conflicts, the leaders were confident that the use of relatively untrained and poorly armed soldiers against a militarily more sophisticated and modern enemy would succeed in Korea. By employing tactics of deception, stealth, and fighting at night, they thought that the Chinese army could overcome technological inferiority; by remaining mobile, mostly traveling by foot over rugged terrain, troops could overcome logistical difficulties. Moreover, as it took time and patience for man to beat weapon, the leaders believed that protracted warfare would bring final victory to a spiritually superior but technologically inferior army.

What made CCP soldiers stronger than their enemies in the leaders' minds were their high spirits and superior morale, sustained by the party's relentless political domination. From its inception, the CCP had maintained direct political control over its armed forces through ideological indoctrination—instilling such ideas as emancipation of all the oppressed, anticolonialism, anticapitalism, and anti-imperialism—and through organizational means—by establishing party committees and political commissars in the army and enforcing their absolute authority. To the CCP leaders, the communist ideology and organizational techniques had worked before and would continue to work. As the victorious PLA became highly politicized and the rank and file highly disciplined, the party embraced a view of the troops as brave, courageous, willing to endure hardship or sacrifice life, and thus capable of fighting any war, no matter how formidable.

Shaped by communist ideology, as well as Chinese political culture and military history, Mao's belief in human superiority over technological superiority suggested his romantic attitude toward the threat and use of force. This characteristic corresponds with what Stuart Schram has termed "military romanticism" in his description of Mao's thought on military affairs.[31] Predictably, however, both a romantic Mao and a pragmatic Mao are apparent in the unfolding events of the war. "Weapons are an important factor in war, but not the decisive factor," Mao wrote, explicitly making the distinction that, "it is people, not things, that are decisive." Yet over the years, the CCP had also championed the concept that, as Mao articulated, "strategically we should despise all enemies, but tactically we should take them all seriously."[32]

A central focus of this study is to illustrate how the interplay of romanticism and pragmatism shaped the CCP attitude, thinking, and behavior regarding the use of force in Korea. Despite its analytic emphasis, this is a military history of the Chinese Korean War experience from June 1950 to July 1953, which I hope will enhance the understanding of the twentieth century's "nastiest little war" and its profound impact on international relations in Asia during the Cold War.[33]

2. MAO'S MILITARY ROMANTICISM

"After three years," Mao Zedong proclaimed at the Twenty-fourth Session of the Central People's Government Council (CPGC) on September 12, 1953, "we have won a great victory in the war to resist U.S. aggression and aid Korea."[1] Mao stated, "We fought U.S. imperialism, an enemy wielding weapons many times superior to ours; and yet we were able to win and compelled it to agree to a truce."[2] As to the credit for the victory, Mao offered a twofold explanation. First, on a political level, "leadership is one factor; nothing can succeed without correct leadership. But we won mainly because ours was *a people's war*, the whole people gave it support, and the people of China and Korea fought shoulder to shoulder." Second, militarily, "[our] battle line . . . is truly a bastion of iron. Our soldiers and cadres are resourceful and brave and dare to look death in the face." To him, this was the "proof of the superiority of our people's democratic dictatorship."[3]

Despite China's obvious inferiority in military and economic strength, Mao was proud to have fought and held off the mightiest and wealthiest power in the world. He explicitly attributed China's "victory" to the function of human force. How did Mao conceptualize warfare in general? How did he formulate a romantic line on warfare? And what inferences can be drawn from Mao's military-strategic thinking that will illuminate Chinese involvement in the Korean War?

I

As a Communist, Mao inherited a distinctively Marxist-Leninist war philosophy. He accepted class struggle as the conceptual framework explaining the origins and nature of modern war. As long as there were classes with conflicting interests and different social strata, Engels asserted, the war between classes would never be extinguished. Lenin attributed the origins of war more directly to the existence of private property. To him, "war is, and will be invariably caused by private property."[4] Based on the teachings of Engels and Lenin, Mao articulated in December 1936 that "war is the highest form of struggle for resolving contradictions, when they have developed to a certain stage, between classes, nations, states, or political groups, and it has existed ever since the emergence of private property and of classes."[5]

Since the existence of class struggle made war inevitable, Mao regarded war and politics as identical. In May 1938, quoting Clausewitz that "war is the continuation of politics," he added that "war is politics and war itself is a political action; since ancient times, there has never been a war that did not have a political character."[6] In his view, only by examining war from a political viewpoint could one fully understand the essence of warfare, because "any tendency . . . to belittle politics by isolating war from it and advocating the idea of war as an absolute is wrong and should be corrected."[7] On the other hand, Mao stressed that war had its own peculiar characteristics and in this sense it should not be equated with politics in general. Violence was a particular feature of war lacking in other types of politics. "When politics develops to a certain stage beyond which it cannot proceed by the usual means," he wrote, "war breaks out to sweep away the obstacles from the way." By such reasoning he arrived at the aphorism that "politics is war without bloodshed while war is politics with bloodshed."[8]

The relationship between war and politics led Mao to believe that "victory is inseparable from the political aim of the war." As he explained, "History knows only two kinds of war, just and unjust. . . . All counterrevolutionary wars are unjust; [and] all revolutionary wars are just." Under any circumstances, those who fought for a just war would prevail because "the banner of mankind's just war is the banner of mankind's salvation."[9] The common masses would only support a war with such a political aim, but that support would create "a vast sea in which to drown the enemy, create the conditions that will make up for [one's] inferiority in arms and other things, and create the prerequisites for overcoming every difficulty in the war."[10] Therefore, all decisions about military intervention must be based on whether the war would be just or unjust.

The public would grasp a just war aim through political mobilization. Mao pointed out that even "a national revolutionary war . . . cannot be won without extensive and thoroughgoing political mobilization." Mao defined political mobilization as a means of "telling the army and the people about the political aim of the war. It is necessary for every soldier and civilian to understand why the war must be fought and how it concerns him." Moreover, he argued that "it is not enough to merely explain the aim to them; the steps and policies for its attainment must also be given, that is, there must be a political programme." Propaganda was the only way to get across one's political messages to the masses. Mao emphasized popular propaganda, especially that disseminated "by word of mouth, by leaflets and bulletins, by newspapers, books, and pamphlets, through plays and films, through schools, through the mass organizations and through our cadres." In his view, an effective propaganda program "must link the political mobilization for the war with developments in the war and with the life of soldiers and the people, and make it a continuous movement."[11]

Among the CCP leaders, Mao in particular regarded political mobilization for war as "a matter of immense importance." In his words, "to wish for victory and yet neglect political mobilization is like wishing to 'go north by driving a chariot south,' and the result would inevitably be to forfeit victory."[12] From the time that Mao assumed CCP leadership in the 1930s, one of the primary policy goals of the Chinese Communists had been to mobilize the support of the masses for their armed struggle. The CCP had devoted enormous efforts to political mobilization in the war with Japan and the civil war with the Nationalists. There was a consensus among the party leaders that the CCP's victories owed a great deal to political campaigns that had marshalled mass support.[13]

As part of its mass mobilization policy, the CCP leadership maintained a long tradition of politicizing its armed forces. Mao was among the few who consistently advocated that the CCP must build its own army and have absolute control over it through political indoctrination. The party created its own combat organization, the Red Army, on August 1, 1927, during the Nanchang uprising against the Nationalist government. As one of the army's senior commanders, Mao repeatedly urged the party leaders to pay close attention to how the army could be politicized. On November 28, 1928, he proposed to the CCP Central Committee that every one in the Red Army must receive a "political education . . . [in order] to become class-conscious." He reasoned that having "learned the essentials of distributing land, setting up political power, [and] arming the workers and peasants, etc. [the soldiers must] know they are fighting for themselves. . . . Hence they can endure the hardships of the bitter struggle without complaint." The responsibility for this political education must rest with "the system of Party Representatives" in the army. Once party branches were organized at the company level, it was the task of the party representatives to "see that the soldiers' committee carries out political training, to guide the work of the mass movements, and to serve concurrently as the secretary of the party branch."[14]

To Mao, it was essential to keep up the troops' morale through the cultivation of group solidarity and a spirit of unity among the rank and file.

Condemning "the purely military viewpoint" within the army, he pointed out in December 1929 that the party must actively attend to the military. All military questions must be discussed and decided on by the party before the rank and file received them; and the party must "draw up Red Army rules and regulations which [will] clearly define its tasks, the relationships between its military and its political apparatus, the relationship between the Red Army and the masses of the people and the powers and function of the soldiers' committees, and their relationship with the military and political organizations."[15] When Mao was the political commissar of the Fourth Red Army, he spent several months with the 2d Brigade, teaching the political officers how to treat the soldiers as brothers and friends, how to act as role models in observing disciplines and enduring hardships, how to get the soldiers to willingly adopt measures of self-discipline and self-education, how to help the soldiers correct mistakes through encouragement or punishment, and finally, how to execute rewards and penalties appropriately. Those methods had dictated the party's political work in the Red Army ever since.[16]

After obtaining complete control of the CCP political and military leadership in the 1930s, Mao did not neglect political mobilization in the military. In his "Problems of Strategy in China's Revolutionary War," written in December 1936, he regretted that his busy schedule prevented him from finishing a chapter on the party's oversight of the army.[17] In early 1944, Mao instructed the CCP's director of the political department, Tan Zheng, to draft a Central Committee document to guide the political work in the army.[18] Tan wrote the first draft, and Mao and Zhou Enlai revised it several times. Finally on April 11, the CCP Central Committee published its "Report on the Issues of Political Work in the Army." "The Chinese Communist Party," read the document, "has created and developed revolutionary political work in the armed forces ever since" the formation of the Red Army in the late 1920s. The party's activities adhered to the principle of "educating the army with the national democratic revolution ideology and the spirit of the peoples' war" and aimed at "achieving the internal unity of the revolutionary army, the unity of the revolutionary people, government, and armed forces, and bringing the revolutionary army under the control of the revolutionary [CCP] party to enhance the army's combat effectiveness." The report pointed out that "this is how our army differs from other armies; this is what we mean by saying that 'political work is the lifeblood of a revolutionary army.'" The CCP guide then described in considerable detail the tasks and objectives of political work in the army, the relationship between political and military officers in positions of command and control, and the principal rhetoric of political propaganda.[19] In another directive to all the lower-ranking commanders, dated

April 20, the Central Committee made it clear that "all the commanders at company level and above must use this document as the primary material in political education, . . . and measure your work and ideas by the standards set up by the document."[20]

Indeed, the system of mass mobilization and political indoctrination of the troops became the most important aspect of CCP military command and control. Most of the CCP military leaders praised Mao's perception of the relationship between war and politics, and between politics and the armed forces, as a remarkable innovation.[21] Seeing it as a political guarantee of military victory, some CCP leaders gained confidence about armed struggle, even though their forces were still poorly trained and equipped.[22] However, Mao and other CCP leaders understood that the people's support and the troops' subordination was not a sufficient indemnity against defeat.

II

"War is the highest form of struggle for resolving contradictions . . . between classes, nations, states, or political groups," Mao wrote in 1936; "unless you understand the actual circumstances of war, its nature and its relations to other things, you will not know the laws of war, or know how to direct war, or be able to win victory."[23] Even so, could a weak nation with inferior military capabilities win a war against a strong nation with superior military capabilities? Mao's answer was affirmative. The key to victory in such a lopsided confrontation, in his view, was the application of *dialectics* in the calculation and execution of the war, which he formulated as principles.

1. *War as a phenomenon was comprehensible*. In his famous essay on military affairs, "On Protracted War," written in May 1938, Mao conceded that the phenomenon of war was "more elusive" and "characterized by greater uncertainty than any other social phenomenon, in other words, that it is more a matter of 'probability.'" Nevertheless, he believed that "war is in no way supernatural, but a mundane process governed by necessity." Even if it was difficult to grasp the enormity of war, he maintained that "whatever the situation and the moves in a war, one can know their general aspects and essential points."[24]

To Mao, war was a social phenomenon that had its own laws and characteristics. Any kind of war would consist of three main elements: a particular set of organizations, a particular series of methods, and a particular process. In the first case, "the organizations are the armed forces and everything that goes with them"; in the second, "the methods are the strategy and tactics for directing war"; and in the third, "the process is the particular form of social activity in which the opposing armed forces attack each other or defend themselves against one another, employing strategy and tactics favorable to themselves and unfavorable to the enemy."[25] Given these elements, Mao believed that war was a peculiar aspect of human life, which could be studied, understood, and what was more important, reshaped.

Thus Mao regarded military-strategic thinking as "the study of the laws of a war situation as a whole." He lectured to the students at the Red Army War College in northern Shaanxi in December 1936 that "a war situation as a whole may cover the entire world, may cover an entire country, or may cover an independent guerrilla zone or an independent major operational front." Any distinct war situation that required comprehensive consideration of its various aspects and stages would form a war situation as a whole. The science of military strategy was "to study those laws for directing a war that govern a war situation as a whole," while the science of military tactics was "to study those laws for directing a war that govern a particular situation."[26]

The key to understanding warfare, Mao found, was to identify war-related contradictions. Mao specified numerous adversarial concepts in war, such as (*a*) "the enemy and ourselves," (*b*) "the front and the rear," (*c*) "losses and replacements," (*d*) "fighting and resting," (*e*) "the concentration [of forces] and dispersion," (*f*) "attack and defense," (*g*) "advance and retreat," (*h*) "concealment and exposure," (*i*) "the main attack and the supplementary attack," (*j*) "assault and containing action," (*k*) "protracted war and war of quick decision," (*l*) "positional war and mobile war," (*m*) "cadres and the rank and file," (*n*) "old and new soldiers," and (*o*) "the regular army and the guerrilla forces." To Mao, not only were these sets unalterably paired, but they each revealed some fundamental problem of war. Yet as long as one understood how these contrarities evolved dialectically, one would have the upper hand, for they were all concerned with the invariable result of war: "victory and defeat."[27]

2. *Military capability shaped victory and defeat in an indisputable way*. Mao maintained that military capability was the starting point for military-strategic thinking. As he defined it, military capability was made up of "almost all the particular sets of contradictions in war." The outcome of a war was predetermined by such elements as soldiers, weaponry, war-related resources, and military strategy. Although war was a complex social phenomenon involving political, economic, cultural, and moral factors, the functioning of all these forces in a war would have to be realized through military capability. History demonstrated, Mao asserted, that war had occurred because of the existence of soldiers and weapons.[28] Mao's statement that "political power grows out of the barrel of a gun," made at the CCP Politburo's emergency meeting on August 7, 1927, became a popular maxim of his military thought.[29]

Mao characterized military capability in rather broad terms. One category consisted of what he defined as "objective conditions," of which the first was population. A country with a large population was more likely to win a war with a smaller nation because the size of human resources would determine the size of the armed forces and the potential for recruitment and replacement. The CCP chairman had long stressed the importance of "employ[ing] our human resources efficiently, carefully, and according to plans."[30] The second objective condition concerned soldiers. Mao distinguished between soldiers and civilians [*laobaixing*] in that only the former received military training, were equipped with weapons, and were organized within a military system. There was thus a gap between "the ordinary civilian" and "the soldier" in terms of military capability.[31] The third objective condition was weaponry, since a military force's combat effectiveness was directly related to the quantity and quality of its weapons and military equipment. In judging the CCP's military capability, Mao often contrasted the enemy's "weaponry and supplies" to that of the CCP forces.[32] The fourth objective condition was economic resources. Mao believed that modern warfare was in part shaped by a country's economic strength. As early as 1933, he warned the CCP leaders of the importance of acquiring the economic resources that were "the material prerequisites for the revolutionary war"; otherwise, "the people will become exhausted in the course of a long war."[33] Finally, Mao pointed out the significance of natural conditions. If, for example, military commanders could take advantage of favorable weather and geography, they could "win a war relatively easier and with much more certainty."[34]

"Subjective conditions" composed another, perhaps more important category of military capability. Here Mao was concerned with the soldier's attitude, belief, political quality, and morale. He regarded a fighting spirit as crucial to an army's military capability. But a superior will to fight largely depended on whether or not the soldier understood what he fought for. "Small as it is," Mao said in 1936, "the Red Army has a great fighting capability because its members . . . are born of the agrarian revolution and are fighting for their own interests and because its commanders and fighters are politically united." Once they grasped the issues at stake, the rank and file would be brave, capable of enduring hardship, and primed to sacrifice their lives.[35] Another way to create and maintain high morale was to build up the relationships between officers and soldiers on the basis of brotherhood and comradeship. Mao in particular advocated "military democracy," in which the officers and soldiers were equals. He also found it necessary to adhere to certain Confucian standards, whereby the superior acted as a role model to his subordinates and was "the first to shoulder heavier work, and the last to enjoy pleasure; . . . the first to advance in offensive marches, and the last to retreat."[36] Finally, Mao paid great attention to winning popular support, both domestic and international. In his view, a war was not only a confrontation between two states' human power [*ren li*] but a contest between two nations' popular will [*ren xin*]. If a war went against the will of people, it would lose popular support, eventually resulting in the declination of that nation's fighting capability. Ultimately, he believed, "the richest source of power to wage war lies in the masses of the people." Once the masses were mobilized and organized, Mao envisioned that "the aggressor, like a mad bull crashing into a ring of flames, will be surrounded by hundreds of millions of our people standing upright, the mere sound of their voices will strike terror into him, and he will be burned to death."[37]

3. *Military capability altered according to the law of the unit of opposites.* Everything in a society was a unit of opposites, Mao believed, and the two opposites intrinsic to military capability were inferiority and superiority. The historical record suggested that wars were usually fought under only two circumstances: an absolutely strong power battled an absolutely weak power, or a relatively strong power battled a relatively weak power. Although Mao found a few cases of the former type, in most instances combatants were states with relatively strong or relatively weak military strength.[38] More important, he maintained that a transformation between the weak power and the strong power might take place in the course of fighting and in a dialectic manner. Under certain conditions, the initially weak power often managed to survive the outbreak of war, gradually enhanced its strength, became relatively or even absolutely stronger than its adversary, and eventually won the war. This law of the unit of opposites, Mao asserted, governed the change "from inferiority to parity and then to superiority."[39]

Assuming that the transformation between "inferiority and superiority" was likely, in what circumstances would it occur? Mao regarded "each side's subjective ability in directing the war" as the key to this change. Acknowledging that "in his endeavor to win a war a military man cannot overstep the limitations imposed by the material conditions," Mao stressed that "within these limitations, however, he can and must drive for a final victory. The stage of action for a military man is built upon objective material conditions, but on that stage he can direct the performance of many a drama, full of sound and color, power and grandeur."[40] Here, Mao believed it was "man's dynamic role" that determined the fate of war.[41] As he explained, "whatever is done has to be done by human beings . . . [and therefore] war and final victory will not come about without human action." For a military action to be effective, there must be people who "derive ideas, principles, or views from the objective facts and [then] put forward plans, directions, policies, strategies, and tactics." To him, ideas were subjective, while "deeds or actions are the subjective translated into the objective, but both represent the dynamic role peculiar to human beings."[42]

Mao saw war as the highest manifestation of an individual's "conscious dynamic role" and the supreme test of the human spirit in transforming the objective world. In his view, if one side's subjective ability in directing war was superior to the other's, its inferior military capability could turn into a superior one. "War is a contest of strength," he wrote in 1938, "but the original pattern of strength changes in the course of war. Here the decisive factor is subjective effort—winning more victories and committing fewer errors." Although the objective factors would make such a change possible, Mao contended that "in order to turn the possibility into actuality, both correct policy and subjective effort are essential. *It is then that the subjective plays the decisive role*."[43] Mao discovered many instances in Chinese warfare that supported his thesis. In the battles of Chengpu (203 B.C.), Kunyang (23 B.C.), Guandu (A.D. 200), Chibi (A.D. 208), Yiling (A.D. 222), and Feishui (A.D. 383), Mao discovered that the weaker states' conscious activity changed their military inferiority into military superiority. In each battle, the combatants were mismatched in their war-waging capabilities when hostilities started, but the weaker side, because of its clever strategy and military command, defeated the stronger enemy.[44]

4. *"Know the enemy and know yourself, and you can fight a hundred battles with no danger of defeat* [*zhiji zhi bi baizhan budai*]."[45] This famous dictum by Sun Tzu, an influential strategist in ancient China, was to Mao a "scientific" truth, and he repeatedly emphasized its aptness in shaping one's conscious activity in war. "In real life," he lectured at the Red Army War College in December 1936, "we cannot ask for 'ever-victorious generals,' who are few and far between in history," but what one could ask for were "generals who are brave and sagacious and who normally win their battles in the course of a war, generals who combine wisdom with courage." The secret to cultivating such attributes in military leaders lay in "[our efforts] to familiarize ourselves with all aspects of the enemy situation and our own, to discover the laws governing the actions of both sides and to make use of these laws in our own operations."[46] The goal of command was to make the fewest possible mistakes while causing the enemy to make as many errors as possible.

Mao believed that an important element of knowing the enemy and knowing yourself was to ensure that "the subjective corresponds with the objective." In other words, "the commander's reconnaissance, judgment and decision have corresponded with the enemy's actual situation and [force] dispositions." He conceded that complete correspondence was extremely rare in actual battles, because "belligerents are groups of living human beings bearing arms and keeping their secrets from each other; this is quite unlike handling inanimate objects or routine matters." But he insisted that "if the direction given by the commander corresponds in the main with the actual situations, that is, if the decisive elements in the direction correspond with the actual situation, then there is a basis for victory."[47] To Mao, the achievement of such correlation would depend on "thorough and necessary reconnaissance" and "piecing together the data of various kinds gathered through reconnaissance." He described a sagacious commander as one who "applies all possible and necessary methods of reconnaissance" and who "ponders on the information gathered about the enemy's situation, discarding the dross and selecting the essential, eliminating the false and retaining the true, proceeding from one to the other and from the outside to the inside." Such a commander would then interrelate the conditions of his own side and those of the enemy, "thereby forming his judgment, making up his mind and working out his plan." Mao stressed that a military commander should carefully go through such a "complete process of knowing a situation" before undertaking a war, a campaign, or even a battle.[48]

To grasp a war situation, Mao maintained, one should also adhere to the principle of flexibility, especially the "flexible employment of armed forces." Particularly "when the weak are fighting the strong," flexible employment of forces "requires subjective ability of a very high order and requires the overcoming of the confusion, obscurity, and uncertainty peculiar to war and the discovery of order, clarity, and certainty in it." Even so, there was "only a very limited and transient certainty" in war, which made complete and rigid planning difficult. Hence, the planning "must change with the movement (flow or change) of the war and vary in scope according to the scale of war." In Mao's analysis, tactical plans, such as plans for attack or defense by small formations or units, often had to be changed several times a day; but a campaign plan could generally stand until the conclusion of the operation, though it might still be subject to partial or wholesale revision. Even if "a strategic plan based on the overall situation of both belligerents is still more stable," he asserted, "it too is applicable only in a given strategic stage and has to be changed when the war moves toward a new stage."[49]

Mao also believed that the achievement of flexibility in directing battles was "the process of practice." Military commanders had to examine "whether the plan [which has] worked out in the proceeding process corresponds with reality." If it did not fully mesh, "then in the light of our new knowledge, it becomes necessary to form new judgments, make new decisions, and change the original plan so as to meet the new situation."[50] This was, Mao stated, what the ancient Chinese strategists meant by the saying "Ingenuity in varying tactics depends on mother wit."[51]

A principal objective of coming to grips with a specific war situation, in Mao's view, was to gain the initiative in battle. He regarded the initiative as "an army's freedom of action as distinguished from an enforced loss of freedom." Such a freedom was "the very life of an army," and once lost, the army was closer to defeat and destruction. Seizing the initiative was crucial for a weak army. Although "the initiative is inseparable from superiority in capacity to wage war," he explained, "to have the absolute initiative is possible only when there is [an] absolute superiority against [an] absolute inferiority." Yet in history, "such absolute superiority rarely appears in the long stages of a war or a campaign but is to be found toward its end." Therefore, it was very likely that a relatively inferior belligerent could acquire relative or even absolute superiority if it struck for and held fast to the initiative at all stages of a war.[52]

How could a weaker belligerent gain the advantage at the tactical level? First, it "can wrest the initiative and victory from the superior side by securing certain conditions through [an] active subjective endeavor in accordance with the actual circumstances." The relatively stronger side would invariably reveal some vulnerabilities, at which point the weaker side should "inflict one sharp defeat on the enemy and then turn on the rest of his forces and smash them one by one, thus transforming the overall situation into one of superiority and initiative."[53] Second, Mao proposed that "deliberately creating misconceptions for the enemy and then springing surprise attacks upon him are two ways—indeed two important means—of achieving superiority and seizing the initiative." Mao derived these principles from an ancient Chinese proverb: "There can never be too much deception in war [*bing bu yan zha*]." By employing deceitful tactics, one could transfer "the uncertainties of war to the enemy while securing the greatest possible certainty for [himself] and thereby gaining superiority, the initiative, and victory."[54] A third way of seeking the initiative was through an "excellent organization of the masses." In Mao's view, it was extremely important "to arouse all the people who are opposed to the enemy to arm themselves to the last man, make widespread raids on the enemy, and also prevent the leakage of news and provide a screen for our own forces." All of these stratagems would keep the enemy "in the dark about where and when our forces will attack, and an objective basis will be created for misconception and unpreparedness on his part."[55]

5. *In striving for the final victory over a stronger enemy, one should insist on a protracted war strategy*. Mao claimed that any prolonged war would pass through three stages. The first period was "the enemy's strategic offensive and our strategic defensive"; the second was "the enemy's strategic consolidation

and our preparation for the counteroffensive"; the third was "our strategic counteroffensive and the enemy's strategic retreat." When a war erupted, the weaker side would almost have to take an overall defensive stand, Mao conceded, but fighting a protracted war would enable the weaker side to switch gradually from the defensive to the offensive. In his view, "the essence, or the object, of war is to preserve oneself and destroy the enemy." As long as one side prolonged the war "to achieve the strategic objective of greatly depleting the enemy's forces, . . . [that side will be] gradually changing the general balance of forces and preparing the conditions for [a] counteroffensive." Therefore, he advised that "in the stages of the enemy's offensive and preservation of his gains, [the weaker side] should wage offensive campaigns and battles within the strategic defense, campaigns and battles of quick decision within the strategically protracted war, and campaigns and battles on exterior lines within strategic interior lines." Only when the enemy's superiority deteriorated should the weaker side launch "a strategic counteroffensive."[56]

Mao regarded the "concentration of troops" as the first and most essential element of fighting a protracted war, because it was "necessary for the purpose of reversing the situation as between the enemy and ourselves" and especially as between "advance and retreat." "Previously," he explained, "it was the enemy who was advancing and we who were retreating; now we seek a situation in which we advance and he retreats. When we concentrate our forces and win a battle, then in that battle we gain the above purpose and this influences the whole campaign."[57] Mao always encouraged the troops to "pit one against ten and pit ten against a hundred" in combat, but in the actual direction of campaigns and battles, he stressed that "we must never do such a thing. . . . Our strategy is 'pit one against ten' and our tactics are 'pit ten against one.'"[58] He specified that "in order to smash the attack of the stronger enemy in conditions where popular support, terrain, and weather are greatly in our favor, it is of course necessary to concentrate [our] main forces . . . for a surprise attack on a segment of one flank of the enemy while containing his center and his other flank with guerrillas or small detachments, and in this way victory can be won."[59]

Effectively executing mobile warfare was another important principle for an extended war strategy. Mao thought that the essence of mobile warfare was "to fight when you can win, move away when you can't win." In resisting a strong enemy's strategic offensive, the weak side should always be prepared to retreat. According to Mao's calculation, first, "it is inadvisable to fight when the force confronting us is too large"; second, "it is sometimes inadvisable to fight when the force confronting us, though not so large, is very close to other enemy forces"; third, "it is generally inadvisable to fight an enemy force that is not isolated and is strongly entrenched"; and fourth, "it is inadvisable to continue an engagement while there is no prospect of victory."[60] Yet all the "moving away" should aim toward fighting, and all strategy and tactics should be built around fighting. Therefore, any "recognition of the necessity of moving away" should be based on the "recognition of the necessity of fighting." To him, this was one of "the fundamental characteristics of . . . mobile warfare." Through retreat, one could be free to employ "several divisions against one enemy division, . . . several columns against one [enemy] column, and suddenly encircling and attacking a single column from the exterior lines of the battlefield."[61] Mobile warfare should be employed not merely to avoid setbacks but also to create opportunities for retaliation when victory was more certain.

Mao also regarded quick decision making as absolutely necessary if a weak army was to prevail. Although tactically a weak force had to fight a protracted war, it must be aware that a long-drawn-out war was detrimental to its efforts as a whole. Therefore, at the campaign and battle levels, "fighting battles of quick decision [*suzhan sujue*]" was the best tactic for inflicting heavy losses on the enemy and preserving one's own strength, which would gradually reduce the enemy's combat effectiveness. Before one could exercise rapid judgment, Mao pointed out, many specific preconditions had to be met, including "adequate preparations, seizing the opportune moment, concentration of superior forces, encircling and outflanking tactics, favorable terrain, and striking at the enemy when he is on the move, or when he is stationary but has not yet consolidated his positions." Unless these requirements were satisfied, he found it "impossible to achieve quick decisions in a campaign or battle."[62] To Mao, a sudden and decisive victory in a campaign or battle was of great strategic significance, because it would severely demoralize the enemy, stimulate the morale of the triumphant forces, and evoke international support. Since a strategically protracted war would translate on the field into battles of quick decision, the two tactics were "aspects of the same thing," which should receive "equal and simultaneous emphasis."[63]

Mao also asserted that a weak army had to fight a war of annihilation. It would be "inappropriate" to advocate a strategy of attrition, because a "'contest of treasures' not between Dragon Kings but between a Dragon King and a beggar would be rather ludicrous." The goal of annihilation was to completely wipe out one enemy unit in each battle. "Injuring all of a man's ten fingers is not as effective as chopping off one, and routing ten enemy divisions is not as effective as annihilating one of them," for the latter would have a much greater psychological impact on the enemy.[64] However, Mao recognized that it was often difficult to achieve total extermination in actual fighting, especially when one's army was inferior to the enemy in equipment. Even so, his instruction was to "encircle part if not all of the enemy forces, capture part if not all of the encircled forces, and inflict heavy casualties on part of the encircled forces if we cannot capture them."[65]

III

Mao Zedong's theories on a weak army's strategy and tactics evolved over a long period, as he witnessed dramatic changes taking place in China. During the first half of the twentieth century, the Chinese people suffered from constant conflicts, both civil wars and foreign invasions. China remained poor, weak, anarchical, and fragmented compared to the advanced Western industrial powers or Japan. As a young soldier in the revolutionary army in the Republican Revolution in 1911 and as a student participating in the May 4th Movement in 1919, Mao was obsessed with the mentality of *wang guo*; that the Chinese people might lose their state and become "slaves without a country." His solution to this potential danger was to fortify the nation's military capability and to enhance the people's military spirit. "Our nation is wanting strength," he wrote in April 1917. "The military spirit has not been encouraged. The physical condition of the population deteriorates daily. . . . If this state continues, our weakness will increase further. . . . If our bodies are not strong, we will be afraid as soon as we see enemy soldiers, and then how can we attain our goals, and make ourselves respected?"[66] Although soldier's physical stamina was important, Mao regarded a man's courage or martial spirit as even more vital to military strength. He stated in 1917 that "[combat] strength depends on drill, and drill depends on self-awareness [*zijue*]. . . . If we wish to make physical conditions effective we must influence the people's subjective attitudes and stimulate them to become conscious of physical education."[67] Mao's belief in human subjectivity had already become a central element of his military thought.

Mao developed his theories on military affairs from 1927 to 1949, and his combat experience greatly influenced his thinking through these years. As the CCP undertook the armed struggle for power during this period, the practical concern was how a weak army could survive and defeat a strong enemy. From 1927 to 1935, the Red Army, which was small, poorly equipped, and inexperienced, encountered KMT forces that were superior in all these areas. As the political commissar of the First Red Army, Mao assisted army commander Zhu De in smashing the KMT's "encirclement and suppression" campaigns in the Jinggang Mountains, Jiangxi province. He then played the crucial role in leading the Communist "Long March" and eventually built a new base at Yanan

[Yenan], Shaanxi province. In his works "Why Is It That Red Political Power Can Exist in China?" (October 5, 1928), "The Struggle in the Chingkang [Jinggang] Mountains" (November 25, 1928), "On Correcting Mistaken Idea in the Party" (December 1929), and "A Single Spark Can Start a Prairie Fire" (January 5, 1930), Mao concentrated on suggesting ways for the Red Army to vanquish the Nationalist forces. His solutions would soon be abbreviated into such memorable quotes as "political power grows out of the barrel of gun," "a system of political work is essential for the people's war," "political work is the lifeblood of all work," "lure the enemy into the deep and strike it when it is unprepared and isolated," and "concentrate a superior force to annihilate one enemy unit."[68] His thought on the strategy and tactics of a weak force enhanced and consolidated his leadership in the CCP's military affairs.

From 1936 to 1938, Mao spent most of his time studying how China could resist and eventually defeat the superior Japanese invaders. He wrote several notable essays on this question, such as "Problems of Strategy in China's Revolutionary War" (December 1936), "Questions of Strategy in the Anti-Japanese Guerrilla War" (May 1938), "On Protracted War" (May 1938), "On a New Stage" (October 1938), and "Problems of War and Strategy" (November 1938). In these writings, several of Mao's principles are reaffirmed, first among them being his faith in the importance of "subjective ability" in directing and fighting a war. Second, by probing into the definition of "weak and strong" from a dialectical perspective, Mao elaborated on the circumstances by which the inferiority or superiority of a power might change—first quantitatively and then qualitatively. Third, when advocating a protracted war strategy for a weaker army, he formulated such military doctrines as "knowing your enemy and yourself" and "achieving the initiative at the tactical level through concentrating troops, fighting a mobile war, making quick decisions, and pursuing the enemy's annihilation." Mao's military thought had matured during these two years and had become an indispensable guide to CCP decision making on armed struggles.[69]

The Chinese Communists brought Mao's theories into full play during the civil war with the KMT forces from 1946 to 1949. While Chiang Kai-shek's Nationalist army was equipped with American weapons and trained by U.S. military advisers, the Chinese Communist forces had fewer troops, no air or naval forces, and little heavy artillery. When the civil war broke out in 1946, the Nationalist forces were already on the strategic offensive while the Communists were in full retreat. Assisted by commander in chief Zhu De, chief of staff Zhou Enlai, and deputy commander in chief Peng Dehuai, Mao took direct command of CCP's military operations. That this experience reinforced his military thought is evident in such writings as "Concentrating a

Superior Force to Destroy the Enemy Force One by One" (September 6, 1946), "A Three-Month Summary" (October 1, 1946), "The Guidance of Operations for the Northwestern Theater" (April 15, 1947), "Our Strategy for the Second Year of the Liberation War" (September 1, 1947), and "Present Situation and Our Tasks" (December 25, 1947). Given his belief that the people's will determined the war's fate, Mao argued that "all the reactionaries are paper tigers." In an interview with American correspondent Anna Louise Strong in 1946, he stated that "the reactionaries all look very scary; yet they do not have insurmountable power. To view the problem from a long-term perspective, it is the people not reactionaries who will enjoy the really powerful force."[70] Mao's most important work during this period was a summary of his ideas on a weak army's strategy and tactics. Titled "Ten Great Military Principles [*shida junshi yuanze*]," it soon became ingrained in the minds of the CCP commanders as well as the rank and file.[71] Achieving one success after another, the People's Liberation Army dealt the final blow to the Nationalists in 1949 and obtained a nationwide victory. This result, to many CCP leaders and soldiers, proved the validity of Mao's military thought.

No single CCP leader had written as extensively on warfare as Mao did, yet other leaders contributed directly to his thinking. Before 1933, Mao had realized the significance of troop concentration, but had no plan for its implementation in battle. It was Zhu De who provided Mao with an answer. "In every assaulting action," Zhu wrote in 1932, "[commanders of] both large and small forces must concentrate the main combat strength in the main direction selected for the attack and shall only spare a small force to divert the enemy's attention in other directions. If [a commander] wants to divide the forces up and take care of every direction, he will suffer from a lack of forces in each direction."[72] Zhou Enlai made his contribution as well. On the basis of his command experience in the Red Army against the KMT's fourth "encirclement and suppression" campaign, Zhou was the first CCP leader to advocate the methodical annihilation of the enemy force piece by piece. "I always believe," he stated in January 1933, "[that] to a weak force, the annihilation of the enemy's main force one by one is much more important than seizure of one enemy city."[73] Liu Bocheng, one of the CCP's best and most experienced military commanders, influenced Mao's deliberations on how to seize and retain the initiative in battle. Liu stressed the need to deploy a balanced force on both defense and offense. If there were too many defensive troops, the army's offensive capability would be considerably reduced; if there were too many assault forces, it was likely that one's defenses would be destroyed by the enemy. As a countermeasure, Liu proposed to wrest the initiative from the enemy by using every possible means to make the enemy either decrease his offensive forces or increase his defensive troops.[74] Mao concurred with these high-ranking commanders and incorporated their ideas into his own writings.

Another influence on Mao's military thought came from the teachings of traditional Chinese strategists. When questioned later about his absorption of the Chinese classics, Mao was said to be "generally whimsical and frequently contradictory in his replies."[75] However, even a cursory reading of his works reveals that he heavily quoted from Sun Tzu and other ancient strategists. Concerning the importance of a national military spirit, for example, the traditional strategist Wu Tzu had asserted that military spirit mainly determined victory or defeat in a war. Pursuing this theme, Wei Liao Tzu wrote, "It is because of people that war is fought, and it is because of people's will that war is fought; therefore, when the people's will is strong, war can be fought; when the people's will is weak, war can never be fought."[76] Of these ancient writers, perhaps Sun Tzu had the greatest impact on Mao and other CCP military leaders. Mao accepted and developed some of Sun's principles, such as correct and flexible command, creation of favorable momentum [*zao shi*] in battle, "ten against one," and "knowing your enemy and knowing yourself."[77]

Some historical lessons of war greatly inspired Mao's reflections on military affairs as well. Because he focused on cases in which a weak force defeated a strong enemy, he frequently cited the battles of Chenggao, Kunyang, Guandu, and Chengpu, which occurred during China's Spring and Autumn period.[78] For instance, the Battle of Chenggao was fought between Liu Bang, king of Han, and Xiang Yu, king of Chu, in 203 B.C. At first, Xiang captured Yunyang and Chenggao (now in Henan province), and Liu's troops were almost routed. Planning a counteroffensive, Liu waited until the moment when Xiang's forces were in midstream crossing the Chi River and then crushed the enemy with his main force. In the Battle of Kunyang, Liu Xiu, founder of the eastern Han dynasty, defeated Wang Mang's Qin dynasty, in 23 B.C. There was a huge numerical disparity between the two sides: Liu's forces totaled 8,000 to 9,000 while Wang controlled 400,000 men. But Liu with 3,000 handpicked troops, mislead Wang's field commanders Wang Shun and Wang Yu, caught Wang Mang unprepared, and routed his main forces. In the Battle of Chengpu in 632 B.C., the state of Chu had the upper hand at the start of the war. The army of Jin, though less trained than the Chu troops, made a deliberate retreat of 30 miles, executed a surprise attack on the two weak flanks of the Chu army, and won the war.[79]

Mao was also very familiar with the analyses of strategy and tactics in *The Romance of the Three Kingdoms* [*sanguo zhi*] and *Water Margin* [*shui hu*], the two most popular titles in Chinese war fiction. Stories told in the *Romance* about the battles of Chibi and Yiling were often mentioned in his writings. The

Battle of Chibi was fought in A.D. 208 between the states of Wu, ruled by Sun Quan, and Wei, headed by Cao Cao. Cao led an army of over 500,000 men in an attack on Sun's 30,000 troops. Knowing that Cao's northern soldiers were plagued by epidemics during their marches in the south and were unaccustomed to naval action, the allied forces of Sun and Liu Bei set fire to Cao's fleet and crushed his army at Chibi, situated on the south bank of the Yangtze River. In the Battle of Yiling, Lu Sun, commander of Wu's army, defeated Liu Bei's numerically superior force in A.D. 222. Liu's troops had scored several victories at the beginning of the war and penetrated deep into the state of Wu as far as Yiling, now in Hubei province. Lu Sun, who was supposed to defend Yiling, avoided battle for over seven months until Liu was at his wit's end and his troops were exhausted and demoralized. Then Lu crushed Liu's forces by taking advantage of a favorable wind to set fire to Liu's tents and thereby cause great casualties.

The Battle of Feishui (A.D. 383) was even more dramatic. Fu Qian, ruler of the state of Chin, led 600,000 infantry, 270,000 cavalry, and 30,000 guards to attack the eastern Jin dynasty. While Fu's forces were lined up and ready to fight on the opposite bank of the Fei River (in Anhui), Xie Xuan, commander of 80,000 men from eastern Jin, decided to exploit the enemy's overconfidence. Xie requested Fu Qian to move his troops back to leave enough room for a battlefield, and Fu complied. When Fu ordered the movement, his troops fell into such a disorder that the retreat could not be stopped or reorganized. Seizing this opportunity, Xie launched an offensive and struck a fatal blow to the strong enemy.[80] Mao was truly obsessed with these stories, not only dwelling on them with enormous relish but citing them as historical evidence of his "weak army" strategy.

IV

Mao firmly believed that a weak army could win in a war against a strong enemy because he was convinced that "man" could beat "weapon." Given Mao's confidence in a human being's *subjective capability* to determine defeat or victory in war, the CCP chairman *romanticized* military affairs. Yet, as he calculated the probability of victory for a weak army, he found his theory logical, realistic, and plausible. As Stuart Schram asserts, given the scope and depth of Mao's thinking, it would be a "gross simplification" to treat of Mao's military doctrines as pure political propaganda.[81]

The idea that warriors, because of their godliness and virtue, can vanquish stronger opponents, is very ancient. "Pericles spoke of it in his funeral oration to the Athenians," one cultural historian observes. "The Christian crusaders counted on it. Jihad, Islam's conception of a holy war, is based on it. The [Japanese] Samurai believed it. So did the Nazis."[82] In the light of his reading of Chinese history and his own combat experience, however, Mao developed a system around a weak army's strategy and tactics. There can be little doubt that this perspective illuminates our understanding of the CCP's behavior in conflict resolution. The involvement of the Chinese Communist forces in the Korean War would be yet another instance that revealed how Mao's war romanticism functioned, sometimes dramatically, during the first years of Communist rule in China after the civil war.

3. PREPAREDNESS ELIMINATES MISHAPS

"We are now on the way to Beiping [later renamed Beijing] just like students in the old days who were about to take capital examinations," Mao Zedong remarked to Zhou Enlai on March 23, 1949, as he climbed into an American jeep at Xibaipo, Hebei province, then CCP's headquarters. "This is the first step of another ten-thousand-kilometer Long March [for us]."[1] The CCP chairman was very concerned about the uncertain future of the new regime, although CCP forces already controlled all of northeastern and northern China and were ready to launch a final blow on the Kuomintang troops scattered in the southeast. After spending three difficult years in Shaanxi and Hebei, the CCP headquarters was moving to Beiping where the Communists were to formally establish the People's Republic Government.

Mao and other CCP leaders had been preoccupied with a long-suspected threat of American armed intervention on the KMT's behalf, and they were clearly prepared to face down the Americans even at this early stage. Given the endless uncertainties, both domestic and foreign, besieging the new government, the CCP leadership was determined to take precautions against what it had long perceived to be the worst contingency: American intervention.

I

In the postwar contest with the Nationalists, the Chinese Communists were sensitive to American support to Chiang Kai-shek's regime. After the Japanese surrender in August 1945, a mad race took place between the CCP and the KMT forces, each trying to reach the occupied territories first in order to harvest the vast quantity of enemy arms and military supplies. With its power bases in north and central China, the CCP enjoyed a distinct geographical advantage over the scattered KMT troops. However, the United States quickly came to the aid of the Nationalists. More than 50,000 U.S. Marines landed in key ports and communication centers to await the arrival of the KMT forces.

The U.S. Air Force also airlifted three KMT armies to Beiping, Tianjin, Shanghai, and Nanjing and transported half a million Nationalist troops to the areas previously occupied by the Japanese. With American assistance, the Nationalists were able to forestall the CCP's expansion in northeastern China (Manchuria) and forced the Communists into retreat. The CCP's suspicion of and hostility toward the US intensified in early October when American naval forces approached Yantai, a port city in Shandong peninsula, and demanded the evacuation of the CCP troops there. Viewing American occupation of Yantai as a potential threat to the CCP, Mao ordered an armed resistance to any landing attempt. Ye Jianying, CCP chief of staff, openly warned that "if U.S. forces insist on landing, . . . they will have to bear the responsibility of serious consequences." The CCP leaders, however, were relieved when the

Map of China (Source: *Central Intelligence Agency. Reproduced courtesy of the University of Chicago Libraries)*

U.S. Navy backed off. The same type of clash occurred in Tianjin, but neither of these incidents escalated into a large-scale conflict.[2]

The outcome of George Marshall's arbitration of the CCP-KMT strife in 1946 reinforced the CCP leadership's suspicion of U.S. intentions. The Marshall mission, the CCP leaders had believed, was supposed to mediate China's civil war impartially, but the proceedings had greatly displeased the CCP. "The United States in reality [is supporting Chiang] through stationing troops [on China's coast] and providing Chiang with military and financial assistance," Zhou Enlai, the CCP's representative at the negotiations, reported to Mao on August 6. "Chiang is ready to expand the [civil] conflict into a full-scale war, and the United States may allow him to resume hostilities before any meaningful outcome of the negotiations would be produced." Zhou concluded that the Marshall mission was anything but neutral toward the CCP.[3] On August 31, Zhou more explicitly warned the CCP headquarters that "the United States and Chiang have already agreed . . . that although American forces would withdraw from China, the United States would continue its secret support to Chiang's civil war efforts. . . . It is clear that the US will no longer play the game of deceit [*pianju*]."[4] Mao concurred with Zhou. "The policy of the U.S. government," he pointed out on September 26, "is to use the so-called mediation as a smoke screen for strengthening Chiang Kai-shek in every way and suppressing the democratic forces in China through Chiang Kai-shek's policy of [mass] slaughter so as to reduce China virtually to a U.S. colony."[5] Earlier in the month, the CCP central leadership had decided to call for a full preparation against the possibility of new KMT offensives coordinated by the U.S. military. Deeply concerned about American military involvement, the CCP launched a propaganda campaign to oppose it and to pressure "the U.S. [government] to withdraw its troops from China completely."[6]

As the Chinese Communist forces began an all-out counteroffensive in 1947, the CCP leadership seriously considered how to prevent the US from overtly intervening on the KMT's behalf. An important article, "Explanations of Several Basic Problems Concerning the Postwar [World War II] International Situation," appeared in an early January issue of *Jiefang Ribao* [Liberation daily], the CCP's official newspaper. Although Lu Dingyi, director of the CCP Propaganda Department, was listed as the author, Mao wrote most of the article, which became an official manifesto of the CCP's anti-American policy. The article referred to the US as "the stronghold of the world's antidemocratic forces" and proclaimed that the Chinese people would "resolutely resist U.S. aggression endeavor of armed intervention against [China's] national liberation movement."[7] In early March, responding to Moscow's inquiry on whether the CCP would accept a Soviet proposal that the Big Three (the USSR, the US, and Great Britain) mediate China's civil war, Zhou

Enlai clearly stated the CCP position: "We only wish that the foreign ministers of the Big Three would [first of all] guarantee: no foreign intervention in China's domestic affairs; complete withdrawal of the American forces in China; cessation of American aid to Chiang's war effort; and the Chinese people's right to resolve their own problems." Otherwise, peace would be out of the question.[8] However, to win international sympathy for the CCP stance, a CCP Central Committee directive to the local authorities in Shanghai and Hong Kong, dated August 21, urged the "exploration of every possible opportunity to disclose the U.S. conspiracy of supporting Chiang's war." To expand the anti-American campaign, the missive instructed that the entire party should work at mobilizing international and domestic support so that "[we] get prepared for large-scale struggle for national [liberation]."[9]

As the civil war gradually turned to the CCP's favor from late 1947 through 1948, the Communist leaders came to believe that the US was not ready for an extensive military action in China. At the same time, they were certain that the danger of American occupation of some of China's port cities still existed. In his report delivered at the CCP Central Committee meetings in late December 1947, Mao pointed out that Britain, the US, France, and the Soviet Union, instead of confronting one another, tended toward accommodation, and "a compromise [among them] is very likely." Under this circumstance, the CCP chairman predicted, it was less likely that the imperialists would immediately intervene in China, though there was little doubt that the US would remain hostile toward the Chinese Communists in the foreseeable future.[10] As the Central Committee stated in the document "On Our Diplomatic Policy Lines Toward the United States," dated March 14, 1948, "we will adhere to two principles in our anti-American policy—to prevent the U.S. imperialists from colonizing China and to overthrow the aggressive rule of the U.S. imperialists in China." Accordingly, the circular specified that the entire party and the military forces should remain vigilant against U.S. armed intervention and, at the same time, seize every opportunity to "explore internal contradictions within the U.S. government and between Washington and Chiang . . . so as to delay and diminish direct U.S. military action to salvage Chiang."[11]

The CCP further assessed the American threat at an enlarged politburo meeting at Xibaipo on September 8–13, 1948. There was general agreement that the KMT would be defeated soon and that immediate U.S. armed intervention was not likely. However, the leaders predicted that the US might attempt to occupy some key coastal cities in eastern and southeastern China. Ren Bishi, one of the five Politburo Standing Committee members, warned at the September 13 session that "the US would increase forces in China to occupy some big cities to forestall our advance [toward victory]."[12] Zhou Enlai shared Ren's view. As early as September 1947, Zhou had anticipated, in his speech to the staff of the CCP headquarters, that as the civil war went on, "the U.S. imperialists would eventually occupy and defend Shanghai," a well-known seaport with a history of Western domination. He declared that should the Americans try to seize Shanghai, "we are surely prepared to fight back."[13] Interestingly, PLA Commander in Chief Zhu De seemed particularly worried about Qingdao, another seaport with a strong Western presence in Shandong province. At the briefing of the CCP's Bureau of Combat Operations on October 16, 1948, Zhu instructed the staff members to watch closely the situation in the port "because [the] strategic significance of Qingdao attracts not only our attention but also the rest of the world." Zhu pointed out that since the U.S. Marines still garrisoned Qingdao, "we shall not plan to attack the place at this moment, and we must wait till we are able to concentrate the main strength of our troops [for such an action]."[14]

The CCP leadership's anxiety about American intervention sharpened as the Chinese Communists approached nationwide victory in 1949. In his drafted CCP Central Committee document of January 8, entitled "The Current Situation and Our Party's Tasks in 1949," Mao asserted that Chiang's rule was doomed unless rescued by the Americans. He then warned that "the US might send armed forces to occupy some of China's coastal cities and directly engage us [there]." However, Mao stressed, "we have already considered this possibility in our combat planning, and we will continue to act on this consideration; otherwise we would be thrown into a helpless position if dramatic change takes place."[15] In the same month, while asserting "the possible trends of [the] current situation," Zhou echoed that "there exists a possibility of U.S. military intervention, but we are fully prepared."[16]

The CCP leadership considered it necessary to plan for this contingency. A primary objective was to organize a counterforce in advance to stare down U.S. aggression. Mao explained in the CCP Politburo document of January 8, 1949, that "the more the Chinese people's revolutionary strength is demonstrated, and the more our resolute attitude [toward the US] is shown, the less possible direct U.S. military intervention will be." Mao even hoped that, faced with the CCP's vigorous countermeasures, Washington might be compelled to "decrease its economic and military aid to the KMT or disengage from the [civil] war."[17]

Early in 1949, the CCP took precautions against the prospect of U.S. intervention occurring when the People's Liberation Army crossed the Yangtze.[18] From February 3 to March 20, the CCP's Central Military Commission, which Mao chaired, ordered both the Second and Third Field armies, totaling more than one million troops, to gather along the northern bank of the

Yangtze by the end of March 1949. The deployment of the Second Field Army—more than 400,000 troops—was targeted against anticipated American military action along China's coast. And for the first time, the CMC decided to establish a combined-front command commission, headed by Deng Xiaoping, to direct both field armies. The central leadership underscored the need for caution and full preparation.[19]

The crossing of the Yangtze began on April 21, and the PLA took Nanjing, the capital of the KMT government, the next day. Although the U.S. military did not respond to the CCP advance, the CCP leaders refused to relax their vigilance on the assumption that U.S. forces would act to prevent the PLA from seizing Shanghai. As a result, when the PLA encircled Shanghai in May, the CMC instructed Deng Xiaoping that the main task of the Second Field Army was still to "prepare for possible U.S. military action while assisting the Third Field Army for the Shanghai campaign." To that end, the CMC wanted Deng to deploy "the main bulk of the Second Field Army in the areas of southern Anhui, eastern Jiangxi, and western Zhejiang." Moreover, the CMC informed Deng that the 20th Army Corps under the direct command of the Central Military Commission would soon gather along the north China's coast—possibly near Tianjin—to protect the Second Field Army's left flank, while the 12th Army Corps of the Fourth Field Army would cross the Yangtze River from the Wuchang area ahead of schedule to safeguard the Second Field Army's right flank.[20] The CMC explicitly stated that "with [these preparations] we can dissuade the United States from realizing its ambition of armed intervention [in China]."[21]

The Chinese Communists occupied Shanghai on May 27, and the U.S. Marines in Qingdao and Shanghai remained calm. Obviously, the likelihood of a sudden American military strike seemed remote. However, the CCP top leaders did not think that they had overreached, but rather believed that their contingency plan had worked. As soon as the Shanghai campaign was over, the CMC issued a new directive to all PLA commanders, entitled "Instructions on How to Prepare for Imperialist Intervention Against the Chinese Revolution." The directive, dated May 28, elaborated on a key admonition: "We must take precaution so as to ensure that *preparedness eliminates mishaps* [*youbei wuhuan*]."

> The main aspect of [our] strategies is that each of the four field armies will continue to advance according to our schedule and to eliminate the remnant KMT forces so as to deprive the imperialists of their running-dogs on the Chinese mainland. Second, [we should try our best] to

> achieve economic self-reliance and self-sufficiency in case of naval blockade of our ports by the [U.S.] imperialists. . . . Third, [we will continue] to deploy sufficient troops in north and east China in order to prevent U.S. naval forces from coordinating with the remnant KMT forces to attack us from behind.[22]

Meanwhile, the CCP leadership tried to avoid provoking U.S. intervention. Between March and May 1949, the Central Committee issued a number of instructions to CCP lower-ranking officials stating that appropriate measures must be taken to ensure that foreigners in China were not mistreated. On April 25, Zhou Enlai, instructed Deng Xiaoping that the lives and property of the Americans and the British "should be protected at our best ability; we shall see to it that these foreigners will not get humiliated, and we should not register them."[23] The next, more important step was Huang Hua's secret mission during May 13–July 2, 1949, to meet with American ambassador John Leighton Stuart in Nanjing. Huang was the head of the Foreign Affairs Division of the CCP authority in Nanjing, but his mission received its mandate from the top CCP leaders. The instructions given to Huang on May 10 by the Central Committee—as drafted by Mao—were to listen to what Stuart would have to say about U.S. intentions regarding Communist control of China rather than reveal the CCP's policy toward the US; if Stuart mentioned the possibility of establishing diplomatic relations, to repeat Li Tao's statement of April 30 that "any foreign government wishing to form diplomatic relations with us must cease its tie with the remnant of the KMT and withdraw its forces from China" (a policy line based on Stalin's recommendation to Mao made that same month); and to not reject outright such suggestions as letting Stuart continue his ambassadorship in China or revising Sino-American trade treaties.[24]

There is reason to believe that a primary purpose of Huang's mission was to ascertain U.S. opinion about the CCP control of China. When Nanjing fell to the PLA, many of the foreign embassies, including the Soviet's, moved to Guangzhou [Canton] with the KMT government, but Stuart and the American embassy did not evacuate. The CCP leaders, particularly Mao, were puzzled. They urgently needed firsthand information about U.S. intentions, especially since the PLA was soon to attack Shanghai, a hot spot likely to trigger foreign intervention. It was not a coincidence that Huang's mission was authorized only two weeks before the scheduled attack on Shanghai. At no time during this period, however, did the CCP leaders consider establishing diplomatic relations with the US. There was no deviation from the CCP Central Committee's policy line: "As for the question of seeking recognition from the western capitalist countries, we should not be in a hurry to deal with it now and need not to be in a hurry to consider it even for a fairly long period after our countrywide victory."[25]

During the Nanjing and Shanghai campaigns, American armed forces in China were actually in the process of evacuation. The U.S. Marines withdrew from Qingdao at the CCP's request in early May 1949, and U.S. naval vessels moved out of Shanghai to Wusongkou (the outlet of the Yangtze to the East China Sea) as soon as Shanghai fell to the Communists. Stuart categorically informed Huang Hua that "there were no American warships beyond Wusongkou."[26] However, the prospect of no immediate U.S. military action did not alter the CCP's belief that the US would harbor a lasting hostility toward a Communist regime in China.

II

The CCP should have felt a great relief when there was no sign of U.S. armed intervention through late 1949; yet the Communist leaders began to focus on the danger of long-term American antagonism toward a Communist China. As Mao addressed the preparatory meeting of a new political consultative conference on January 15, 1949, "I think it is necessary to call people's attention to the fact that the imperialists and their running dogs, the Chinese reactionaries, will not resign themselves to defeat in this land of China. They will continue to gang up against the Chinese people in every possible way."[27] To him, the U.S. government might execute its animosity toward China in three ways: first, "they will smuggle their agents into China to sow dissension and make trouble"; second, "they will incite the Chinese reactionaries, and even throw in their own forces, to blockade China's ports"; and third, "if they still hanker after adventures, they will send some of their troops to invade and harass China's frontiers." All of these, Mao stressed, were "not impossible."[28]

What then could the CCP possibly do to inhibit the US from acting out its hostility against China? Based on his understanding of the postwar Soviet-American confrontation, Mao calculated that his new regime would have to identify itself with the Soviet Union. His reasoning was simple: It would never be wrong to ally with an enemy's enemy. Yet to form such an alliance would not be easy, given the tortuous relationship between the CCP and Moscow. The CCP leadership was keenly aware that Stalin remained skeptical of the Chinese Communists, particularly worrying that Mao was another Tito.[29]

In an attempt to alleviate Stalin's distrust, the Communist leaders decided in May 1949 to dispatch a secret mission of top leaders to Moscow. Vice-chairman Liu Shaoqi and Zhou Enlai, assisted by Wang Jiaxiang, were in charge of the preparations. In late June, Liu led a five-person delegation to Moscow. The Communist Party boss in northeast China, Gao Gang, well known and much liked at the Kremlin, also joined the group. In Moscow, Liu had four meetings with Stalin and his top aides to discuss problems concerning the international situation and Sino-Soviet relations. Liu was supposed to convince Stalin that the Chinese Communists were not Titoists; ensure Soviet support, including diplomatic recognition and economic and military assistance; and conduct preliminary talks about a possible Mao visit to Moscow of some future date. At these meetings, Liu reported back, Stalin made three important points. First, the Soviet Union had erred in not offering as much help to the Chinese Communists as it should have and regretted having "hampered your revolution to some extent, . . . because we did not know China very well." Second, the CCP, after the nationwide victory, should immediately establish its government; otherwise, "the foreigners would take the advantage [of your anarchy] to intervene collectively." Stalin's final point was that "the world revolution is now moving eastward, therefore, you Chinese comrades should be prepared to assume more responsibility [for carrying the revolution]. This is our wish from the bottom of our hearts."[30] To show their willingness to help the Chinese, the Soviet leaders offered 360 pieces of anti-aircraft artillery to "strengthen China's coastal defenses."[31]

The CCP leadership now seemed encouraged by Moscow's new, positive attitude toward the CCP. The Central Committee then decided that Mao should visit Moscow and have a face-to-face meeting with Stalin. Mao himself was not sure to what extent the Kremlin would be able to accommodate CCP demands, not how his visit would be perceived. In order to probe Stalin's intentions, Mao sent a telegram on November 9, 1949, to Wang Jiaxiang, then CCP's representative to the Soviet Union, instructing him to ask Stalin if he would want Zhou Enlai to accompany Mao to Moscow. Mao was hopeful that if Stalin permitted Zhou, the CCP's best negotiator and diplomatic expert to come with him, it would indicate the Kremlin's sincere desire to assist the CCP. Either because of Mao's ambivalence or Moscow's reluctance, Mao departed for Russia in early December, without Zhou Enlai.[32]

Mao was given a splendidly cordial welcome upon his arrival in Moscow on December 16. Stalin and almost all of the Soviet top leaders met with Mao at the Kremlin at 6:00 P.M. that day. The Soviet leader praised Mao: "You are a great man. You have made a great contribution to the Chinese people, and therefore, you are the Chinese people's good son. I wholeheartedly wish you good health!" When Mao complained about the difficulties that the CCP radical elements had caused him, Stalin interrupted him: "Now you are a winner, and as a winner, no criticism should be imposed on you. This is a universal law."[33] The Soviet leader seemed very interested in finding out what Mao wanted from the USSR. Though Mao could have told Stalin plainly that he hoped to achieve a substantial Sino-Soviet relationship, he did not. "For this trip," Mao explained, "we expect to create something that should not only look nice, but taste delicious." This Chinese-style metaphor was so ambiguous that when it was translated into Russian, no one really understood what it meant. As Shi Zhe recalled later, "Stalin was very serious and kept asking Mao to clarify it." Refusing to do so, the CCP chairman totally disappointed and, to some extent, confused the Soviet leaders.[34]

For the next two weeks, Mao remained ambivalent regarding the real intentions of his visit to Moscow, although Stalin seemed ready to comply with whatever request Mao might make. In a short meeting as well as three personal telephone calls, Stalin repeatedly urged Mao to spell out his needs. With his long-standing suspicion of the Soviets, Mao still equivocated, insisting that Zhou Enlai should come to Moscow.[35] Mao continued to play the game of ambiguity when he told the *Tass* news agency on January 2, 1950, that "the length of my stay in the Soviet Union will largely depend on the time actually needed to settle the issues concerning the interests of the People's Republic of China." He never mentioned a word about what these issues were or how they were to be settled.[36]

The Kremlin leaders began to run out of patience. On the day after Mao's comments to *Tass*, Anastas Mikoyan and Vyacheslav Molotov informed Mao that Stalin had authorized them to talk about the true purpose of his visit. Beginning to credit Stalin's sincerity, Mao listed three possible outcomes. First, "we may sign a friendship and military alliance treaty as well as new economic cooperation agreements"; second, "we may sign an informal agreement to establish some general guidelines for the future Sino-Soviet relationship"; and third, "we may just sign a communiqué to confirm the friendly relationship between the two countries." Mao noted that in the last two cases, "Zhou need not come." He was impressed when Molotov and Mikoyan replied resolutely, "We will go for the first." Pleased with the proposal, Mao immediately cabled Beijing and asked Zhou to leave for Moscow in five days. Perhaps not wishing to appear too anxious, he instructed Zhou to "take the train and do not fly."[37]

Nevertheless, Mao expected to have a serious dialogue on a Sino-Soviet military alliance treaty. As he stated in his January 5 telegram to the CCP Central Committee, "We must have a full preparation for the coming talks [with the Soviets], which should include all the issues that our Central Committee is concerned with. Now that it is going to be a formal negotiation, we should proceed with it in all ways possible, and make all our positions clear [to the Soviets]."[38] Mao also specified that "the basic spirit of the alliance treaty should be to prevent Japan and its ally [the United States] from invading China"; "we will be able to use [the treaty] as a big political asset in dealing with imperialist countries in the world."[39]

When the negotiations started, the Russians did not seem forthcoming on certain points. Zhou especially could not obtain a clear commitment that the Soviet Union would assist China in the event of foreign invasions, an objective he regarded as crucial to an alliance treaty. The first Soviet-drafted version of the treaty stated that if one side was invaded by a third party, the other side "is supposed to [*de yi*] offer assistance." To Zhou, this was not potent enough because it did not make explicit the binding liability of a military alliance. Zhou and his aides worked strenuously to wring a clarification of this point out of the Soviet negotiators. The Chinese were genuinely pleased with the final text, which provided that "if one side is attacked by a third party, the other side *must devote all its efforts* [*jiejin quanli*] to provide military and other assistance."[40]

For economic assistance, the Soviet Union agreed to provide 300 million rubles in loans over five years at only 1 percent per annum interest. This accorded with Mao's expectations, since he had been informed by Stalin in April 1949 that the USSR was unable to make a huge loan to the CCP. Moreover, as Mao contended on January 3, 1950, "it will be appropriate for our own sake not to borrow too much in [the] next few years."[41] Coming from a diligent Chinese peasant family, he believed that loans were debts and debts ought to be paid back sooner or later.[42]

The Chinese leaders were satisfied with the creation of a military alliance between China and the Soviet Union. Mao told the sixth meeting of the Central People's Government Council, convened to consider ratification of the Sino-Soviet alliance treaty, that "[since] the imperialists still exist in the world, we therefore need friends and allies under this circumstance. . . . Now that the treaty has confirmed the friendship of the Soviet Union and formed the alliance relationship, we will thus have a good hand of assistance if the imperialists prepare to invade us."[43] Addressing the foreign ministry officials on March 20, Zhou declared that the primary objective of the Sino-Soviet military alliance was "to oppose [military] collaboration between Japan and other imperialists. By 'other imperialists,' [we] mean the United States." Song Qingling, widow of Sun Yat-sen and then vice-chairman of the People's Republic, also asserted that the power of the Sino-Soviet alliance "surpasses that of an atomic bomb."[44]

Having secured a military pact with the Soviet Union, the CCP leaders turned to their smaller allies: the Vietnamese and North Korean Communists.

The Sino-Vietnamese border had historically been vulnerable to foreign incursions. The CCP leaders were concerned in late 1949 that a French reoccupation of Indochina, combined with the increased U.S. military presence there, would be detrimental to China's border security. In order to diminish that danger, the Chinese leaders were determined to support the Vietnamese liberation movement on the grounds that Communist hegemony in Vietnam or Indochina would constitute a buffer zone.

Political and military cooperation between the Chinese and Vietnamese Communists developed rapidly after the CCP's success in China. Established in May 1941, Ho Chi Minh's League for the Independence of Vietnam, or Vietminh, had conceived the strategy that would eventually drive the French from Vietnam. In late December 1949, Ho sent his representative to Beijing to seek the PRC's diplomatic recognition and the establishment of formal relations. When Mao, then in Moscow, was informed of the Vietnamese request, he immediately instructed Liu Shaoqi that "recognition and diplomatic relationship should be granted to the Vietminh government at once."[45] At the same time, Mao personally drafted an official reply to Ho Chi Minh, in which he affirmed that "the establishment of our diplomatic relationship . . . will serve the purpose of strengthening the friendship and cooperation of our two nations in our common course." On January 19, Beijing proclaimed its willingness to open diplomatic relations with the Vietminh, thus becoming the first country to do so. Moreover, in order to find more supporters for the Vietminh, Mao appealed to Moscow and the Eastern European Communist countries and urged them to grant diplomatic recognition as well.[46]

Ho Chi Minh made a secret visit to Beijing in late January 1950, hoping to ascertain what the Chinese could do to advance his cause. Liu Shaoqi and Zhou Enlai clearly understood Ho's needs, but they could not make any commitment without Mao's endorsement. They suggested that he go immediately to Moscow and talk with Mao and Stalin. Realizing the importance of such a summit meeting, Ho hurried to Moscow.[47] There he conferred with the two Communist leaders about ways they might assist the Vietnamese revolution. Though Stalin expressed his deep concern about the Vietnamese struggle, he preferred that "the Chinese comrades take over the principal responsibility of supporting and supplying the Vietnamese people." Welcoming this opportunity, Mao promised to consider how that could be appropriately accomplished when he returned to Beijing.[48] In order to secure Mao's pledge, Ho addressed a memorandum to Zhou Enlai, outlining the main points of the Stalin-Mao-Ho talks and asking Zhou to verify them. He also informed Zhou that he would wait for him in Beijing to discuss detailed arrangements for Chinese military assistance.[49]

What the Vietnamese Communists wanted actually coincided with the CCP's security concerns regarding Indochina. Zhou and Liu Shaoqi had made it very clear to Ho in early 1950 that the Vietnamese struggle against the French was part of the larger Chinese struggle against imperialism in Asia, simply because China's southern border would be exposed to a direct threat if Vietnam was reoccupied by the imperialists.[50] In a telegram to Ho in May 1950, Mao underscored the importance of "the eternal unity of the peoples of the two countries, China and Vietnam, and their common effort in the cause of peace in Asia."[51] To safeguard China's southern border, the Chinese could either supply the Vietminh with war materiel, dispatch military advisers to Vietnam, or send in troops to engage the French directly. Hoang Van Hoan, then the Democratic Republic of Vietnam's ambassador to Beijing, recalled that the top Chinese leaders "expressed their determination without any hesitation that China would provide the Vietnamese people all the necessary material assistance and would be prepared to send troops to fight together with the Vietnamese people if necessary."[52] Hoang does not mention who said this and when, but if true, it seems that the Beijing leaders had offered an almost blank check to the Vietnamese.

Indeed, the Chinese had already been assisting the Vietnamese. Early in 1950, Chen Geng, commander of the 4th Army Corps stationed in Guangxi province, had a covert meeting with Ho Chi Minh in Nanning, the provincial capital. After Ho left, Chen ordered his troops to move closer to the Sino-Vietnamese border. He directed his soldiers to transport all the weapons captured from the KMT and "to take good care of them," because, Chen explained, "we need these weapons to carry out our internationalism."[53] Throughout that spring, the Chinese delivered a sufficient amount of artillery ammunition, trucks, and military equipment to equip five Vietminh infantry divisions, one artillery division, one anti-aircraft artillery regiment, and one guard regiment.[54] Meanwhile, the Chinese had constructed several training camps in Guangxi and Yunnan provinces, where a total of four Vietminh infantry regiments received intensive combat training under Chinese instructors.[55]

However, the Vietnamese leaders wanted the Chinese to "be directly involved in [their combat] efforts against the French colonialists and American imperialists." In April 1950, Ho sent a formal request to the CCP Central Committee, asking the PRC to dispatch military advisers for the Vietnamese forces at the divisional level and above and to send officers to command the Vietminh's regiments and battalions. Mao was cautious about Ho Chi Minh's demand. It was likely, in his view, that an overt involvement of Chinese forces in Vietnam might provoke a vigorous American reaction. In his reply to Ho, Mao made it clear that "our people will only act as advisers and will never command [Vietnamese] forces directly."[56] In late April, the CMC decided to form a military advisory group and appointed Wei Guoqing, a PLA army corps commander, as its head. The CMC's order specified that this group would go to Vietnam with the mission of "assisting the Vietnamese party and government in their political power construction and military struggle."[57]

Arriving in Vietnam in the early summer of 1950, the Chinese military advisers were intensely involved in the Vietminh's military buildup. At and above the divisional level, the Chinese coached the Vietnamese commanders on matters of strategic planning, military organization, political mobilization, and logistics. Moreover, the Chinese supplied the Vietminh's three best divisions (the 304th, 308th, and 312th) with advisers down to battalion level, giving them charge of not only training but combat planning.[58] Under Chinese patronage, the Vietminh soon possessed a conventional army of considerable offensive capability. As the North Koreans were preparing an all-out attack on South Korea in June, the Vietnamese Communists were planning a full-scale assault on the French forces along the Sino-Vietnamese border. At Ho Chi Minh's request, Beijing sent Chen Geng to Vietnam to direct the border campaign in early July.[59]

The CCP authorities regarded the Korean peninsula, like Indochina, as another dangerous spot that might complicate China's security. In their view, Korea was of too much geopolitical importance to be ignored. Believing that the US had long "dreamed" of dominating East Asia, Hu Sheng, a CCP senior political analyst, observed in late 1949 that the Korean peninsula stood as a "bridgehead" connecting Japan and northeast China.[60] When U.S. Secretary of State Dean Acheson asserted on March 15 that the US would never attempt to acquire anything from Asia, Zhou Enlai retorted that the Truman administration wanted to "cheat us again." The US would always want to control Taiwan, Korea, and Indochina, and that was why "the U.S. government is still supplying the KMT with bombers to bomb the Chinese mainland; . . . the US is doing the same thing to support such puppet regimes as Baota and Syngman Rhee . . . so as to suppress the Vietnamese and Korean liberation movements to strengthen U.S. control over those places."[61]

To alleviate the fear of an American invasion from the Korean peninsula, Beijing could have offered the North Korean Communists the same type of assistance they rendered to the Vietminh. The CCP leaders obviously understood the significance of Communist control in that region, and the CCP troops had fought the Japanese side by side with more than 90,000 Korean soldiers in northeast China. Yet Beijing never made quite the same level of commitment to the North Koreans as it did to the Vietnamese. It was the Soviet Union that actually played the major role in assisting the North Koreans.[62] As long as Moscow kept offering military supplies and maintaining a considerable number of military personnel and advisers in North Korea, it was wise for the Chinese to stay uninvolved. However, in the literature on the Korean War, South Korean historian Pak Toufu found evidence that Beijing's military officers consistently participated in Kim's decision making during his liberation war. The Chinese delegates, he claimed, attended an important strategic planning session at Moscow in mid-December 1948 and a meeting discussing military implementation at Harbin, northeastern China, in January 1949. Furthermore, at the Harbin meeting, Chinese representatives Zhou Baozhong, the commander of the PLA Jining Military Region, and Lin Feng, the chairman of the Northeast Executive Committee, reportedly agreed to "return all the 28,000 officers and soldiers of Korean origin [in northeastern China] to North Korea in three different times before September 1949."[63] There have been no studies by Chinese historians either to confirm or refute these findings.

Yet scattered Chinese references do suggest a close military relationship between Beijing and Pyongyang. Beijing signed three agreements with the North Koreans on January 7, 1950, dealing with the establishment of Sino–North Korean postal services, telegraphic communication, and telephone lines. As these systems would enhance Beijing-Pyongyang military cooperation, the CPGC ratified these documents and put them into effect on February 1.[64] As for the soldiers of Korean origin, Nie Rongzhen, then PLA's acting chief of staff, recalled that in January 1950, Kim Il-sung sent his aide Kim Kwang-hyop to Beijing to discuss the matter. He relayed to the CCP Politburo Standing Committee the North Korean leader's request that all the officers and soldiers of Korean origin be returned to North Korea after they were organized into a combat-ready army in northeastern China. After a few rounds of negotiation, Nie reached an agreement with the North Korean representative that "altogether 14,000 soldiers of Korean origin would return to North Korea along with their weapons and equipment."[65] In the spring of 1950, Beijing's military authorities increased the PLA force deployment in northeastern and northern China. Although these troops were to conduct military training and protect the economic reconstruction there, their actual mission was to defend the Sino-Korean border, given the coming North Korean attack on South Korea. During his inspection on April 2, 1950, of a cavalry force that was soon to move into northeastern China, Zhu De warned the soldiers that "you should by no means relax your vigilance. You should be ready at all times to wipe out any imperialist invaders."[66]

III

Along with forming military allies, the CCP leaders took on the task of strengthening China's coastal defenses. Coterminous with the western Pacific, China had more than 10,000 miles of coastline. A number of port cities, including Dalian [Darine], Lushun [Port Arthur], Tianjin, Yantai, Qingdao, Shanghai, Fuzhou, Xiamen [Amoy], Shantou, and Guangzhou [Canton], connected China to the Pacific sea-lanes and had historically served as "front gates" to the Chinese mainland. Over the past century (1839–1945), as the leaders were keenly aware, China's coast had been subject to invasions from Britain, France, Japan, Russia, Germany, the US, Austria, and Italy, as many as 470 times.[67] With these encroachments on China's coastal boundary fresh in their memory, the Chinese Communists considered it imprudent to be complacent about a possible U.S. military threat from the sea.

It had never been easy for China to defend its coast, and it was even more difficult for the Chinese Communists in the early days of their rule. The new government lacked the necessary means to establish effective coastal defenses. Although the People's Liberation Army comprised more than five million troops, it was no better than a light conventional force.[68] At the same time, the United States, the perceived enemy, maintained absolute air and sea superiority in the western Pacific. With naval and air bases in Japan, Taiwan, and the Philippines, American armed forces in East Asia were capable of seizing any Chinese port. Moreover, the KMT forces controlled most of the islands off the Zhejiang, Jiangsu, Fujian, and Guangdong coasts by late spring of 1950. Assisted by its air force, the KMT Navy set up an effective blockage against inshore and offshore CCP transportation in the East and Southeast China Seas. Constant KMT assaults disturbed the security of China's coasts.[69] Compounding the logistical problems was the state of the nation's economy, which had completely collapsed under the burden of decade-long wars. Beijing authorities found it very difficult to finance the armed forces, let alone to find extra resources to build a strong coastal defense.[70]

Regardless, the CCP leaders tried to make the best of some stopgap measures, choosing to protect the most vulnerable areas instead of defending the entire coast. This idea fit squarely into Mao's principle of "concentrating one's attention and efforts to deal with major problems." In a telegram to Fourth Field Army Commander Lin Biao on October 31, 1940, Mao instructed that "our national defense should focus on three areas, centering around Tianjin, Shanghai, and Guangzhou." As for force deployment, he directed that "after completing the battles in Guangxi [province], the Fourth Field Army should dispatch five regular armies to the Guangzhou area to assume the responsibility of defending Guangdong and Guangxi [provinces]."[71] These three port cities formed an isosceles triangle from the North China Sea to the southeastern China coasts, and Mao evidently regarded them as areas of great strategic significance, intending each to reinforce the defense of the others.

Instead of maintaining a positional defense along the coast, the Chinese Communists also decided to build an in-depth defense—a defensive zone of several layers with forces deployed in such a way as to maneuver and reinforce one another. This arrangement was based on a calculation of both sides' military capabilities. China's best asset was its large conventional force, which was especially good at ground battles. Since it could not resort to naval and air support, China could instead allow the enemy to land and even move inland. Fighting on familiar terrain, Chinese troops could concentrate the main strength of the army on mobile warfare or battles of quick decision. In all likelihood, China would seize the initiative. The U.S. armed forces, the CCP leaders reasoned, chiefly relied on naval and air intervention and superior firepower; without a large infantry, once they became a land force, they would become vulnerable, especially to close combat. This was an essential element of traditional Chinese strategy: *hou fa zhi ren*, to gain mastery by striking only after the enemy has struck. For this purpose, Mao ordered the Fourth Field Army headquarters in late October 1949 "to deploy three regular armies in Henan [province] and the rest of the field army along the railways of Hunan, Hubei, and Jiangxi [provinces] so that [these troops] can be quickly transported either south [between Shanghai and Guangzhou] or north [between Shanghai and Tianjin] whenever required."[72] Earlier that month, Mao had also directed the 19th Army Corps, consisting of three infantry armies (the 63d, 64th, and 65th) and headed by Yang Dezhi, to move to Baoji, a city near Tianjin in Shaanxi province, to be "national defense mobile forces for reinforcement purposes." The Tianjin area, with "Yang Chengwu's three armies and six second-rate infantry divisions," should be strengthened so that "if anything serious happens, we will have enough forces to react."[73]

Rather than rely on a central command for coastal defenses, the CCP leaders opted for regional posts. On December 26, 1949, the CMC announced the establishment of the Central South China Military Command [*zhongnan junqu*] and named Lin Biao the commander. With his headquarters in Hankou, Hubei province, Lin directed all the forces stationed in Guangdong, Guangxi, Hunan, Hubei, and Jiangxi provinces. As the first echelon of defense, Lin placed the 15th Army Corps, composed of the 43d, 44th, and 48th armies and headed by Deng Hua in Guangdong, and the 13th Army Corps, composed of the 38th, 39th, 48th, and 49th armies and directed by Cheng Zihua (replaced by Huang Yongsheng in January 1950), in Guangxi.

The 12th Army Corps (the 40th, 41st, 45th, and 46th armies) in Hunan formed a second tier of defense. Three infantry armies (the 42d, 50th, and 51st), three infantry divisions (the 153d, 155th, and 158th), four artillery divisions (the 1st, 2d, 5th, and 8th), one anti-aircraft artillery division, and four regiments of engineering corps were directly attached to Lin's headquarters as strategic reserves.[74]

Meanwhile, the CMC established the East China Military Command [*huadong junqu*]. With Chen Yi as the chief commander, the entire Third Field Army was put under its control. According to the CMC directive of January 1950, Wang Jianan's 7th Army Corps, consisting of the 21st and 22d armies plus ten local units (altogether, 93,300 men), was to garrison Zhejiang; Ye Fei's 10th Army Corps (the 28th, 29th, and 31st armies), assisted by eight local units (totaling 152,300 men), would defend Fujian. The CMC also formed the Shandong Military Command (under the East China Military Command) and appointed Xu Shiyou to direct more than 113,700 troops for the protection of the Shandong peninsula and northern coast of Jiangsu. Chen Yi set up his headquarters in Shanghai with the 97th, 98th, 99th, and 100th infantry divisions to guard the city. The 9th Army Corps, comprising the 20th, 23d, 26th, and 27th armies (altogether, 191,800 men) and headed by Song Shilun, would move to the western suburbs of Shanghai to serve as the strategic reserves.[75]

The establishment of these new commands was an important step taken by the PRC to bolster China's coastal defense. First, the new structure strengthened command and control. The PLA's field armies had been under the direct supervision of the CMC throughout the civil war. With the regional commands in place, field commanders were in a position to make both short-term and long-term military plans. Second, being deployed in the coastal areas and renamed as "the National Defense Army [*guofangjun*]," the rank and file now had a clearer idea of their mission. Their training and preparations became more closely related to this task. Third, the disposition of such a large number of troops along the coasts would help consolidate the CCP's control over these areas. As the CMC instructed in December 1949, the coastal armed forces were to bear three grave responsibilities for the year 1950: defending China's coast against foreign invasion; carrying on the fight against the KMT remnants on the offshore islands; and assisting economic construction and production.[76] In the spring of 1950, both the East and the Central South China commands spared several thousand men and women to participate in the land reform in the surrounding countryside.[77]

However, the CCP leaders understood that the deployment of three million troops along the coast would meet only short-term security needs. A long-term national defense would require modernization of the armed forces. It is interesting that the CCP leadership chose the construction of a modern air force as its first priority. Mao had begun considering the buildup of an air corps as early as January 1949. In a CCP Politburo document entitled "The Current Situation and Our Party's Task in 1949," Mao remarked that "we must be devoted to the construction of an air force so that [we will be able to] use it [in our military struggle] in 1949 and 1950."[78] Commander in Chief Zhu De also sounded urgent in his letter to Mao in early July that "we shall arrange to send pilots to the Soviet Union for air force training immediately. Hopefully, [these pilots] will learn how to fly after six months [in Russia]."[79] Concurring with Zhu's idea, Mao instructed Zhou Enlai on July 10 to dispatch 300 to 400 air force personnel to the Soviet Union for six to eight months of flight training. He further authorized the purchase of 100 military planes from the USSR "so that we can form our own air force."[80] On July 26, Mao cabled Liu Shaoqi in Moscow that he should go directly to Stalin with this request. "Our air force capability is very small," Mao explained to Liu. "We now only have sixty-eight pilots capable of flying [combat aircraft], and we only possess thirty-six fighters, ten bombers, and twelve transport planes. Most of these planes need to be repaired and cannot be used for some time." He wanted Liu to inform Stalin that "we are determined to build our [own] air force in one year, and that is our first priority [*shouyao renwu*]. Therefore, we will need to buy [military] aircraft from the Soviet Union and invite Soviet air force experts to assist [us]."[81] Meeting with Stalin on July 27, Liu asked that the Soviet Union provide China with 100 to 200 Yak fighters and 40 to 80 bombers, accept 200 pilots and 500 Chinese ground crew for training in Soviet air force institutions, and send air force advisers to China. Stalin promised to do his best in fulfilling China's request.[82]

With the Soviet assurance in hand, the CCP leadership immediately intensified preparations for building its own air force. In July 1949, the CMC decided to establish a temporary air force command to take charge of the organizational work. Liu Yalou, the 14th Army Corps commander, accepted the appointment, and all the staff and personnel of the 14th Army Corps headquarters were incorporated into the proposed air force command.[83] In late July, Liu traveled to Moscow, as Zhou Enlai instructed, to work out the details of the pledged Soviet assistance.[84] Meeting with Soviet Defense Minister Alexander M. Vasilevskii several times, Liu secured the sale of 434 Soviet military aircraft to China. As agreed upon by Vasilevskii and Liu, Soviet air force experts would assist the Chinese in setting up pilot training centers in the Northeast, and the Soviets would supply the needed equipment and materials for the facilities. When on October 5 Stalin approved the Liu-

Vasilevskii agreement, Liu left Moscow for Beijing the next day.[85] Now that the Soviet promise had materialized, the CMC announced the official establishment of the people's Air Force Command on November 11, and formally appointed Liu Yalou as its commander. Anxious to have an air force, the CMC gave Liu only two weeks to put the new command into operation.[86]

Capable but extremely irascible and self-confident, Liu embraced the new challenge. Instead of a nationwide recruitment, he focused on the backbone of the army. As he recommended to the CMC in late July 1949, candidates who "have good political background [CCP member], are around the age of twenty, have had elementary or middle school education, and serve as platoon or company leaders," would meet the requirements for pilot training. Meanwhile, Liu advocated "accelerated methodology [*sucheng fa*]" for the flight training. He arranged the training curriculum to meet his requirement that the trainees would be able to fly solo after 150 to 200 hours of basic instruction. The main objective, Liu stressed, was to maximize the production of pilots within a minimum amount of time. To him, the pilots need only acquire basic techniques during training, and then they could improve their skills while on combat duties.[87] Liu's impetuosity did not seem to bother the top leaders. Mao Zedong only warned during his private meeting with Liu on July 31 that although China had to build a strong air force, "we must be very careful with our budget [when we plan for] purchasing [military] planes and equipment and inviting [Soviet] experts, [because] we are now facing enormous financial difficulties and the Soviet Union won't provide [us] free assistance and service."[88]

Mao's caution did not seem to restrain Liu. In his October 30, 1949, directive to the pilot training centers, Liu made November 30 the deadline for the completion of all construction and ordered that "[flight] training must begin by that date."[89] Eager for quick success, in early November the new air force declared the opening of six training centers in Beijing, Jinan, Shenyang, Jinzhou, Changchun, and Harbin. With 1,672 candidates gathered in Changchun for preliminary instructions and awaiting the arrival of Soviet planes and experts, the centers were inaugurated on December 1.[90] After only a few months the Air Force Command proclaimed its readiness to organize an air force unit. In his April 1, 1950, report to the CMC, Liu announced that he had trained enough pilots to fill seven air force divisions; all he needed was more personnel for ground crews. The CMC leaders were pleased at Liu's progress and approved his request.[91] Liu informed Mao on April 21 that the 4th Air Force Brigade, CCP's first air force unit, would be deployed in Nanjing.[92]

As urgent as the need was for an air force, the CCP also felt pressed to build a navy; as specified by the June 8, 1949, CCP Politburo document, it had to be "capable of defending both [eastern and southeastern China] coasts and the Yangtze River."[93] Mao had emphasized at a Chinese People's Political Consultative Conference (CPPCC) meeting on September 21, that "our national defense will be consolidated so that no imperialists will ever again be allowed to invade our land. Therefore, we will not only have a powerful army but also a powerful air force and a powerful navy."[94] On October 10, Mao again pointed out that any navy constructed by the CCP "must have the capability of defending our coast and must be powerful enough to prevent imperialist invasion."[95]

As early as January 21, 1949, the CMC had directed the Third Field Army headquarters to plan for the creation of a naval force. Deputy Chief of Staff Zhang Aiping assumed this special responsibility. In the early spring of 1949, the KMT's Second Fleet and 5th Convoy Group defected to the Chinese Communists, which yielded two cruisers and twenty-five other warships and gunboats with full crews. With these vessels and personnel, Zhang formed the first CCP naval unit, the East China Navy, on April 23.[96] Over the next few months, the continued defection of the KMT naval forces added another seventy-three warships and gunboats to the new navy. In December 1949, the CMC assigned 12th Army Corps Commander Xiao Jinguang to organize the People's Navy, which was officially inaugurated in Beijing five months later.[97]

Viewing the acquisition of more vessels as its first priority, the navy confiscated private and commercial vessels, including eighteen transports owned by the Shanghai Commercial Bureau and fifty-six fishing boats belonging to the Shanghai Water Resources Company. By the end of 1949, the navy had seized as many as 169 commercial vessels with a total displacement of 64,865 tons; all of these were converted into warships.[98] Meanwhile, a salvage operation began in September 1949 in the Yangtze, and within six months, the East China Navy had pulled out seven sunken vessels, including two cruisers of the KMT Navy. With inadequate technology and tools and with the constant harassment of KMT air raids, the navy's salvage mission was not as fruitful as expected.[99] Beijing then turned to foreign markets. Although the infant government had little foreign currency with which to buy advanced naval vessels, the Soviet loan of $150 million cleared in February 1950. The PRC thus managed to purchase secondhand and retired naval and commercial vessels from the British colony of Hong Kong. Between late 1949 and early 1950, China bought forty-eight used warships totaling 25,470 tons; most of them were British manufactured, though there were some American and Japanese remnants from World War II.[100] The CCP leaders had actually hoped to rely on Soviet products, but Moscow was unwilling to provide free support. Despite its fiscal difficulties, Beijing submitted to Moscow in the early spring of 1950 a lavish shopping list for naval equipment: over the next three years, China planned to buy 205 Soviet gunboats and submarines totaling 55,300 tons, 420 aircraft for a naval air force, and enough coastal artillery guns to equip thirty-eight companies.[101]

The Chinese Communists at first counted on Soviet naval experts for training, but soon found the Soviet instructors none too helpful. As a result of the Liu Shaoqi–Stalin talks during the summer of 1949, 90 Soviet naval specialists had arrived in China between October and November, and 600 more came in 1950.[102] However, the CCP naval commanders could not find enough Russian interpreters, which put an insurmountable language barrier between the instructors and their Chinese students. More important, the Chinese felt that the Soviets did not understand their compressed timetable for mobilizing a navy, and they had difficulty in persuading the Soviet advisers to skip such fundamentals as mathematics, physics, and mechanical engineering. The Soviet training method, Zhang Aiping commented, was like "water away at a distance which can't save those who are dying of thirst here [*yuanshui bu jie jinke*]." An immediate requirement of China's naval training program, Zhang explained in August 1949, was to teach the Chinese how to sail vessels, operate engines, and fire guns, not to learn some useless theories. To him, it was like showing someone how to turn on an electric light: It was not necessary to understand how the light worked in the first place.[103]

Zhang eventually ignored the Soviet experts and established his own curricula, since he was determined to have his naval trainees complete the course quickly. In December 1949, he issued a "Three-Month Rush Training Plan," which required all the training centers to spend three months demonstrating only how to run vessels. The plan stated that "[our naval] training must adhere to the principles of 'teaching and learning the most useful techniques and the simplest measures of operation.'" The sole objective was to "have intensive training on individual techniques so that [the trainees] will be able to operate naval vessels after three months."[104] As a result, by February 1950, the East China Navy's training centers had rushed 4,800 trainees through the minimum preparation, focusing merely on operating a naval vessel.[105] Since the Soviet advisers refused to give way to CCP's impatience, Zhang had to recruit former KMT naval personnel and other maritime specialists as instructors. The faculty of the Dalian Naval Training Center, established on November 23, 1949, consisted of 26 percent former KMT naval personnel, 33 percent former professors at Beijing and Qinghua universities, 13 percent university students majoring in engineering, 2 percent technicians from local shipyards, and only 6 percent Soviet advisers. The CCP naval commanders were extremely proud of their "self-reliance" in raising their modern naval personnel.[106]

The navy had to accelerate its training because it was immediately needed to support the infantry's assaults on the KMT on the offshore islands. In late 1949, the PLA had met with great obstacles in its drive against the KMT's island positions. In an attack on the Dengbu Islands off the eastern Zhejiang coast on October 3, the 61st Division (of the 21st Army) dispatched five battalions. The troops managed to occupy the islands but lost control of them when the KMT Navy blocked them; the PLA suffered a total of 1,490 casualties.[107] An even bigger setback was the outcome of the Jinmen [Quemoy] Islands attack later that same month. The 10th Army Corps was able to land but, with no naval support, eventually lost 9,086 men to the KMT naval counterattack.[108] The field army commanders came to believe that the participation of the People's Navy was the key to seizing the KMT-occupied offshore islands, and they urged its immediate deployment.

The Fourth Field Army Command incorporated a naval element in the planned attack on the Wanshan Islands in late May 1950. Composed of forty-eight small islands, the Wanshan group was known as the "southern big gate" to the Zhujiangkou [the Gulf of Pearl River], Guangzhou. The KMT had deployed more than thirty warships and gunboats to defend these islands. The PLA field commander Hong Xuezhi calculated that, without naval backing, any amphibious push would be another Jinmen failure.[109] The People's Navy assigned two cruisers—the American-manufactured *Guishan* of 358 tons and the *Guochu* produced by Britain during World War II—and ten gunboats at Hong's disposal. However, these vessels were in poor condition: several gunboats did not have navigation or communication equipment, and most of the officers and crew lacked naval battle experience and only knew how to turn on the engine and fire the guns.[110] With such liabilities, this small naval force ventured an attack on May 25 and was initially beset with mishaps. As soon as all the vessels sailed out, they lost contact with one another. The gunboat *Jiefang* almost collided with a KMT ship, only to discover that it was surrounded by more than twenty enemy vessels. Believing the enemy had not identified them, Captain Lin Wenhu launched the attack alone. In a few hours, the *Jiefang* sank one KMT gunboat and damaged three others. When the KMT Navy counterattacked the next morning, the *Jiefang*, joined by the rest of the CCP fleet, fought with determination. Lin and his crew employed the ground tactics of "close battles" and "bayonet charges"; they moved very close to the KMT vessels below the range of the enemy's heavier guns and then fired machine guns at the enemy crew and threw grenades onto the KMT ship. This small CCP naval force reportedly sank four vessels, damaged another twelve, and forced the KMT Navy to retreat from the Wanshan Islands. More important, the CCP leaders were encouraged by this unexpected victory—a small, weak naval force defeated a strong enemy navy. Mao highly commended his young navy, declaring that "this is the first glorious success of the People's Navy and [you] deserve [our] wholehearted congratulation."[111]

IV

Although economic reconstruction and political consolidation were the most urgent tasks during the first months of their rule, the Chinese Communists were meticulously concerned with national defense. The CCP's apparent sense of insecurity had derived from a fear that the US would militarily intervene in China to serve its expansionist aims in Asia. It is important to note that Mao among other leaders consistently saw Korea as one of the hot spots where any U.S. military action would be detrimental to China's security. Without questioning how realistic this perceived threat was, Mao relentlessly pursued military preparations for a worst-case scenario. Nourished in the context of turmoil and strife, Mao's long-held belief that "preparedness will eliminate mishaps" stood firm.

More important, Mao believed that China could stand up against the superior American military power should a conflict arise. In his view, the deployment of a large number of the PLA forces had compelled the Americans to evacuate their positions in China and had thus forestalled direct U.S. armed intervention in 1949. He became even more confident after securing a military alliance with the Soviet Union and establishing good relationships with the North Korean and Vietnamese Communists. He was also pleased to see that the buildup of the People's Navy and People's Air Force proceeded with such great speed, as the Chinese Communist forces became stronger than ever before. This seemed to confirm Mao's belief that "the revolutionary forces always start from scratch and develop from weak to strong and from small to large [*cong wu dao you, cong ruo dao qiang, cong xiao dao da*]."[112]

However, Mao failed to recognize the potential danger of his inflated optimism, especially in a time of unexpected crisis. There is reason to believe that the CCP chairman had never intended to engage the United Nations forces directly in Korea, but in the end he did just that.

4. "WE CAN'T SIT STILL WITH FOLDED HANDS"

From June to October 1950, the dramatic escalation of the military conflict in Korea shocked the world. The war began on June 25 with the North Korean Communist troops' surprise attack on South Korea. The vastly superior North Korean People's Army (NKPA) swept over the 38th parallel, the artificial line dividing the two Koreas, and within a few days had slashed through South Korea's defense line and routed Syngman Rhee's troops.

The US responded immediately. Within twenty-four hours, the Truman administration had decided to intervene militarily on South Korea's behalf. Washington first sent the U.S. Seventh Fleet to "neutralize" the Taiwan Strait and then dispatched U.S. armed forces to Korea from their post–World War II occupation bases in Japan. Meanwhile, the United Nations Security Council condemned North Korea's aggression and recommended that member nations furnish aid to South Korea. On July 7, General Douglas MacArthur, supreme commander for the Allied powers, was named supreme UN commander to direct the joint military force of sixteen nations in Korea, with the US supplying the vast bulk of forces and materials. The US/UN military intervention turned Korea's civil war into an international conflict played out on China's doorstep. After the success of MacArthur's daring amphibious operation at Inchon in mid-September, the US/UN troops proceeded to roll back the Communist forces through North Korea. By early October, they occupied part of North Korea, and US/UN vanguard units were a few miles away form the Yalu River, the boundary line separating northeastern China and North Korea. This chapter explores the Chinese response to the outbreak of war and the prospect of US/UN occupation of North Korea.

I

Probably surprised by the timing of the Korean conflict,[1] Beijing authorities were alert to the developing war situation and, in particular, worried about the quick and unyielding U.S. military response in North Korea. Given their abiding fear that the US might take provocative action either from the Korean peninsula, the Taiwan Strait, or Indochina, the Chinese Communists viewed the American armed intervention in Korea as strong evidence of U.S. hostility toward China. They did not believe that the increased American involvement on the peninsula was to defend South Korea, nor were they convinced that the U.S. Seventh Fleet's presence in the Taiwan Strait was intended to neutralize that area.

The CCP leaders viewed Washington's reactions to the Korean War as part of a grand scheme of U.S. expansion in East Asia. Mao Zedong pointed out at the CPGC's eighth session on June 28 that "there is absolutely no ground for the United States' intervention in the internal affairs of countries such as Korea, Philippines, and Vietnam." He reminded his audience that "it was only on January 5 of this year that Truman announced that the United States would not intervene in Taiwan. Now he himself has proved that statement to be a [pack of lies], . . . he has torn to shreds all international agreements regarding the nonintervention of the United States in the internal affairs of China." All these "aggressive actions," Mao stressed, were an "exposure by the United States of its own imperialist face."[2] Zhou Enlai also commented on the same day that China was not surprised by the "aggressive" moves of the US in Korea and the Taiwan Strait because "the predatory behavior of the American government is well within the Chinese people's expectation." Zhou declared that "for a long time, the Chinese people have continuously brought to light the U.S. imperialist plot to invade China and to dominate Asia." In his view, American military actions were "no more than an open exposure of and putting into practice a long-prepared plan [of aggression]."[3]

However, Beijing's initial reaction was dictated by the old Chinese saying *yu ze li*, meaning that a precise anticipation of a crisis guarantees an advantageous position. As soon as Washington committed ground forces to Korea, Beijing authorities assessed how the American intervention might endanger China's security, and they concluded that Korea would become a focal point in East Asia for the ongoing Cold War. When the NKPA advance met strong resistance around the Pusan perimeter in July 1950, Mao discerned "the possibility that the Korean War might become stalemated and the US would expand its military action." To him the danger was "being exacerbated on a daily basis." Given this eventuality, he asserted, the Chinese people had no choice but to brace for the worst.[4] Mao explained to his advisers that "we have to prepare for an emergence of war mania; we have to prepare for [the possibility] that the United States might provoke a third world war, or carry it out for a protracted time, or even use atomic bombs." Should the US dare to

Map of North Korea (Source: *Central Intelligence Agency. Reproduced courtesy of the University of Chicago Libraries)*

expand the military conflict into China, the CCP chairman was confident that "we should by no means be intimidated by such an aggressive war. . . . [We] will be obliged to fight to the finish." Given the tense situation, Mao urged that "in any case, we shall get fully prepared so that we won't be caught by surprise and rush into the war unprepared."[5]

Under Mao's direction, China began to make military preparations. On July 7, Zhou Enlai, then the CMC's standing vice-chairman, chaired a national security meeting. The participants were the high-ranking military commanders of the CCP that Zhou could summon to Beijing on short notice. They included Zhu De, PLA's commander in chief; Nie Rongzhen, acting chief of staff; Nie's aide Li Tao, director of combat operations; Luo Ronghuan, director of the General Political Department; Yang Lisan, minister of the General Logistics Department; Xiao Jinguang, commander of the People's Navy; Liu Yalou, commander of the People's Air Force; Xu Guangda, commander of the armored forces; Su Jin, deputy commander of the artillery forces; Teng Daiyuan, commander of the railway corps; Lin Biao, commander of the Fourth Field Army; Tan Zheng, deputy political commissar of the Central South Military Command; He Jinnian, deputy commander of the Northeast Military Command; and Wan Yi, commander of the Fourth Field Army Artillery Forces.[6]

At the meeting, there emerged a consensus that the Sino-Korean border defense must be strengthened immediately, since "it is necessary to prepare an umbrella before it rains [*wei yu choumou*]." For this purpose, the participants suggested first the establishment of an individual northeastern border defense command, to be headquartered in Shenyang, Liaoning province. They recommended that first deputy commander of the Third Field Army Su Yu, one of CCP's best field commanders, head this new unit, with navy commander Xiao Jinguang, deputy director of the General Political Department Xiao Hua, and deputy chief of staff of the Fourth Field Army Li Jukui serving as Su's deputies. Second, the commanders proposed the deployment of troops from the Fourth Field Army, the CCP's most experienced combat force. More important, since they had spent years in northeastern China during the anti-Japanese war and the civil war, the troops were familiar with the terrain and were accustomed to fighting in cold winters. The Fourth Field Army's 13th Army Corps consisted of the 38th, 39th, and 40th infantry armies, stationed in Henan, Guangdong, and Hunan provinces as strategic reserves; they should be the first to move to the Sino-Korean border. The commanders, however, had doubts about 13th Army Corps Commander Huang Yongsheng. Luo Ronghuan, who had formerly been second-in-command of the Fourth Field Army, suggested that 15th Army Corps Commander Deng Hua replace Huang. All the participants concurred. The commanders also attached the 42d Army—already in Manchuria—and three artillery divisions to the 13th Army Corps. Third, with an obvious sense of urgency, the commanders emphasized the importance of prompt decision making and quick action. They specified that all the troops now designated as the Northeast Border Defense

Army (NBDA) must gather along the Sino-Korean border no later than the end of July, that the PLA General Logistics Department should begin to stockpile arms and supplies right away, and that the General Political Department should immediately lay out detailed plans for political mobilization.[7]

After the session, Nie reported to Mao, who endorsed "all the resolutions adopted at today's meeting" and directed "immediate implementation" of the resolutions.[8] Three days later, Zhou Enlai called another national defense meeting to discuss the details of force deployment along the Sino-Korean border. This time only four commanders—Tan Zheng, Zhao Erlu (then chief of staff of the Fourth Field Army), He Jinnian, and Wan Yi—were called in. Zhou urged in particular that the Fourth Field Army and Northeast Military commands fully support the formation and disposition of the NBDA. He then talked in detail with the commanders about specific locations to station troops, set up supply depots, and establish air defense."[9]

Mao signed the CMC "Resolution on Defending the Northeast Border Security" on July 13. The order officially appointed Su Yu as the NBDA commander, Xiao Hua as political commissar, Xiao Jinguang as deputy NBDA commander, and Li Jukui as logistics commander. The order directed that four infantry armies (38th, 39th, 40th, and 42d), three artillery divisions (1st, 2d, and 8th), one anti-aircraft artillery regiment, one regiment of engineers, and three transportation regiments, totaling 250,000 troops, would be put under the new command. The directive also indicated that Deng Hua and 15th Army Corps political commissar Lai Chuanzhu, 13th Army Corps chief of staff Xie Fang, and 13th Army Corps political department director Du Ping were to form a front command in Andong (Dandong), only a few miles away from North Korea's Sinuiju. While the NBDA Command would set up its headquarters in Shenyang, all the combat units were to gather between Andong and Kaiyuan. Finally, the CMC order required all the commanding officers to report to their new posts immediately and all the troops to assemble at their designated sites within twenty-five days.[10]

Implementation of the CMC order, however, proved to be a formidable task. None of the appointed NBDA commanders, except Li Jukui, who was based in Shenyang, were able to report to duty. Su Yu was seriously ill and hospitalized in Qingdao. Xiao Jinguang, who had only recently assumed his post as commander of the People's Navy, found it difficult to depart for the new assignment at short notice. Deputy director of the General Political Department Xiao Hua was also preoccupied with his job, since the director of the department, Luo Ronghuan, had taken sick leave. Zhou suggested to Mao that the establishment of the NBDA Command be postponed and the NBDA forces be put under the Northeast Military Command for the time being. Mao accepted the suggestion, and the northeastern district took complete charge of the NBDA from July through September.[11]

The muster of the NBDA forces also encountered enormous difficulties. Since December 1949, the 38th Army had been stationed in Xinyang, Henan province, while the 39th Army had stayed in Luohe, Henan province. As strategic reserves of China's coastal defense, these two armies were expected to maintain combat readiness. However, in addition to military drills, the troops were preoccupied with farming and other nonmilitary work. The 40th Army was exhausted after its participation in the campaign against the KMT remnants on the Hainan Islands in the late spring of 1950. Indeed, none of these three armies were ready for their new assignment. Du Ping, as director of the 13th Army Corps political department, had earlier reported to the General Political Department that the strength of the troops was greatly weakened because of "too much farming and too little training." Du found that the soldiers had used military equipment to dig navigation tunnels and plough farmland; battle steeds had been turned into pack horses; and most of the heavy weapons were rusty. In one case, Du reported, some sparrows had built a resort in the barrel of a mountain cannon. More to the point, the rank and file were worn out by the heavy labor, and this overwhelming fatigue had depressed troop morale.[12] Du Ping recalled later that many units of the 38th and 39th armies departed for the front from their muddy rice fields, showing obvious reluctance to leave their farms. It was truly difficult for these troops to adjust to an immediate combat situation.[13]

The reorganization of the 13th Army Corps Command faced obstacles as well. When the CMC ordered the switch of commanders between the 13th and 15th army corps, only Deng Hua was able to go to Shenyang, leaving his political commissar, Lai Chuanzhu, behind to ensure a smooth transition. Deputy Commander Hong Xuezhi, was deeply involved in the operations against the remnant KMT along the Guangdong coast, and the Guangzhou authorities refused to release him. Most of the commanders thought that the change was too risky because it violated a traditional Chinese principle of warfare: "no switch of commanders on the eve of a battle [*linzhen huan jiang*]." Although the Fourth Field Army Command had clear instructions from the CMC on the transfer of command, both Lin Biao and Luo Ronghuan were ill, so the task of ensuring compliance fell to deputy political commissar Tan Zheng. Tan called a meeting of the high-ranking commanders at the field army headquarters in Hankou. Before and during the meeting, he talked with Du Ping several times to convince Du that the CCP central leadership's decision to switch the army corps commanders was based on "careful consideration" at Beijing's national defense meetings. All the leaders in Beijing had agreed, Tan emphasized, that "Deng Hua suits this position better than Huang Yongsheng," and "Chairman Mao concurred with them." Tan wanted Du to guarantee that every lower-ranking commander would support Deng and the new command. "Since the deployment of your troops in northern China preludes a large-scale and tough war," he warned Du, "you should be fully prepared for any serious change [of the war situation]."[14] On July 19, the CMC cabled Du Ping that "the [northeastern] border defense is urgent, and you are honored to assume the task." The CMC also urged Du to come to Beijing "as early as possible so that we can give you a confidential briefing [on the war situation] in person."[15]

Reluctant and unprepared, the main bulk of the 13th Army Corps moved to the Northeast in mid-July. The 38th Army arrived in Fengcheng on July 24, and the 39th Army reached Liaoyang and Haicheng the next day. Coming directly from Guangdong, the 40th Army gathered in Andong on July 26, while the 42d Army moved from Qiqiha'er into Ji'an.[16] The troops were settled into their positions, yet there was still a command vacuum. The commander of the Northeast Military District, Gao Gang, was engrossed in the economic and political affairs of that region, and he had no intention of taking charge of these troops. To resolve this problem, on August 5, Mao pressed Gao to assert a more active leadership over the NBDA forces.

1. Now that all the NBDA troops are in position, we, however, do not anticipate that these troops would assume combat tasks in August, but [we] expect that these troops should be combat ready by early September. Comrade Gao Gang must see to it that a high-rank command meeting involving each army and division commander be held in mid-August to explain the objectives, meanings, and main directions of [our] battles and to assure that every unit will finish all the preparations and be ready to take actions by the end of this month. Be sure to maintain a high morale and get the troops fully mobilized; and be sure to free the troops' mind of doubts and misgivings. We will send Xiao Jinguang, Deng Hua, and Xiao Hua to attend this meeting.
2. On the basis of the above-stated guidelines, you are authorized to make decisions regarding such matters as force dispositions in accordance with circumstances. If you should think that it is of our advantage to deploy the 38th Army along the Siping railway area, please go ahead to issue such an order.[17]

Despite Mao's urging, the supervision of the NBDA remained ineffective.

Deng Hua was unable to exercise complete control over the troops. In early August, he complained to the CMC that he did not have enough command personnel and specifically requested that his long-time partner, the 15th Army Corps deputy commander and chief of staff Hong Xuezhi, assist him. Mao and Zhou accepted Deng's request and asked Lin Biao to make the arrangements. Hong happened to be on the way to Beijing, and upon his arrival, he was escorted from the railway station directly to Lin's house. When Lin informed Hong of the CMC decision on his new assignment, Hong was "absolutely unprepared." Lin explained to Hong that "the main body of the NBDA forces comes from our Fourth Field Army, and you are familiar with these troops. Now that Deng Hua is having difficulties in commanding them alone, you ought to assist him in handling everyday affairs." Lin ordered Hong to go to the Northeast as soon as possible. Finding it hard to reject his long-time superior, Hong reluctantly accepted his new task and was put on the train for Shenyang that afternoon.[18] After Hong left, Lin informed Nie of Hong's acceptance and asked the General Staff Department to formally appoint Hong as the first deputy commander of the 13th Army Corps.[19]

On August 13, shortly after Hong arrived in Shenyang, Gao Gang convened a meeting of high-ranking NBDA commanders at his headquarters, with Xiao Jinguang and Xiao Hua representing the CMC. Gao briefly spoke about the central leadership's assessment of the Korean War situation. However, his speech, Hong commented later, was "of the nature of [political] mobilization."[20] Deng Hua then talked about strategy and tactics. "The enemy's frontal defense is so tight," Deng pointed out, "and its firepower is so well-organized that a frontal attack against such a defense line won't be effective." On the other hand, "what the American troops fear most is being cut off from their communications and retreat lines." Given these strengths and weaknesses, Deng believed that "we shall try to carry to its full effect such tactics as 'determined and audacious penetration,' 'close-combat battles,' and 'night operations.'" Although these were traditional maneuvers of the CCP armed forces, Deng instructed each army and division commander to concentrate on them in their drills and preparations.[21]

Other commanders at the meeting expressed their deep concerns about the lack of transportation and antitank artillery, the shortage of medicine and field doctors, and, especially, the current low level of training and mobilization. They agreed that these problems, if not resolved immediately, would handicap the troops' combat effectiveness later. After the meeting, Xiao Jinguang hurried back to Beijing and informed Mao about the field commanders' misgivings. Taking Xiao's report very seriously, Mao cabled Gao Gang on August 18 that "the general lines discussed [at the meeting] are all correct" and that the problems besetting the NBDA "can and must be taken care of." He then agreed to extend the deadline for the completion of troop training and preparations, but he urged Gao to "step forward" to supervise the NBDA forces and make sure that military readiness would be achieved by the end of September.[22]

With increased pressure from Beijing, the NBDA intensified its preparations in late August. The 13th Army Corps Command set up its headquarters in Andong. The army corps political commissar Lai Chuanzhu joined the group, and the field command began to work in earnest. The commanders divided up responsibilities among themselves: Deng, assisted by Chief of Staff Xie Fang, focused on studying the strategy and tactics of US/UN forces and formulating appropriate Chinese countermeasures; Hong was responsible for training; and Lai and Du Ping took charge of political mobilization.[23] Only at this point did the NBDA troops actually begin to shape up for an anticipated war with the US.

II

When the NKPA had a hard time breaking through the US/UN defense line around Pusan, the Beijing leaders became increasingly anxious about any sudden change in Korea. At a CCP Politburo meeting on August 4, Mao pointed out: "If the U.S. imperialists win [the war in Korea], they may get so dizzy with success that they may threaten us. We therefore must come to [North] Korea's aid and intervene in the name of a volunteer army, although we will select the best timing [to do so]." To him, the war could evolve in several ways, including "coming to an end quickly or protracting, expanding, and even involving atomic bombs." Even if the US decided to use atomic weapons against China, Mao observed that "we cannot but allow them to use it because we do not have [the bomb] and thus we are in no position to stop them." But, he asserted, "we are not afraid [of the atomic bomb], and we just have to get prepared." Zhou Enlai made similar remarks at the meeting: "if the US prevails over [North] Korea, it will be swollen with arrogance, and [it might move further to] endanger the peace [in the Far East]." In order to ensure a North Korean victory, Zhou believed, "China's factor must be counted in." However, he cautioned that "since China's involvement may cause serious changes of the international [situation], we can only prepare long-term plans [for any contingency]."[24]

In envisioning how the U.S. action in Korea might encroach on China's security, the Chinese leaders believed that the Northeast would become the cockpit. In their calculation, an initial stage would involve American air raids of the area and the major cities along the eastern China coast. A U.S. air attack would then be followed by KMT amphibious assaults from the Taiwan Strait where Chinese Nationalist air, naval, and ground forces still occupied a number of offshore islands and Taiwan. In this scenario, the U.S. Seventh Fleet would coordinate the KMT assaults. It was also likely that the French in Indochina might step up their military activities along the Sino-Vietnamese border. Indeed, this projected course of action guided Beijing's military planning in the months following the outbreak of the Korean War.

There seems little doubt that Beijing wanted to ensure a numerical advantage in terms of troop deployment against the enemy in the Northeast. Should a large-scale war break out in the area, they thought, the NBDA's four infantry armies were not enough. At the August 26 CMC meeting, Zhou was concerned about how to replace the NBDA losses once it engaged in combat. He considered "selecting 10,000 men from all other PLA forces for the NBDA replacements" or "sending our troops into [Korea] in rotation," in order "to dispose sufficient troops at the rear ready to move up to the frontline to replace these [units] which need rest and reorganization." To him, the second option seemed better. For this purpose, the General Staff Department decided to deploy eight more infantry armies in northern China as strategic reserves. According to the plan, the 9th Army Corps consisting of four armies and regarded as one of the best forces in the Third Field Army, would be stationed along the "Jin-Pu" (Tianjin-Pukou) railway line, and the 19th Army Corps along the Long-Hai railway, so that the troops could be quickly transported into the Northeast when needed.[25] Mao endorsed this scheme and personally arranged the deployment. In his August 27 telegram to Peng Dehuai, then the commander of the First Field Army and the Northwest Military District, he instructed Peng to release the 19th Army Corps. As Mao explained, "In order to prepare for [unexpected changes in] the current war situation [in Korea], we shall build up altogether twelve [infantry] armies in northeastern China (four armies already there) as an expedient force for emergency." However, he told Peng that he would not "make any decision on the use of these troops until the end of September."[26] Uneasy about the removal of the 9th Army Corps from Shanghai, the East China Military District headquarters appealed to Mao to reconsider. Given the importance of defending Shanghai, Mao compromised by letting the 9th Army Corps assemble along the Xuzhou-Jinan railway to reinforce either Shanghai or the Northeast.[27]

With a large number of troops deployed in northern China, Beijing authorities realized that it was imperative to improve the troops' weaponry. According to the CMC statistics of May 1950, the PLA was composed of 61.1

percent infantry, 20.4 percent artillery, 1.6 percent engineers, 3.6 percent communication and support units, and a small anti-aircraft artillery unit with no armored force or anti–chemical warfare capability. With regard to ordnance, the entire army only had 17,000 pieces of artillery, most of which were manufactured by the Japanese between 1905–1936. Their best heavy artillery was the American-made MI-155 howitzer, though the PLA only had thirty-five of these. Deeply concerned about the PLA's poor equipment and weak firepower, Zhou Enlai proposed at a national defense meeting on August 26 that China purchase a large amount of munitions from the Soviet Union, especially for air, tank, and long-range and anti-aircraft artillery forces. With such weaponry, Zhou added, "we shall at least build four more air force regiments, three more tank brigades (altogether nine regiments), eighteen anti-aircraft artillery regiments, and enough heavy artillery guns to equip ten infantry armies."[28]

The CCP leadership's immediate task was to improve the PLA's artillery firepower. On August 1, 1950, the CMC established the PLA Artillery Command and named Chen Xilian its first commander. The CMC leaders instructed Chen to organize ten heavy artillery divisions and eight anti-aircraft artillery regiments right away.[29] Meanwhile, Beijing persuaded the Soviet military to provide by the end of the year 4,000 long-range artillery guns, including cannons, howitzers, rocket launchers, and mountain artillery pieces. The Soviet products, mostly manufactured in the 1930s, were not as good as the American artillery, but they were better than what the PLA was then equipped with. Moreover, the supply of ammunition was guaranteed.[30] The Chinese also secured an agreement with Moscow that the Soviet Union would assist China in outfitting two new anti-aircraft divisions and eighteen regiments with Soviet anti-aircraft guns and ammunition.[31]

For its armored force, the PLA possessed 410 tanks by May 1950, mostly of Japanese World War II manufacture with some American M-3s and M-4s captured from the KMT. However, these tanks were scattered among all the field armies. The CMC decided in June to establish a central command for the armored forces and appointed 2d Army Corps Commander Xu Guangda as its head. Xu immediately inspected the tank troops and was alarmed to find out that, due to the lack of regular training, none of the tank units was operational. In late August, he suggested to the CMC that all the tank troops be combined and reorganized into three brigades. He also recommended the establishment of centers to train the existing tank troops and new recruits. In Xu's view, the most urgent need was to raise the level of skills to meet the requirements of modern warfare. With the CMC's approval, Xu constructed the first facility in Tianjin in early September and four more shortly thereafter. Xu repeatedly requested that all the training courses focus only on the techniques of driving, firing, and communications. In these areas, Xu obtained Soviet assistance. In October, ten Soviet tank regiments moved into northern China, turned over their vehicles to the Chinese, and showed the Chinese how to operate the Soviet T-34s on a one-on-one basis for three months. In November, Moscow also delivered another large contingent of tanks to China.[32]

Along with the efforts to modernize its ground force, Beijing intensified the buildup of its air force. At the outbreak of the Korean War, China was in the process of training the first group of pilots under Soviet advisers, with no squadron combat-ready. As a result, the CCP leaders asked the Soviet air force to help defend China's coasts. Welcoming China's invitation, the Soviet Union dispatched an air force division to the Shanghai-Nanjing-Xuzhou area in March 1950. As the conflict in Korea heightened, Beijing sought another Soviet air force division for the defense of northeastern China. By late August, Moscow had sent a division with 122 MIG-15 fighters and 16 training aircraft, which was immediately deployed in the Northeast.[33] Uncertain whether the Soviet air divisions would join the Chinese against the Americans, Beijing accelerated the strengthening of its own air force. At a meeting in August 1950, the Air Force Command formulated ambitious plans for 1950–1953, including:

- Enhancing the capability of the already established seven pilot training centers beginning in November 1950 so as to produce 25,400 pilots in the next four years;
- Preparing to form ninety-seven air force regiments [in the near future]: the first class graduates (1950–1951) will form [the first] twenty-three regiments; the second class (1951–1952) will form [another] forty-five regiments; and the third class will make up twenty-nine more regiments;
- Equipping [the air force] with 4,507 [war] planes including 2,640 combat aircraft;
- Forming one airborne brigade directly under the People's Air Force Command;
- Constructing eleven aircraft repair plants and building 107 military airfields. . . .
- Expanding the People's Air Force into a total number of 290,000 [in the next three years].[34]

Interestingly, the CMC leaders were not satisfied with these goals. On September 2, Zhou Enlai directed the Air Force Command to include the buildup of one more jet fighter division in the plans. Under pressure, the Air

Force Command reported—three weeks late—that Air Force Training Center No. 4 would specialize in jet fighter instruction, and each center would recruit 126 more candidates for jet fighter training and 112 more for bomber training. The revised projections seemed to satisfy Mao and Zhou.[35]

The central leadership's intense anxiety, however, pushed the air force into reckless training. In early August 1950, the organization of 4th Air Force Brigade, the very first CCP air force unit, was proclaimed in Shanghai. The brigade consisted of one attacker, one bomber, and two fighter regiments. In Shanghai, the 10th Regiment, initially based in Longhua and then at the Dachang and Hongqiao airfields, began intensive training in MIG-15 jet fighters under the supervision of the Soviet advisers. In mid-August the 11th Regiment, which was stationed at the Jiangwan airfield in Shanghai's northeastern suburb, received instruction in Soviet Lar-II piston fighters, while the 12th Regiment in Nanjing, equipped with Soviet Tu-II bombers, and the 13th Regiment in Xuzhou, equipped with Soviet Ill-11 attack planes, began their exercises at the same time. Air Force Commander Liu Yalou urged the brigade political commissar Li Shian in early August that "training must be intensified to the extent that an air force of considerable combat effectiveness will be produced within a minimum period of time so as to pass 'the threshold of combat' quickly and smoothly." Under this mandate, the instructors had to skip the study of flight theories and instead concentrate on operational skills only. After three months of practice, the majority of the trainees were reportedly capable of solo flight, though they had flown an average of only sixteen hours. These pilots assumed the air defense of Shanghai in mid-October.[36]

Meanwhile, Beijing authorities were deeply concerned about the southeastern China coast, especially the Taiwan Strait. At the July 10 national defense meeting, all the participants agreed that the troops should postpone the preparations for the attack of Taiwan, given the presence of the U.S. Seventh Fleet in the strait. Accordingly, the troops assembled along the southeastern China coast halted their amphibious assault training.[37] The CCP leaders regarded the Fujian and Guangdong areas as the most vulnerable. In a telegram to the Central South Military Command on July 27, Mao stressed the importance of building an in-depth coastal defense. "As for where to deploy the 43d Army," he instructed, "it serves [a defense purpose] better to concentrate the army's main strength in the Leizhou peninsula and to place only one division on the Hainan islands."[38] As Mao explained on August 25, "It is very likely that the enemy forces in Taiwan might launch an amphibious attack on the Chao[zhou]-Shan[tou] and Hailufeng areas." Therefore, he directed that

> you must (1) strengthen intelligence and reconnaissance work to make sure that we will have reliable and accurate information before the enemy starts its amphibious attack; (2) augment force deployment [and] in this regard, please consider moving one infantry division and several artillery units from Guangzhou to the Chaoshan-Hailufeng coast and set up an army level command to direct the overall defense so as to guarantee that we can resolutely smash the enemy's attack; (3) speed up preparations and mobilization of all the party, government, troops, and civilians, try to eliminate the wishful thinking for peace in the minds of our cadres, and free the production task of the regular troops and local militia so that they can concentrate on combat preparations.[39]

The CCP leadership also expected the young navy to join the coastal defense. Su Yu, first deputy commander of the Third Field Army, spoke with the naval commanders in mid-July on the CMC's behalf. He charged the navy to be responsible for dredging the transportation lanes of the Yangtze, assisting in eliminating the KMT remnants on the offshore islands along the Jiangsu-Zhejiang coast, constructing a naval base on the Zhoushan Islands, and, especially, preparing contingency plans to counter the enemy's landings.[40] Given these instructions, the naval commanders came to agree in August 1950 that "our long-term [security interests] and immediate needs require us to construct a naval force . . . capable of fighting offshore battles, both defensively and offensively." For this purpose, the navy decided to reorganize itself to enhance its combat effectiveness and then to build a new fleet of torpedo boats and submarines and a naval air force.[41]

The navy assigned top priority to the construction of a torpedo flotilla, submarine, and coastal artillery force. In August 1950, a torpedo training center was set up in Qingdao with the mission to produce enough personnel for a fleet in six to twelve months. The center, supplied with six retired Soviet torpedo boats, mainly relied on Soviet naval advisers. A class of 897 students graduated after fourteen months of training. With the newly arrived Soviet torpedo boats, these graduates formed China's first torpedo flotilla, which was immediately deployed along the eastern China coast.[42] However, the navy could not raise a submarine force on its own. In April 1951 China sent 275 naval personnel to the Soviet Union for submarine training, and the navy was able to construct its first submarine base in Qingdao over a year later.[43] Also setting up a training center in Qingdao, the navy welcomed 258 graduates in October 1950; equipped with Soviet 130mm coast guns, this group formed the first coastal artillery force. In a short time, as many as ninety-nine battalions, most supplied with Soviet 130mm coast guns and howitzers, had been organized.[44]

Another urgent task the navy undertook was to determine ways of protecting Wusongkou. Since the spring of 1950, the KMT Navy had tightened up its blockade over the southeastern China coast, consequently sinking five vessels near Wusongkou between June and July. The KMT had also increased its troops strength on several important offshore islands, including Maan, Chengsi, and Tanhu Mount, from which the Nationalists constantly harassed fishing boats and shelled the inshore areas. At a meeting of the East China Military Command on August 28, Zhang Aiping, commander of the East China Navy, offered to clear up the mines around Wusongkou. With the help of Soviet advisers, Zhang had four warships refitted into mine-sweepers and equipped with Soviet mine-sweeping apparatus. The mine-sweeping action began in early September, and the navy claimed that it had removed most of the mines by late October.[45] At the same time, the navy coordinated the army's assaults on the KMT troops on the Jiangsu-Zhejiang offshore sites, which resulted in the seizure of the Tanhu Mount, Chengsi, and Pishan islands.[46] The PLA's control of these islands and the contiguous waters bolstered the defense of the Shanghai area.

Aside from its protection of China's coasts, Beijing also took precautionary measures to enhance the security of the Sino-Vietnamese border. At the outbreak of the Korean War, Ho Chi Minh was planning an offensive campaign in the Sino-Vietnamese border (the so-called border campaign). He asked the CCP to send a high-ranking commander to direct the attack and provide logistical support for the Vietnamese troops. Since the success of the operation would enable the Vietnamese Communists to control the border area, thus securing a buffer zone for China, Beijing decided to come to Ho's aid. As a preliminary step, the CMC put the deputy commander of the Guangxi Military District, Li Tianyou, in charge of logistics. Heading a "supporting commission" to the border region, Li set up a rear-service base and two field hospitals just within China's border for the Vietnamese troops. Shortly afterward, the CMC sent Chen Geng, the commander of the Yunnan Military District and a close friend of Ho Chi Minh's, to Vietnam to direct the border campaign.[47]

Secretly departing for Vietnam on July 7, 1950, Chen arrived at Ho Chi Minh's headquarters three weeks later. Known as the "ever-victorious general" during China's civil war, Chen accepted his mission with impassioned optimism. "Now that the North Korean People's Army is marching southward and already breaking through the enemy's defense along the Han River," his diary entry on July 8 read, "I am getting more confident about the coming battle in Vietnam, which will, as a coordinating action with that of [North] Korea, be an [important] part of a two-pronged blow [on the US]."[48] In the upcoming campaign, he expected to wipe out at least five French battalions in one battle. Should the attack succeed, "it would be a decisive victory as far as the future of Vietnam is concerned."[49] Mao also anticipated fruitful results from the Vietnamese border offensive. On July 28, he wired Chen to stress that "this battle is of great significance and you should try your best to assist Vietnamese in making a military breach of [Indochina's] situation."[50] After two months of combat preparation, the Vietnamese Communists opened the offensive on September 16 with a surprise attack on the French. When the campaign ended on October 10, the Vietnamese claimed that they had eliminated five French battalions—a total of 3,800 casualties—and now controlled a 250-mile-wide area adjoining China.[51]

When the Korean situation suddenly turned against the North Koreans in mid-September, the Chinese leaders became cautious about military actions in Indochina. Sensing an imminent threat from Korea, the leaders believed that China's open involvement in Indochina might provoke a U.S. military action there or in the Taiwan Strait. In his two telegrams to the Central South Military Command, dated September 16, Mao instructed: "You should deploy one division at the area south of Nanning [Guangxi province] to wipe out the leftover KMT bandits, and prepare to assist one division of the 43d Army in eliminating the [KMT] remnants before they escape into Vietnam." But, he added, "you should be very careful and make sure that these two divisions ought not to get too close to the Vietnamese border. . . . [Should that happen], it would mean a big trouble [for us]." Predicting an intensified conflict in the area, he wanted the main forces to "undertake necessary adjustments in military training and productive work. . . . The troops ought to spend a sufficient amount of time in combat training so that their weapons won't get rusty, equipment won't be unprepared or in shortage, and combat spirit won't get too low. In order to maintain [military preparedness], the troops must not be assigned with too much productive work."[52]

Seriously considering military intervention in Korea in early October, Beijing ordered a cessation of the large-scale offensive in Indochina. "We are pleased to hear of the Vietnamese victory," Mao cabled Chen Geng on October 16, "but the Vietnamese troops should proceed to rest and reorganize" instead of mounting assaults on the French. He advised that "the Vietnamese force is still a young army and [its combat effectiveness] can only be enhanced through more battles in the future [but] now it must take a break and proceed for more training." However, Mao's real concern was to prevent any escalation of the hostilities in Indochina.[53] The CMC soon recalled Chen Geng, although most of the Chinese advisers remained in Vietnam and China continued to offer military aid through the end of the Korean War.

III

The CCP leaders had been closely watching the development of the war in Korea. In their views, any drastic fluctuation in the situation unfavorable to North Korea might call for Chinese military involvement to block the US from expanding the conflict into China. Believing in Sun Tzu's dictum that "knowing yourself and knowing your enemy, you can fight a hundred battles with no danger of defeat," the Chinese leaders considered it imperative to grasp fully the war situation in Korea.

As early as June 28, Nie Rongzhen proposed to Zhou Enlai that China dispatch a military observation group to Korea and that Chai Chengwen, then the director of military intelligence of the Southwest Military District, head this mission. Zhou concurred and personally arranged for Chai's assignment. On the night of June 30, Zhou, deputy foreign minister Zhang Hanfu, and first deputy minister of military intelligence Liu Zhijian gave instructions to Chai in person. "Now that the war has broken out in Korea," Zhou explained, "the U.S. Truman government has not only sent troops to Korea and the Taiwan Strait but also is implementing a general plan of [military] deployment for further aggression in Asia." Since the US intended "to link the Korean issue with that of Taiwan and the Far East," Zhou believed, China was in a great need "to send some people [to Korea] to maintain a direct contact with Comrade Kim Il-sung." However, Zhou disliked the idea of sending Chai as a Chinese military observer and decided instead "to place Chai's mission under China's embassy [to Pyongyang]," thus leaving no evidence of the presence of Chinese military personnel. Given the urgency of the task, Zhou wanted Chai's group to depart for North Korea in a week. Deputy intelligence minister Liu soon selected five members of his senior staff who were "capable of both intelligence analysis and combat organization" and four personnel to handle radio communication with Beijing.[54]

On the morning of July 8, Zhou briefed Chai and his team. He explained that "we anticipate that the United States will muster more countries to send troops to Korea, and therefore the prospect of a prolonged war in Korea is so difficult to avert that a series of issues will emerge to complicate the overall situation [in the Far East]." Given this circumstance, the group's mandate was "to establish a close contact with the North Korean Labor Party [leadership] and the North Korean People's Army [command] and send back information on any change of the battleground as quickly as possible."[55] China's military intelligence group arrived in Pyongyang on July 10 and were presently welcomed by Kim Il-sung. "At the outbreak of the war," Kim told Chai, "I already requested Premier Zhou that China send army and division-rank commanders to Korea.

Finally, you are here." At Chai's request, Kim instructed the NKPA's General Political Bureau to assist the Chinese intelligence officers. Kim also directed the establishment of a special telephone line between his headquarters and Chai's group so that, as Kim said, "you can reach me whenever you want."[56]

Meanwhile, intelligence analysts in the General Staff Department were busily assessing Korea's war situation. Their goal was to deduce what actions MacArthur might take to reverse North Korea's offensive posture. Based on available information concerning the combat experience of MacArthur and the U.S. Eighth Army, the staff came to believe that it was very likely the US/UN forces would launch an amphibious attack on the midsection of the Korean peninsula, thereby cutting the NKPA in half from the rear. The intelligence analysts reasoned that MacArthur had won his five stars principally because of his success in directing the landing operations against the Japanese during World War II. Moreover, the Eighth Army had become famous as an "amphibious army," participating in more than sixty landing actions in the Pacific theater since its formation in June 1944. Consequently, the evidence suggested that MacArthur was actually organizing such an operation by having several marine divisions transported from the US to Japan. In mid-August, Lei Yingfu, Zhou Enlai's special assistant for military affairs, reported to Zhou on the possibility of a U.S. amphibious attack on North Korea. In Lei's judgment, MacArthur's likely landing site was Inchon. Finding Lei's assessment compelling, Zhou immediately reported to Mao, who then sent for Lei and the director of combat operations, Li Tao. This time, Lei pinned down Inchon as the near-certain place for MacArthur's assault. Mao was completely convinced.[57]

The 13th Army Corps Command in Andong arrived at the same conclusion. Deng Hua had planned to go to Korea "to personally observe the battleground," but he never made the trip because he was tied up at his headquarters.[58] Anxious to "know" the enemy, Deng called an army corps command meeting in late August to analyze the possible moves of the US/UN forces in Korea. The attendees all agreed that an enemy amphibious action would be the most devastating to North Korea. On behalf of the command, Deng sent the following report to the CMC on August 31, 1950: "Given the long, narrow, and hilly terrain of the Korean peninsula," the space for a force of numerical superiority to maneuver is small and limited. Although our [North Korean] troops are fighting on an internal line and enjoying offensive initiatives in [their] battles, we are surrounded by sea on three sides, and the enemy enjoys sea and air superiority and might land at our rear to attack our weak points." In his view, "the U.S. imperialist troops are now trying to hold tight to the Pusan area with small-scale counterattack so as to win enough time for reinforcement and preparations for a large-scale counteroffensive somewhere else." Deng further contended that:

> the intention of the enemy's counteroffensive is estimated to be as follows: first, to land part of its troops on some coastal area in North Korea for harassing and holding operations and advance its main forces northward along main highways and railways gradually; second, to make a large-scale landing of its main force on our flank rear areas (near Pyongyang or Seoul) and at the same time employ a small force to pin down the [North Korean] People's Army in its present positions, enabling it to attack from the front and rear simultaneously. In that case the People's Army would be in a very difficult situation.[59]

Alert to a possible US/UN amphibious action, Zhou Enlai called Chai Chengwen and Ni Zhiliang, Chinese ambassador to Pyongyang, to a briefing in Beijing on September 1. Chai agreed that MacArthur might launch an invasion of North Korea, whereupon Zhou interrupted him and asked, "If sudden change of the [Korean] situation requires us to participate in the war, what would be the problems that we will encounter?" Chai replied, "In my view, an immediate problem concerns [difficult] transportation and [shortage of Korean language] interpreters." As he explained, "We cannot guarantee railway [transportation], and highways [in Korea] are narrow and in poor condition; neither can we acquire supplies [in North Korea] because there is no food or munitions there; and it is also impossible for a large army to live on capturing enemy supplies." Zhou took Chai's analysis very seriously and urged all the CCP Politburo Standing Committee members to read his report.[60]

The top leaders recognized that the North Koreans needed to be warned about the potential for attack. Coincidentally, Kim Il-sung's personal representative Lee Sang-jo, came to Beijing in late August to brief the Chinese leaders on North Korea's war plans. During the meeting, Mao observed that "the United States is a real tiger and capable of eating human flesh." Pointing at three seaports, including Inchon, along North Korea's western coast on the map of Korea, he stressed that "we ought to prepare for [the possibility] that American troops might take a circuitous course through landing at any one of these ports to strike the rear of the Korean People's Army." The CCP chairman urged the North Korean emissary to report to his leader that the NKPA "must begin military preparations for possible U.S. amphibious attack immediately."[61]

Despite Beijing's warning, Pyongyang authorities were unprepared for the US/UN assault. When the US/UN forces landed at Inchon on September 15, the NKPA disintegrated right away, and its offensive in South Korea soon collapsed. Shortly after, Kim sent Pak Il-yu, minister of interior affairs, to Andong. At the 13th Army Corps headquarters, Pak told the Chinese commanders that "the entire front is getting worse" and that the NKPA's main forces were cut off by the U.S. troops rolling eastward from Inchon. "On behalf of the [North] Korean party and government," Pak requested that "China send troops into Korea to assist [us]." Making no commitment, the commanders only promised to relay the request to the CCP central leadership immediately, though they assured Pak that "once the central leadership issues an order [to intervene], we will move in at once." While Pak spent the night at Andong, the 13th Army Corps Command sent an urgent telegram directly to Mao.[62]

On their part, the leaders in Beijing were already deeply worried about the drastic setback of the North Koreans. As soon as he heard of MacArthur's Inchon landing, Zhou Enlai directed the dispatch of five more high-ranking officers to Korea, including Zhang Mingyuan, deputy minister of rear services of the Northeast Military Command; Cui Xingnong, intelligence director of the 13th Army Corps; He Lingdong, deputy director of the 39th Army's staff department; Tang, Jingzhong, chief of staff of the 42d Army's 118th Division; and Li Fei, deputy intelligence director of the artillery command. Their main task, Zhou specified, was to "observe the general situation [in North Korea], inspect Korea's topography, and prepare the battlefield [for China's military action]." On September 17, Zhou spoke to the officers in person to underscore the importance of their mission. Seeing it as a preliminary step toward full Chinese involvement, Kim Il-sung warmly welcomed this new group in Pyongyang and instructed his aides to provide whatever assistance the Chinese required. With little delay, this group hurried to the battlefront.[63]

North Korea's resistance to the US/UN advance deteriorated in late September. As the Truman administration approved MacArthur's plan to "liberate" North Korea, the crossing of the 38th parallel by US/UN forces seemed imminent. Without immediate Chinese intervention, the North Korean leaders believed that the NKPA would be crushed. Late in the evening of October 1, Kim Il-sung called an emergency meeting with Chinese ambassador Ni Zhiliang in Pyongyang, formally requesting that the Chinese government dispatch the 13th Army Corps across the Yalu River within the next few days. In order to win more time for the entry of Chinese forces, Kim told Ni, the remnant NKPA troops would "fight with life and blood" to delay the enemy's advance.[64] At the same time, Kim and Vice-premier Pak Hon-yong sent Mao a long letter, which first explained the "very serious situation" that the North Koreans faced:

> Although the People's Army is carrying out an indomitable resistance against the enemy's landing forces, our troops on [the South Korean] front are already in a very disadvantageous position. Since the outbreak of the war, the enemy forces have been bombarding our front and rear areas day and night with thousands of [war] planes of various kinds. The enemy is able to make a full play of its [air] power because we practically have no air defense capability. With its air force shielding [our positions], the enemy is able to move a large motorized force [to attack us] everywhere on the front. We have suffered severe losses in manpower and equipment. Our rear services—especially transportation and communications—are so severely damaged that our troops have lost all mobility. [Now] the enemy's landing forces have already joined hands with their forces on the front thus cutting off [our connection with] our forces in the south. As a result, the People's Army in the south is in a dangerous position as it is being disintegrated: it has run out of supplies, lost contact [with us], and become isolated from each other by the enemy forces. . . . As far as we can anticipate, the enemy will continue to move north of the 38th parallel. If we cannot prevent this unfavorable situation from deteriorating, it is more than likely that the enemy will accomplish its objective [of occupying North Korea].

Nevertheless, the North Korean leaders reiterated their determination "to overcome every problem to prohibit the enemy from colonizing Korea and turning it into a [U.S.] military base" and "to fight for the independence, liberation, and democracy of the Korean people with every last drop of our blood." At present, Kim told Mao, "we are making every effort to reorganize new divisions, and we are trying to gather the more than 10,000 [NKPA] troops trapped in the south in areas where they will be safer and in a better combat position, and [we are] mobilizing our whole nation to fight a protracted war." Even so, the North Korean leaders predicted that "should the enemy continue to attack the areas north of the 38th parallel, we could not survive if we merely relied on our own strength." Kim appealed to Mao that "we cannot but ask for your special assistance, that is, when the enemy moves into [North Korea], we expect that the People's Liberation Army directly participate in our fighting."[65]

It is important to recall that the Chinese field commanders consistently favored military intervention in the event that the tide turned against the North Koreans. The 13th Army Corps commanders had agreed at a mid-August meeting that the best time for the Chinese to take action was after the U.S. forces crossed the 38th parallel but before they could consolidate their foothold in North Korea.[66] In his report to the CMC on August 31, Deng

Hua regarded it expedient for China to enter the war only when the US/UN forces attacked north of the 38th parallel. "Then we will not only be politically justified [to intervene] but also [it will be] militarily advantageous," he explained. "It will be much easier to strike the enemy forces when they stretch longer and wider; and we will have much smaller burden regarding our coast defense and much shorter lines of supply and transportation."[67]

By comparing and contrasting China's military strength with that of the US/UN forces, the field commanders appeared confident that the enemy was beatable. At a late September command meeting, they calculated that although the enemy enjoyed absolute sea and air superiority and relative superiority in firepower, equipment, and mobility, it suffered from several vital weaknesses. First, the U.S. forces were politically unmotivated, because "they are invading other people's country, fighting an unjust war, and thus encountering opposition from not only the American but other peace-loving peoples around the world," whereas the Chinese forces would "fight against aggression, carrying on a just war, and thus will have the support of our people and other peace-loving peoples; and more important, our troops have a stronger political consciousness and higher combat spirit." Second, the U.S. troops were inferior in terms of combat effectiveness, because "although they have excellent modern equipment, their officers and soldiers are not adept in night battles, close combat, and bayonet charges." By contrast, the CCP troops "have had rich experience over the past ten years in fighting an enemy of modern equipment . . . and are good at close combat, night battles, mountainous assaults, and bayonet charges." Third, the U.S. forces were not tactically flexible, since "American soldiers always confine themselves to the bounds of military codes and regulations, and their tactics are dull and mechanical." On the other hand, the CCP forces were "good at maneuvering flexibility and mobility and, in particular, good at surrounding and attacking enemy's flanks by taking tortuous courses, as well as dispersing and concealing [our own] forces." Fourth, American soldiers were not capable of enduring hardship. "They are afraid of dying and merely relying on firepower [in combat, while] . . . on the contrary our soldiers are brave and willing to sacrifice life and blood and capable of bearing hardship and heavy burdens," attributes that would remedy the disadvantage of inferior firepower. Finally, the U.S. forces had greater logistical problems. The US was "carrying on a war across the [Pacific] Ocean and has to ship most of the necessities from the American continent—even if it can use supply bases in Japan, [for instance] it is transporting drinking water from Japan—and therefore its supply lines are much longer, eventually making it difficult for them to reinforce manpower and supplies." Meanwhile, the Chinese would be close to the rear bases and "backed by [their] fatherland." The organization of supplies would also be much easier; because "we have less trucks and artillery, we won't consume that much gasoline and ammunitions."[68]

Based on these calculations, the 13th Army Corps commanders developed some strategic and tactical guidelines. "Strategically," they reported to the CMC in late September, "we will adhere to fighting a protracted war [in Korea]." Tactically, "[we] will employ our traditional methods such as concentration of [our] superior force [to attack weak enemy positions], penetration, circling and disintegration, close combat, night strikes, and quick battles to force a quick solution."[69] The CMC leaders concurred, and in a CMC document dated September 20, they explicitly stated that if China became involved in the Korean War, "we will primarily rely on ourselves and fight a protracted war." The document maintained that "we [must] always concentrate our manpower and firepower to gain an absolute superiority, and then disperse, surround, and wipe out numerically inferior enemy force." Only by adhering to these principles, "could we gradually wear down the enemy so that we can switch to an advantageous position and fight a protracted war [in Korea]."[70]

Although China's entry in the Korean War seemed almost certain late in September 1950, timing remained a crucial issue. From a political standpoint, China would be in a much better position to intervene when the US/UN forces crossed the 38th parallel and marched toward the Sino-Korean border. Therefore, Beijing abruptly amplified its warnings against MacArthur's continuous advance. On September 22, a foreign affairs ministry spokesman issued an official statement, for the first time since the outbreak of the Korean War, that "we clearly reaffirm that we will always stand on the side of the Korean people—just as the Korean people have stood on our side during the past decades—and resolutely oppose the criminal acts of American imperialist aggression against Korea and their intrigues for expanding the war." On September 24 and 27, Zhou Enlai twice cabled United Nations headquarters to protest against a U.S. air intrusion over Andong. Appearing as *Renmin Ribao's* headline news, Zhou's statement read: "The flames of war being extended by the United States are burning more fiercely." Should the UN General Assembly "still be plaint to the manipulation of the United States and continue to play deaf and dumb to these aggression crimes of the United States," Zhou asserted, it would "not escape a share in the responsibility for lighting up the war-flames in the [Far] East."[71] These widely publicized official declarations served as much to mobilize domestic support for Chinese intervention as to warn against US/UN movement into North Korea.

On October 1, an intelligence report reached Beijing indicating that US/UN vanguard units had begun crossing the 38th parallel. Twenty-four hours later, another report confirmed that American troops were moving into North Korea in large numbers. Mao spent a sleepless night talking with other top CCP leaders about the Korean situation, and during those discussions, the CCP chairman finalized his decision to intervene. "We have decided," he informed Stalin the next day, "to send troops into Korea in the name of the People's Volunteer Army to fight the United States and its running dog, Syngman Rhee's forces, and to aid the Korean comrades." Mao explained to the Kremlin leader that "this is a necessary step because, should the Americans occupy the whole of Korea, the Korean revolutionary force would be completely destroyed and the American invaders would become more rampant; [all of these] would be detrimental to the entire East." The CCP chairman then conveyed his assessment of the prospects for China's military action in Korea:

> Now that we decide to dispatch Chinese forces to fight the Americans in Korea, we think that, first of all, we shall aim at resolving the conflict, that is, to eliminate the U.S. troops within Korea or to drive them and other countries' aggressive forces out [of Korea]; second, now that Chinese troops will soon open fire on the U.S. forces (although we fight in the name of a volunteer army), we must prepare for the possibility that the US would declare a general war on China or it would at least bomb China's major cities and industrial bases and attack our coastal areas with its naval forces. . . . Of these two issues, [we are] more concerned about whether Chinese troops could wipe out the American forces within Korea's boundary to bring about a successful resolution of the Korean conflict. As long as our troops are able to eliminate the Eighth Army (one of America's old armies with considerable combat effectiveness), the danger of the second issue—U.S. declaration of war on China—although still in existence, would not be that grave because by that time the situation would turn to favor the revolutionary forces and China. In other words, since the Korean conflict can actually be resolved on the basis of defeating the US (although it is likely that the US won't recognize [North] Korea's success for a long time . . .), even if the US would declare a general war on China, such a war would be limited in scale and would not last long. However, we think that the most dangerous prospect [of this conflict] is that the Chinese forces could fail to annihilate the U.S. troops in substantial number and wind up in a military stalemate in Korea while America already declares a general war on China and attacks [our] territory. Should this happen, our ongoing economic construction would be devastated, and China's national and petty bourgeoisie would openly oppose our policy [or resisting the US and aiding Korea] because they are very scared of fighting [with the US].

What would China do in the initial stage of intervention? Mao descended to particulars for Stalin: "Under present circumstances, we will begin to dispatch the twelve [infantry] divisions already deployed in South Manchuria into North Korea—not necessarily down along the 38th parallel—on October 15." In the first phase, these troops "will mainly be in a defensive disposition." Their immediate goal, he explained, will be to "fight the enemy forces which are threatening to attack the areas north of the 38th parallel but aim at annihilating [the enemy's] small units so as to get to know each side's [combat] situations." Meanwhile, the Chinese troops would wait for Soviet weapons "so as to become better equipped, and only after that will they coordinate with the [North] Korean comrades to counterattack U.S. aggression forces." In addition to these twelve divisions, he told the Soviet leader that China had gathered twenty-four more infantry divisions along the Long-Hai, Jin-Pu, and Bei-Ning railways as second and third echelons of reinforcement and would send them to Korea next spring or summer "if circumstances so require."

Concerned about the inferior firepower of the Chinese troops, Mao asked for Soviet assistance. "As the information that we have collected shows, one U.S. army (consisting of two infantry and one motorized divisions) is equipped with 1,500 various kinds of artillery pieces ranged between 70mm to 140mm including tank and anti-aircraft guns; one of our armies (three infantry divisions) only has 36 artillery pieces." Moreover, he conceded that "the enemy enjoys air domination while our air force, which is still in the process of flight training, will have 300 planes combat-ready no earlier than February 1951. Therefore, at the present stage, our forces do not have the capability of eliminating one U.S. army in a single campaign." Once the Chinese began to engage the Americans in combat, Mao anticipated that the US would probably "use an entire army to fight with us, and then we would have to concentrate manpower four times larger than the enemy's (that is, to gather four of our armies to deal with one enemy army) and to deploy firepower one-and-a-half to two times stronger than that of the enemy's (that is, to dispose 2,200 to 3,000 artillery guns of above 30mm to meet the enemy's 1,500 artillery guns of the same range)." In conclusion, the CCP chairman stressed that "only with such a force deployment can we be assured to annihilate an entire [U.S.] army."[72]

Awaiting Stalin's response, Beijing authorities acted quickly on their decision in favor of military intervention. On October 2, Mao instructed the 13th Army Corps to "end all preparations ahead of our schedule," and get ready to move into Korea "as we have so prepared in the past." He directed Deng Hua to keep him updated on the troops' readiness because he needed to know exactly when the forces could be dispatched. Mao also summoned Gao Gang to Beijing.[73] Zhou Enlai was occupied with the foreign ministry's suggestion that China issue a last-minute warning against a U.S. attack on North Korea, to be sent to Washington via India's embassy in Beijing. Since Mao had already made up his mind to intervene, Zhou chose his words carefully. In his view, the message should not disclose Beijing's unalterable decision to enter the conflict; otherwise, China might offend neutral countries such as India. Describing how China would react if the US continued to advance in North Korea, Zhou used the Chinese verb *guan*. He then spent several hours discussing with his English translator Pu Shouchang how to render the word "appropriately."[74] At 1:00 A.M., Zhou called Indian ambassador K. M. Panikkar to his office for an emergency meeting. "The American forces are endeavoring to cross the 38th parallel and aim at expanding the Korean conflict," he stated to Panikkar. "If they really want to do so, we will not sit still and do nothing. We surely will respond [to this contingency] [*women yao guan*]. Please inform your prime minister of this position [of our government]."[75]

Meanwhile, Mao was attempting to achieve a consensus among the top CCP leaders. During a CCP Secretariat [*shuji chu*] meeting on October 2, he scheduled an enlarged Politburo meeting for October 4 at 3:00 P.M. All the Beijing members—Zhou Enlai, Zhu De, Liu Shaoqi, Ren Bishi (just back from medical treatment in Moscow), Liu Bocheng, Lin Biao, and Nie Rongzhen—were in attendance. Of the members who were outside of Beijing, Gao Gang was present, and Peng Dehuai arrived late in the afternoon. Beyond the Politburo circle, Mao brought in such nonmembers as the commanders of the air force, the navy, the armored and artillery forces, and the railway engineering corps. The Politburo meeting had become a top-rank command gathering.[76]

Strong opposition, however, surfaced at the meeting. Gao Gang voiced one dissenting argument, insisting that if China entered the war, the one-year-old People's Republic, which had barely survived its own domestic problems, would encounter grave political and economic crises: China's economic reconstruction would have to give way to the production of war materiel, and the Chinese people, who had had less than one year of peace, would quickly become disenchanted with another war. More important, China did not have the means to engage the US in a general war; for example, China only produced 610,000 tons of iron between 1949 and 1950 while the US produced 87.7 million tons of iron and steel in the same period.[77] Another objection, expressed by Lin Biao, was based on military calculations. Warfare in Korea—a long, narrow peninsula with three sides surrounded by water—would inflict massive losses on China's ground forces, which had no air or naval support and limited artillery firepower. To Lin, a wiser and safer solution was to strengthen the border defense, accelerate the buildup of air, naval, and artillery forces, and assist the North Koreans in fighting a guerrilla war. Lacking confidence in China's intervention, Lin also firmly declined Mao's suggestion that he command the Chinese forces in Korea, though he used his illness, neurasthenia, as the reason for his refusal. Acting Chief of Staff Nie Rongzhen, among other leaders, expressed surprise at Lin's "fear" of engaging the Americans in Korea.[78]

Nevertheless, Mao was bluntly persistent that China's entry into the Korean War was necessary. From a geopolitical standpoint, he asserted, the American intention to occupy North Korea was part of its grand strategy to dominate the Far East and the whole of Asia. With a foothold consolidated in the Korean peninsula, the US would be free to undertake further aggression in the Taiwan Strait, the Philippines, and Indochina. Once a strategic encirclement of China was achieved, China would be compelled to fight a two- or even three-front war at some future date. From a military point of view, Mao judged that the U.S. armed forces in Korea could be defeated. Despite their superiority in firepower, the American troops suffered from such strategic weaknesses as a long and cumbersome supply line, insufficient manpower, low morale, domestic opposition, and disunity among allies. Furthermore, not only had the Chinese Communist forces battled enemies with superior military capability before, but after defeating Chiang Kai-shek, the PLA had greatly improved its combat effectiveness in fighting a large-scale war. Mao reminded the group that the Soviet Union would provide military assistance, and its air forces in the Far East would assist China in protecting Manchuria and might provide air cover for the Chinese troops in Korea. From a political stand, Mao pointed out that China's domestic stability and economic construction would be disrupted even if China passively allowed American troops to reach the Yalu River. First, China's electric power plant in southern Manchuria, iron and steel plants in Anshan, coal-mining bases in Fushun, and the heavy industries in Shenyang would be under direct threat. Second, the burden of stationing a large number of troops at the northeastern border for a neutral defense was unacceptable. "We would have to wait there year after year, unsure of when the enemy will attack us," Mao observed. Third, it was wishful thinking that China could concentrate on economic construction now, with the threat of harm hanging over the nation. A later military conflict would destroy economic achievements as surely as a precipitate one. At the end of the meeting, Mao sighed deeply and said, "After all, it *feels* sad to stand by with folded hands and watch your neighbor [suffering from] a national crisis."[79]

It is interesting that Mao seems to have counted on Peng Dehuai's support of his position. On October 2, he had instructed Peng to fly from Xian to Beijing in time for the Politburo meeting. Given Lin Biao's refusal to accept command, Mao saw Peng as his second choice. Peng had been one of the CCP's top military leaders since the Red Army period, and he was especially known for fighting bravely under duress. Although Peng arrived at the October 4 meeting an hour late, he was there in time to hear Mao's remarks on why China should intervene in Korea. Peng later recalled that he could not sleep that night. Going over and over Mao's arguments, he became convinced of the necessity of China's intervention. Early the next morning, Peng was surprised when Mao sent Deng Xiaoping to invite him to the chairman's office for a private meeting. "Old Peng, you didn't have time to speak out yesterday," said Mao. "We do indeed face enormous difficulties, but what favorable conditions do you think we have?" Peng replied, "Chairman, I thought this issue over and again last night, and I support your decision [on military intervention]." Mao then declared that he preferred Peng as commander of the Chinese troops in Korea. When Peng agreed to assume the command, the chairman said "nostalgically," "Now I can rest at ease!" At the next Politburo meeting that afternoon, Peng expressed his firm support of Mao's policy: "It is necessary to dispatch troops to aid Korea. Even if [China] is devastated [by the U.S. forces] in war, it would only mean that our liberation war lasted a few years longer. Should its troops be poised on the bank of the Yalu River and Taiwan, the US will be able to find a pretext to invade us at any time."[80]

Mao's decision to enter the Korean War finally prevailed among the leaders at the October 5 meeting. On October 8, the day after the UN resolution empowered the US/UN forces to unify Korea, Beijing authorities issued a formal order of armed intervention. On the CMC's behalf, Mao instructed that "the Northeast Border Defense Force is renamed the Chinese People's Volunteers [CPV] and it should get ready to move into the [North] Korean territory immediately." The CMC appointed Peng Dehuai as the CPV commander and assigned Gao Gang to direct supplies, transportation, and other rear services.[81] On the same day, Mao informed Kim Il-sung of the CCP Politburo's actions and asked Kim to send Pak Il-yu to Shenyang, where Pak, Peng, and Gao would go over detailed arrangements for the deployment of the Chinese troops in Korea.[82]

As Mao had given him a mere ten days for preparations, Peng left for Shenyang with only his personal secretary. That evening he met with Pak to discuss how the Chinese and North Korean forces could best coordinate and foster "a cordial and friendly atmosphere" for the coming struggle. Meanwhile, the ambassador to Pyongyang, Ni Zhiliang, and Chai Chengwen paid a visit to Kim's underground headquarters near Pyongyang. Before they entered Kim's office, Ni and Chai heard Kim "arguing fiercely" with Pak Hon-yong, the former head of the South Korean Communist Party, who was seemingly discouraged by the war situation. After the Chinese visitors relayed Beijing's firm determination to aid North Korea, Kim expressed his relief and toasted Ni and Chai: "Please convey our heartfelt gratitude to Chairman Mao and the CCP central leadership. We have fought and defeated Japanese imperialists shoulder to shoulder before; now let us fight together again to defeat the U.S. imperialists."[83]

In the meantime, Beijing authorities wanted to ensure Soviet military assistance before their troops began fighting in Korea. On October 8, Zhou Enlai flew to Moscow, accompanied by interpreter Shi Zhe and Kang Yimin, his confidential secretary. Joined by Lin Biao, who was to receive medical treatment in Moscow, Zhou went to see Stalin at the Kremlin leader's summer resort on the Black Sea on the afternoon of October 11. Stalin and other Soviet leaders, including Mikoyan, Georgi Malenkov, Lavrenti Beria, and Molotov, met immediately with the Chinese delegation. The Soviets acceded to Zhou's request that should China send ground troops into Korea, Moscow would provide supplies (including enough tanks and artillery guns to equip ten Chinese infantry divisions) and would dispatch its air forces to protect China's northern and eastern coasts. A few hours after the meeting, however, Molotov informed Zhou that the Soviet Union would only "loan" the Chinese the promised munitions and supplies and, more critically, that the Soviet air force was "not yet ready to assist in the Chinese military action in Korea and could only set out in two-and-a-half months." Wary that the Chinese were incapable of matching the US in combat, the Kremlin leaders also opposed a large-scale Chinese offensive against the Americans because it could eventually provoke a general war between the US and the USSR. Clearly, the Kremlin was backing off from its commitment of military assistance. To inform Mao of this change, Stalin and Zhou sent him a joint telegram that night.[84]

Caught by surprise, Mao held back the dispatch of the Chinese troops into Korea. On October 12 he instructed Peng that "the decision on the 13th Army Corp's entry into Korea is now called off and the troops should stay within our border." In the same telegram, he asked Peng and Gao to fly to Beijing for an emergency meeting.[85] Meanwhile, Mao canceled the directive to move the 9th Army Corps from Shandong into the Northeast. He told all the commanders that "there is no need to explain either inside or outside the party [about this sudden change]."[86] Mao then chaired another Politburo meeting at Zhongnanhai the next day. On the question of whether China should enter the war even if the Soviet military would not assist, all the participants leaned toward an affirmative answer. Mao immediately contacted Zhou in Moscow: "The result of our Politburo discussion is a unanimous decision that it is advantageous to send our troops to Korea. . . . Such a positive action will be beneficial not only to China and Korea, but also to the East and world peace." If China did not enter the war and instead "allow[ed] the enemy to approach the Yalu River," Mao reasoned, "the consequence would be detrimental to all of these areas and more to northeastern China, [because] our entire northeastern border defense forces would be tied down there and the [electric] power plants in South Manchuria would be under direct enemy's threat." Still hopeful that the Soviet Union might come to China's aid, Mao directed Zhou to stay in Moscow for a few more days. Zhou was to ensure that the Soviet Union would allow the Chinese to obtain Soviet military materials on credit so that Beijing could allocate enough resources for domestic economic reconstruction while fighting the war in Korea. Zhou was also to confirm that the Soviet air force was committed to eventual participation in Chinese military actions in Korea and especially to the protection of Beijing, Tianjin, Shenyang, Shanghai, Nanjing, and Qingdao. Should the Soviet leaders guarantee this air support, Mao claimed, "we won't be afraid of [U.S.] massive air raids; at worst, [our troops] would have to endure some losses in the event of air attack in the next two-and-a-half months."[87]

Zhou immediately notified the Kremlin of Beijing's final decision on China's entry into the war even without Soviet air cover. Stalin was surprised and "deeply moved." He repeatedly told Zhou: "The Chinese comrades are, nevertheless, good comrades." Although he could not allow the USSR to be drawn into the war, Stalin understood that the Chinese would be at a severe disadvantage because of superior American firepower. Stalin approved Beijing's request for sufficient munitions and supplies to equip 100 Chinese infantry divisions, to be purchased with a Soviet loan of 5.6 billion rubles. The Soviet leader also agreed to assist the PLA in safeguarding China's coast.[88] After Zhou left Moscow on October 16, two Soviet air force divisions, which had been stationed in Shenyang and Shanghai, handed over all of their aircraft (altogether, 231 planes) to the Chinese People's Air Force before returning to Russia in mid-October. From late October through December 1950, the Soviet air force dispatched thirteen divisions, including nine MIG-15 and MIG-9 fighter divisions, three attack-aircraft divisions, and one bomber division to northern, eastern, and southern regions in China, with the understanding that they would only assist in China's air defense and would not fly over Korea.[89]

IV

Many Western scholars attributed Beijing's entry into the Korean War to the US/UN thrust toward the Yalu River. Had the United States adopted different tactics in the aftermath of Inchon, William Stueck argues, Chinese intervention might have been averted altogether. Rosemary Foot also stresses the crossing of the 38th parallel, contending that Washington acted because of the expected domestic political benefits to be derived from the movement north and the lack of strong restraints from the allies, countermoves from Moscow, or objections within the U.S. bureaucracy.[90] The Truman administration never believed that the Chinese Communists would intervene because, as Washington officials calculated on October 12, the "disadvantages of [China's] participation in the war appeared to outweigh the advantages." Although intervention would give China the chance for a "major gain in prestige," American officials asserted, "the Chinese Communists undoubtedly *fear the consequences of war with the United States,*" since Beijing's "domestic programs are of such magnitude that the regime's entire domestic programs and economy would be jeopardized by the strains." Therefore, the best move for Beijing was to continue "covert assistance to the North Koreans."[91]

However, it now seems arguable that Beijing's decision to intervene, though catalyzed by the breach of the 38th parallel, was no less significantly shaped by Mao's optimistic willingness to confront the US in Korea. Although he was well aware of US/UN firepower and air superiority, the CCP chairman was not at all intimidated. Indeed, he even believed that the Chinese ground forces, if they maneuvered well, could wipe out the U.S. Eighth Army, the backbone of the US/UN forces, in one fell swoop. Although hopeful that Stalin would commit Soviet air power to Korea, Mao was too anxious to face down the "arrogant" Americans to call off the operation when the Soviet leader refused to provide the Chinese infantry with air cover.

The Chinese field commanders shared Mao's perceptions and attitudes. Their confidence was largely based on the contrast of their own "subjective advantage" against the enemy's "objective difficulties." They never realized that they exaggerated the strength of the Chinese infantrymen, who had had no experience in modern warfare. Exultant to have triumphed in a civil war against the "U.S. trained and equipped" KMT troops, their victory padded the illusion that China could beat American troops. Now, after months of military preparations for intervention—even though the final decision had been pending—the Chinese military was geared for war. Like an arrow on a drawn bowstring, nothing could easily prevent its release.

5. LURING THE ENEMY IN DEEP

"War is a contest of strength," Mao wrote in his famous 1938 essay *On Protracted War,* "but the original pattern of strength changes in the course of war."[1] To him, such a shift would occur in three stages over the course of a war: first, a strategic offensive for the stronger side and strategic defensive for the weaker side; second, a period of strategic stalemate; and third, the weaker side's strategic counteroffensive to force the formerly strong enemy into strategic retreat.[2] In the first stage, the stronger side's advantage would take a turn for the worse under the pressure of a war of attrition. The reversal, Mao maintained, "manifests itself in hundreds of thousands of casualties, the drain on arms and ammunition, deterioration of troop morale, popular discontent at home, shrinkage of trade, . . . condemnation by world opinion."[3] To accelerate the change, the weaker side "should wage offensive campaigns and battles within the strategic defensive, campaigns and battles of quick decision within the strategically protracted war, and campaigns and battles on exterior lines within strategic interior lines."[4] The key to victory was not capturing enemy territory, but reducing the enemy's effectiveness and preserving one's own strength. Indeed, these ideas dictated China's strategy in the early period of its military action in Korea.

I

China's initial goal was to conduct a strategic defensive in North Korea, and Mao laid out his blueprint in a telegram to Zhou Enlai, then in Moscow, on October 14, 1950.

> (a) The U.S. 1st, 2d, and 24th [Infantry] divisions, together with the British 25th Brigade and [ROK] puppet 1st Division, are gathered at the Kaesong-Kumchon areas along the 38th parallel, north of Seoul, prepar-

> ing to assault Pyongyang. Today's intelligence indicates that the U.S. 2d [Infantry] Division is moving toward Kumchon for the purpose of consolidating its position there. It seems that the U.S. [Command] has not made a final decision on whether or not to attack Pyongyang or when. (b) The [ROK] puppet Capital and 3d divisions have arrived at Wonsan and the [ROK] 6th, 7th, and 8th divisions are moving steadily toward the Wonsan area to receive supplies by sea. (c) With its 1st Marine Division stationing in Seoul, 25th Division guarding the Taejon-Suwon line, and 7th Division in the Taegu-Pusan line, the U.S. 8th Army is headquartered at Taejon. Two [ROK] puppet divisions are hindered [by the NKPA] in the south. Most of the areas in [North] Korea are not yet occupied by the enemy. (d) Each combat-effective NKPA unit directed by Kim Il-sung is bravely resisting the enemy along the 38th parallel; while more than 50,000 have withdrawn to the areas north of the 38th parallel, majority of the NKPA forces in the south remain in South Korea.

Taking the battlefield situation into consideration, Mao pointed out that the best the Chinese forces could do at this point was to assist the NKPA in defending the line between Pyongyang and Wonsan. To achieve this, he informed Zhou, Peng Dehuai planned to move one CPV army into the mountainous areas near Tokchon, about 120 miles northeast of Pyongyang, and three infantry armies and three artillery divisions into Huichon, Chonchon, Kanggye, and areas north of Tokchon. This deployment would serve a twofold objective. First, it "may force the American and puppet forces to hesitate and even cease advancing onward." To Mao, this would mean that "the areas, at least the mountainous areas, north of the Pyongyang-Wonsan line will remain unoccupied [by the enemy] and our troops don't have to rush into combat but gain more time for training and equipping." Second, with this arrangement, Mao envisioned that the CPV would be able to marshal their main forces to assault the ROK troops coming from Wonsan and deploy enough troops to block the enemy's attack from Pyongyang. "As long as we can completely eliminate one or even two or three [ROK] divisions," he concluded, "the [overall] situation would become more relaxed."[5]

On the same day Mao informed Zhou Enlai of his specific plans for fighting a defensive war in Korea. First, he had already ordered Peng Dehuai not to plan for any offensive actions. The CPV's immediate task was "to build two or three defensive perimeters in the Tokchon areas north of the Pyongyang-Wonsan railway and south of the Tokchon-Yongwon road." As long as the US/UN forces remained in Pyongyang and Wonsan during the next six months, the CPV would not engage them. "We will consider attacking

Pyongyang and Wonsan," he stressed, "only when our forces are fully equipped and our air and ground firepower is greatly improved or [even becomes] overwhelmingly superior to the enemy's. In short, we will take no offensive action in the next six months." Second, regarding the timetable of the CPV action, he told Zhou that he had set October 19 as the day when the CPV would begin to move into Korea. "It will take seven days for a vanguard unit to cover 200 kilometers [about 120 miles] to Tokchon," he calculated. "The vanguard will need one or two days to rest and then begin to construct fortifications in the area south of the Tokchon-Yongwon line on October 28. It will take ten days for the entire [CPV] army of 26,000 men (twelve infantry and three artillery divisions) to cross the Yalu River, that is, [our main forces] will not finish crossing the river until October 28." Third, should the US/UN forces stay in their present positions between Pyongyang and Wonsan and allow the CPV sufficient time to construct defense works, Mao even planned to "send half of the troops back to the Chinese territory for further training and equipment and dispatch them to [North Korea] at the time [when] we are ready for a major offensive." Finally, in order to coordinate with the Chinese defensive maneuvers, Zhou was to request that the Kremlin use its influence to ensure that "the NKPA continue its resistance and try to delay the US/UN advance as much as possible."[6]

Indeed, Mao was keenly worried about the seemingly demoralized NKPA. Although its headquarters remained in North Korea, Pyongyang had decided in early October to evacuate civilian officials and family members of military officers to China's Northeast. Mao had assigned Gao Gang to help these North Koreans resettle.[7] But his greatest concern was whether the NKPA could reorganize its resistance and hold fast to the Pyongyang-Wonsan line until the Chinese forces arrived. In his telegram to Kim Il-sung on October 10, Mao noted that in its advance north, the US/UN main force was leaving its rear weakly defended. "It is strategically necessary and advantageous that all those NKPA troops who have difficulties withdrawing to the north should stay in South Korea to open up a front in the enemy's rear." It was certain that 40,000 to 50,000 NKPA forces fighting guerrilla warfare in South Korea would "greatly contribute to the military struggles in the north." Moreover, Mao expected the NKPA to defend the transportation line between Pyongyang and Sinuiju because "the enemy seems to have an intention to launch another amphibious assault along the coastal line from Chinnampo to Sinuiju for the purpose of cutting off [our] transportation line."[8]

However, the dispatch of the Chinese troops did not proceed as smoothly as Mao had hoped. Although well-known for his ability to organize battles quickly and efficiently, Peng Dehuai was having difficulties carrying out his new mission. Since the CMC had not kept him apprised of its plans before his appointment, Peng was unfamiliar with the battlefield. Moreover, the combat forces were mostly from the Fourth Field Army, not from his own First Field Army. Contrary to the Chinese military maxim of "knowing the enemy and knowing yourself," Peng lacked knowledge and so had reason to be apprehensive.

On October 9, the day after he arrived at Shenyang, Peng called the first CPV command meeting. Gao Gang began by briefing the commanders on how the CCP Politburo deliberated and decided on China's entry into the war. Despite his opposition in China's intervention, Gao promised that he would do his best to organize logistics, and he exhorted the commanders to obey Peng's orders absolutely.[9] Peng spoke next. "I arrived in Beijing on the fourth [of October], accepted this assignment on the fifth, and came to Shenyang on the eighth," he told the commanders. "I, indeed, can be described as 'being pitched into the work in haste [*cangcu shangzhen*].'" He then observed, "You are the main forces of the Fourth Field Army, and I never had the chance to direct you during the Liberation War. Therefore, I may not be good enough to command [you and your troops]." Peng had the reputation of being extremely tough and strict. After learning of his appointment, the 13th Army Corps Commander Deng Hua had cautioned First Deputy Commander Hong Xuezhi that "we ought to wait upon him with great care [because] Chief Peng has a strong sense of responsibility, and always sets strict demands in combat. Once he finds even a minor error, he will lose his temper and sometimes gets so angry that he would have you court-marshaled." Seeing Peng's modesty at the meeting, both Deng and Hong were relieved: "Chief Peng is the PLA's deputy commander in chief and CMC's vice-chairman. Certainly you can direct our forces very well and lead us to victory. We will surely follow your orders."

Pleased with this vote of confidence, Peng turned to issues of strategy and tactics. "Our current task," he pointed out, "is to preserve and protect a revolutionary base [in North Korea] whereby to annihilate the enemy forces at appropriate time while [we] will actively assist the Korean people fighting against the invaders." Given the technical and ordnance superiority of the US/UN forces and the narrowness of the Korean peninsula, he conceded that "the mobile war strategy that we employed in our civil wars does not fit in the Korean battleground." In his view, the best plan was to fight "a combined positional and mobile warfare." He explained that "we will firmly resist the enemy advance so as to keep it from forwarding even one more step; meanwhile, we will make a quick decision to strike out by penetrating into the enemy's rear wherever there is a weak point." Finally, Peng reiterated that "our present task is to preserve a base but, more important, is to annihilate the enemy's strength. Therefore our defense is not completely defensive. It should enable us not only to eliminate the enemy but also to defend our positions."[10]

The 13th Army Corps commanders had no objection to Peng's strategy but raised some questions about the deployment of the troops. According to the original CMC plan, the army corps would first move two armies across the Yalu River, while the rest of the forces in the Northeast awaited Soviet equipment. Deng and Hong found this scheme unrealistic. First, without air or artillery support, two armies would not be enough to establish and maintain a defense base in North Korea. Second, the U.S. Air Force was stepping up its reconnaissance over the Yalu, and if it detected the concentration of Chinese forces there, it would certainly bomb all the river bridges. Should these bridges be destroyed, any subsequent crossing would be handicapped. Deng and Hong then suggested that all four infantry armies and three artillery divisions move into Korea simultaneously. Concurring, Peng immediately requested the CMC to modify the original plan. He also urged the Northeast Military Command to strengthen the air defense of the Yalu River.[11] Mao sent his approval on October 11 and also informed Peng that an anti-aircraft artillery regiment from Shanghai was headed to Andong to protect the bridges. Mao mentioned his regret that none of the Chinese air force planes was as yet combat-ready.[12]

The field commanders also had serious misgivings about the lack of reserves. Explaining their concerns to Peng at Andong, Deng and Hong asked him to pressure the CMC to augment reinforcements to twenty-four divisions and to muster them in the Northeast before the spring of 1951. They specifically wanted the CMC to deploy another infantry army to protect the supply lines of the 13th Army Corps. Mao satisfied the field commanders by moving the 9th Army Corps from Shandong to the Northeast ahead of schedule and the 66th Army from Tianjin to the Sino-Korean border to guard the rear of the 13th Army Corps.[13]

Aside from these strategic issues, the field commanders considered it urgent to mobilize the rank and file. There had been doubts expressed about why Chinese troops should fight and die for North Korea. Some soldiers did not understand the CPV's war objective; others were fearful of superior U.S. air and artillery firepower; still others had no idea of how to combat the American troops. Always taking political mobilization seriously, Peng held a meeting with all twelve division commanders and political commissars in mid-October. He told the participants that China had no other choice but to intervene, since "U.S. imperialists are attacking the [North] Korean revolutionary government and people with seven U.S. [infantry] divisions and

Syngman Rhee's forces, and their troops have already crossed the 38th parallel and are pressing north." Given the real threat of aggression, Peng concluded, "I personally think that the central leadership's decision [on intervention] is 100 percent necessary and correct."

> If we did not take the initiative to dispatch forces to aid the [North] Korean revolutionary government and people, the reactionaries within and outside [China] would bluster forth threats more fiercely and the pro-American elements would become more active. Should we allow U.S. imperialists to occupy Korea, that would constitute a direct threat to us, [because] the US would be able to transfer its forces to Vietnam and Burma [or elsewhere] so as to make trouble everywhere, which would place us in a passive [and disadvantageous] position. It would also bring about devastating consequences to the international communist movement, for some countries would then make up their minds to lean to U.S. imperialists.

"Is it all right that we would not fight the war until after three or five more years and let us relax our breathing?" Peng's answer was "maybe," but he saw a graver danger in a policy of "fighting no war now but waiting till three or five years later." "By then our industries constructed with great hardship during these three or five years would be damaged; by then U.S. imperialists could complete the arming of Japan, which would be involved with a larger number of forces, and we would encounter greater difficulties in prohibiting [foreign] invasion; by then U.S. imperialists will probably finish arming West Germany, which would be able to produce such a large quantity of iron and steel that we could not ignore it; and by then revolutionary movements in other Western European nations would probably be suppressed and the [world] revolutionary strength would be reduced." Given these prospects, Peng declared, "it is more beneficial to fight [the war] now [than later]."[14]

To boost the commanders' morale, Peng insisted that the Chinese troops were capable of engaging the US/UN forces in Korea. In his view, the US/UN coalition suffered from numerical inferiority. He quoted statistics from the CMC that indicated "America has altogether twenty-one infantry divisions of which seventeen divisions are highly combat effective, and a total amount of 1,460,000 troops including the army, navy, and air force. . . . [The US] is capable of mobilizing another 500,000 to constitute a total of two million by June of next year, which will consist of 834,000 infantry men, 579,000 naval forces, 150,000 marines, and 584,000 air force personnel." At the present time, Peng believed, there were in Korea seven U.S. infantry divisions, each with 12,000 men; seven South Korean divisions, each composed of 6,000 soldiers; a British brigade; and a small number of troops from other countries. In his judgment, the enemy had dispersed its forces too thin, and the farther north it advanced, the thinner its formation would be. Since the enemy had to spare troops to suppress the North Korean guerrillas in South Korea, Peng estimated that the maximum number of forces the US/UN headquarters could assemble on the front line would be three U.S. and three ROK divisions, which "we are more than capable of dealing with." Peng conceded that "the U.S. Air Forces, only a small number deployed in Korea, though, dominate the sky at this stage," but he reminded the commanders that "air forces [alone] cannot determine the outcome of war; the enemy tank and artillery forces are also superior to ours for the time being, . . . [nevertheless] the US/UN superiority cannot last very long and the difficulties the enemy faces will rapidly grow."[15]

The key to defeating the US/UN forces was the correct use of strategy and tactics. "We are not planning to fight a large-scale war at the present time," Peng told the division commanders. "[Our military action] does not mean a declaration of war on the US but enter the war merely in the name of a people's volunteer army to aid [North] Korea's revolutionary war." And the CPV's first mission was to build a defensive line in North Korea. "Although our main task is to protect a strip of land," he explained, "we must try to weaken the enemy strength and seize every opportunity to wipe out even one enemy battalion or regiment [at a time] resolutely and completely." With regard to tactics, he instructed that "we must dare to organize close combat with satchel charges, bayonets, and grenades, which the enemy troops fear the most." To minimize the impact of the enemy's firepower, Peng directed that all troops focus on building defense works that were deep and heavily covered. "Each squad should be divided into three or four groups and dig several bunkers, spreading out in the shape of a plum blossom to form cross fires at a distance of twenty or thirty meters so as to support each other. . . . [We] ought to feign some fortifications to attract the enemy artillery fire so as to waste its ammunition. Our artillery forces should also be well camouflaged to avoid being detected [by the enemy's reconnaissance]."[16]

While the CPV tried to prepare for the oncoming battle, the central leadership in Beijing pressed for an earlier movement into North Korea. At 1:00 A.M., October 15, Mao informed Gao Gang that the CPV would begin to cross the Yalu on October 18, or no later than October 19. He directed Gao to make sure that the food and supplies demanded by the 13th Army Corps was transported to the front in advance, and he stressed that "there must be no delay."[17] Four hours later, he cabled the CPV headquarters, pointing out that "the U.S., British, and the puppet [ROK] forces at the 38th parallel already occupied Kumchong on [October] 13 and seem to be preparing an assault on Pyongyang from there. U.S. Marine divisions appear ready to land at Chinnampo to assist the attack of Pyongyang, while, [our intelligence] reports indicate, the puppet 6th and 8th divisions, which originally were to gather in Wonsan, have turned to attack Pyongyang." Since an enemy assault on Pyongyang seemed imminent, one army should set out as the advance unit on October 17 so that it could reach the Tokchon area by October 23. This army, Mao specified, would rest one day and then construct defense works on October 25. Another army must begin to march on October 18, followed by the other forces. The CCP chairman ordered that all forces must be across the river within ten days and that sufficient food and munitions must be stored in temporary depots in North Korea before the troops moved in.[18]

As his sense of urgency grew, Mao changed his mind and on the afternoon of October 17, he told the CPV Command to prepare to dispatch two armies instead of one as the advance forces and to head out on October 19. Meanwhile, he asked Gao Gang and Peng Dehuai to fly by Beijing for further consultation.[19] After confirming with Peng, Gao, and Zhou Enlai, who had just returned from Moscow, Mao altered his plan one more time. At 9:00 P.M., October 18, he instructed all four infantry armies and three artillery divisions to begin the crossing of the Yalu on the evening of October 19. To achieve a covert entry, Mao prescribed that "every day the troops should start crossing the river at dusk, cease action at 4:00 A.M., and finish covering up before 5:00 A.M., and [every unit] must strictly and carefully follow up this plan." In order to "learn by experience," he taught, "[you] should only plan to move two or three divisions across [the river] on the night of 19th and then determine whether to increase or decrease the number of troops [to get across] for the next night."[20]

Mao evidently regarded a surreptitious dispatch of the Chinese forces to Korea as extremely important. He informed China's regional military commanders on October 19 that "the Volunteers will begin to move into [Korea] today. They will first obtain a firm foothold in the areas in North Korea not yet lost [to the enemy] and then look for opportunities to fight a few battles of mobile warfare." He then urged the commanders to guarantee the secrecy of China's military action. Meanwhile, he instructed the CPV headquarters that "all of our volunteer army's scouting units must disguise themselves as the North Korean People's Army and should not reveal their [Chinese] volunteer army identity so that [we] can confuse the enemy." Since the key to transforming the war situation "is whether we can catch the enemy off guard, in the next few months, we will only do it and not speak about it [*zhizuo bushuo*], that is, we will not allow [Chinese intervention] to appear in the newspapers and just keep it among the high-ranking leaders within the party."[21]

However, the war situation in Korea underwent a sudden change. On the morning of October 19, Pak Il-yu, sent by Kim Il-sung, came to see Peng at Andong. Pak reported that the US/UN forces had started a massive attack on Pyongyang on October 18, causing the already fragile NKPA defense to disintegrate completely. Pak passed along Kim's urgent demand for the immediate participation of the Chinese forces. Worried about the deteriorating situation, Peng decided to enter North Korea right away, leaving Deng Hua to direct the crossing of the Yalu. Shortly after Peng left, Deng called a command meeting, at which he observed that any scenario based on the US/UN forces remaining between Pyongyang and Wonsan was now irrelevant. The CPV, he asserted, might encounter three possible situations once they moved into North Korea: "(1) The enemy forces may reach our gathering areas before we get there; (2) the enemy forces may engage us shortly after we arrive but before we can consolidate our defense positions; and (3) the enemy forces may run up against us on our way [to the destination]." Deng believed the only option for the CPV was to move as fast as possible into defensible areas—perhaps along the line between Kusong in the west and Oro-ri in the east—and thereby to stall the enemy advance and cover the NKPA evacuation. Deng then ordered the troops to speed up the crossing while strictly complying with the rules of secrecy. Every soldier, he specified, should be in complete disguise and advance as quietly as possible; vehicles should drive with no headlights, and every unit should shut off radio and telegraphic communications.[22]

The 13th Army Corps's four infantry armies, three artillery divisions, and one anti-aircraft artillery regiment embarked on the secret crossing of the Yalu on the cold and rainy night of October 19. More than 260,000 troops waited in Andong, Changdian, Ji'an, and Linjiang to reach the other side of the river. The 119th and 120th divisions of the 40th Army were transported by train from Andong to Sinuiju and marched toward the Tokchon area, while the army's 118th Division crossed the river from Changdian and moved toward Onjong. Following the 40th Army, the 39th Army's 115th Division gathered in the Namsidong area to guard the right flank of the army's main force, with the 116th and 117th divisions moving toward the Kusong and Taechon areas. The 42d Army walked across the river from Ji'an and Linjiang using pontoon bridges constructed by the 4th and 6th Engineer regiments, and then headed for Sochang-ri and Oro-ri. The 38th Army followed the 42d Army and advanced toward Kanggye.[23]

II

As the Chinese forces were being ferried across the Yalu, the US/UN forces carried their offensive northward, much faster than the Chinese leaders had anticipated. The U.S. 1st Army Corps captured Pyongyang on October 19. The next day, the ROK 2d Corps moved into areas only about eighty miles away from the planned CPV staging sites, and the ROK Capital Division took Oro-ri and Hongwon in the east, already occupying the places where the Chinese 42d and 38th armies were to assemble. Mao predicted on October 21 that the ROK 3d Division would advance on Hamhung, the ROK 6th Division would turn northward from Paup to Tokchon or Huichon, and the ROK 7th and 8th divisions would pass Sunchon, Kunu-ri, and Anju to occupy Taechon, Yongsong, or Kusong. "The ultimate destination for these five [ROK] divisions," he believed, "is the line between Kanggye and Sinuiju."[24] But the Chinese had only transported five divisions across the river on the first night, and the 13th Army Corps vanguards had to cover themselves in the daytime and could only move slowly at night. It was impossible for the main forces to reach the designated areas before the enemy forces.

Nevertheless, the Chinese leaders saw an opportunity to counter the US/UN advance via mobile warfare. Apparently, the US/UN forces had not detected the entry of the Chinese troops in large numbers. As they advanced northward in two parallel columns, the US/UN troops were spread thin, and the east-west gap between the two lines was getting wider. Given the enemy situation, the Chinese could concentrate their main forces to launch a surprise attack on one US/UN column. "Neither the US or the puppet forces have by far expected the entry of our Volunteers," Mao cabled Peng Dehuai at 2:30 A.M. on October 21; "that is the reason why they dare to advance in two separated (east and west) lines." Given the exposed positions of the ROK 6th, 7th, and 8th divisions in the west, he viewed this as "an excellent opportunity to wipe out the three ROK divisions and win a first victory after entering the war" and "stabilize the war situation."[25]

Excited about this development, Mao himself designed the battle plan. First, the 13th Army Corps would gather three armies to subdue the three divisions of the ROK 2d Corps in the west "one by one." It was vitally important that "since [ROK] 6th Division is stronger [than the other two] in terms of combat effectiveness, . . . our 40th Army, if (the whole army) can reach the Tokchon-Yongwon area on October 23, should bypass (from the eastern side to the south near the railroad) [ROK] 6th Division to its rear in order to make way in the enemy's front for our main forces (38th or 39th armies)." Second, the 13th Army Corps should deploy the 42d Army for a blocking action in the east. He anticipated that it would take about seven days for the ROK Capital and 3d divisions to reach Changjin. One division of the 42d Army should be sent to check these two ROK divisions in the Changjin area, and "the 42d Army's main forces should be deployed in the areas south to Maengsan to cut the railway line between Wonsan and Pyongyang and to prevent the enemy forces in Wonsan and Pyongyang from reinforcing [the ROK 6th Division]." Finally, Mao urged the field commanders to "encourage the whole army [corps] to fear neither death nor the hardship and to strive for a complete victory."[26]

However, Mao's immediate concern was with CPV organization at the top. At this point, Peng Dehuai was already in North Korea, while the entire staff of the CPV Command was still in Andong. The 13th Army Corps headquarters had just crossed the Yalu, and disrupted communications had broken the chain of field command. At 3:30 A.M., October 21, Mao cabled Deng Hua, asking: "Have you already marched forward?" He then ordered that the 13th Army Corps Command must join Peng Dehuai and be immediately transformed into the CPV Command "for the sake of [effective] command." He stressed that "it is now a matter of seizing a combat chance and completing battle organization so as to commence fighting in a few days, instead of preparing for an offensive action after a period of defensive actions."[27] However, Deng had lost contact with Peng. Cui Lun, who was the CPV's deputy signal director, recalled that the truck carrying him and a transceiver had lost track of Peng's jeep on the way to Kim Il-sung's headquarters. Not until the morning of October 21 was Peng located. Peng immediately contacted the 13th Army Crops headquarters, instructing Deng, Hong Xuezhi, and Han Xianchu to join him and leave army crops chief of staff Xie Fang to lead the rest of the command staff.[28]

Peng now considered altering the original plans. Meeting with Chai Chengwen on the morning of October 20, he had expressed his surprise at the speed of the US/UN advance. The next morning, he was even more shocked when Kim told him how little the NKPA could do to delay the enemy's northward movement. North Korea's four regular divisions were already beating a total retreat. Kim hinted that the responsibility for the entire battlefield had to be shouldered by Peng and the CPV.[29] "It is now extremely important," Peng cabled Mao at 4:00 P.M. on October 21, "that [we] control the areas of Myohyang-san and Sinchang-dong and construct defensive positions there so as to isolate the enemy in the east from its forces in the west." In his view, "if we can control the two key points . . . we can attack the enemy forces either in the west or in the east with our concentrated forces of absolute [numerical] superiority." For this purpose, he directed that all available trucks assemble and prepare to transport two regiments to Myohyang-san and one regiment to Sinchang-dong to build a defensive perimeter there ahead of the ROK troops.[30]

Mao responded at 7:00 A.M. the next morning. He agreed that the 13th Army Corps should send one division into the area around Changjin to block the ROK forces in the east, but he showed more interest in attacking the ROK 2d Corps in the west. In his view, a victory could be ensured by luring the enemy forces into the areas favorable to the Chinese. Regarding the regions north of Chonju, Pakchon, and Kunu-ri as good battlegrounds, Mao instructed that "our forces must stay twenty kilometers away from these areas; otherwise the enemy might detect [our intention] and cease advancing or even turn back." Should the ROK divisions enter the Pakchon and Kunu-ri areas, "it will be most advantageous for our forces to surround the [ROK] 6th and 8th divisions," with the 40th Army surrounding one and the 39th Army encircling the other simultaneously. Anticipating that the ROK 7th Division would seek to rescue its companion forces, he asserted that "we can [then] prepare to deal with this division later." Interestingly, he thought it was unlikely that the U.S. troops in Pyongyang might come to the ROK forces' aid. Enthusiastic about a prospective victory, Mao urged "prompt deployment of forces" and "immediate implementation of the battle plan." Otherwise, he warned, "[we] might not have enough time to act if the decision is made too late."[31] Two hours later, Mao instructed the 13th Army Corps headquarters to quickly transport as many troops as possible by trucks to Myohyang-san and Haengchon-dong and to keep the CPV main forces away from the Pakchon and Kunu-ri areas to let the South Korean troops move in.[32]

Without much hesitation, Peng agreed to diverge somewhat from the defensive strategy to an offensive action. "It is unlikely that our forces control Tokchon ahead of the enemy," he stated in his telegram on October 22 to Deng Hua and Hong Xuezhi. "We must transport one division either from the 39th or the 40th armies by trucks to the Myohyang-san and Sinchon-ri areas south to Huichon to construct fortifications there." In his plan, as the ROK 6th, 7th, and 8th divisions continued their northward trek, the main forces of the 39th and the 40th armies would outflank the enemy force from the line between Onjong and Unsan on the east; the 38th Army would set out from Sinchang-dong to envelop Yonwang and Tokchon on the southeast; and the 42d Army would advance on Changjin. Peng emphasized that "the faster the troops can move, the better position we will be in."[33] At 3:00 P.M. that same day, Peng cabled Deng and Hong again, stressing that the CPV's immediate task was to "lure the [ROK] forces in deep so that [we] can wipe them out one by one." To that end, "[we must] try to avoid being tied down by the American forces." Therefore, he instructed that the 40th Army should dispatch one division to build defense works in the areas southward to Huichon; the 39th Army should gather in the Unsan–Sachon-dong area with one regiment to block the Unsan-Pakchon road; the 38th Army should enter the areas northeast of Huichon; and the East China Anti-aircraft Artillery Regiment would follow the 38th Army to position themselves near Huichon.[34]

Table 5.1. CPV Command: October 19–November 5, 1950

CPV Commander	Peng Dehuai
Political Commissar	Peng Dehuai
Deputy Commanders	Deng Hua
	Hong Xuezhi
	Han Xianchu
Chief of Staff	Xie Fang
Director of Political Department	Du Ping
13th Army Corps Commander	Deng Hua
Political Commissar	Deng Hua
Deputy Commander	Hong Xuezhi
	Han Xianchu
Chief of Staff	Xie Fang
Director of Political Department	Du Ping
38th Army Commander	Liang Xingchu
Political Commissar	Liu Xiyuan
Deputy Commander	Jiang Yonghui
39th Army Commander	Wu Xinquan
Political Commissar	Xu Binzhou
Deputy Commander	Tan Youlin
40th Army Commander	Wen Yucheng
Political Commissar	Yuan Shengping
Deputy Commander	Cai Zhengguo
42d Army Commander	Wu Ruilin
Political Commissar	Zhou Biao
Deputy Commander	Wu Jicheng
50th Army Commander	Zeng Zesheng
Political Commissar	Xu Wenlie
Deputy Commander	Shu Hang
66th Army Commander	Xiao Xinhuai
Political Commissar	Wang Zifeng
Deputy Commander	Chen Fangren
CPV Artillery Commander	Wan Yi
Political Commissar	Qiu Chuangcheng
Deputy Commander	Kuang Yumin
Front Logistics Commander	Zhang Mingyuan
Political Commissar	Du Zheheng

Uncertain about the upcoming battle, Peng did not plan for an all-out offensive. The CPV, in his view, was still unprepared to launch a major attack. He knew, however, that he had to convince Mao. On the evening of October 22, Peng reported to Mao that "the basic guideline regarding our military action for the next six months still ought to be the establishment [of a defensive position in] the northern areas including Changjin, Huichon, and Kusong and protecting the ferry points [of the Yalu] at Changdian, Ji'an, and Linjiang so that we can win enough time to get fully prepared for a large-scale counteroffensive later." Since the Chinese forces had no air support, he asserted, "we shall even give up defending [North Korea's] coastal cities including Sinuiju" because the CPV was not capable of defending them against superior U.S. air, naval, or tank forces. By evacuating these areas, he believed that "we may compel the enemy to disperse its forces further and avoid unnecessary losses of our troops." Peng assured Mao of his determination to attack two or three ROK divisions if there was a possibility of success, but he intimated that Mao and other leaders should not have too high expectations. "With this attack," he explained "[our ultimate goal is] to extend and consolidate a foothold in the mountainous areas north of the line between Wonsan and Pyongyang and to support [NKPA's] guerrilla warfare in South Korea." Sensing the difference between his stand at the end of the report and Mao's orders, Peng asked for Mao's instructions.[35]

In his reply the next day, Mao regarded Peng's plans as "safe" and agreed that "we shall take safety into serious consideration and should never risk unreliable measures." However, he was evidently displeased with Peng's caution. From a military point of view, the combat situation in Korea should be determined by "whether we can take advantage of the enemy's complete unawareness [of our entry] so as to wipe out three or even four puppet divisions with a surprise attack (the puppet 3d Division may follow ROK 6th Division and ROK 1st Division may possibly be involved in)." Should the CPV achieve "a major victory," the US/UN headquarters would have to reconsider its strategy. "It probably would not attack Sinuiju, Songchon, or Chongju at least for a considerable period of time," Mao anticipated. "The ROK Capital and 3d divisions might retreat from Hamhung to Wonsan, and then we would be able to defend Changjin." He saw this development certainly constituting "a major problem for the enemy," because the US/UN forces might lose control of Sinanju and Sunchon and have no troops with which to defend the railway between Songchon and Yangdok, thus "exposing a big breach [of its defense line] to us." But, should the CPV's planned attack be unsuccessful—"that is, we shall fail to wipe out the main forces of ROK 6th, 7th, and 8th divisions, allows them to escape, or resist firmly to wait for rescue and the reinforcement of the ROK Capital and 1st divisions and perhaps some U.S. troops"—then the CPV would be compelled to withdraw. As a result, Mao insisted, "the overall situation would turn to the enemy's favor and it would be more difficult for us to defend Huichon and Changjin."

Mao also pointed out that whether or not the CPV could achieve a notable victory with the proposed attack would depend on "how much the enemy air raids would subdue our soldiers to hinder our assaulting actions." In his judgment, U.S. air raids would not create insurmountable problems because the CPV could "march and fight at night so that the enemy, even with a large number of planes, could not inflict heavy casualties [on us] or make our movement difficult; our forces may carry on field operations and attack the isolated enemy positions." He strongly believed that "other than [the enemy forces in] Pyongyang, Wonsan, Seoul, Taegu, and Pusan which we cannot attack without air forces, we may manage to annihilate the enemy in all other places [of North Korea] one by one. Even if the US would send in several more divisions, we would still be able to wipe them out one after another." In all likelihood, the US might be "compelled by our attack to initiate [cease-fire] negotiations; or we may recapture these cities one by one after we acquire sufficient air and artillery power." However, Mao conceded that "if the enemy air strike would cause heavy damages [on our forces] and force us to cease fighting, we would then be put in a very difficult position, because we cannot acquire air support now." Moreover, "if the US would add another five to ten divisions of reinforcement in Korea before we eliminate a few of the American and ROK divisions through mobile warfare or assaults of the isolated enemy positions, the situation would turn against us." Otherwise, he was optimistic that "it would be in our favor." Mao firmly pressed Peng to plan a more aggressive action. "I believe," he explained, "that we shall make every effort to fight for a complete victory in this battle; we must try our best to maintain a high morale to fight effectively even under the enemy air raids; we ought to decimate the enemy as much as possible before their reinforcement from America or other countries are transported into Korea."[36]

Recognizing Mao's aspiration for a major victory, Peng and other field commanders believed that they needed more troops. Discussing the situation with Peng at Kim's headquarters, Deng Hua and Hong Xuezhi pointed out that if the entire 39th Army moved east, there would be no troops left to defend Sinuiju and Chongju, areas crucial to CPV supply lines. They suggested that the 66th Army, which was guarding supply and rear services in northeastern China, relocate to the Sinuiju-Chongju region. Peng concurred and requested the CMC to make the arrangements. On the morning of October 23, Mao informed him that a vanguard division of the 66th Army had already set out for Sinuiju and that its other two divisions would gather in Andong the next day as reserves. Mao added that the 50th Army would move to Andong, along with the 9th Army Corps in northeastern China, to serve as strategic reserves to the 13th Army Corps.[37] The additional forces seemed to soothe the field commanders' worries.

An effective field command still eluded the commanders, since the CPV headquarters had yet to function fully and effectively. Peng did not bring any staff with him from his First Field Army except his personal secretary. The CMC had to transfer personnel from the General Staff Department and the Northeast Military Command at short notice, and these people had never worked under Peng or with one another. Setting up his headquarters at Tae-yu-dong, a mountain cave formed from an abandoned gold mine, Peng merged the 13th Army Corps top staff into the CPV Command on October 23.[38] He named Deng Hua, Kim's representative Pak Il-yu, Hong Xuezhi, and Han Xianchu as deputy commanders of the CPV, Xie Fang as the CPV chief of staff, and Du Ping as director of the CPV Political Department; Deng and Pak were also named deputy political commissars. He then put Hong and Xie in charge of the headquarters' routines. Mao approved Peng's command structure, but in his telegram on October 25, he ordered the formation of the CCP Party Committee of the CPV with Peng as the secretary and Deng and Pak as vice-secretaries.[39]

Before the new CPV command was ready to function, the Chinese forces fired the first shot at the South Korean troops in Onjong on the morning of October 25. At 2:00 A.M., Chief of Staff Xie Fang was surprised to receive a telephone call from Deng Yue, commander of the 40th Army's 118th Division, reporting that his scout units had discovered some enemy forces marching along the Onjong-Pukchin highway. Interestingly, Deng was not sure whether the foe was South Korean or American because none of his scouts understood the "foreign language [*yanghua*]." It took Deng several hours to identify the enemy troops as part of the ROK 6th Division. The Onjong-Pukchin road wound its way through a valley about fifteen miles long and half a mile wide and surrounded by mountains. To set a trap, the CPV headquarters ordered the 118th Division to occupy the heights north of Onjong and the 120th Division to control the hills on the eastern side of the highway.[40]

Before dawn on the morning of October 25, a heavy moist fog rose from the nearby Kuryong River and concealed the Chinese movement. It was a perfect setting for a surprise attack. Around 7:00 A.M., the ROK 1st Division's vanguard, preceded by tanks, approached the position of the 360th Regiment of the 120th Division, whereupon the Chinese soldiers fired at the ROK troops and forced them into retreat. At 10:00 A.M., the 118th Division's 354th

Regiment also assaulted an infantry battalion and a reinforced artillery company of the ROK 2d Regiment. Charging down to the highway and cutting the enemy line into three sections, the Chinese troops destroyed the entire ROK battalion and captured a few hundred prisoners of war including one American military adviser. The main problem the Chinese troops encountered that day was taking prisoners, because no Chinese soldier could speak Korean or English. They kept shouting "*jiaoqiang busha* [lay down your weapon and we'll spare your life]." Later that day, the CPV 360th Regiment stalled a vigorous counterattack by the ROK 1st Division but incurred heavy casualties in its 3d and 5th companies. Having lost almost his entire company, 3d Company leader Li Baoshan made a suicidal charge into the enemy positions with two bangalore torpedoes and so became the first CPV hero to sacrifice his life for victory. At dusk, the ROK 1st Division withdrew to Unsan, and the two CPV regiments pursued the enemy as far as Onjong.[41]

This unexpected combat in Onjong was unwelcome to the Chinese leaders. In his telegram to Peng at 5 P.M., October 25, Mao was disappointed that "the enemy is beginning to find out our entry [in Korea]. . . . It can be anticipated that our troops will be exposed more to the enemy today and tomorrow." Undaunted, however, he urged the CPV to waste no time in surrounding one or two ROK units in order to attract reinforcements and so to destroy a larger number of US/UN troops.[42] Peng reported back at 9:00 P.M. that since the ROK troops were advancing in small units, often carried by tanks and trucks, and were spreading all over North Korea, "it becomes very difficult for us to surround and attack two or three entire [ROK] divisions, and it is unlikely that we can disguise our entry any more." Therefore, in his view, "now it is necessary that each army and division will surround and attack the one or two enemy regiments in front of them (starting tonight) so that we can destroy one or two enemy divisions in total for the first battle"—which, he reminded Mao, merely "aims at stopping the enemy advance and stabilizing the [war] situation."[43] In his responses the next day, Mao agreed with Peng but warned that "the U.S. 24th Division and U.K. 27th Brigade have already crossed the Chongchon River from Sinanju and, therefore, the [CPV] 39th Army should not engage the US/UK troops." In his judgment, the CPV should still target the ROK 1st, 6th, and 8th divisions and try to wipe them out in a series of small assaults. He suggested that the 40th Army attack the ROK 6th's Division's 7th and 9th regiments advancing on Onjong, the 38th Army move south to break up the ROK 8th Division at Huichon into small pockets and destroy them, and the 39th Army set up a blocking position in the Unsan area to prevent the Anglo-American forces from reinforcing the ROK 1st Division.[44]

Following Mao's order, the CPV Command decided on October 27 to deploy six divisions against the ROK 8th Division and a unit of the ROK 6th Division and two divisions against the ROK 7th Regiment. According to this plan, two divisions of the 40th Army would move into the area southwest of Huichon on the night of October 28, while the 38th Army would gather in Huichon before dawn on the twenty-ninth. The 125th Division of the 42d Army would position itself southeast of Huichon as the 38th Army's reserves. The 39th Army was to maintain already constructed defensive works north of Unsan in order to guard the flanks of the attacking forces and to surround Unsan after the Huichon battle was over. Finally, the 40th Army's 118th and 50th Army's 148th divisions would launch a two-pronged attack on the ROK 7th Regiment.[45] Unfortunately, the enemy situation changed before all the CPV movements were completed. The 38th Army was still about thirty-five miles from Huichon when the ROK 8th Division pulled out of Huichon to help rescue the 7th Regiment. Joining the ROK 1st Division and units of the 6th Division, the ROK 8th Division confronted the CPV in Onjong. At 10:00 P.M. on October 27, Mao asked Peng to modify his plan immediately.[46]

Peng then redeployed the forces with an emphasis on attacking the enemy on the move. Anticipating that the ROK 8th and 1st divisions would come to the aid of the 7th Regiment, Peng directed the CPV 118th and 148th divisions to surround, but not to engage, the ROK 7th Regiment so as to attract the enemy reinforcements into the Onjong area. The 40th Army should maintain a holding action on Onjong to win time for the 38th and the 39th armies to gather north of Unsan.[47] Mao endorsed this change but pointed out that the key to the success of this new plan was, first, to surround the ROK 7th Regiment and allow it "to cry for help in two to three days so loudly that the ROK 1st, 6th, and 8th divisions will have to rescue it and then we will have a battle to fight"; and, second, to open the offensive only when "all of our three armies are completely poised for actions."[48] Nevertheless, Peng's hopes of luring the ROK troops in deep turned out to be wishful thinking. By the evening of October 28, the main forces of the ROK 1st and 8th divisions stopped moving northward and sent only four battalions to attack Onjong, while the ROK 7th Regiment turned south. The U.S. 24th Division and the U.K. 27th Brigade entered the areas southeast of Chongchon and moved toward Chongju.

Disappointed at this development, Peng ordered an immediate assault of the ROK forces. He instructed the 118th and 148th divisions to attack the ROK 7th Regiment, and the bulk of the 40th Army to annihilate the four ROK battalions in Onjong. He then directed the 39th Army's 115th Division to join the CPV's main forces to surround the ROK 1st Division in Unsan. In order to block the ROK 6th and 8th divisions from retreating across the Chongchon River, Peng ordered the 38th Army to penetrate through Huichon to Kunu-ri to cut off the enemy lines of retreat.[49] On the evening of October 28, the CPV began the operation. The 40th Army fought all night and destroyed the ROK battalions in Onjong. After capturing about 400 South Korean POWs, twenty howitzers, and sixty trucks, the army rolled south. Fearful that the enemy might escape, the 118th Division started its attack on the ROK 7th Regiment before the 148th Division was in position to assist. Around midnight, division commander Deng Yue reported that he had eliminated the ROK regiment entirely. As part of the three-pronged assault, the 39th Army had completely enclosed the ROK 1st Division by late afternoon on the twenty-ninth. However, the 38th Army had moved too slowly, impeded by several mishaps. The North Koreans retreating northward had blocked road traffic, and an enemy air raid had hit the army headquarters, knocking communications out of order for a considerable length of time. And in Huichon, the army commander hesitated and held back the army because he mistook the ROK troops there for Americans, who were not to be engaged as yet. At dusk on October 29, the ROK units all evacuated. Tired and discouraged, the troops of the 38th moved toward Kunu-ri.[50]

At this juncture, the U.S. Eighth Army headquarters redeployed its forces on the western front. It sent the U.S. 1st Cavalry Division from Pyongyang to reinforce the ROK 1st Division in Unsan and ordered the ROK 8th Division to join the ROK 7th Division in the Tokchon area. The U.S. 24th Division and the U.K. 27th Brigade advanced on Sinuiju with its rear guarded by the U.S. 2d Division moving from Anju. The US/UN forces apparently enhanced their frontline strength and improved the coordination among the attacking units. Despite this change in the enemy situation, Peng insisted that the CPV continue the offensive, because, in his calculations, the Chinese forces still outnumbered the enemy troops. At 9:00 A.M., October 30, he reported to Mao that he would employ the 39th and 40th armies in a frontal charge and the 38th Army in a penetrating movement into the enemy's eastern flank and rear. He told Mao that he was going to deal first with the ROK 8th, 7th, and 1st divisions and then the U.S. 1st Cavalry Division. Meanwhile, the 66th Army would keep the U.S. 24th Division and U.K. 27th Brigade at bay. Mao approved Peng's much more ambitious plan. In his response to the CPV Command at 8:00 P.M. that night, he stressed that "as long as the 38th Army and one division of the 42d Army can block the enemy's way back to the Chongchon River and each army or division of the main forces dares to thrust deep into the enemy lines to cut them up in small pockets and destroy them one by one, a major victory still will be in our hand."[51]

All the CPV forces assigned to the frontal attack were supposed to act simultaneously at 7:30 P.M., November 1. The 39th Army, however, discovered early that afternoon that the enemy troops in Unsan were about to move. Afraid that the ROK 1st Division might evacuate, the army commander decided to launch the attack at 5:00 P.M. In fact, the 8th regiment of the U.S. 1st Cavalry Division was in the process of replacing the 12th Regiment of the ROK 1st Division. The 39th Army hurled the 117th and 116th divisions against the enemy positions in Unsan. At daybreak, the army commander reported that the U.S. 8th regiment had been decimated. After two days of fighting, the 39th Army claimed that it had killed 700 American troops and annihilated small units of the ROK 12th and U.S. 5th regiments, which were sent to rescue the U.S. 8th regiment.[52] At the same time, the 40th Army attacked the ROK 8th Division near Yongbyon but made no progress in the face of vigorous enemy resistance. However, the 38th Army's flanking movement proved to be the key to the CPV's success in the battle. On November 2, when the 38th Army reached Won-ni, Mao cabled the CPV Command three times urging the army to rush to Anju and Kunu-ri. If the 38th Army could quickly build a strong blocking position there, either to check the northward reinforcement of the U.S. 2d Division, forestall the southward retreat of the ROK forces, or even threaten Pyongyang, Mao was convinced that "our victory will be genuinely guaranteed."[53]

Nevertheless, on November 3, before the 38th Army could reach its destination, the U.S. Eighth Army headquarters ordered an overall retreat. Realizing that the enemy evacuation would nullify the CPV movements, Peng immediately ordered all CPV units to pursue and pin down the enemy forces on the front. It was, however, a race between American wheels and Chinese feet. The pursuing Chinese troops were battered by fierce US/UN air raids and constant artillery bombardment, and their progress was greatly hindered by heavy rain on November 4 in the areas north of the Chongchon River. Not surprisingly, all the US/UN forces safely reached the southern bank of the Chongchon River. After several days of relentless fighting, the Chinese troops were weary and, even worse, were running out of food and munitions. Unaware of the battlefield conditions, Mao cabled Peng at 10:00 P.M. on the fourth, ordering the CPV to fight on and, in particular, to "get prepared to wipe out the enemy forces if they counterattack." He contended that "the enemy's defense organization is in disorder and [especially] the defense of Pyongyang is weak, as two regiments of the U.S. 2d Division had already left for Sunchon." Mao wanted the 38th Army to advance on the enemy's front to support the CPV main forces' breakthrough.[54]

Cognizant of the difficulties the CPV had gone through, Peng Dehuai had already decided to cease all offensive actions. In his earlier telegram to Mao at 3 P.M. on the fourth, Peng reported that "the [first] counteroffensive in North Korea is over." Since the 38th Army delayed its penetration to Kunu-ri and the 66th Army failed to cut off the U.S. 24th Division's line of retreat, he explained, the enemy forces were able to escape quickly and safely. During the battle, Peng pointed out, "our troops were not thoroughly galvanized and very fearful of the [enemy] air raids and thus only devastated six to seven regiments of the enemy forces." To him, the CPV forces were not in a position to carry on the offensive because "our troops are very tired, and it has been very difficult to transport food and munitions due to the fact that the vehicular roads are too narrow and our trucks cannot move in daytime but drive without headlights at night." Moreover, he continued, the cold winter was coming, which would make it "increasingly difficult to preserve the strength of our troops who have to sleep outside and [sometimes] in the snow." Given these problems, Peng stressed that the troops had to rest and reorganize before they could undertake another offensive drive.[55] Peng's report seems to have convinced Mao, who agreed the next morning to halt the pursuit. The CCP chairman, however, directed that while the troops recuperated, the CPV Command should prepare for the next attack in the area north of the Wonsan-Sunchon railroad, where "we can wear down the enemy's strength and carry out the battle along the Pyongyang-Wonsan line with the areas north and west of Tokchon, Kujang, and Yongbyon as your rear."[56]

The CPV forces on the western front ceased the offensive completely on November 5. In the east, the 42d Army had been engaged in a fierce blocking action at Chosin Reservoir with the ROK Capital and 1st divisions backed by the U.S. 1st Marines Division. The 42d evacuated its defensive positions on November 7. During this first-phase offensive, the CPV estimated 15,000 enemy casualties and 10,000 of its own.[57] However unexpected this initial encounter, the CPV commanders believed that they had accomplished a great deal: the troops had settled in North Korea and experienced their first combat.

Mao was less temperate than the commanders and seems to have gained tremendous confidence from this first offensive. On October 30, passing on a report from the CPV headquarters to the 9th and 19th army corps on the combat characteristics of the ROK forces, he bragged:

> (1) The enemy's combat effectiveness is low. His assaults and counterattacks must always be accompanied by firepower support because he fears close combat (afraid of bayonets and grenades). (2) Also he lacks the morale for carrying out offensive operations. Only small units (consisting

of a squad or a platoon at most) attacked our positions. They withdraw quickly if they fail to achieve their objectives and often flee as soon as we organize for a well-launched attack. (3) Their artillery fire is quite heavy, but their riflemen are poor at making shots. Before each of their offensives and withdrawals, the enemy troops have to have fierce cover fire. Living in their trucks, they attack only during the daytime and withdraw by nightfall. (4) After they lose their position [to us], they have three or four aircraft immediately raid and bomb this position which is revealed by air reconnaissance and land gunfire. (5) Their fortifications are simply constructed, because of the lack of sufficient tools. Artillery positions are mainly located out in the open field or on the road. Their equipment is too heavy to be mobilized in the mountains. (6) After the sun rises every morning, usually one to four of their airplanes fly at low altitude within ten to twenty miles of our positions to carry out reconnaissance and strafe. (7) Their special agents are quite active. Most are pretending to be refugees and carrying military maps, pistols, grenades, etc. The agents fire upon our positions, setting fire to ammunition, trucks, and villages, and also contacting their airplanes (with white towels). (8) It is not too difficult to handle the enemy's tanks. The 15th Brigade of the enemy's First Division was originally equipped with five tanks. We have destroyed four of its tanks.

The CCP chairman firmly believed that the CPV's small-scale battles had annihilated about one division of the South Koreans. "It is certain," he declared, "that we can eliminate all enemy units."[58]

III

The CPV headquarters soon began to plan for another offensive. Peng judged that the US/UN forces would eventually continue their advance northward, since he saw them settled into their positions along the southern bank of the Chongchon River. More important, the enemy seems to have underestimated the strength of the Chinese troops.[59] In Peng's view, the CPV's best strategy was still to lure the US/UN forces into areas favorable to CPV counteroffensives. True to Peng's assessment, the US/UN forces began an overall forward attack on November 8 supported by an intensive bombing of all ferry points on the Yalu River. Both the U.S. 10th Marine Corps and the Eighth Army resumed their northerly push.

Learning of the renewed US/UN advance, the CPV commanders met on November 8 to discuss how to draw the enemy farther north. As they reported to Mao, "we will adhere to a strategy of luring both the [US/UN] eastern and western columns deep into [North Korea], and [we will then] gather our main forces to surround and annihilate one [enemy column]." To implement this plan, the commanders resolved that the 9th Army Corps would secretly move two armies (the 20th and 27th) into the Changjin area and deploy one division to lead the U.S. 1st Marine Division into a trap to be set by the corps's main forces. The 38th and 42d armies would gather their main forces in the Tokchon area to form a double flanking attack of the enemy forward elements. One division and one regiment would be dispatched, first to delay enemy movement on the Tokchon road and then to divert those forces into the trap set by the 38th and 42d armies. The 40th Army would withdraw to the Yongbyon area and wait to coordinate with the 38th Army's southward penetration after it had outflanked the enemy forces. The 39th Army would organize a frontal holding operation in the Taechon area once the envelopment was accomplished. Finally, the 66th Army would gather in Kusong and Chongju as reserves while the 50th Army defended the western coast. As most of their trucks were damaged, the CPV commanders were very concerned about supplies and requested more transportation vehicles from Beijing.[60]

Mao was pleased with the CPV Command's decision to conduct another major offensive. He cabled Peng on November 9 that "your present plan is very good, . . . and [you should see to it that] it be implemented steadily and successfully." If the CPV would fight "one or two battles on the eastern and western fronts between late this month and early December to destroy another seven to eight regiments of the enemy forces," Mao expected, "[we would be able to] extend the [present] front line to the Pyongyang-Wonsan railway areas, and thus achieve a fundamental victory." In response to the request for more trucks, Mao was certain that "the first shipment of Soviet vehicles will soon arrive and the losses of trucks, although very heavy, can be replaced." Interestingly, he did not express much concern about the CPV's shortage of vehicles. He calculated that "in all likelihood, if an average of 30 trucks will be damaged every day, [we will lose] 900 every month, only adding to a total of 10,000 each year." But there were many ways to reduce the loss, including "repairing the damaged truck, or using parts of the damaged, or capturing [the enemy's]." The CPV's immediate task, he maintained, was to "construct several (not one) vehicular roads leading to the Tokchon, Yongwon, and Maengsan areas—an extremely important strategic task [that] ought to be carried out with dedication and diligence." Meanwhile, he instructed the Northeast Military Command to "try every possible means to guarantee the supplies of food, munitions, and winter clothing to [the troops at] the eastern and western fronts."[61]

Hoping for a bigger victory in the next offensive, Peng called the first CPV Party Committee meeting at his headquarters on November 13. The 38th Army Commander Liang Xingchu, 39th Army Commander Wu Xinquan, 40th Army Commander Wen Yucheng, 42d Army Commander Wu Ruilin, and 66th Army Political Commissar Wang Zifeng joined the CPV commanders. Peng evaluated the CPV performance during the first battle. A major failure, he asserted, was that "we routed the enemy forces more than annihilated them." Other than some objective difficulties, including unpreparedness and unfamiliarity with the battlefield, Peng regarded "the subjective mistakes of command" as the primary cause of the problem. "Some comrades still did not understand that the use of [our] main forces to outflank the enemy from its rear is the most effective way of eliminating the enemy strength." To him, the 113th Division (the 38th Army) commanders made a tactical error by dispatching only one regiment to cut off the retreat of two ROK regiments and resting its main forces twelve to nineteen miles away. "You have to understand," Peng stressed, "that annihilating one enemy regiment is much better than routing one enemy division." He was disturbed that "some high commanders overestimated the enemy strength and did not dare to infiltrate into the enemy rear but employed a frontal holding position against the powerful enemy and therefore bungled the good chance of smashing the enemy." Specifically referring to the delayed penetration movement of the 38th Army, Peng angrily called on 38th Army Commander Liang to stand up and then severely reprimanded him. He also censured the 66th Army for its failure to tie up the U.S. 24th Division at Kusong.[62]

Declaring that he would not tolerate any more such mistakes, Peng outlined his plan for the coming campaign. "We will employ a strategy of luring the enemy forces into our internal line and wiping them out one by one," he explained, offering several compelling reasons for such a strategy. First, "[our] transportation lines will be shorter and the supplies will be easier to obtain"; second, "[we are] now familiar with the terrain and the routes of the enemy movement"; third, "the enemy forces will be so dispersed as they move north that we can easily destroy them one by one"; and fourth, "the enemy transportation lines in the rear will be more vulnerable to our [guerrilla] assaults." He specified that the CPV main forces would be gathered in the Myohyangsan, Unsan, and Pyongnam-chin areas while small units would maintain contact with the enemy troops and lure them into established CPV traps. If the US/UN forces could not be ensnared, Peng stated that "we are obliged to strike out." In his view, there were only two ways of striking out: "we can surround one enemy unit and attack the enemy reinforcements"; or, "we can coordinate the 38th and 42d armies in a penetrating movement to Sunchon and Sochon and have the 40th Army cover the maneuver." Finally, Peng believed that "if we can annihilate two or three U.S. and ROK divisions, the Korean war situation would fundamentally turn [to our favor]."[63]

The CPV's military preparations for the campaign soon began. Despite the heavy U.S. air bombing, the 9th Army Corps, consisting of the 20th, 26th, and 27th armies and a total of 150,000 men, secretly crossed the Yalu River at the Ji'an and Linjiang ferry points and by November 19 had moved into their positions in the Chosin Reservoir region. These new troops greatly augmented the CPV strength in the east.[64] Meanwhile, two battalions of the 42d Army disguised themselves as North Korean troops, and, together with a special NKPA unit, infiltrated the US/UN rear. Their mission was to contact the remnants of the NKPA 2d and 5th corps in South Korea and to disrupt the US/UN supply lines with guerrilla raids. As instructed by the CPV headquarters, each army also dispatched a special force charged with the task of conducting an independent guerrilla operation in South Korea.[65] Meantime, the Northeast Military Command accelerated the transportation of supplies when it established a new service line to supplement the existing three lines and sent the 1st Railway Engineering Division into North Korea to repair vital railways and bridges. Each army's engineering battalions plunged into the construction of three vehicular roads connecting Huichon and Sinchang-dong, Yongwon, and Tokchon. Due to the vigorous efforts of 60,000 hardworking Chinese service personnel, the CPV supply situation was noticeably improving.[66]

The CPV appeared better prepared this time than in mid-October. Nevertheless, Peng's strategy had not foreseen how cautious the US/UN advance would be. In the west, the U.S. Eighth Army frequently stopped to probe the Chinese positions, thus covering only five miles in one week. At the November 16 CPV Command meeting, Deng Hua pointed out that the longer it took the enemy to enter the CPV trap, the more likely it was that the enemy would detect Chinese intentions. The CPV should undertake appropriate measures to persuade the enemy to relax its vigilance. Accepting Deng's suggestion, Peng ordered immediate cancellation of the small units' delaying operations and an evacuation northward of all CPV troops. He also directed each army to try to give the enemy the false impression that "we are being intimidated into retreat." For this purpose, the CPV released 100 captured POWs (thirty Americans and seventy South Koreans) on the western front expecting them to convey a message that the Chinese forces could no longer withstand the superior US/UN troops. In order to "hook a big fish," Peng explained to his staff, "you must let the fish taste your bait. MacArthur boasts that he has never been defeated. We'll see who is going to wipe out whom!"[67] The CPV headquarters also tightened up the control of information about troop movements. Mao had earlier instructed Peng that "for the purpose of misleading the enemy, [the CPV Command] at present should not issue battle reports in the name of the combined Chinese-Korean command but solely through the NKPA headquarters. The reports, however, could mention the participation of a Chinese volunteer army (the term 'Chinese People's Volunteers' is for internal use only) and the bravery of this force in the battle." He made it clear that he would personally edit each draft of these reports before they were released.[68]

The Chinese tactic of deceit seemed to work. Shortly after the CPV units disappeared from the front, the US/UN forces sped up their advance. By November 21, the U.S. Eighth Army's vanguard reached the area between Yongwon and Pakchon and stood poised for an all-out offensive. Mao was elated. "The enemy," he cabled the CPV Command on November 18, "still estimates that our troops [in Korea] are no more than 60,000 to 70,000 and regard[s] our forces as 'not unbulliable.' This [judgment] is to our advantage." Moreover, he asserted, "neither the United States, nor Britain and France has the slightest idea of how to deal with us, and they are shrouded by pessimism felt all over their countries." Therefore "as long as our forces can win a few more victories and wipe out a few more thousand enemy troops, the entire international situation will turn [to our favor]."[69]

On November 21, the CPV commanders met to finalize the planned offensive. In assessing the enemy situation, the commanders believed that the ROK 2d Corps's three divisions east of the Chongchon River were poised to attack Mampo through Huichon and that the U.S. Eighth Army's main forces gathered west of the Chongchon River were aiming for Sinuiju. They then decided that the 38th Army's 112th Division would draw the three ROK divisions into the Myohyang-san and Sinchang-dong areas while the main forces of the 38th and 42d armies plus one division of the 40th Army would attack the two flanks and rear of the ROK 2d Corps simultaneously. After breaching the U.S. Eighth Army's eastern flank, the 38th Army would turn west, link with the 40th Army, and roll up the U.S. 1st Cavalry and 2d Infantry divisions. If the U.S. 24th Division and the U.K. 27th Brigade advanced to Kusong and Taechon by the time the attack on the ROK forces began, the 39th and 66th armies would launch a pincer assault on the U.S. 24th Division while the 50th Army would try to tie up the U.K. 27th Brigade to keep it from reinforcing these ROK units. If the U.S. 1st Cavalry and 2d divisions entered the areas south of Unsan before the U.S. 24th Division moved into Kusong, the 39th, 40th, 38th, and 66th armies would combine to surround and attack these two American divisions. For the eastern front, the CPV headquarters instructed the 9th Army Corps to deploy the 20th and 27th armies to engage the 5th and 7th regiments of the U.S. 1st Marine Division; the 26th Army would be stationed in Changjin as army corps reserves.[70]

Mao, however, had some reservations about this plan. In his telegram to the CPV Command at 7:00 P.M. on November 24, he pointed out that after the outflanking attack against the ROK 2d Corps commenced, it was likely the U.S. 1st Cavalry and 2d divisions would turn east to rescue the ROK forces. Given their mission to obstruct the U.S. reinforcements, the 39th and 40th armies could not spare troops to assist the 38th and 42d armies, yet the failure to quickly punch a hole in the enemy flank might be detrimental to the overall campaign. Mao then suggested that all three divisions of the 42d Army concentrate on the ROK 8th Division in Yongwon and the entire 38th Army attack the ROK 7th Division in Tokchon, leaving the 40th Army to block the U.S. 2d and 1st Cavalry divisions. After that, the 38th and 42d armies could turn west for a two-pronged envelopment of the American forces at the Chongchon River. Mao also directed the 9th Army Corps to reposition the 26th Army behind the U.S. 1st Marine Division in order to cut off its retreat route and to check the possible reinforcement of the ROK 7th Division.[71] The CPV headquarters revised its plan in accordance with Mao's instructions and issued a final order for an all-out offensive, which specified that the troops on the western front would open combat at dusk on November 25 and the 9th Army Corps would move at dusk the next day. The main objective, the order stated, was to allow the enemy troops to advance and then to attack them before they could consolidate their new positions. Given the importance of the 38th and 42d armies' operations, CPV Deputy Commander Han Xianchu offered to assume direct command of the two armies.[72]

The U.S. Eighth Army launched what MacArthur called the "home-by-Christmas" offensive on the morning of November 25. The US/UN forces reached the line between Chongju in the west and Yongwon in the east by sunset. Shortly afterward, the CPV offensive began with the 38th Army's penetrating movement. The 38th Army had been known throughout the Chinese civil war as the best unit in the Fourth Field Army, but Peng's sharp criticism of the army's delay in the first campaign had shamed the commanders and made them anxious to regain their glorious reputation. The 114th Division's frontal attack was intended to pin down the ROK 7th Division in the Tokchon area and to cover the enveloping movement of the 112th and 113th divisions. Before noon on the twenty-sixth, the 113th Division had broken through the ROK 6th Division's positions and cut off the 7th Division's retreat, while the 112th Division controlled the area west of Tokchon. Scout companies of the army and the 113th Division, headed by deputy army scout director Zhang Kui and disguised in ROK uniforms, slipped through the ROK-occupied areas and destroyed the Oh-yong bridge, a strategically important point at the rear of the ROK 2d Corps. After a three-pronged attack in the early afternoon, the 38th Army reported that it had annihilated more than 5,000 ROK troops, captured seven American military advisers, and occupied Tokchon by 7:00 P.M.[73]

The 42d Army advanced on the ROK 8th Division's positions on the evening of November 25. As the 125th Division initiated a frontal assault, the 124th and 126th divisions swept south to surround the enemy on its eastern flank and rear. Unfortunately, the South Korean reserve regiment detected the Chinese movement and blocked the CPV drive. Afraid of being outflanked, the ROK 7th Division soon fell back. The 125th Division then pushed forward and took Yongwon but failed to eliminate the ROK 7th Division's main force. However, the other two divisions managed to smash the ROK rear guard. Meanwhile, the 40th Army launched a frontal attack on the U.S. 2d Division south of Huichon and forced the enemy to retreat. The American troops counterattacked and forestalled the 40th Army's progress.[74] The 38th and 42d armies succeeded in breaching the enemy's right flank, which compelled the U.S. Eighth Army to suspend its advance. On the afternoon of November 26, anticipating that the enemy might retreat, Peng ordered the 39th, 66th, and 50th armies to join the offensive.[75]

The battle situation quickly changed on November 27. The US/UN forces west of the Chongchon River conducted an orderly and swift evacuation. The 39th Army captured only one American engineering company near Unsan, and the 66th and 50th armies came up empty-handed. At the same time, the Turkish Brigade, part of the U.S. Eighth Army's reserves, advanced from Kaechon to Tokchon to reinforce the ROK 2d Corps, and the U.S. 1st Cavalry Division moved from Sunchon to Sinchang-ri to protect the right flank. Peng then suspected that the enemy might try to build a defense line between Anju and Wonsan, where the US/UN forces could best concentrate their strength. Peng determined that the Chinese response must be to prevent the US/UN troops from retreating and to inflict as much damage as possible on the fleeing enemy. Deciding to concentrate on the two divisions of U.S. 9th Army Corps, he directed the 38th Army to march its main forces south and send one division to hold at Samso-ri. He sent the 40th and 39th armies to outflank the U.S. divisions and squeeze them into the Kunu-ri area. The 42d Army would also move farther south through Sinchang-ri to maintain the line between Sunchon and Sochon. Should these operations succeed, Peng believed, the CPV would choke the enemy's avenue of retreat and destroy its main forces.[76]

The 38th Army, however, found its penetrating movement very difficult. Samso-ri was more than 30 miles away from Tokchon, and the army had to proceed on foot. Because the Turkish Brigade's forward elements were already on their way to block the 38th Army's advance, the Chinese troops had to fight their way through to Tokchon. Keenly aware of the importance of his army's mission, army commander Liang sent the 113th Division directly to Samso-ri and then personally led the 122d and 114th divisions in a two-pronged attack on the Turkish positions. Around midnight, the army's main forces approached the Turkish encampment. Under Liang's direction, the 343d Regiment commander Sun Hongdao had his troops remove their boots and quietly climb up a nearby hill. The Turkish soldiers, mostly asleep by their campfires, were caught by surprise, and the battle ended with little resistance. By daybreak, both the 122d and 114th divisions had moved to Wawon, not far from Kunu-ri.

The 113th Division had set out for Samso-ri at 6:00 P.M., November 27, with only its light weapons. Before its departure, CPV Deputy Commander Han had personally ordered the division commanders of the 113th that they should advance regardless of cost or casualties and, once in position, they must be equally resolute in preventing the enemy's retreat. The 113th Division troops took shortcuts across mountain trails, ridgelines, and gullies and practically ran all the way. At daybreak, however, they were still some distance from Samso-ri. Division commander Jiang Chao suggested taking a break, but deputy commander Liu Haiqing insisted on moving on. Liu argued that since they were already in the enemy's occupied area, they might as well take off their disguises and try to pass for ROK forces. Liu's trick worked amazingly well. For the first time, the Chinese forces were able to advance in open fields in the daytime. Without encountering a single enemy air raid or roadblock, the division's main forces seized Samso-ri around 8:00 A.M. on November 28 and immediately erected defensive positions there. After covering forty-five miles on foot within fourteen hours, the 113th Division arrived in time to stymie the US/UN retreat. Although tired, hungry, and thirsty, the 113th Division fought a vigorous blocking action.[77]

The successful movement of the 38th Army ensured the encirclement of two divisions of the U.S. 9th Army Corps. Very pleased with the 38th Army, Mao congratulated the CPV Command in his telegram to Peng at 5:30 A.M., November 28. Mao emphasized that "[your] present combat task is to gather the 42d, 38th, 40th, and 39th armies to attack the main forces of the U.S. 1st Cavalry, 2d, and 25th divisions." As long as the CPV destroyed these three divisions, he predicted, "the entire battle situation will favor us." Therefore, Mao assigned the 42d Army to attack the U.S. 1st Cavalry Division in the Tokchon-Sunchon area and the other three armies to attack the U.S. 2d and 25th divisions in the Kunu-ri and Kaechon areas. "This is a very important campaign, and I urge that every army [commander] carry it out in your best effort."[78] Interestingly, Peng became even more ambitious and aspired to finish off all four American divisions and the British brigade in the west. He directed the 42d Army to complete its enveloping maneuver toward Sunchon and Sochon to cut off the enemy escape routes from Anju and then to advance on Pyongyang; the 38th Army, to consolidate its defensive positions in the Samso-ri area and to send one division to ambush the U.S. 5th Cavalry regiment near Kaechon; and the 40th Army, to continue its pursuit to Kaechon and Kunu-ri and then proceed south to Anju. He also urged the 39th and 66th armies to speed up their pincer movement on the U.S. 25th Division in Yongbyon; then the 39th Army would cross the Chongchon River in Kunu-ri and advance on Anju by the Kaechon-Sinanju railroad, and the 66th Army would join the 50th Army to clean up the enemy remnants south of the Chongchon River. Acknowledging that "this battle is of great significance to the Korean war situation," Peng pointed out that "every army must overcome all possible obstacles and win a major victory even in exchange for a huge cost."[79] Mao endorsed Peng's plan as "very feasible," yet he cautioned that "[you] ought to prepare to finish this entire campaign in about twenty days. You can divide it up into several big or small battles or combats and spend one or two days on each one in the shortest and three or four days the longest. Our troops should also take a few short breaks for reorganization." In this way, he calculated, "we would lose less lives and save more [materials]."[80]

Neither Peng nor Mao allowed that they might have misjudged the battlefield situation. The US/UN forces began an overall retreat in the west on the morning of November 29. Supported by the air force, the U.S. 2d Division, together with units of the 25th and 1st Cavalry divisions, repeatedly assaulted the CPV 113th Division's positions at Samso-ri, expecting to retake the ferry over the Taedong River to Sunchon. The Chinese troops vigorously resisted the American attack. Without any heavy artillery, they fought the enemy for two days with light machine guns, light mortars, rifles, grenades, and sometimes rocks and fists. Some soldiers made suicidal counterattacks. The 113th Division finally succeeded in keeping the enemy forces from crossing the Taedong River at Samso-ri. The U.S. 2d Division then turned west and evacuated through Anju.[81] As the 40th and 39th armies were pressing the U.S. 25th and ROK 1st divisions and the Turkish Brigade to the Kunu-ri area, the only escape open to the enemy was through Anju to Sochon. The CPV Command repeatedly urged the 42d Army to hurry because "whether [or not we] can seize hold of Sochon before the enemy reinforcing forces arrive so as to completely cut off the enemy runaway is the key to the success [of this battle]." To Peng's great disappointment, however, the 42d Army did not advance on Sochon fast enough. On the night of November 29, its vanguard regiment could not break through the U.S. 7th Cavalry regiment at Sinchang-ri. The whole army moved haltingly, eventually failing to form a second flank at Sochon.[82]

On the morning of December 1, the US/UN forces from both the western and eastern banks of the Chongchon River crowded into Anju. Facing no roadblocks, they managed to reach Sochon by sunset after abandoning almost all the heavy artillery, tanks, trucks, and ammunition. Since the US/UN forces had already withdrawn, Peng called off the pursuit at 5:00 A.M., December 2. He directed each army to mop up the battlefield and rest for four to five days "in order to reorganize the troops, supply food and munitions, and prepare to fight on." Indeed, the Chinese troops badly needed a respite from the fighting.[83]

In the Chosin Reservoir, the CPV 9th Army Crops was unable to achieve its objective against the U.S. 10th Marine Corps. According to Peng's plan, the army corps was to start the attack on the evening of November 26, but the commanders had problems moving all twelve infantry divisions into position and therefore postponed the offensive for twenty-four hours. The troops were supposed to surround the two regiments of the U.S. 1st Marine Division and then engage the U.S. 7th or 3d Marine divisions' reinforcing units.[84] However, just as the 20th Army's four divisions (58th, 59th, 60th, and 89th) completed outflanking the enemy forces and the 27th Army readied for attack, an unexpected, heavy snowstorm hit the battlefield, and the temperature plummeted to −30° C. The 9th Army Corps was one of the best forces of the Third Field Army, but it had fought mostly in eastern China during the civil war. The troops had never experienced such cold weather before and were unaccustomed to the mountainous terrain of Korea. Most of their Soviet-made heavy machine guns froze and were useless. Even worse, many men died of hypothermia due to the lack of winter clothing. One-third of the army corps suffered from frostbite over a four-week period.[85]

Despite a two-day nonstop offensive, the 20th and 27th armies failed to destroy the enemy troops at Yudam-ri. The commanders were surprised to discover that the American forces had been increased to four infantry regiments, three artillery battalions, and one tank battalion—a force twice as large as they had previously estimated. They immediately decided to gather the 80th, 81st, and 94th divisions of the 27th Army to attack the enemy forces in Sinheung-ri and directed the 20th Army to envelop Yudam-ri in order to block the enemy reinforcements from Sochang-ri. Peng accepted this change and instructed the army corps to turn south after this battle and station in the Hamhung area, where "it is much warmer and you can spend the entire winter there." For the next two days, both the 20th and 27th armies fought fiercely, eventually forcing the U.S. 10th Marine Corps into a withdrawal toward Hamhung on the morning of December 1. The army corps command then ordered the 26th Army to coordinate with the 20th Army in a blocking action. Unfortunately, the 26th Army was too far away from the front—because of insufficient food supply, the army had to station in Changjin—and did not reach its position in time to relieve the 20th Army. As a result, the enemy forces were able to reach Ohno-ri where they were reinforced by the U.S. 3d Marine Division and safely evacuated.[86]

While the CPV was resting and waiting for supplies, Mao began to consider how to break the US/UN western defensive line, since he still wanted to carry the CPV's offensive down to Pyongyang and Wonsan. On December 2, he directed Peng to seize Sunchon with a small force and secure it as a springboard for bringing the CPV main forces into the Pyongyang-Wonsan area.[87] But Peng believed the enemy would continue its retreat south. "Because of the two severe blows [by us] on the western and eastern front," he telegraphed Mao at midnight on December 4, "it is likely that the enemy may either retreat and build a new defensive position along the Pyongyang-Wonsan line or return to its previous defensive line along the 38th parallel." Before planning for another offensive, he suggested organizing several probing actions to identify the enemy's intentions. For this purpose, he would send three divisions to assault Sunchon, Songchon, and Pyongyang, respectively. "If the enemy intends to hold Pyongyang," Peng explained, "[we] will dispatch one army and one or two NKPA divisions in a feigned attack on Pyongyang and assemble five armies to roll up south through Sungchon to Kangdong . . . to threaten Seoul." This attack would compel the enemy forces in Pyongyang to retreat south, he calculated; "then we can pursue and outflank the enemy on the move." For the eastern front, he planned to "have the NKPA 5th Corps advance on Hamhung and Wonsan for the purpose of pressing the enemy further south, . . . so that [our 9th Army Corps] can seek a chance to assault the enemy forces in retreat." On the other hand, he pointed out, "if the enemy abandons the [defensive] line between Pyongyang and Wonsan, we will chase it down to the 38th parallel and then wait for an opportunity to attack Seoul."[88]

Coincidentally, thirty minutes before Peng sent out his telegram, Mao had cabled the CPV headquarters that "we are genuinely sure that the enemy forces in Pyongyang are in the process of retreat and the [US/UN] main forces are already between Pyongyang and the 38th parallel." He instructed Peng to "send one division to attack Pyongyang tomorrow and occupy it if it is possible." After reading Peng's midnight message, however, Mao completely concurred and in the early hours of December 5, ordered the CPV Command to proceed.[89] The 40th, 39th, and 42d armies advanced in three columns toward the 38th parallel, encountering little resistance. On December 6, the Chinese forces captured Pyongyang, which symbolized the final victory of the second-phase offensive. Although the CPV did not completely achieve their campaign objectives, both Mao and Peng were very pleased with the outcome. Regaining most of the North Korean territory, the Chinese forces reportedly inflicted 36,000 US/UN casualties (including 24,000 American); 30,700 Chinese soldiers were dead or missing in action.[90] By way of summary, Peng made an interesting observation: "The South Korean forces are no good at fighting, but [it is] difficult to catch [them when they retreat]; the U.S. forces are good at fighting, and that is why more American soldiers are killed than captured alive."[91]

IV

Undoubtedly, the Chinese forces were unprepared for the immediate and large-scale battles they encountered when first entering Korea. Beijing authorities had inadequate information about the enemy situation and the CPV command, control, and communication structures had yet to be established. The Soviet weaponry and equipment were still some distance from the front, and the combat troops suffered from a shortage of supplies, including food, munitions, medicine, and even winter clothing. Moreover, there was a widespread fear of the superior American air and artillery firepower among the rank and file.

Nevertheless, this evident unpreparedness did not prevent the Chinese leaders from undertaking bold actions to meet ambitious goals. It is true that Mao's initial aim was to establish a defensive line between Pyongyang and Wonsan, but he was also under the illusion that China's military intervention would sufficiently invigorate the North Korean Communists so as to turn around the war situation. He was anxious to prove the ability of the Chinese forces to reverse the tide of war when he decided to abandon the defensive strategy and undertake offensive actions. Strategically, he found it advantageous to "lure the enemy in deep," not only because he wanted to take advantage of MacArthur's underestimation of the Chinese strength, but also because he believed that the Chinese troops were better at mobile warfare than the US/UN forces. Based on the CCP's civil war experience in which the Communists had scored constant victories by fighting mobile warfare, Mao, among other leaders, never questioned how realistic it was to compete with the US/UN mobility in Korea. Interestingly, none of the CPV penetration operations really succeeded. It was hardly feasible for the Chinese soldiers to outmaneuver the motorized enemy forces under any circumstance, let alone in the mountainous terrain, under constant U.S. air bombardment, with the poor supply facilities of the CPV, and in the biting cold.

The Chinese leaders seem to have overemphasized the importance of "subjective" ability. Mao never believed that American air raids would cause insurmountable problems. As long as the troops maintained high spirits, he thought, they would be able to withstand the superior American firepower. Peng Dehuai harshly criticized the 38th Army commander for his "subjective mistakes," but he overlooked the objective difficulties that the army faced. He was puzzled as to why the famous "iron and steel army [*tie jun*]"—the nickname earned by the 38th Army in the civil war—had suddenly become soft in Korea.

More important, the Chinese leaders were convinced that they had achieved the first victory not by sheer good luck but by superior strategy and tactics. After the initial battles, the belief that "we can defeat American armed forces" became increasingly prevalent among the commanders.[92] That belief later led to unrealistic expectations that the CPV would work miracles.

6. BETWEEN THE OFFENSIVE AND THE DEFENSIVE

"What is flexibility?" Mao queried the Yanan Association for the Study of the War of Resistance Against Japan in a 1938 lecture. "It is the concrete realization of the initiative in military operations; it is the flexible employment of armed forces." Mao regarded flexibility as "the central task in directing a war, . . . particularly when the weak are fighting the strong." In his view, flexibility consisted of "an intelligent commander's ability to take timely and appropriate measures on the basis of objective conditions after judging the hour and sizing up the situation (the 'situation' includes the enemy's situation, our situation, and the terrain)." He asserted that the important task for a flexible command was to "make changes such as from the offensive to the defensive or from the defensive to the offensive, from advance to retreat or from retreat to advance, from containment to assault or from assault to containment, from encirclement to outflanking or from outflanking to encirclement, and to make such changes properly and in good time according to the circumstances of the troops and terrain on both sides." The ability to make these changes, he believed, was essential to "command in battles, command in campaigns, and strategic command."[1]

The Chinese military leaders demonstrated considerable flexibility in the initial fighting in Korea. With a prompt change from a defensive plan to offensive actions, the CPV pushed the US/UN troops back to the 38th parallel. How would they fight the next stage of the war?

I

The CCP central leadership had already decided to keep advancing when the CPV approached the 38th parallel. In retrospect, it probably would have been a more rational decision had the Chinese forces not penetrated too far south. Strategically, Beijing had achieved its initial objectives: the Chinese recovered for North Korea most of its lost territory; a buffer zone between

China's Northeast and the US/UN forces was reestablished; and China's resolve to resist American aggression in Asia was clearly demonstrated. Militarily, the CPV troops had almost reached the limit of their combat capability by undertaking two major offensives back-to-back without sufficient preparations. They badly needed reinforcement, rest, and reorganization before they could open another campaign. Intoxicated with the unexpected success, however, Beijing authorities drove their armies southward for a new offensive.

The North Koreans inadvertently fueled the Chinese decision to embark on another campaign. As the CPV forces were about to seize Pyongyang, Kim Il-sung was on the way to Beijing for his first wartime meeting with Mao Zedong. In the evening of December 3, Kim met with Mao, Zhou Enlai, and Gao Gang in Mao's office in Zhongnanhai. Kim highly praised the Chinese troops' "bravery" and expressed his "heartfelt" gratitude to the Chinese leaders. He then asked Mao to predict the evolution of the war situation. "As far as I can see," Mao asserted, "there exists a possibility of resolving the conflict quickly, but anything unexpected may happen to protract the war." Kim was anxious to know how much longer the Chinese would fight in Korea. Mao responded that "we are prepared to fight at least one [more] year, but [in my opinion] the [North] Korean side should get prepared to fight a protracted war in which [you will] mainly rely on yourself and partly on outside assistance." This was not what Kim wanted to hear. He pressured the Chinese leaders to aim for a quick end to the war. "We should not give the enemy breathing time," Kim declared. "We ought to advance in the crest of the victory to seize Pyongyang and Seoul and to press the enemy to withdraw from [the whole of] Korea." Noting the Chinese leaders' concerns about supplies, he promised that "our party's local authorities will support the Chinese People's Volunteers as much as possible and see to it that CPV's food and supply problems be solved." Referring to Stalin's suggestion of establishing a united command to direct both the CPV and NKPA forces, Kim assured the Chinese leaders that his reorganized troops would be subject to the CPV Command unconditionally.[2]

Overly optimistic about a swift victory in Korea himself, Mao yielded to the North Korean leader's request for another CPV offensive. A CMC telegram to the CPV headquarters, dated December 4, revealed Mao's determination to advance southward "in the flush of victory":

> It is possible that the [Korean] war may be resolved quickly; it is also possible that the war might be protracted. We are prepared to fight for at least one year. It is likely that the enemy may want to negotiate a cease-fire now. [We] would negotiate only when the enemy agrees to withdraw from Korea but first to withdraw back to the south of the 38th parallel. It is

most advantageous that we shall not only seize Pyongyang but also capture Seoul and we will mainly aim at eliminating the enemy [strength] and first of all wipe out the ROK forces. [With this action] we will be in a stronger position to compel United States imperialists to withdraw from Korea.

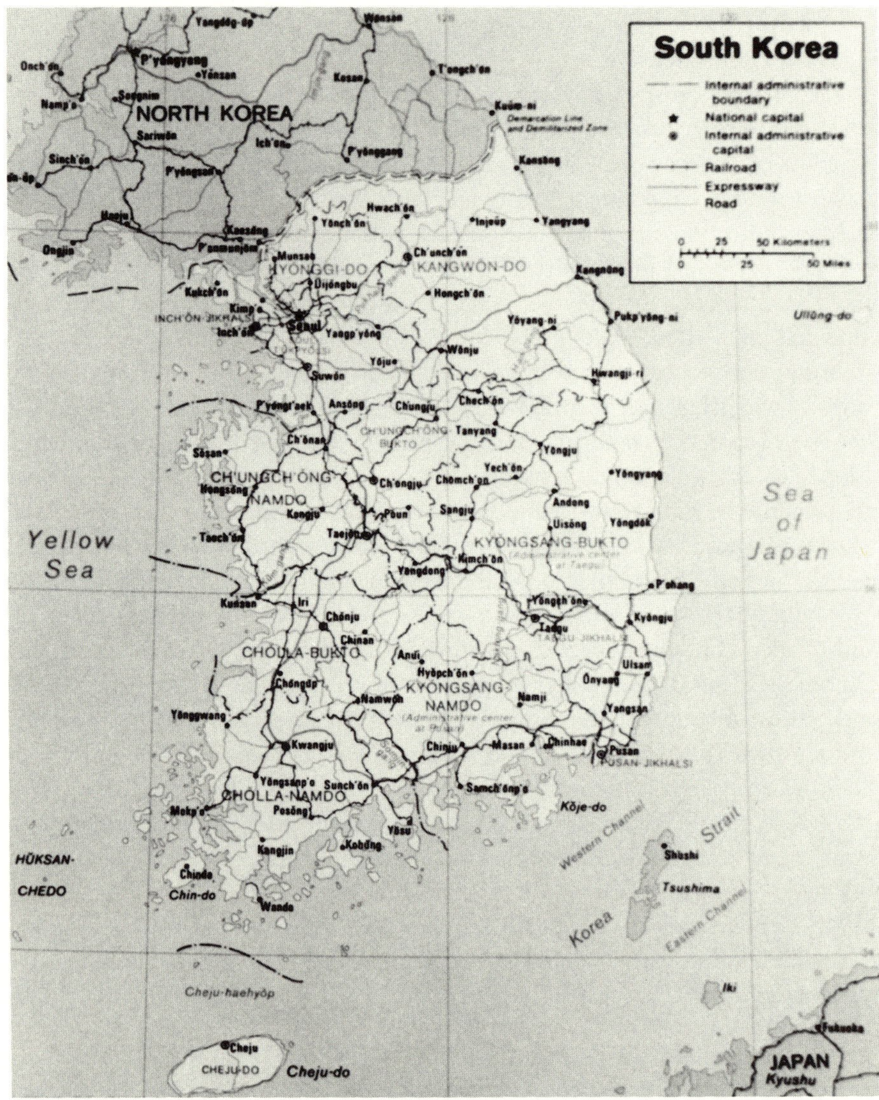

Map of South Korea (Source: Central Intelligence Agency. Reproduced courtesy of the University of Chicago Libraries)

Mao viewed it as very likely that the United Nations might agree to let the Korean people select their own government with UN supervision and Chinese and Soviet participation in the political process. He also pointed out that "just like those of Chiang Kai-shek, U.S. imperialists' promises and agreements are by no means trustworthy, and we therefore ought to prepare for the worst."[3]

However, the field commanders did not deem it wise to mount another offensive right away. From a strictly military point of view, they calculated, the CPV forces had already been stretched to their limitations, and a continuous push would drain their strength and spirit. When Kim came to see Peng on December 7, shortly after his trip to Beijing, his zeal for a nonstop advance even south of the 38th parallel alarmed the CPV commander. The next day, Peng cabled Mao and Gao Gang, urging flexibility in the deliberations about the next action. "If we are able to wipe out the [ROK] puppet 1st and 6th divisions and the U.S. 24th and 1st Cavalry divisions or at least inflict a heavy loss on them," he explained, "we would then cross the 38th parallel to attack Seoul if there is a chance of success. But if we fail to destroy the above enemy troops, we must not advance deep into south even if we are capable of capturing Seoul." In his view, the CPV forces would suffer from the problems with supplies and combat fatigue. He thus regarded it as imperative "to not move into the areas ten kilometers [six miles] north of the 38th parallel and allow the enemy to stay along the 38th parallel so that we can strike its main strength again next year." Peng was also worried about the lack of forces on the front. In his estimation, "to replace each [infantry] army's casualties would require as many as 150,000 troops—30,000 for the 13th Army Corps (three armies), 60,000 for the 9th Army Corps (four armies), and 5,000 for the 42d, 50th, and 66th armies respectively." It would at least take three months for these replenishing forces to gather on the front. Moreover, all troops were in critical need of resupply, rest, and reorganization.[4]

The field commanders' concerns gave Mao pause in considering another offensive. However, two factors seemed to reinforce his determination to act immediately. An intelligence assessment of the enemy situation suggested that the Truman administration was preparing for a total withdrawal from Korea soon. In his telegram to Peng on December 11, Mao informed him: "It is reported from a secret source that U.S. Army Chief of Staff [Gen. Joseph L.] Collins, who was authorized [by Washington] to inspect the Korean front, commented after a meeting with MacArthur and [U.S. Eighth Army Commander Lt. Gen. Walton H.] Walker that the situation concerning the US/UN forces in Korea is becoming hopeless." Collins had reportedly conceded that "the American military was unable to retain a long-term defense."

Mao believed that Collins had already ordered MacArthur to prepare vessels in South Korean ports for evacuation. "According to the news reports of foreign presses," he continued, "[the enemy] is now evacuating Seoul. . . MacArthur has already prepared a large number of vessels at Port Hangnam, south of Hamhung, and publicly announced that the 10th Corps (headed by Maj. Gen. [Edward M.] Almond) will evacuate from that port." Although he was not sure whether this intelligence was accurate, he asserted that "it will prove to be true soon or at least when our 13th Army Corps reaches Kaesong or Seoul." With little doubt about the likelihood of a US/UN withdrawal, Mao instructed Peng not to release this information to the rank and file because they might "get relaxed."[5]

Another factor that spurred Mao to have the CPV mount another offensive was a cease-fire overture put forth by thirteen neutral countries. K. M. Panikkar, Indian ambassador to Beijing, passed the proposal on to the PRC leadership on December 7, asking China to suspend hostilities along the 38th parallel and then negotiate a peaceful solution. The Chinese leaders quickly concluded that this was an American trick to win a respite before renewed military action. Zhou asked Panikkar, "Why were these thirteen countries never opposed to the American invasions of China and Korea? Why haven't these thirteen countries asked for a complete withdrawal of all foreign forces from Korea? Why did these thirteen countries never speak out when the American forces crossed the 38th parallel? Why was the Philippines, who joined the US intervention, included as one of the [proposal's] sponsors?" Unsatisfied with Panikkar's answers, Zhou declared that since the US/UN forces ignored the 38th parallel, the Chinese troops would do the same.[6]

Mao felt keenly that accepting this proposal would hurt China's political prestige, for the simple reason that one should oppose anything that his enemy supported. In his telegram to Peng on December 13, he explained that "the United States, Britain, and some other countries want us to stop advancing toward the 38th parallel so that they can reorganize their forces for another offensive. [Under this circumstance], our forces have no choice but to cross the 38th parallel, [because] our stop at the 38th parallel would cause us serious political disadvantages." In his view, the CPV must cross the 38th parallel and "eliminate several more enemy units in the Kaesong area, near Seoul." Should the enemy defend Seoul, he instructed, "our main forces may return to the area north of Kaesong and get reorganized for an assault on Seoul at some future [time], and meanwhile we may dispatch a few divisions near the northern bank of the Han River to assist the NKPA fighting against the puppet forces there." If the enemy relinquished control of Seoul, the CPV combat forces could then rest in the areas between Pyongyang and Seoul.[7]

On December 17, very confident about the upcoming offensive, Mao ordered the evacuation of the 9th Army Corps to China's Northeast for rest and reinforcement. Six CPV armies on the western front were sufficient to coordinate the NKPA's attack of South Korea because, he explained, "[we merely] intend to annihilate 10,000 to 20,000 U.S. and puppet troops for each battle during this period; and more troops are not really needed." He thought that "only at the time of a final decisive campaign need we enhance our manpower on the front."[8] Mao had already demonstrated his optimism in his talk with Kim Il-sung in early December, when he proclaimed that the Chinese would eventually defeat the US/UN forces in Korea because the Americans "have a lot of steel but little spirit [*gangduo qishao*]" and American steel could not match the Chinese spirit. He reasoned that "the CPV combat experience [in the past] has proven that our forces are absolutely capable of defeating the U.S. forces no matter how superior their equipment and air power are."[9]

Peng accepted Mao's request for another offensive but with obvious reservations. At a meeting of CPV commanders on December 15, he stated that "because of political considerations, the central leadership requires us to cross the 38th parallel. Therefore we are obliged to do so." But, to him, "a key issue is how." Regardless, he doubted if such an action would compel the enemy to withdraw from Korea. Deputy commander Hong Xuezhi was also skeptical, because he had discovered the US/UN main forces standing firm in their established positions south of the 38th parallel. the CPV, in his view, would be at a disadvantage if they were to storm the heavily fortified US/UN encampments. Alert to this possibility, Peng decided that, rather than aim at eliminating the enemy, the next offensive would merely aim to cross the 38th parallel; "if we succeed in doing that, we will claim a victory, and what to do next will depend on circumstances." He also maintained that the combat troops should still target the ROK forces and should not penetrate too far into South Korea.[10]

Four days after the meeting, Peng sent a long telegram to Mao explaining his caution. First, he asserted that the war in Korea was drawing out, and a prompt ending was unlikely. "The enemy has changed from the offensive to the defensive," he pointed out. "Its present positions are very favorable to its coordinated operation [of the air, naval, and ground forces] because its [supply line] is shorter, its forces are concentrated, its front is narrowed, and its defense in depth is consolidated. Although the enemy morale is lower than before, they still have more than 260,000 U.S. and puppet troops at their disposal." He surmised that, politically, "[since] immediate American withdrawal from Korea would be detrimental to the imperialist camp, Britain and France would not allow the Americans to [leave Korea] right away." Militarily, even if the US/UN forces suffered a few more defeats, they would retreat to their bridgehead positions in Pusan and Ichon and would not completely withdraw from Korea. "In my opinion," Peng stressed, "the Korean War will remain protracted and arduous." Second, he observed that the growing aspiration for a quick victory would do more harm than good. "After achieving the two major victories, the morale and enthusiasm of the [North] Korean party, government, and people is vehemently bursting, and the influence of the Chinese People's Volunteers is greatly enhanced." However, "an unrealistic optimism for a quick victory is rapidly growing among every sector of our [and Korean] sides. . . . [Yet] we have not inculcated in our troops a better understanding of how, in particular, we can transform our strategy from fighting mobile battles in mountains to storming [the enemy's] fortified positions."

Third, the lack of supplies, the exhaustion of the troops, and the coming cold winter would hamstring the CPV from mounting another large-scale offensive. Peng reported to Mao that "our transport line is two and three times longer than during the first and second phase offensives; yet our army service depots have no more than 300 trucks at their disposal." Overcoats for the troops had not been transported to the front, and the 42d Army still did not have cotton boots. "Those who had cotton boots have worn them out. Many [people's] cotton jackets and blankets were burned by the enemy incendiary bombs; with no [supply of] cotton boots, many have been barefooted." Moreover, Peng complained that "the supply of food, vegetables, salt, and oil is so low that the troops' health condition is deteriorating and more and more troops are getting sick." In his judgment, these problems would worsen as the troops advanced farther south; without some fast solutions, "the war is bound to protract." Therefore, Peng insisted that the CPV should not be expected to accomplish more than they were capable of. "If our attack does not go smoothly," he told Mao, "we will stop fighting right away. Whether we can and will control the 38th parallel will depend on concrete conditions." Finally, Peng pleaded with Mao to understand his concerns.[11]

Mao responded on December 21. "Your assessment of the enemy's situation is correct," he conceded, and "[we] must be prepared for a protracted war." However, he argued that "the United States and Britain are exploring the old status quo of the 38th parallel in the people's mind for political propaganda purposes and trying to force us to accept a cease-fire." Therefore, he believed that "our forces must cross the 38th parallel now for another campaign and rest and reorganize afterwards." He agreed with Peng that "before launching the offensive, the troops ought to rest for a few days as long as it is feasible. Since we hold the initiative, we must remain calm so as to avoid wearing down our own strength." He then assured Peng that the Northeast Military

Command would find more trucks for the transportation of the needed winter clothing. But Mao insisted that "if we can eliminate the whole or most of the [ROK] puppet forces, we will force the Americans to fight alone, and it will be impossible for them to stay in Korea for long; if we can destroy a few more U.S. divisions, it will be even easier for us to resolve the Korean conflict."[12]

Mao continued to pressure the field commanders to act resolutely, though he confirmed Peng's argument that "a stand for a quick victory is harmful." Between December 24 and 26, he twice cabled Peng that "the current situation that the [ROK] puppet forces are gathered together is in our favor; [because] it would be difficult [for us to attack them] if they are dispersed." Mao regarded it as "wise" to pin down the ROK main forces along the 38th parallel so that the CPV would not have to move too far to engage the enemy and would therefore avoid the problems of a long supply line. To that end, he allowed the CPV to withdraw to the north, thus making room for the ROK forces to reorganize a clear (and assailable) defense line and giving the CPV an opportunity to rest. Mao also asked Peng to delay the plan to dispatch the NKPA 2d and 5th corps into South Korea since it would distract the enemy strength on the front.[13]

Given Mao's determination, the CPV headquarters issued an operational order for the third-phase offensive on the morning of December 22. Since its objective was to cross the 38th parallel, Peng directed that the campaign would mainly consist of frontal attacks on the ROK, 1st, 6th, and 2d divisions and one unit of the 5th in the areas east of the Imjin River and west of the Pukhan River. The CPV 50th, 39th, 40th, and 38th armies, supported by the 1st Artillery Division and the 29th Artillery Regiment, were to assault first the ROK 1st Division and then the ROK 6th Division. If these assaults went well, the entire phalanx would advance on Uijongbu and Seoul. The NKPA 1st Corps would feint an attack on Munsan to protect the CPV's right flank. The 42d and 66th armies would cross the Pukhan River at Hwachon to tie down the ROK 2d and 5th divisions in the areas north of Chunchon and protect the left flank of the CPV. If the main forces' operation succeeded, the 42d and 66th would then proceed forward to block the Chunchon-Seoul railway. Peng also instructed the NKPA 2d and 5th corps to break the connection between the ROK 1st and 2d corps and move into the Hongchon area.[14]

In order to catch the enemy by surprise, the CPV commanders were very careful in timing the attack. They checked the Chinese calendar and found that there would be a full moon between late December and early January, which would greatly favor Chinese night operations. Moreover, they noted that the last week of December was full of significant holidays (Christmas and New Year's Eve) for the American and other Western troops. Taking all of these factors into account, the CPV Command selected December 31 as the day to open the offensive.[15] Meanwhile, the CMC sent another regiment of engineering corps into North Korea to repair the road from Anju to Pyongyang. Two more railway engineering regiments also arrived at the front line. Since the food supplies transported from the Northeast met only 25 percent of the CPV needs, Beijing managed to persuade the North Korean authorities to provide 30,000 tons of grains and vegetables to the CPV attacking units.[16]

Of paramount urgency was to get the troops combat-ready for the coming battles. In his order of December 22, Peng included a five-point instruction on tactics that he wanted each army command to practice and observe in the fighting:

1. For each combat, you must gather absolute superior man and fire power for the purpose of making a breach in the enemy defense line so as to divide up, surround, and then annihilate the enemy forces one by one. Therefore, you must prepare a reserve force to ensure continuous and tenacious advance into [the enemy] depth.
2. You must mass the artillery forces for supporting operations and, in particular, providing fire protection for the crossing of the rivers. The engineering corps and infantry reserves must assist the artillery forces in repairing roads, building ferry bridges, constructing fire positions, defending against enemy air raids, and preparing to move forward [after the initial action].
3. You must organize reconnaissance to identify the conditions of the enemy outposts and the rivers and bridges on our attacking routes. You must try your best to build bridges so as to make the crossing of the rivers easier and safer.
4. You must take anti-air defense very seriously. You must [carefully] feint, disperse, conceal bunkers, and organize anti-aircraft batteries.
5. Each army must carefully plan and dispatch several small detachments of picked troops deep behind the enemy front to harass its rear.[17]

After several nights of stealthy movement, the six CPV armies reached the staging positions by the morning of December 27. Peng remained ambivalent, however. The next evening, he cabled Mao to offer his thoughts about whether the CPV should retain the 38th parallel after crossing it. "For this campaign," Peng suggested, "we have mainly stressed the significance of crossing the 38th parallel [in our mobilization] (it is actually not that important politically); it will be more difficult for us to explain [to our troops] why we seize the 38th parallel and give it up afterwards." In his view, "since we intend to occupy the 38th parallel, we may as well retain it if there are no other concerns involved." He also advised against an attack on Seoul. "We shall allow the enemy to possess it," he proposed. "If the enemy abandons it as it did Pyongyang, we may let the [North] Korean People's Army occupy it and send our four to five armies (excluding the 9th Army Corps) back to the areas north of the 38th parallel for food supplies and reorganization." If the operations of the main forces went well, he planned to have either the 66th or the 50th army seize Chunchon and Hongchon and build supply depots there, because "the enemy planes would frequently bomb the bridges over the Imjin and Han rivers to frustrate our transportation." He assured Mao that since the ROK 1st and 6th divisions were composed of many new recruits, it would not be too difficult for the CPV troops to eliminate them.[18]

In order to dispel the field commander's misgivings, Mao sent a long telegram to Peng the next day. First, he approved of Peng's plan for the post-campaign rest and reorganization. "The so-called 38th parallel," he explained, "is an old impression in the people's minds, and will no longer exist after this campaign. It therefore does not matter whether our troops will rest and reorganize south or north of the 38th parallel." But he was adamant that "if we do not launch this offensive, and if our forces spend the entire winter resting and reorganizing, it would arouse the capitalist countries to speculate a great deal [on our intentions] and cause the democratic nations to disdain us; should we gain another victory in early January as you have planned by annihilating a few more ROK divisions or American units, . . . we would greatly impress the democratic front and the peoples of the capitalist countries, thereby to strike a new blow at the imperialists and enhance pessimism among them." However, he acknowledged the difficulties that the CPV faced. Mao informed Peng that Stalin "has volunteered to provide 2,000 more trucks to solve your [transportation] problems" and that a total of 40,000 replacements—the twenty best soldiers from each PLA infantry company in China—would reach the front by February 1951. He then pointed out that "the enemy's new commander Lt. Gen. [Matthew B.] Ridgway is already in Seoul to replace the dead Walker. As soon as he arrived, Ridgway ordered each unit of the American and [ROK] puppet forces to hold tight to the defense line." He was pleased that this enemy action "makes it easier for us to attack the ROK forces one by one. It would favor us more if [Ridgway] is determined to defend Seoul after this campaign." His only worry was that the US/UN forces would "evacuate [Seoul and the areas north of the 37th parallel] to build a defense line in the narrow areas between Taegu and Pusan."[19]

Despite Mao's optimism, the CPV's preparations for the third-phase offensive did not proceed smoothly. The NKPA 2d and 5th corps secretly moved into the mountainous area southeast of Hongchon but brought only enough food for three days. Kim Ung, who commanded these troops, requested that the campaign begin immediately; otherwise, his forces would run out of provisions. But the CPV troops were not yet ready, and the artillery forces were still on their way to the front. CPV Deputy Commander Han Xianchu reported to Peng on December 30 that, to speed the deployment of the artillery units, the infantry troops had already constructed the artillery works. He had asked each artillery regiment to carry a few of the best batteries into position by horse-drawn carriages. "[Even with these arrangements], they will not reach their positions until tomorrow," Han admitted. "Strictly speaking, we are not fully prepared." Then, a disastrous incident occurred on the morning of December 30. Shortly after moving into position, the 1st Artillery Division's two regiments were hit by a U.S. air raid. With no time or effective means to camouflage artillery in the snow, nineteen artillery guns were destroyed. The 26th Artillery Regiment was left with sixteen artillery pieces, and the 25th Artillery Regiment with only eight.[20]

Despite these difficulties, the six CPV armies and three NKPA corps launched the offensive at 5:00 P.M. on December 31, 1950. That night, a cold wind chilled the soldiers to the bone, and the snow fell thick and fast. The temperature suddenly drooped to −20°C. In such conditions, the 40th, 39th, and 38th armies had to cross the Imjin River and climb over several mountains. To describe the battle as arduous would be an understatement. Han Xianchu massed about 100 artillery pieces to pound the ROK 1st Division's outposts for five minutes. The South Korean troops, perhaps caught by surprise, did not fire back until thirty minutes later. The 39th Army, followed by the 50th Army, quickly marched over the Imjin River and advanced ten miles that night. At 5:00 A.M. the next morning, they succeeded in breaking the link between the ROK 1st and 6th divisions. However, unable to deploy a strong blocking force, the 39th Army failed to stop the ROK 1st Division's evacuation. The 40th and 38th armies also penetrated the enemy positions, but with no enveloping operations, their frontal charge merely drove the ROK 6th Division into retreat. On the left flank, the 42d and 66th armies pushed through mountain spurs covered with thick and icy snow and succeeded in routing the enemy. Assisted by the 124th Division of the 42d Army, the main forces of the 66th Army surrounded and destroyed two regiments (the 31st and 32d) of the ROK 2d Division and one regiment of the ROK 5th Division. They also smashed one ROK artillery battalion and captured more than sixty pieces of light and heavy artillery. This was the biggest victory of the entire campaign.[21]

By the morning of January 3, 1951, each CPV and NKPA combat unit had advanced eight to ten miles south. The Chinese–North Korean attack led

U.S. Eighth Army Commander Ridgway to consider the alarming prospect of more than 100,000 US/UN troops and their heavy equipment blocked from the bridges over the Pukhan River. At 3:00 P.M. on January 3, he ordered an overall withdrawal and abandoned Seoul. Surprised by the enemy retreat, Peng directed Han Xianchu to attack at once Seoul, Inchon, and Yangpyong, and he deployed the 42d and 66th armies and the two NKPA corps against Hongchon. Most of the pursuits did not meet much resistance, though the 50th Army engaged in a fierce fight with the delaying units of the U.K. 29th Brigade on the night of January 3. Pounding the British heavy tanks with grenades and satchel charges, the 149th Division reportedly destroyed or captured thirty-one tanks and devastated the Royal Rifle and 8th Cavalry regiments. The next afternoon, the NKPA 1st Corps and two divisions of the CPV 39th and 50th armies entered Seoul, now an empty city in flames. On January 5, Peng ordered the CPV 50th Army and two divisions of the NKPA 1st Corps to cross the Han River, establish a bridgehead on the southern bank, and seize the Kimpo airport and Inchon's port. Meanwhile, he had all the other attacking forces end their chase and rest for three days along the northern bank of the Han River.[22]

Peng remained cautious, despite the successful offensive. Although combat casualties were fairly low, a large number of CPV troops were severely frostbitten and unable to continue the fight. Some had even died of exposure. The troops had virtually no frostbite preventive; they coated their faces with pork fat and wrapped their feet in straw, but such primitive measures were ineffective against the severe winter in Korea. The 196th Division of the 66th Army had the most casualties from the cold, and its 586th Regiment was entirely devastated. "For this campaign," Han Xianchu reported to Peng on January 5, "we have so far lost the backbone of our troops. Two regiments of the 116th Division [of the 39th Army] have suffered more than 1,000 casualties, and one regiment of the 199th Division [of the 40th Army] has lost more than 300. Many regiments and battalions are completely combat-ineffective, with some divisions only half full." He also pointed out that troop morale had noticeably declined, because "the [troops] are extremely tired and there are just too many difficulties: the [Korean] civilians south of the 38th parallel have all left with their houses all burned down and no food left. Our troops cannot rest well nor do they have enough to eat; their strength is drained away." Han urgently informed Peng that "the attacking forces need food, munitions, and boots very badly," and with no immediate reinforcement, "it is impossible to rely on the present manpower to continue the offensive."[23] Meanwhile, the CPV intelligence department reported on January 8 that the enemy forces were no longer retreating and it was likely that they might want to lure the CPV deep into South Korea and replay the Inchon landing.[24] Taking all these factors into account, Peng ordered an immediate end to this offensive. In his directive of January 8, he instructed each army to move its main force back toward the 38th parallel for rest and reorganization. The NKPA troops and small units of the CPV 38th and 42d armies were to cover the withdrawal of the main forces and to watch the enemy movement.[25]

Peng's directive put an end to the CPV third-phase offensive. After seven days and nights of fighting, the Chinese forces, assisted by the NKPA troops, crossed the 38th parallel and forced the US/UN forces to retreat some eighty miles south. According to the Chinese reports, they had killed, wounded, or captured more than 19,000 US/UN troops at the cost of 5,800 CPV and 2,700 NKPA casualties.[26]

Nevertheless, the North Korean authorities were not satisfied. Shortly after Peng called off the pursuit, Kim Il-sung and Pak Hon-yong came to the CPV headquarters to protest the campaign's abrupt halt and to ask why the CPV forces did not advance "on the crest of the victory." The North Korean leaders mentioned the comment of the Soviet ambassador to North Korea that the Chinese and North Korean forces should push on when the enemy was in an overall retreat. Peng, however, stood firm and made it clear that it would be militarily detrimental to continue the offensive at this point. He insisted that the Chinese troops needed to recuperate through the winter. Kim would not give up: "In my opinion, the time for the troops to rest and reorganize should be no longer than one month." Raising again the Soviet ambassador's criticism that "[the Chinese] exaggerate the difficulties," Pak urged Peng to "continue the victorious pursuit and liberate South Korea." Infuriated at the North Korean leaders' pressure, Peng promptly rejected their request.[27] Kim and Pak had the Soviet ambassador inform the Kremlin of Peng's insistence on ending the offensive. Interestingly, Stalin, in a reassuring telegram to Mao, "wholeheartedly" praised Peng's success in defeating the powerful enemy with such inferior weaponry. The Kremlin leader also concurred with Peng's decision to not advance too far into South Korea and promised the Chinese that the Soviet ambassador would cause no further trouble. Shortly after this incident, the Soviet Union agreed to deploy two air force divisions to the Sino–North Korean border to protect the Jian-Kanggye and Andong-Anju transport lines.[28]

II

The breakthrough of the 38th parallel and, in particular, the seizure of Seoul again made Chinese leaders in Beijing dizzy with success. An editorial in

Renmin Ribao, sponsored by the CCP political propaganda department, proclaimed on January 5 that "the recovery of Seoul has proven one more time the invincible strength of the Chinese People's Volunteers and the [North] Korean People's Army. The absolute superiority of U.S. air, naval, tank, and artillery forces has been proven useless in both the defensive and offensive battles against the great Chinese-[North] Korean troops." It further boasted: "Today the Chinese-[North] Korean forces have demonstrated to the whole world that they are a strong army [in defending] peace and they have the invincible power to frustrate the American invading forces and drive them out of Korea so as to restore peace in Korea." That same day the CCP organized a huge public rally in Beijing, which resounded with shouts that "we should drive the enemy out to the sea."[29]

The growing furor for a quick victory, however, troubled the CPV field commanders. Reading the *Renmin Ribao* news, Peng Dehuai exclaimed that "[they] only pay attention to our success in the battlefield and have no idea of the cost we have paid or the difficulties we have faced." Deng Hua was also concerned that "now that [they] celebrate the recovery of Seoul, what would they have to say if the military situation requires us to evacuate Seoul in the future?" At a meeting of CPV high-ranking commanders on January 8, Deng pointed out that "since we are still inferior to the enemy in terms of equipment and technology, . . . we have to fight mobile warfare and night combats. We will definitely encounter greater difficulties in the battlefield."[30] In his report to Mao, Peng also maintained that the adversities of the battlefield rendered a swift victory unlikely. The CPV forces were suffering from combat fatigue and a shortage of manpower, food, munitions, and other supplies after three offensives in a row, whereas the enemy still supported more than 230,000 troops in its established defensive positions and enjoyed much shorter supply lines. He agreed that, to be successful, the next CPV offensive would have to annihilate the American main strength, but in order to achieve this, the CPV troops on the front needed more time to rest, resupply, and reorganize. Moreover, the 3d and 9th army crops had to be deployed around the 38th parallel right away, which, in Peng's judgment, would take at least two or three months. He also discovered that the participation of the North Korean forces in the war had caused friction between the CPV and the NKPA commanders. To resolve any conflicts, Peng suggested holding a four-day joint command meeting attended by CPV and NKPA officers at the rank of army commanders or above to "summarize the [combat] experience, reach a common understanding, and prepare for the spring offensive." He asked Mao to send one of the top CCP leaders to attend this meeting. Anxious to have all problems settled, Peng offered to accompany Kim Il-sung to Beijing for a top-level conference if necessary.[31]

Responding in mid-January, Mao acknowledged Peng's concerns. "The enemy will not voluntarily withdraw from Korea before its main strength is destroyed," he asserted, "because the U.S. aggressors have to hold their [strategic] positions in the Far East and the world. . . . They are still confident that their weaponry and equipment superiority will enable them to hold on in South Korea." Regarding the development of the war situation, he believed that there existed two possibilities. First, "under the pressure of the powerful Chinese and [North] Korean armies, [the enemy] may make a show of resistance and then evacuate Korea. This possibility can only become real when we are fully prepared [for a decisive action] and let the enemy know that we are fully prepared. Only when our military strength becomes more powerful will the enemy retreat in the face of difficulties." Second, "the enemy may carry out a vigorous resistance in the Taegu-Pusan areas and withdraw from Korea only when they are no longer capable of bearing the burden of fighting with us. If this is the case, we must still get fully prepared before we launch another offensive." Mao granted that under either circumstance, the CPV and NKPA troops had to spend two or three months recuperating and preparing for another offensive in the spring of 1951. Meanwhile, he informed Peng, 100,000 new North Korean recruits who had been in training in China's Northeast would soon assemble on the front so that the NKPA could be reorganized into fifteen infantry divisions and reequipped with newly arrived Soviet weapons. Finally, Mao called Peng's attention to a third possibility: that "the objective conditions may compel us to engage in another battle in February and force us to continue the fight before [our troops] will have a chance to rest, reorganize, and prepare for the final, decisive offensive."[32]

Although Mao underestimated the possibility of an immediate US/UN counteroffensive, General M. V. Zakharov, then head of the Soviet military advisory group to the PLA general staff, did suggest that the CPV forces prepare for such a contingency. He pointed out that the enemy had recently intensified its air reconnaissance, and with the U.S. 3d Division now deployed on the front line, it might make a surprise attack of the CPV bridgehead positions on the southern bank of the Han River. Zakharov proposed that the CPV move its main forces closer to the front in order to defend the 38th parallel. When this suggestion was brought to Mao's attention, the CCP chairman insisted that even if the enemy did launch a strike against the CPV bridgehead, it would not pose a big problem.[33]

The field commanders also thought that an immediate US/UN counterattack was unlikely. At a CPV Command meeting on January 22, there was general agreement that "the recent deployment of the U.S. 3d Division [on the front] is to enhance the enemy frontal defense rather than to prepare for an assault on our bridgehead positions in the southern bank of the Han River." Therefore, it was unnecessary to move the CPV main forces farther south. Deng Hua, in particular, argued that "even if the enemy intends to attack our bridgehead positions, we do not have to sacrifice a large amount of manpower and materials to defend these positions. A better way is to conduct a mobile defense," which meant to abandon those positions when attacked and to counterattack whenever ready. After the meeting, Peng cabled Beijing to report that "the present [CPV] force dispositions must be in accord with preparations for [our] planned spring offensive . . . to deploy [our] main forces for the frontal defense would disrupt the troops' rest and reorganization."[34]

Paying little attention to the enemy's situation, the CPV leaders proceeded with their command reorganization. On the morning of January 25, the CPV-NKPA joint command meeting was inaugurated at the CPV headquarters. More than 120 CPV and NKPA army commanders were present, and Kim Il-sung showed up two days after the meeting had convened. Peng Dehuai discussed the combat experience of the three offensives by first considering, "how to correctly treat the enemy's superiority in weaponry and equipment." Peng contended that "as long as we depend on the commanders' flexibility and the infantryman's bravery, we are capable of winning victories against the superior enemy." He specifically praised the CPV's persistence in "fighting night combat (but daytime combat was possible and necessary when [we] penetrated into the enemy rear or pursued the scattered enemy forces in retreat), boldly seeking to outflank, surround, and divide up [the enemy forces], bravely penetrating the enemy rear in depth, and organizing a small unit of handpicked brave men to assault the enemy artillery positions and commanding posts so as to confuse the enemy's command, control [and communication]." More important, he stressed that "we have always concentrated [our] man and fire power to constitute a superiority against the isolated unit of the enemy forces so that [we could] wipe them out one by one." Regarding defense, he noted that "[we] have stressed an active mobile defense. As for these positions that we had to defend, we always placed our main forces either along the side or in the rear and employ[ed] them for counterattacks according to circumstances (often right after the enemy forces broke through our defense positions)."[35]

The most serious topic of the meeting was how the CPV and NKPA forces would coordinate in battles. Mao had sent a special instruction, which Peng announced at the meeting, that "the Chinese People's Volunteers must try their best to learn from the [North] Korean Labor Party and the [North] Korean People's Army, must wholeheartedly support the Korean people and the government of the People's Republic of [North] Korea . . . and the Korean people's leader Kim Il-sung."[36] On behalf of the CCP central leadership, Gao

Gang addressed the importance of Chinese–North Korean unity in the war. In his speech, Kim Il-sung extolled the sacrificial efforts of the Chinese forces and also urged the NKPA and the CPV commanders to "learn from each other." Next, Liu Haiqing, deputy commander of the 113th Division (the 38th Army), Zhang Feng, deputy commander of the 116th Division (the 39th Army), and NKPA 5th Corps commander Pang Ho-san gave successive reports on their experiences in the recent campaign. Their appearance together was deliberate—a symbol of how the Chinese and North Koreans could benefit from cooperation.[37] When discussion sessions commenced on January 27, however, the CPV and NKPA commanders, who had been split up into six groups, began to hurl fierce criticisms at one another. The North Koreans, in particular, excoriated the CPV's decision to cease pursuit at the close of the third-phase offensive. They insulted the Chinese commanders as conservatives for refusing to advance on an enemy that was "in a helpless retreat."[38]

It was soon apparent that the enemy was not as helpless as the North Koreans had believed. On the same day that the CPV/NKPA joint command meeting opened, the US/UN forces began to attack the CPV/NKPA defense positions. Though small scale at first, the assault had expanded into a front-wide counteroffensive by January 27. General Ridgway had gathered four U.S. divisions, two British and one Turkish brigades, and two ROK divisions in a two-pronged attack on Seoul and employed three U.S. and five ROK divisions plus one U.S. airborne regiment for supporting operations in the east. Wary of being penetrated or outflanked, the US/UN forces were advancing slowly but steadily this time.[39]

The US/UN action took the CPV commanders by surprise, and they were especially alarmed to see how quickly the enemy transformed from the defensive to the offensive. The CPV forces were in the process of reorganization, and their reinforcements were still in training in the Northeast. The 9th Army Corps, resting in Wonsan and Hamhung, was not yet combat-ready. The 19th, 20th, and 3d army corps, which had gathered in northeastern and northern China to be reequipped with Soviet weapons, could not move to the front in such a short time. The present CPV/NKPA troops would soon lose numerical superiority, and were already at a disadvantage in terms of firepower and equipment. Receiving a confirmed report of the enemy attack, Peng cabled Mao on the night of January 27, declaring that the situation had become very critical. He suggested that Beijing announce straightaway its support for the neutral countries' call for a cease-fire, with the concession that the CPV/NKPA forces would "withdraw 15 to 30 kilometers [about ten to twenty miles] north" of the 38th parallel. Peng was convinced that "if the enemy continues to move north, it would be very difficult [for us] to hold our bridgehead positions, and we would have to launch an all-out counterattack to wipe out at least one enemy division; but a major offensive at this point would spoil [our] plan for rest and reorganization, postpone the spring offensive, and [moreover] since our forces have as yet to resupply food and munitions, [we] would be barely ready [to fight back] early next month in the earliest." Peng emphasized that "if politically we cannot afford to give up Seoul and Inchon, we would have to counterattack, which would be an action strained by tremendous difficulties no matter how one would look at it."[40]

Mao, however, ignored Peng's warnings and instead ordered an immediate counterattack. In his January 28 telegram to the CPV headquarters, he regarded it as "inappropriate" to either retreat ten to twenty miles north or accept a time-limited cease-fire. He contended that "the enemy is expecting our forces to evacuate [our present positions around] the Han River before it would agree upon a cease-fire . . . [its intention is] to compel us to accept a truce agreement under their fire threat thereby to put China and North Korea in a [politically] unfavorable position. This shall we never accept." To challenge the enemy scheme, Mao directed the CPV headquarters to prepare to launch "a fourth-phase offensive" that would aim at annihilating another 20,000 to 30,000 American and ROK troops and occupy the areas north of the Taejon-Andong line. He asserted that "it will be very advantageous no matter how one looks at it if the Chinese-[North] Korean forces can seize the areas north of the Taejon-Andong first and then spend two to three months preparing for a final offensive." On the issue of CPV unpreparedness, Mao argued that "it is not a great difficulty even if our forces have not been resupplied with munitions; we still possess the capability of . . . destroying some U.S. units and four or five ROK divisions if we try our best." He wanted Peng to press this point at the joint command meeting and see to it that the troops were galvanized into action.[41]

Mao's order aimed for an ambitious but unrealistic goal. He would not allow the Chinese troops to retreat north; rather, he expected them to advance toward the 36th parallel, about sixty miles south of the CPV's present position. Since the troops on the front were barely capable of resisting the enemy assaults, Mao had set an almost impossible task for the Chinese forces. Realizing that he would be unable to persuade Mao to change his mind, Peng read Mao's instructions to the joint command meeting on January 29, and then sent all the commanders back to their posts. The best Peng could hope for in this upcoming offensive was to minimize losses and satisfy Mao at the same time. The CPV headquarters soon developed the operational plans to implement Mao's directive. Given that the US/UN forces were advancing side by side, an all-out frontal counterattack would be disastrous. Peng thus decided to employ the 38th and 50th armies on the southern bank of the Han River to delay the enemy advance on Seoul, have the CPV/NKPA forces pull back in the east to allow the ROK forces to move ahead of other US/UN columns, and assemble the 39th, 40th, 42d, and 66th armies in the Hoengsong area to attack the overextended ROK forward elements. Han Xianchu was assigned to direct the resistance in the west with Deng Hua commanding the combat forces in the east. Anticipating fierce fighting, Peng requested the 19th Army Corps to move to Andong and the 26th Army to move to Chorwon as reserves. He also directed the NKPA 2d, 3d, and 5th corps to cover the advance of the CPV attacking forces into the Hoengsong area.[42]

Still pessimistic, Peng underscored the dangers of the coming offensive in his report to Mao on January 31. "As regard to the situation of our forces," he explained, "boots, food, or munitions have not been provided. Each person can only be supplied with an average of five *jin* [about five-and-a-half pounds] of food provision, and even that can be barely completed by February 6. It is impossible to march barefoot on the snowy ground; . . . the main forces of the 13th Army Corps will have to cover around 200 kilometers [about 120 miles] to reach staging areas in Hongchon and Hoengsong." He calculated that the troops could only be combat-ready by February 12. These serious problems, in his view, overwhelmed the CPV numerical advantage. "This fourth-phase offensive," he stated, "is going to be an equal contest of the enemy and our infantrymen. Although we enjoy a higher combat spirit than the enemy, we will suffer from numerous difficulties." Therefore, he anticipated that "even if we could eliminate 20,000 or 30,000 more enemy troops, [the US/UN forces] with their technical superiority would still be capable of depleting us and preventing us from taking two or three months of rest and reorganization. The third-phase offensive was fought with great difficulties (fatigue) and this (fourth-phase) offensive will be fought with even greater difficulties." The worst outcome, he feared, would be that "if the advance of our main forces is checked [by the enemy], it is very likely that the [overall] war situation in Korea would turn against us."[43]

On February 5, Peng cabled Beijing again, urging Mao to lower his expectations of the CPV campaign. He insisted that "we could only try our best to hold back the enemy advance so as to prepare the battlefield [for our offensive action later] step by step and meanwhile, to accelerate our preparations . . . for a protracted and tough war [in Korea]." Though it was possible that an immediate CPV counterattack might compel the enemy to stop advancing or even turn it back to its previous positions, it was more likely that the enemy might take advantage of a weak CPV defense in the west and keep pressing Seoul to force a CPV retreat in the east. If that happened, the Chinese forces might have to withdraw all the way back to the areas north of the 38th parallel and to sacrifice territory for time so as to make "a [more] determined counterattack on the enemy in the future."[44]

It seemed that Mao finally took Peng's concerns into consideration. He decided on February 7 that the Chinese forces would rotate in the fighting in Korea. In a telegram to Peng two days later, he confirmed that "it is obvious that the enemy won't withdraw from Korea unless its main strength is decimated." At this stage, the US/UN intention was "to look for chances to advance on [our positions] after consolidating its defense line and finishing reorganization; this will not only help expand its possessions but prevent us from taking some time off for reorganization." To him, the US/UN assaults on North Korea's coasts and the bombing of the CPV supply lines were "coordinating attempts to accomplish this objective." Mao consequently agreed that "we must prepare for a prolonged war . . . so as to achieve a final solution of the Korean conflict." Accordingly, he informed Peng that the 3d Army Corps (the 12th, 15th, and 60th armies), the 20th Army Corps (the 67th and 68th armies), and the 47th Army would begin to enter North Korea in early March to join the 19th Army Corps (the 63d, 64th, and 65th armies) to replace the six armies presently on the front. Meanwhile, the CMC accelerated the organization of tank, anti-aircraft artillery, rocket, and howitzer units. These "special forces," equipped with Soviet weapons and trained by the Soviet advisers in northeastern China, would arrive in Korea soon.[45]

The field commanders, however, regarded these arrangements as "distant water that won't put out the fire close at hand [*yuanshui bu jie jinke*]." Before the CPV forces had even started their combat preparations, the 50th Army and the 112th Division of the 38th Army met a fierce US/UN attack along the southern bank of the Han River. The 50th Army originated in the KMT 60th Army, which, headed by army commander Zeng Zesheng, had surrendered to the PLA during the civil war. Entering Korea in October, the 50th had not participated in any significant battles of the previous campaigns; this attack was a real challenge to the former Nationalist troops. With no fortified works or long-range artillery support, the army barely survived the first five days of fighting (January 26–31). The troops then built fieldworks by sprinkling water on the soil and letting it freeze solid. To avoid heavy losses from the enemy firepower, they were deployed in an in-depth defense with a small unit forward and the main forces hidden at the sides or rear. Attempting no last-ditch defense, they mainly relied on counterattack to regain lost ground: evacuate when the enemy assaults were too fierce, let the enemy occupy the positions in the daytime, and strike back at night when the enemy troops were tired and often had no air support. The 148th Division was the first to employ these tactics and the rest of the army soon followed suit. Peng highly commended the 50th Army for its creativity and instructed all the defending forces to learn from it.[46]

The aggressive attack of US/UN troops gradually wore down the 50th Army's defense. On February 4, Peng sent out the 38th Army's main forces (the 113th and 114th divisions) and one unit of the NKPA 1st Corps for reinforcement. He also placed the 26th Army of the 9th Army Corps in the Uijongbu and Chongpyong-chon areas to build a second layer of defense to back up the 50th and 38th armies. When the US/UN forces broke through the 50th Army's first defense line on February 7, Peng had the 50th evacuate to the Han River's northern bank to keep it from becoming trapped once the river thawed.[47] The 38th Army, however, remained on the southern bank with the mission to further delay the enemy advance and to protect the right flank of the attacking forces in the east. With the 50th Army gone, the 38th Army stood alone against the US/UN forces. The army's 112th Division had already suffered huge losses, and its 336th and 334th regiments had been rendered totally combat-ineffective; yet the assaults of the U.S. 24th and 1st Cavalry divisions, the U.K. 27th Brigade, the ROK 6th Division, and a Greek battalion were becoming increasingly devastating. Realizing that this was the most severe battle that the army had ever fought, army commander Liang Xingchu and army political commissar Liu Xiyuan called together all the division commanders to figure out how to survive the attack. At the meeting, however, some commanders complained that Peng should not have used the best attacking troops for defense; some suspected that Peng was sacrificing the backbone of the Fourth Field Army; and others asserted that "Chief Lin [Biao] would never allow the 38th Army to suffer this heavy loss." Liang was also upset but stood firm against retreat. Determined to prove that his army was superior in both offense and defense, he issued an order stating that this was a life-or-death engagement and that the entire army would defend its positions to the last man.[48]

Aware of the 38th Army's predicament, Peng planned to alleviate its burden by having the 42d Army and the NKPA 2d and 5th corps attack the US/UN forces in the Hoengsong area ahead of schedule. Mao, however, vetoed the idea. In his telegram to the CPV headquarters on the morning of February 4, he pointed out that since "the enemy forces are advancing side by side in the east and west and well linked together," a premature attack on the enemy's eastern column would not forestall its advance in the west because the CPV defense was too vulnerable there. "To avoid being caught in such an unfavorable position, Deng Hua's attacking group must not be engaged in battles in haste" and should wait until all the assault forces were ready. Therefore, Peng had to give up his plan and instead urged the 39th, 40th, and 66th armies to hasten toward the Hongchon area.[49]

At last, the CPV offensive in the east was ready to begin. By February 9, units of the U.S. 2d Division and one French battalion had entered Chipyong-ni, and the ROK 8th and 5th divisions had moved into Hoengsong. Finally, the enemy columns were protruding targets in these two areas, but with insufficient forces to attack both places at once, Peng found it difficult to choose which to assault first. Han Xianchu and Deng Hua each chose a different place. Han wanted to attack Chipyong-ni because, he reasoned, the 38th Army's positions were closer to Chipyong-ni and an offensive action there would immediately relieve the pressure on the 38th Army. In addition, the main forces would risk further fatigue by marching the longer distance to Hoengsong. Preferring to attack Hoengsong first, Deng argued that the U.S. 2d Division had already fortified its defense positions in Chipyong-ni, but the ROK forces still were on the move; moreover, it was easier to fight the South Korean troops than the American forces. The two front commanders obviously had different priorities. Peng vacillated between their proposals for two days but could not decide. Finally, he authorized Deng "to make a final decision regarding which to attack first, but to take action no later than February 11."[50]

Deng Hua was determined to attack Hoengsong. He employed the 42d and 40th armies and the 117th Division of the 39th Army for a frontal assault on the ROK 8th Division, dispatched the 66th and 40th armies to envelop the enemy rear, and sent the NKPA 3d and 5th corps to block the ROK 5th Division. At 5:00 P.M., February 11, Deng issued the final order to launch the attack. The next day, the main forces surrounded three regiments of the ROK 8th Division, but the 66th Army's penetrating movement was unexpectedly obstructed by the ROK 3d Division, whose disposition there had never been detected by the CPV reconnaissance. Moreover, the 40th Army had failed to set blocking positions in the enemy's line of retreat, thus allowing the U.S. 2d and the ROK 3d and 5th divisions to withdraw to Wonju. Regardless, it was a considerable victory for the CPV: the troops had routed the entire ROK 8th Division, devastated four artillery battalions of the U.S. 2d and ROK 3d and 5th divisions, and reportedly captured more than 7,800 US/UN prisoners.[51]

Shortly after the Hoengsong battle, Deng Hua urged all the attacking forces to advance on Chipyong-ni, but his optimism was ill-advised. First, he had no adequate intelligence on the enemy forces in Chipyong-ni. He was informed that there were less than 4,000 American and French troops there, but, as he later discovered, the actual complement was more than 6,000. Second, believing that the US/UN forces in Wonju would continue retreating and would not reinforce Chipyong-ni, Deng was confident that the isolated enemy forces in Chipyong-ni could not withstand the CPV's assault. He therefore placed no blocking forces against possible enemy reinforcements. Third, surmising that the enemy would soon abandon a defense and retreat south, he ordered an immediate attack, hoping to drive the enemy troops out of their defensive positions and destroy them in flight. The CPV assault on Chipyong-ni was thus hastily organized. The three divisions of the attacking forces belonged to three different army commands: the 199th Division to the 40th Army, the 115th Division to the 39th Army, and the 126th Division to the 42d Army. Deng placed these troops under the command of 40th Army Commander Wen Yucheng, who in fact had no direct communication with the two other division headquarters. When the 119th and 126th divisions began the attack on the evening of February 13, the 115th Division was far away from its staging site. The CPV was unprepared for the vigorous US/UN resistance. The 23d regiment of the U.S. 2d Division and one French battalion, supported by a U.S. artillery battalion and more than twenty tanks, constructed fortified positions and were determined to hold fast, whereas the CPV troops were tired from continuous combat and had no strong supporting artillery. Despite their repeated charges, the Chinese forces could not break through the US/UN defense line. The battle situation underwent a drastic change on the night of February 15 when the 5th regiment of the U.S. 1st Cavalry Division broke its way into Chipyong-ni and the ROK 6th Division and one unit of the U.K. 27th Brigade moved closer. Given the arrival of the enemy reinforcements, Deng Hua had to call off the attack and ordered a retreat.[52]

The failure to seize Chipyong-ni was a serious setback during the fourth-phase offensive. Deng criticized his own negligence in command, but Peng saw more ominous problems than the battle commanders' mistakes. "The enemy offensive this time," he explained to Mao on February 17, "is different from the first and second phase offensives: [the enemy] has deployed more troops and closed up gaps between its eastern and western columns; [the enemy forces] are advancing side by side with frequent contacts with each other and considerable in-depth formations." By contrast, the six CPV armies on the front were handicapped by a shortage of reinforcement and supplies. "[Our] forces are [like] 'the new crop which is still in the blade while the old one is all consumed [*qinghuang bu jie*].'" Since "the enemy takes [full] advantage of its excellent equipment, air support, and fast transportation," Peng predicted, "it is likely that the US/UN forces would continue advancing [on us, perhaps] with the intention to reach the 38th parallel before our second echelon formation and reinforcing troops arrive on the front." Therefore, he concluded, "one can easily sense that the enemy will never withdraw from Korea unless U.S. main strength is substantially destroyed. This makes certain that the war will protract."[53]

As Peng considered how to stop the persistent US/UN onslaught, he found himself in a dilemma. The present CPV forces were incapable of halting the enemy advance, and it would take another two months for the reinforcements to reach the front. But the political concerns of the leaders in Beijing did not allow for the loss of the 38th parallel, because, as Peng understood, "it would be difficult to explain to the democratic camp and Korean comrades." Given this predicament, Peng chose to fight a mobile defense: to evacuate the positions that the enemy could easily storm and then counterattack before the enemy consolidated its new foothold. His main design was to delay the US/UN advance at minimum cost by exchanging territory for more time. As he calculated, the delaying operations would at least impede the enemy's progress for two months, which would provide ample time for the 19th, 3d, and 9th army corps to reach the front and establish positions north of the Han River. He further planned that the CPV 38th, 50th, 42d, and 66th armies and the NKPA 1st, 2d, 3d, and 5th corps would build an in-depth defense zone, ninety miles wide and twenty miles deep, along the northern bank of the Han River. The CPV 26th, 40th, and 39th armies and the 19th Division of the NKPA 1st Corps would form a second defensive perimeter from Munsan through Uijongbu to the eastern coast. Peng envisioned that the first formation would fight for one month and then withdraw to the rear of the second defense line, and the second formation would continue the fight for another month. In his order of February 17, he stressed that "the essence [of this defensive strategy] is to avoid wearing down our own strength by the superior enemy firepower. [For this purpose] each unit ought to divide into several small group formations to take turns fighting, resting, and reorganizing."[54]

Since his decision for a mobile defense contradicted Mao's goals for this campaign, Peng rushed back to Beijing on February 20. It is unfortunate that the minutes of the Mao-Peng talks have yet to be released. Peng recalled later that he elucidated his contention that the Korean War could not be won quickly, and "the Chairman gave a clear instruction for conducting the War to Resist U.S. Aggression and Aid Korea: 'Win a quick war if you can; if you can't, win a slow one.'" He was satisfied with this trip because Mao finally agreed that the CPV should adhere to "the principle of flexibility."[55] After Peng left for Korea, Mao reconsidered the war situation and conceded on March 1 that "the enemy will not withdraw from Korea unless its main strength is devastated, but it will take time to destroy the enemy's main forces; therefore, it is likely that the Korean War will protract and we must be prepared to fight at least for two [more] years." The best strategy, in his view, was to rotate the Chinese combat forces in Korea. "We have decided to form our forces in three echelons: the first echelon consists of the nine armies—altogether thirty divisions—presently fighting in Korea; the six armies on the way to Korea [the 19th and 3d army corps] and the [9th Army Corps's] three armies (two are resting and reorganizing in the Wonsan-Hamhung areas) as a second echelon will reach the 38th parallel by early April to replace the first formation; [we plan] to select and dispatch six more armies to Korea which, together with four armies of the first echelon, will form a third group—altogether thirty divisions—that will get combat-ready by mid-June."[56]

The CPV forces on the front conducted a cautious but tenacious mobile defense. The field commanders were primarily concerned with avoiding heavy losses. No troops, they directed, should defend their positions at the cost of many casualties. Peng in particular pointed out that since the enemy would fiercely bombard the CPV positions with artillery, tanks, and air power before the infantry attacked, the CPV forces should place only a small unit in the outposts to watch for enemy movement and deploy the main forces in the rear or sides, ready to counterattack before the enemy infantry secured their positions. He also wanted the artillery to target the enemy tanks to reduce the enemy's fire support.[57] This strategy seems to have worked. The first echelon accomplished its task of delaying the US/UN advance and evacuated the battlefront on March 12. The second group carried on the resistance through early April and safely withdrew to the north of the 38th parallel. By this time, the 19th and 3d army corps had already reached the front. Having detected the arrival of the CPV reinforcements, the US/UN forces held back and built a defensive line between the Han River through the Imjin River to Yangpyong—the so-called Kansas Line. This operation ended with the CPV and NKPA forces pushed north of the 39th parallel after suffering more than 53,000 casualties.[58]

III

The CPV fourth-phase campaign was a serious reversal, but Mao still hoped to undertake another large-scale offensive. In early March 1951, he anticipated that the US/UN forces, after gaining control of the 38th parallel, would (a) "take advantage of our fatigue and continue to attack north"; (b) "stop at the 38th parallel for some time (ten to twenty days)"; or (c) "stay at the 38th parallel for a considerable length of time (two or three months) and not resume attacking until they have their outposts fortified." Regarding the first two possibilities as less likely than the last, he asserted that "once the enemy finds out the arrival of our reinforcements in a large number, the third possibility will not only exist but become real, that is, [the enemy] will lock us in a stalemate along the 38th parallel." Since it was essential to "diminish this possibility," he planned to gather all the troops along the 38th parallel to counterattack the US/UN forces before they could get a firm foothold. He expected the CPV to "wipe out another 10,000 of the American troops and completely destroy Syngman Rhee's forces around the 38th parallel and then advance south onto the Han River."[59]

What the field commanders wanted, however, was to get better prepared before embarking on another offensive. Describing the planned action as "a decisive battle," Peng believed that more forces should be deployed in Korea in order to retain a numerical advantage. He calculated that for the next operation, he would need "nine to eleven" CPV armies and two NKPA corps as well as the newly equipped rocket artillery, tank, and air forces. Since it would involve a sizable number of infantry troops and motorized forces, he was especially concerned about the transportation of food, ammunition, and gasoline. Peng doubted that the rear services had the capacity to support the offensive as Mao envisioned. He also felt it was essential to select a favorable staging area, one that would be convenient for mobilizing tens of thousands of troops and a large amount of materials.[60] CPV Deputy Commander Hong suggested in late March that not only was the Kumhwa-Chorwon area an ideal battlefield, but its location would enable the CPV troops to quickly establish forward positions. Other CPV commanders concurred. However, Peng viewed the broad, open terrain of Chorwon as advantageous to the enemy tanks and insisted that the troops should move to the line from Kaesong through Hwachon to Yangyang, where the mountains would be a boon to the Chinese foot soldiers.[61]

Despite his misgivings, Peng was becoming anxious to start the offensive and he argued for an earlier launch date at the enlarged CPV Command meeting on April 6. In attendance were the 9th Army Corps commander Song Shilun, the 19th Army Corps commander Yang Dezhi and political commissar Li Zhimin, the 3d Army Corps deputy commander Wang Jinshan and deputy political commissar Du Yide, and North Korean leader Pak Il-yu. Peng asserted that "the United States is determined to carry on the war with us and 'peace' is by no means likely [in the near future]. . . . [And] numerous evidences indicate that the enemy is prepared to fight a larger scale war. Any illusion for peace and wishful thinking for winning [the war] by a fluke will soon be smashed." To support his argument, Peng quoted from a CPV intelligence assessment:

> The enemy forces in Korea consist of fourteen divisions (seven U.S. divisions and seven ROK divisions), three brigades (two British brigades and one Turkish brigade), and small units of several other countries, altogether 240,000. . . . The enemy may gather at least 120,000 reinforce-

> ments. [U.S. Secretary of Defense George] Marshall announced on March 27 that the U.S. armed forces would be enlarged to a total of 3.5 million and two national guard divisions would be shipped to Japan to replace the U.S. 2d Marine and 11th Airborne divisions; 30,000 KMT troops in Taiwan have already been transported to the Cheju Island in January; at least two ROK divisions are under training in Japan and being equipped with American weapons; Washington planned to mobilize 80,000 new recruits in January and February and another 80,000 in March, and it is likely that those recruited in January and February would arrive at the [Korean] front by the end of April.

Given the US/UN reinforcement plans and "recent inspections by MacArthur and Ridgway on the eastern front," Peng believed that "it is most likely that the enemy will launch a frontal attack in the east coordinated by an amphibious operation on Wonsan or Tongchon, which would aim at controlling the north of the 39th parallel so as to prevent us from attacking its forces from the eastern mountainous areas."[62]

In Peng's view, it was more favorable for the CPV to fight back now than later because "the enemy is tired, its troops have not been replenished, its reinforcements have yet to gather [on the front], and its military strength is relatively weak [at this point]." Therefore, he insisted that "if the enemy advances fast, [we] will begin the counteroffensive around April 20; if the enemy moves slowly, [we] will act in early May." Should the CPV postpone the offensive, "we will encounter a greater difficulty [especially] when the enemy finishes reinforcing its forces on the front and gets ready to undertake amphibious landing." This campaign's objective, Peng specified, was to "destroy a few more US/UN divisions and crush the enemy plan [for a major attack]." Only by accomplishing that goal would the CPV "regain the initiative." To him, this was not an overly ambitious plan: the CPV simply had to "carve up the enemy forces into many pockets and wipe them out one by one." In particular, the Chinese forces would break through the US/UN defense line in the Kumhwa-Kaepyong area, cut it into two sections, and then surround and attack the isolated enemy troops. For this purpose, he wanted the 3d Army Corps to attack the Chorwon-Kaepyong area, the 9th Army Corps to advance on the area between Hwachon and Hoengsong, and the 19th Army Corps to seize the Seoul-Uijongbu area.[63]

Peng was absorbed in the details of preparing for the offensive. He directed that "each army corps must carefully pick a scout unit of 200–300 troops and assign experienced commanders to head it . . . which ought to be equipped with necessary [South Korean] currency, clothing, food, explosives, light weapons, transceiver, and Korean and English language interpreters, and get ready to penetrate into the enemy rear at the beginning of our offensive, with the mission to destroy the enemy transportation lines, vehicles, supply depots, and capture the enemy personnel to learn the enemy's conditions." To solve the food-shortage problem, Peng instructed all attacking troops to carry enough food for at least five days and the rear servicemen to transport another five-day food supply. He also required that "each unit command must find enough drivers or employ those captives who can drive to save the trucks abandoned by the enemy. If each company can capture and save one truck, our transportation situation will be greatly improved." Moreover, each army was to construct roads within its garrison area instead of relying on the engineering corps, and each army commander was to "see to it that the [infantry] troops help unload trucks and protect them." He threatened that he would not tolerate any "irresponsible acts [of the infantry] such as wantonly damaging trucks and beating up drivers or refusing to make way for the transport trucks."[64]

Peng reported his operational plan to Mao on April 10, and three days later, the CCP chairman indicated his approval "with no reservation." The field commanders were to "determinedly implement it if conditions permit." Concerned about the possibility of US/UN amphibious assaults, however, Mao proposed that "in order to prevent the enemy from landing at Wonsan, [I think that you] should place the main force of the 42d Army in the Wonsan area so as to guard [the coast]."[65] Anticipating Mao's endorsement, Peng issued "Instructions on Command and Tactics for the [Fifth-Phase] Offensive" on April 11. The directive elaborated on the principle of "concentrating a superior force to annihilate the enemy one by one" by declaring that "we will surely win, if we succeed in isolating the enemy forces in the east from its [forces] in the west, and carving the enemy's large units into small ones so that we can build an absolute superiority in man and fire power to destroy them one by one in combat." Since the US/UN forces would take advantage of the limitations of the CPV "one-week offensive" and would no longer be afraid of being surrounded at night, the instructions stressed that "this time, our combat forces must prepare to fight in the daytime." Peng wanted all high-ranking commanders "to carefully prepare, organize, and command [their troops], adequately understand the battle situation, try hard to organize anti-aircraft defenses, and appropriately coordinate with each other." The central task was to "make sure that our troops will *no longer fear* fighting daytime combat."[66]

Meanwhile, the US/UN forces slowed their advance, and finally stopped in the Chorwon, Kumhwa, and Kumsong areas. To tempt the enemy troops to move farther north, the CPV headquarters decided on April 15 to pull their soldiers back from the front. Peng ordered the 39th, 40th, and 26th armies to retreat northward beginning on the night of April 17. At the same time, he urged the attacking troops to enter their staging positions.[67] By now, preparations for the fifth-phase offensive seemed encouraging and satisfactory. As many as twenty-seven infantry divisions had joined the 13th Army Corps on the front. The 19th and 3d army corps, in action for the first time, were at full strength and entirely equipped with Soviet weapons; the 9th Army Corps had rested for four months and had replaced its casualties. The CPV firepower was also enhanced. As many as four field artillery divisions (the 1st, 2d, 7th, and 8th), two long-range artillery divisions (the 31st and 33d), four anti-aircraft divisions (the 61st, 62d, 63d, and 64th), and one rocket-gun division (the 21st) had gathered on the front. Four tank regiments (the 1st, 2d, 3d, and Independent 6th), which had entered Korea in February 1951, now strengthened the CPV offensive capabilities. Moreover, the CPV rear services were greatly improved. On April 16, the CMC established the CPV Logistics Command with CPV Deputy Commander Hong Xuezhi as its head and Zhou Chunquan as political commissar. A logistical corps of more than 180,000 personnel had plunged into transport of food, ammunition, and other materials by truck, rail, and manpower, with the help of three railroad engineering divisions (the 1st, 2d, and 3d) and nine engineering regiments (the 3d, 7th, 10th, 14th, 15th, 16th, 17th, 18th, and 22d). More important, two Soviet air force divisions in North Korea and eight CPV air force divisions in China's Northeast were committed to the protection of the transport and supply lines. By early April, more than 150,000 tons of food and three to five cardinal number of ammunition had been transported to the front.[68]

Peng seemed to be increasingly confident of a decisive victory. In a telegram to the CMC on April 18, he announced that "[with this offensive,] we are determined to eliminate three U.S. divisions (excluding one regiment), three British and Turkish brigades, and ROK 1st and 6th divisions in the west of the Pukhan River." He reported that the CPV would first concentrate on the ROK 6th Division, the U.K. 27th Brigade, the U.S. 3d Division, the Turkish Brigade, and the U.K. 29th and ROK 1st divisions and then deal with U.S. 24th and 25th divisions. For this purpose, Peng explained, the CPV 3d Army Corps would launch a frontal attack on the U.S. 3d Division and the Turkish Brigade in the Yonchon area; the 9th Army Corps would first attack the U.K. 27th Brigade and then outflank the U.S. 24th and 25th divisions from the southeast while the 39th and 40th armies guarded the army corps's left flank against reinforcement from the U.S. 1st Marine and 1st Cavalry divisions; the 19th Army Corps would dispatch one army to cross the Imjin River and penetrate through Uijongbu to cut the enemy retreat line; the main forces of the 19th would first attack the U.K. 29th Brigade and then roll northeast to Pochon to harass the left flank of the U.S. 24th and 25th divisions. Finally, Peng intended for the NKPA 1st, 2d, and 6th corps to protect the western coast. He assured the CMC that all troops would be combat-ready by dusk on April 22.[69]

As it happened, on April 22, the U.S. 24th and 25th divisions and the Turkish Brigade resumed their advance on Chorwon and Kumhwa while the other US/UN forces remained in their positions. The CPV commanders took the overextension of these US/UN troops as a good combat opportunity and at 5:30 P.M., ordered an all-out offensive. On the left flank, the 9th Army Corps quickly broke through the enemy line and advanced ten to twelve miles north by the next morning. The 40th and 39th armies managed to set up blocking positions against the U.S. 1st Marine Division's reinforcements from east of the Pukhan River. However, the 3d Army Corps, the central attacking force, met strong resistance, and the 19th Army Corps on the right flank failed to accomplish its enveloping movement. One key problem was the ineffective coordination between the artillery barrages and the infantry charges. Sometimes, before the foot soldiers had begun their assault, the artillery forces had already ceased fire; and sometimes when the infantrymen moved forward, the artillery units could not follow quickly enough to provide fire support. Another drawback was the combat inexperience of the newly employed troops. Based on their success in subduing the American-equipped and-trained KMT forces during the civil war, the commanders and soldiers of the 3d and 19th Army corps were overly optimistic about their numerical and "spiritual" superiority. Instead, the massive charges of the 19th Army Corps were handicapped by the narrow terrain of the Imjin River valley, and the troops suffered heavy casualties because of the enemy's firepower.[70]

The initial CPV attack was not as successful as expected. The commanders were distinctly surprised that, instead of retreating, the US/UN forces conducted a vigorous in-depth resistance. The U.K. 28th Brigade, along with two battalions of the Canadian 25th Brigade and the 7th regiment of U.S. 1st Cavalry Division, consolidated their positions in the Kaepyong area while releasing some troops to reinforce Seoul. Although the 3d and 19th army corps continued the assault on the enemy line during the next four days, the CPV failed to cut the US/UN forces north of the 38th parallel into pieces—an essential objective. To avoid more casualties, Peng considered ending the offensive. In a telegram to Mao on April 26, he explained that "the enemy forces are so closely knit together that there exists no gap and tactically, they advance and retreat steadily and entrench themselves at every step. We could not make a breach unless we penetrate into [the enemy] depth and bear a fierce fight." He admitted their inability to "achieve the objective of advancing to Uijongbu and cutting the enemy retreat line after three days and nights [of] fighting." More urgent, however, was the possibility that the enemy might "attempt its alternative of amphibious operations." It would be extremely devastating if the US/UN forces landed at Inchon or other ports of North Korea while the CPV's main forces were pinned down on the front. Given the US/UN air and naval superiority, the long coast of Korea, and the arrival of a large number of the U.S. reinforcements in Japan, Peng believed that "[the enemy's] intention to launch an amphibious attack on our rear is clearer than before." If the enemy began its landing operations soon, the CPV would face serious difficulties fighting a two-front war. Therefore, rather than "advance too far into the south," he planned to send only three CPV armies and two NKPA corps to the 37th parallel to tie up the US/UN front around the Han River. The bulk of the CPV would then move back to the north of the 38th parallel.[71]

With the NKPA Inchon defeat still fresh in his mind, Mao shared Peng's belief that "the enemy definitely has an intention to lure us into the south and land in the north." Yet he rejected Peng's suggestion to suspend the advance of the CPV main forces. In his judgment, the US/UN forces would remain "undecided for some time because its strength is not completely filled up (perhaps not until May) and its reinforcements (the newly arrived troops in Japan) are not yet combat-ready; during this period, the enemy will carry out a seesaw battle with us for the purpose of depleting [our strength]." This did not have to be "detrimental," if the CPV Command ensured that its armies were not expended and at the same time "disposed the enemy strength so as to delay the enemy landing or northward advance."[72] Peng gave in to Mao's argument and did not order an immediate cessation of the CPV's frontal attack. However, having noticed the buildup of the superior firepower of the U.S. 1st Cavalry Division around Seoul, he finally called off the planned attack on Seoul on April 29, withdrew the main forces to the areas north of Uijongbu, Pochon, Hwachon, and Chunchon, and moved the 40th and 26th armies to the north of Pyongyang as strategic reserves against possible US/UN amphibious operations.[73] Interestingly, the commanders of the 3d and 19th army corps did not appreciate Peng's caution. Embarrassed by the setbacks of their first battle in Korea, they demanded to carry on the offensive. Peng had to urge the army commanders to "acknowledge" their problems and "learn a lesson" before making unnecessary sacrifices.[74]

At this juncture, however, the enemy situation seemed to favor another CPV attack in the east. With the US/UN forces heavily concentrated in the west, the east was primarily defended by the ROK troops. Sensing this opportunity, Peng decided on April 28 to secretly shift the 9th and 3d army corps to the east with the mission to first attack the ROK forces and then speed west to outflank the US/UN forces. Meanwhile, he directed the 19th Army Corps to tie down the US/UN main body in the west and then join the enveloping operations with a frontal attack across the Imjin River.[75] On May 6, the CPV headquarters ordered the 9th Army Corps (minus the 26th Army), the NKPA 3d and 5th corps, and the CPV 12th Army to surround and attack the ROK 3d, 5th, 7th and 9th divisions; the 3d Army Corps (without the 12th Army) and two divisions of the 39th Army to prevent the U.S. 10th Marine Corps from reinforcing the ROK forces; and the 19th Army Corps to make sporadic sorties to hold up the US/UN main strength in the west. Peng underscored that the combat troops "must have the courage to penetrate into the enemy in depth" and that the 19th Army Corps "must select two or three targets (each manned at battalion strength) and gather absolutely superior man and fire power to destroy them." He directed that "each unit must be settled into attacking positions with sufficient food and munitions on the night of [May] 9 or [May] 10 and get combat-ready by dawn of the 14th and be prepared to take the action on the dusk of either the 15th or 16th." Two days later, he stressed again that a complete victory depended on three elements: "a serious feint against the US/UN forces in the west, a well-disguised movement to the east, and bold, prompt enveloping operations."[76]

The 9th Army Corps played the key role in the planned assault. Army corps commander Song Shilun called a two-day (May 8–9) unified command meeting at his headquarters with the 3d Army Corps commanders and the NKPA commander Kim Ung to discuss procedures for optimum coordination. On May 9, Song directed each unit under his command to start moving to the east that night. According to his plan, the 3d Army Corps would enter the Chunchon area under the cover of the 39th Army, the 19th Army Corps would gather in Yanggu, and the NKPA 2d, 3d, and 5th corps would arrive at Inje by the morning of May 15.[77]

At 6:00 P.M. on May 10, the CPV/NKPA offensive in the east commended. Caught by surprise, the ROK troops could not hold their positions and went into a hasty retreat. However, the mountainous terrain made CPV/NKPA pursuit and encirclement extremely difficult. Hundreds of thousands of foot soldiers crowded onto the few roads and could barely catch up with the motorized ROK troops. The CPV 20th Army and the NKPA 5th Corps surrounded the ROK 3d and 9th divisions but failed to destroy them as the South Korean troops disappeared into the mountains. The 27th Army advanced rapidly but only routed the ROK 5th and 7th divisions. The main forces of the 3d Army Corps met strong resistance from the U.S. 2d and 1st Marine divisions north of Hongchon. On May 20, the situation turned against the Chinese when the US/UN forces in the west pressed on the 19th

Army Corps's positions and reinforced the east by quickly sending the U.S. 3d and the ROK 8th divisions there. The overall fighting soon became stalemated. The CPV/NKPA troops ended up in the undesirable position of conducting a fierce fight while running out of food and munitions.[78] Afraid of heavy losses, Peng decided to halt the offensive at 4:00 P.M. on May 21. He ordered the 19th Army Corps to return to the region north of Yonchon, the 3d Army Corps to Chorwon and Kumhwa, and the 9th Army Corps to the east of Hwachon. Each corps was to begin to fall back echelon by echelon on the night of May 23.[79]

The CPV withdrawal turned into a disaster. Peng had warned the 19th Army Corps command on May 22 that the US/UN forces would again chase the retreating CPV with their motorized troops.[80] Yet no one anticipated that the US/UN forces would make a sweeping counterattack on the morning of May 23—twelve hours before the scheduled CPV withdrawal. Moreover, several columns of US/UN "special forces," assisted by airborne troops, daringly and swiftly penetrated north to cut the Chinese communication and retreat lines. Confronted with an entirely new situation, the CPV troops panicked. The 3d Army Corps suffered the most severe losses. The army corps command had the 15th Army move north on the night of May 22, which left a large gap between the 12th and 60th armies' positions. The US/UN rapid breakthrough isolated these two armies from each other. In addition, the army corps command's communication network was devastated by a US/UN raid on May 23, and it took the command three days to become operational again. Deputy army corps commander Wang Jinshan was unable to organize an orderly withdrawal. Even worse, when the 180th Division (60th Army) commander found his retreat line cut off, he decided to dissolve the troops. With no information about this division's status, Mao and Peng authorized several rescue operations. Since the division commander had shut off his radios, there was no way to contact the 180th. As a result, the entire unit lost 7,000 troops, of which 5,000 were captured by the U.S. 24th Division. Only division commander Zheng Qigui and several hundred soldiers managed to return to safety. Within a few days, the 3d Army Corps had lost more than 16,000 men.[81]

To resist the unexpected US/UN counterattack, Peng immediately organized an in-depth defense. On May 27, he directed the 63d, 64th, 15th, 26th, and 20th armies and the NKPA 5th, 2d, and 3d corps to form the primary line of resistance from the Imjin River through Hwachon to Kansong. The 42d and 47th armies joined these forces a few days later. By early June, the US/UN force had ceased advancing, and the CPV headquarters declared the end of the fifth-phase offensive. The CPV had fought for fifty days and nights and lost 85,000 troops.[82]

IV

The CPV's two offensives from December 1950 to May 1951 ended as major setbacks, and Mao's consuming aspiration for a quick and decisive victory was directly responsible. He evidently overestimated the favorable momentum that the Chinese forces had seemed to create after they had entered Korea. Certainly, the CPV scored an unexpected victory in October and November 1950, but to expand that victory was unrealistic since the Chinese troops had already reached the limit of their combat capability. Nevertheless, believing that human power would eventually overcome objective difficulties, the CCP chairman kept pushing the CPV to advance "in the flush of victory [*chengsheng qianjin*]."

Mao and the other CCP leaders truly believed in the importance of flexibility in war, but they did not employ the principle as a safeguard against risky actions. Certain that the Chinese Communist forces were masters of flexibility in warfare, the leaders became hopelessly overconfident and impatient. The usefulness of combat flexibility was largely dependent on an adequate understanding of an opponent's situation, as Mao had vigorously stressed; but when Mao himself overlooked the CPV's fatal weakness and mounting problems and underestimated the enemy's strength, he could not effectively exercise flexibility.

More important, Chinese leaders overvalued the importance of political prestige. In late December 1950, Mao seemed to be preoccupied with only one thing: crossing the 38th parallel, which, to him, would demonstrate China's resolve and ability to stand up against external pressures. Conversely, staying behind the parallel would be a sign of weakness. This preconceived political consideration evidently overwhelmed any realistic military calculation. It became even more difficult for the Chinese leaders to be flexible in the battlefield when the North Korean authorities began to press vehemently for much riskier actions than the Chinese forces could afford. The North Korean demands prevented the Chinese leaders from reaching an accurate assessment of China's best interest in the war.

The CPV did not recover much territory or destroy a large number of US/UN troops, as the leaders had projected; instead, the Chinese armies suffered heavy losses. Indeed, it was high time for the Chinese leaders to discard their blinding optimism and their counterproductive anxiety for a quick victory in Korea and consider a more realistic course of action.

7. FIGHTING A STALEMATED WAR

In Korea, the Chinese Communist forces were fighting battles unprecedented in their military history. Strategically, as Mao's military doctrines dictated, they should have started with strategic defensive, gradually shifting through a stalemated war to a strategic counteroffensive. Tactically, they were supposed to fight flexible mobile warfare rather than positional battles. However, instead of maintaining a defensive posture, the CPV fought five offensive campaigns in a row, of which none achieved what the military leaders had expected. The setbacks that the CPV suffered in the fifth-phase offensive in particular indicated that the US/UN forces were capable of not only preserving their strength but inflicting heavy casualties on the Chinese. In the late spring of 1951, the Chinese leaders seemed to come to grips with the fact that the war would be protracted. This chapter examines their reassessment of the enemy strength and their subsequent adjustments in strategy.

I

As the spring of 1951 waned, Chinese military planning transformed from large-scale offensives to "piecemeal" warfare. "The past campaigns have shown," Mao cabled Peng Dehuai on May 26, "that our enveloping, outflanking, and penetrating operations at both campaign and battle levels have encountered such great difficulties that we were prevented from achieving the goals of completely annihilating several U.S. divisions or even a whole U.S. division or regiment." He conceded that this was "because the American armed forces still maintain a very strong confidence [in fighting with us]." Therefore, he directed that "from now on, we must not be too ambitious in every battle." Instead of targeting the US/UN forces at division or regimental levels, each CPV army should only "aim at completely destroying one or two battalions of U.S., U.K., and Turkish troops." Mao was very sanguine about this change. Since the CPV maintained eight infantry armies on the front, he calculated that "if each army can wipe out one enemy battalion entirely [we] will annihilate as many as eight enemy battalions completely each time we fight, [an accumulation of which] will be a heavy blow to the enemy."[1] For the next few months, he wanted the CPV headquarters to plan, not all-out assaults, but attacks on one U.S. or British battalion at a time. If this strategy proved effective, he thought, "after three or four more battles in which we would cause each U.S. and British division to lose three or four entire battalions, [we] will definitely deplete the enemy's morale and shake its confidence." Only at that point "should we consider targeting one, two, or even three entire enemy divisions in each battle." Reminding Peng of the civil war experience, in which "we went from small-scale annihilation to large-scale offensives," he pointed out that in Korea, "we have only gone through a period of small-scale annihilation with our five offensives and we have not gone far enough. Only when we fight a few more battles can we end the small-scale annihilation period and step into a stage of large-scale offensives." With regard to a future battlefield, he asserted that "if the enemy wants to advance, the farther north [it moves] the better, as long as it would not go across the Pyongyang-Wonsan line."[2]

Mao discussed his piecemeal strategy further on May 27 in talks with 3d Army Corps Commander Chen Geng and CPV Chief of Staff Xie Fang in Beijing. Such an approach, he explained, bore a vivid analogy to "eating *niupitang* bit by bit." *Niupitang* was a sticky candy that was very popular in Mao's home province, Hunan. Since it always stuck together in one large piece, you had to cut it up and eat it a little bit at a time. Picturing the US/UN forces as a giant lump of sticky candy, it would be more effective if the CPV chopped them up bit by bit. The small successes would accumulate into a big victory. To implement this strategy, Mao requested that the CPV headquarters rotate the troops on the battlefield in order to retain the numerical advantage; galvanize the troops for fighting a protracted and arduous war; and reorganize the command system by abolishing army corps command.[3] Meeting with Deng Hua, 38th Army political commissar Liu Xiyuan, 39th Army commander Wu Xinquan, 40th Army Commander Wen Yucheng, and 42d Army commander Wu Ruilin on June 4, Mao elaborated on his *niupitang* strategy again and stressed the need for "patience" in order to wear down the US/UN forces. In his June 13 telegram to Peng, he mentioned his new concept and asked Peng to arrange a command meeting with Deng Hua, who would brief him on the details. Being a Hunan native, Peng perfectly understood the *niupitang* analogy, and he was pleased with the change in Mao's thinking.[4]

In late June, Peng summoned all high-ranking CPV commanders to discuss how to effect Mao's piecemeal strategy. After Deng Hua and Xie Fang briefed the army commanders on Mao's new policy, Peng explained his assessment of the situation. First, he attributed the CPV's setbacks to the fact that "we made several mistakes in directing the offensives; our rank and file lacked the experience of fighting against an enemy with modern [equipment] and suffered from ineffective military leadership. With superior equipment, the enemy was able to subdue the mobility of our forces, and moreover, [we were handicapped by the fact that] three sides of Korea are surrounded by the sea and the [peninsula's] terrain is long and narrow." Given these subjective and objective problems, he asserted that "it is unlikely at present that we can completely wipe out a few U.S. or British divisions in one campaign." Second, Peng argued that the Korean War could not be ended unless the US/UN main strength was eliminated. Therefore, he insisted that "[we] must wear the enemy down to a considerable degree, and race against time to get better prepared so that we can gradually overcome these subjective and objective difficulties." Instead of fostering expectations about a swift victory in Korea, the CPV "must determinedly adhere to the policy of protracted warfare." Third, Peng contended that the piecemeal strategy was the most appropriate for the next stage of war. He then specifically required each CPV army to

> (1) make a steady—not rash—advance but always with established positions behind; (2) take turns to assault the enemy forces and try to wipe them out one by one; (3) fight seesaw warfare to wear down the enemy's effective strength; (4) take offensive actions only after getting fully prepared so as to avoid engaging in unprepared battles: (5) start with piecemeal assaults and gradually shift to larger-scale offensives; (6) concentrate superior man and fire power to catch the enemy troops in a pincer; (7) take flexibility into serious consideration and act in accordance with [our] capability; (8) coordinate offensive and defensive operations closely; (9) always aim at achieving a quick solution in combat; (10) open up a front for guerrilla warfare in the enemy rear; and (11) make a full play for [our] propaganda campaign to disintegrate and demoralize the American and [ROK] puppet troops.[5]

What Peng envisioned, in essence, was an overall defensive action with small-scale assaults. However, there was considerable opposition to his plan. First, the North Korean leaders were not pleased with a frontwide defensive strategy. On June 3, Kim Il-sung came to Beijing, and in meetings with Mao and Zhou Enlai, he argued that the US/UN control over a large area north of the 38th parallel would be detrimental to the CPV/NKPA military and political positions. If cease-fire negotiations were to open soon, he insisted, the CPV should at least be in possession of the 38th parallel before assuming a defensive posture. Kim vehemently demanded an immediate offensive to restore the 38th parallel.[6] Among the CPV rank and file, many also favored an offensive campaign. Because of their success in mobile warfare during China's civil war, the Chinese troops disliked positional defense. The avowal that "[we] would rather assault three [enemy positions on] hills than defend [our own positions] for one hour" was often heard within the CPV ranks. Those commanders whose units did not do well during the fifth-phase offensive also hoped for another offensive in order to restore their lost honor.[7]

Peng himself seems to have wanted to finish the job as well. At the end of the CPV high command meeting, he directed his aides to prepare operational plans for a sixth-phase offensive that would merely aim at retaking the US/UN possessions north of the 38th parallel. As he reported to Mao on July 1, he believed that "it should be acceptable to both sides to restore the demarcation at the 38th parallel." If the US/UN forces decided to retain control of areas north of the 38th parallel, he told Mao, "we will take the offensive in August." For the first stage of such an offensive, the CPV would "fight a seesaw battle in the areas north of the Han and Soyang rivers and south of the 38.5 parallel." Then the CPV would "organize a major assault on the enemy outposts every other month." For this purpose, he planned to have the 20th, 26th, 42d, and 64th armies and two NKPA corps resist the US/UN northward advance through mid-August so that the attacking forces of the 19th and 3d army corps could get fully prepared for the first assault. If these troops were not settled into their positions by mid-August, then the 38th and 40th armies and the 20th Army Corps (consisting of the 67th and 68th armies) would join the resisting forces for a tactical counterattack early in September. "Before our counterattack," he stressed, "it will be militarily and politically more advantageous for us to allow the enemy forces to advance some ten kilometers [about six miles] north."[8] Shortly afterward, the CPV headquarters issued to each army and division commander a long directive drafted by Deng Hua, entitled "On the Protracted War in Korea." The order confirmed the importance of tactical offensives within a strategic defensive and called on the CPV to prepare for seesaw battles around the 38th parallel.[9]

Peng remained focused on the recovery of the 38th parallel by means of one more offensive as prerequisite to negotiating a truce. On July 24, he suggested to Mao that another all-out counterattack be opened in either August or September, in which the forces would advance beyond the 38th parallel and then return to it to build a line of resistance there. In his response two days later, Mao deemed it "absolutely necessary" to launch an offensive in September before the war might come to an end.[10] Mao's approval greatly boosted the field commanders' enthusiasm about another offensive. Wang Jinshan, deputy commander of the 3d Army Corps, reported to the headquarters that his troops were already well rested. As the troops had "exchanged their lessons learned through the fifth-phase offensive and know better how to fight the sixth-phase offensive," he argued, "the [CPV] headquarters should finalize the attacking order as soon as possible." Other commanders shared Wang's opinion. The 47th Army commander Cao Lihuai, who had been known as a relentless warrior among the Chinese senior commanders, kept pressing Peng for immediate action because "his troops missed the fifth-phase offensive and definitely want to get into this one."[11] On August 17, Peng finally issued a preliminary order for the sixth-phase offensive. This time, he planned to gather thirteen CPV armies and four NKPA corps for the ground attack and twenty-two CPV Air Force regiments for air support. His operational plan, however, reflected the emphasis on the piecemeal strategy and seesaw warfare. First, "each army would mainly concentrate on the U.S. and British outposts manned at battalion strength and try to wipe it out quickly in the first wave of assaults; then build defensive fortifications against immediate enemy counterattacks; and advance farther south if the US/UN forces retreat." Second, if the first-round assaults failed or became stalemated, "all the attacking forces must withdraw gradually and by echelon so as to lure the US/UN forces deep into the areas north of the 38th parallel and then drive them back to the 38th parallel through another full-scale offensive."[12]

Despite the bellicose sentiment in the field, Deng Hua regarded an offensive in September as premature. He reported his opposition to both Peng and Mao on August 18 from Kaesong, where he, CPV Chief of Staff Xie Fang, and the North Korean representatives were negotiating a cease-fire with the US/UN delegates. According to his "firsthand information," the US/UN forces had already constructed a twenty-mile-long, in-depth defensive perimeter with concrete works, numerous mines, and superior air and artillery support along the 38th parallel. The enemy, Deng suspected, might intend to induce the CPV to storm its heavily fortified positions and decimate the Chinese troops with its close-knit network of firepower. Such a large-scale storming action against the well-fortified enemy defense positions would be too costly. Referring to the present line of resistance as a potential cease-fire demarcation, Deng asserted that "it is not at all disadvantageous to both sides, because, although the area [we're occupying] in the west of the Imjin River and south of the 38th parallel is small, it contains many more resources and a larger population." From a military point of view, he added, "although it is easier for the enemy forces to conduct amphibious attack given that their positions [in the east] are close to Wonsan, it is even easier for us to outflank the enemy and threaten its rear since our positions [in the west] are closer to Seoul." He thus recommended delaying the sixth-phase offensive plan. It was more realistic, in his view, to retain the current line of resistance and "take some small-scale tactical counterattacks to forward the front line and obtain a better knowledge of the enemy fortified positions."[13]

Deng's argument was brought to Mao's immediate attention, and between August 19 and 21, he cabled Peng twice to convey his hesitation about the planned offensive. To storm the enemy fortifications with no strong fire support, he believed, would produce the same result as the fifth-phase offensive, ultimately making no substantial headway toward the resolution of the Korean conflict. To ease the disappointment of the field commanders, he directed the CPV headquarters to continue the combat preparations, though he set no deadline for actions. Indeed, battle readiness would help the CPV/NKPA negotiation efforts. "Now that we have massed a large number of troops [along the main line of resistance] and already built up [our] air and artillery forces," he explained, "the enemy has to take [our force build-up] into consideration in the [truce] negotiations." But if the CPV undertook the offensive and ended with another setback, Mao believed, "we would inevitably expose our weakness [to the enemy]." Should the Chinese and North Korean negotiators obtain a compromise from the US on the issues of demarcation and the demilitarized zone in September, Mao judged that "we would be in a better position [politically] if we won't take another offensive [at this moment]."[14] Deng collaborated with Mao's efforts to persuade Peng to postpone the offensive. In his telegram to Peng on August 26, he listed three possible outcomes of a full-scale CPV offensive against a triphibious (air, naval, and ground) enemy defense line: "First, we completely break through the enemy [defense] lines and annihilate part of the enemy forces; second, we completely break through the enemy lines but disperse the enemy forces; third, we fail to break through the enemy lines and are forced into retreat." He pointed out that "with any one of these possibilities—the third in particular—we would invariably suffer high casualties." On the contrary, "if we induce the enemy to leave its [established] positions to attack us on a large scale, we would be capable of smashing it and destroying part of its forces without much cost [of our strength]."[15]

Reconsidering the sixth-phase offensive plan, Peng presided over an enlarged CPV Party Committee meeting beginning September 4 that involved all army commanders. Though unwilling to give up his plan completely, he agreed to postpone it until early November. "It is less and less possible," he explained, "that we will conduct large-scale mobile warfare [in the next stage of war], and it is more and more likely that we will have to fight positional battles." From September to November, he stressed, the infantry troops should "learn how to fight positional battles for both offensive and defensive purposes" and how to cooperate with the artillery, tank, and air forces. He specified that the forces on the front should maintain constant readiness in case of enemy offensives and should simultaneously organize small-scale assaults on the US/UN outposts manned at company or battalion strength to gain more experience at storming enemy fortifications. Peng directed the troops to be fully devoted to the buildup of an in-depth defense system that was capable of resisting US/UN amphibious and frontal attacks. For this purpose, he wanted each army corps to construct at least one "standard and strategically important" vehicular road by November.[16]

With the delay of the sixth-phase offensive action, the CPV headquarters assigned priority to the construction of a defensive barrier north of the 38th parallel. To strengthen the frontal defense, Peng adjusted the troop deployment in late August and early September. He had the 65th Army of the 19th Army Corps move into the Kaesong area and the 67th and 68th armies of the 20th Army Corps replace the 27th Army and the 5th NKPA Corps in the Kumsong area. To enhance the defensive firepower, he assigned one rocket artillery, one antitank artillery, one tank, and two or three howitzer regiments—all newly equipped with Soviet weapons—to each CPV army on the front line. He urged each army corps to form a close-knit network of antitank and anti-aircraft artillery forces in the areas where US/UN tank and airborne assaults would most likely occur. Peng also established two coastal defense commands in mid-September. The Western Coast United Command, headed by CPV Deputy Commander Han Xianchu, directed the 38th, 39th, 40th, and 50th armies and the NKPA 1st and 4th corps on the front with the 11th Army stationed in Andong as reserves. Ninth Army Corps Commander Song Shilun, as the head of the Eastern Coast United Command, had at his disposal the 20th and 27th armies and the NKPA 7th Corps, with the 16th Army, recently posted at Tonghua in northeastern China, in reserve.[17]

Before the CPV's reorganization was complete, the US/UN forces intensified their ground assaults. Late in September, the U.S. 25th and 7th divisions, along with units of the ROK 2d and 6th divisions, began a probing attack on the western front. Anticipating that the enemy would undertake a larger-scale offensive, Peng issued an order on October 2 calling for "determined resistance of the enemy advance." Each army was to "take a heavy toll of enemy troops through [small-scale] counterattack if circumstances are in our favor." To distract US/UN attention, he directed the 9th and 20th army corps to move on the enemy positions in the middle and eastern front.[18] The situation suddenly changed the next day, when the U.S. 1st Cavalry, the U.S. 3d Division (including one Philippine battalion and one Thai regiment), and the U.K. 1st Division launched a two-pronged attack on the CPV 64th and 47th armies east of Kaesong.

Kaesong soon became a focal point of the fighting. Believing that the enemy lacked reserves, the CPV headquarters instructed the troops to concentrate on a "mobile positional defense." Each division would deploy small units on the heights, with the main force hidden in bunkers during the preliminary US/UN shelling. The small units would repeatedly assault US/UN infantry troops and then evacuate. Right after the enemy occupied the heights but before it consolidated its positions, the CPV would counterattack, first by shelling the enemy troops and then by having the main forces, sheltered at the rear of the heights, attack the exhausted enemy infantry. A key requirement, the commanders demanded, was to fight close combat and at night so as to reduce the threat from the US/UN air and artillery. These tactics seemed to be effective. Between October 3 and 18, the 47th Army battled the U.S. 1st Cavalry Division and units of the U.S. 3d Division over several heights in the Kumhak-san area. Possession frequently changed hands over hills 346.6, 287.2, and 345.6, with both sides suffering heavy losses. Meanwhile, the CPV 64th Army, fighting the U.K. 1st Division in the Kowang-san area, occupied two major heights and then evacuated and counterattacked them five times. On October 18, the 47th and 64th armies became too fatigued to fight and abandoned their first line of defense. Although the Anglo-American troops advanced about two miles north after two weeks of fighting, they were also too tired to proceed.[19]

In mid-October, the US/UN offensive shifted to the Kumsong area in the east. The U.S. 2d and ROK 8th divisions attacked the CPV 68th Army on October 8; five days later, the U.S. 7th and 24th divisions and the ROK 2d and 6th divisions moved on the CPV 67th Army. In these assaults, the US/UN forces successfully relied on mobility. Instead of providing front fire support, several hundred tanks penetrated deep into the CPV positions to break up the Chinese defense lines. This new US/UN tactic caught the Chinese troops off guard. Arriving in Korea in June 1951 and at the front late in September, the 67th and 68th armies had so little time to fortify their outposts that they initially experienced heavy losses, especially from the US/UN tank assaults. The commanders then discovered that the mountainous terrain forced the enemy tanks to crowd together, which made them easy targets. They immediately adjusted their tactics: Each division gathered all its artillery guns to shell the massed enemy tanks first. Special antitank forces were placed on either side of the roads to ambush the passing US/UN tanks, and each division's engineering corps built roadblocks. Soon the CPV casualty numbers dropped, and the two CPV armies managed to hold fast to their positions. On October 22, the US/UN forces halted the fighting. Since the US/UN troops only advanced about four miles after two weeks of combat in the Kumsong area, the CPV 67th and 68th armies proclaimed the engagement a great success.[20]

The CPV headquarters highly commended the troops' defensive performance. Although the CPV suffered a huge loss, they gained confidence and experience in positional defense. In a report on how the 67th and 68th armies fought their positional battles, 20th Army Corps Commander Yang Chengwu boasted that, adhering to an active defense strategy, "we are capable of wiping out the enemy forces in large numbers." And "active defense," he explained, required "(1) toughness and tenacity in combat and unwillingness to give up defensive positions; (2) a close coordination of the artillery, antitank, anti-aircraft, and infantry firepower; (3) repeatedly wrestling for any lost positions; and (4) disposition of a large number of reserves so as to ensure that the longer we fight, the stronger we will be." Yang declared that these tactics were very effective in fighting the U.S. troops because they were dependent on firepower, were afraid of heavy casualties, and lacked reserves.[21]

Another discovery from this action concerned the usefulness of tunnels for the CPV, not only defensively but also offensively. The CPV had previously relied on small individual bunkers against US/UN air and artillery raids. In an instruction on the tactics of small-scale battles, dated September 16, 1951, the CPV headquarters urged the troops to dig tunnels on "our main defensive positions, especially our key positions."[22] During the defensive battles, one company of the 64th Army dug a U-shaped tunnel, large enough to hide a hundred men with their food and munitions. The company leader found that this type of tunnel not only protected his troops but served as a base to counterattack the enemy. In one day, this company had reportedly destroyed more than 700 British troops at the cost of 21 casualties and still held its ground. The 65th Army, which had been known for its success in using tunnel warfare against the Japanese in northern China, also dug a number of V-shaped tunnels that proved extremely effective during the defensive combat. Very excited at these reports, the 19th Army Corps Commander Yang Dezhi phoned Peng Dehuai to recommend that all CPV forces dig tunnels. Viewing tunnel warfare as a solution to the CPV's weakness in firepower and equipment, Peng immediately ordered every CPV unit to construct tunnels for both defensive and offensive purposes.[23]

The CPV commanders became more enthusiastic about the positional defense when they learned that the troops had consumed fewer arms and less ammunition. The military leaders in Beijing were particularly relieved because supplying the CPV was an enormous and grueling task. By the end of October, China had sent to Korea more than 1,150,000 troops, including nineteen infantry armies, nine artillery divisions, five tank regiments, twelve air force divisions, four railroad engineering divisions, and eight logistical corps. To sustain the CPV war efforts, the two-year-old government spent about half of its revenue on the armed forces through 1951. The military expenditure for the Korean War became a huge burden on the nation and devastated its economic reconstruction. Launching a nationwide campaign to increase production and practice economy [*zengchan jieyue yundong*], the central leadership intended to reduce military expenditures by 20 percent in 1952. Since Mao believed that the overall defensive would cost much less than all-out offensive operations, he told the CPV headquarters to "economize manpower, materials, and finance; adhere to a protracted active defensive, hold fast to the present front line; force the enemy to expend as much manpower and resources as possible; and fight for a victorious end of the war." Per Mao's instructions, the General Staff Department was planning to send 260,000 to 300,000 CPV troops back to northeastern China so as to "substantially reduce the burden of supplying."[24]

Peng finally seemed convinced that another all-out offensive was unnecessary. On October 29, he informed each army commander that the CPV headquarters "decided not to plan for any major offensives from November to the end of the year [of 1951] unless unexpected circumstances require [us] to do so." Instead, he ordered the armies (the 64th, 47th, 42d, 26th, 67th, and 68th) along the main line of resistance to conduct small-scale assaults on the US/UN positions from Kaesong to Kumsong. "Each army," he directed, "ought to choose one enemy position manned at company or battalion strength and have it wiped off the map [for a battle]. . . . [For this purpose], each army must carefully prepare operational plan, organize an accurate and powerful fire support, determinedly hold fast every position that is seized, and at the same time, prepare for smashing the enemy counterattack." Peng stressed that "this [small-scale] offensive is of great importance and [you] must see to it that we achieve complete success [every time]."[25]

Determined to challenge US/UN superiority in firepower and equipment, the commanders of these six armies soon picked twenty-six US/UN positions, manned at battalion level. The CPV forces opened simultaneous strikes against these targets on October 30 and were engaged in a seesaw battle for nearly one month. The 47th Army won a quick victory. On the evening of November 4, it gathered 114 artillery pieces and 11 tanks to support an attack by eleven infantry companies on three positions of the U.S. 1st Cavalry

Division, each site being defended by one company. Because of improved cooperation between the infantry and artillery forces, the CPV troops were able to seize these positions in three hours. They then broke off the attack and assumed a defensive posture. After inflicting numerous casualties on the two U.S. battalions when they counterattacked the next day, the Chinese troops evacuated at dusk. Reinforced by another nine infantry companies, they fought back at midnight and smashed the weary and unprepared U.S. troops. The entire army repeated this type of maneuver through late November. The 64th Army's assault was also successful. Rather than fight at night, the troops unexpectedly took action in the daytime: they collected sixty artillery pieces to shell the enemy's fortifications first and then employed a dozen tanks to directly support the storming attack of three infantry battalions. The army reported that it had destroyed one battalion of the U.K. 28th Brigade. Along the whole front, the CPV broke through twenty-one of the picked targets and succeeded in seizing nine US/UN positions after dogged back-and-forth combat.[26]

As winter approached, the CPV commanders decided to reduce small-scale assaults and concentrate on tunnel construction, but the freezing weather limited what they could accomplish. Some tunnels collapsed because of poor construction, and some failed to withstand US/UN heavy bombardments. On April 17, 1952, the CPV headquarters instructed each army to upgrade the tunnels to make them functional for "air, artillery, and gas defense, and waterproof, damp-proof, fire and frostbite prevention [*fangkong, fangpao, fangdu, fangyu, fangchao, fanghuo, fanghan*]"[27] Between April 26 and May 1, the CPV headquarters also summoned all army chiefs of staff to discuss how to build better tunnels. The meeting established detailed criteria for a standard tunnel: the top of the main cavity should be at least 100 feet thick; every tunnel must have more than two exits, and its inside should be 4 feet wide and 5½ feet high; all tunnels should be well connected to trenches and other fieldworks.[28] With these guidelines, the CPV forces had significantly improved their tunnels by May. At the same time, the troops learned how to use tunnels more effectively. In defense, the tunnels would be shelters against US/UN shelling; for offensive actions, the soldiers would extend the tunnels closer to the enemy's outposts so that the assault troops could move more quickly and reduce their casualties. During the defensive battles in the summer of 1952, the CPV increasingly executed tunnel warfare.[29]

At this point the CPV no longer seemed afraid of fighting positional battles in Korea. At a meeting of CPV army corps commanders on June 6–9, 1952, the commanders all confirmed that strategically the CPV ought to adhere to "a protracted war" and, tactically, to "an active defense." They vowed that "we must never give up our major positions along the main line of resistance."

In their consensus, to retain the momentum of an active defense, the CPV should repeatedly assault the US/UN positions with well-picked small units so as to keep the enemy in a perpetually restless mood. They also pointed out that a successful positional defense required ample reinforcements, and therefore, every army corps must place at least one army in reserve. Finally, they considered it imperative that each infantry unit assist the engineering corps in transforming the fieldworks into more solid fortifications for a long-term defense.[30] The CPV had clearly and determinedly transformed into a defensive force in Korea.

II

Despite their passion for offensive actions, the CPV troops were compelled to maintain defensive positions, partly because of the critical problems plaguing rear services. In July 1951, a severe flood—the worst in forty years—swept North Korea. The mountain torrents destroyed most of the brigades and roads, which consequently crippled the already fragile CPV ability to transport food, munitions, and other materials to the front.[31] The flood posed an immediate challenge to China's war efforts. "Strictly speaking," then acting chief of staff Nie Rongzhen recalled, "not until the Korean War did we begin to fully realize the importance of rear services in modern warfare."[32] The Chinese Communist forces had never had a standard logistical system before entering the war in Korea. Throughout the civil war, they had mainly relied on capturing KMT weapons and acquiring food and other necessities from the local people. The old way to obtain supplies—namely, the reliance on captured enemy materials on the front [*cangku zai qianfang*]—became obsolete in Korea.

The CPV's logistics had remained meager and inefficient ever since China's entry into the conflict. When the 38th, 39th, 40th, and 42d armies first gathered along the Chinese–North Korean border, they had minimal supply systems in place. On July 26, 1950, the CMC established the Logistical Department of the Northeast Military Command (hereafter, Dong Hou) to be in charge of these armies' rear services, with Fourth Field Army Deputy Chief of Staff Li Jukui as the director. Although Nie Rongzhen emphasized the urgency of logistical preparations when he talked to Li in early August, Li could barely find enough skilled personnel to staff his department. Planning to form by late September three rear-service branches, each consisting of 2,600 men, he was able to set up only one branch with two depots, two field hospitals (seven clinics), one truck regiment, one impedimenta, and one guard battalion. It was not until late October that the other two branches finally came into being. By then, the main CPV forces had already entered North Korea, and were about to begin the first-phase offensive. Dong Hou was further hampered because most of its servicemen came from combat troops with no experience or training on logistics and because it had no engineering or communication corps or anti-aircraft forces at its disposal.[33]

Regardless, the military leaders in Beijing expected the small and poorly staffed logistical department to guarantee the supplies. They required Dong Hou in the summer of 1950 to "prepare 300,000 sets of sheets, a three-month supply of grain, meat, and vegetables; gather 1,000 trucks with gas storage sufficient for six months and 2,000 drivers and assistants; set up field hospitals capable of treating 100,000 patients with 20 surgeon groups, and establish repair shops for weaponry, equipment, and vehicles."[34] Working diligently, by the end of September, Dong Hou had stored 16,470 tons of food, 400 tons of vegetable oil, 430 tons of salt, and 920 tons of reserved vegetables and corralled 2,000 mules and horses. On order were 340,000 cotton-padded clothes, 360,000 pairs of cotton and leather shoes, 700,000 pairs of gloves and socks, and 5,000 field cauldron pieces. It had also stockpiled hundreds of tons of combat munitions.[35]

As military materiel piled up in the Northeast that summer, Li Jukui was worried about insufficient storage space. He went to Beijing in late August and suggested that they ship these supplies across the Yalu River and secretly store them in North Korea. Yang Lisan, head of the PLA General Logistical Department, could not decide and instead sent Li to Zhou Enlai. Zhou thought the idea was premature because, he explained, "we are planning to fight in a foreign country and we have not decided as to when to cross the [Yalu] River or when to take the action. For the sake of secrecy, [we] would be better off [if we do] not transport any materials across the river at this moment." As a result, Li had to spread tons of supplies over eight sites along the Sino-Korean border, including Dandong, Ji'an, Fengcheng, Tonghua, Benxi, Meihe-kou, Shenyang, and Siping. With the CMC's approval and the North Korean authorities' permission, however, Li was able to send deputy director Zhang Mingyuan and several other logistical officers to Korea in early September to explore possible depot locations.[36]

A traditional Chinese military doctrine teaches that "food and fodder should go before troops and horses [*bingma weidong liangcao xianxing*]." Yet not until three days after Mao's decision to participate in the war did the CMC allow Dong Hou to convey military materials across the Yalu. Although the department used all available trucks and trains and continued to transport the supplies day and night, the CPV logistics failed to meet the needs of the combat troops—for several key reasons. First, because of poor management, the materials shipped to North Korea were not quickly dispersed. After being unloaded, they sat for days before they were moved to the field depots. Lacking the cover of anti-aircraft artillery, a large amount of materials were destroyed by US/UN air raids either at the unloading sites or on the way to the field depots. Second, movement was terribly slow, for the trucks and trains had to go through crowds of troops on their way to North Korea. The infantry marching on the same roads often refused to make way for the trucks carrying their supplies, since they did not understand the new system. Third, Dong Hou had not been told to supply an immediate offensive action. Since the CMC's original plan was to establish a defensive line between Pyongyang and Wonsan, with no offensive attempted for the next six months, the logistical department had made its procurement decisions accordingly. When the military leaders changed the plan late in October, Dong Hou was caught unprepared. It had to supply not only the 13th Army Corps but also the 9th Army Corps and the 50th and 66th armies, which had originally not been assigned to combat duties.[37]

Peng Dehuai had been apprehensive about the logistics from the beginning. Before he went to North Korea, he summoned Li Jukui to the 13th Army Corps headquarters in Andong on October 18. "Since our troops will completely rely on the supplies transported from our homeland this time and our enemy will never make it easy for our transportation," Peng concluded, "you must prepare for a bigger budget to store 20 percent more than we actually need." He pressured Li to see to it that the troops would have enough food and munitions once they reached the front. When Li replied that he could not promise anything, Peng was displeased with that answer and declared that he would tolerate no delays in the transportation of supplies. Peng told Li to ask for Beijing's help in solving his problems.[38] Realizing the seriousness of the CPV logistical situation, the CMC sent three appeals in mid-October to the Northeast, Central South, Northwest, and Southwest military commands asking that they dispatch more rear-service personnel to Korea. Mao put a "Most Urgent" mark on the second CMC instruction and stressed that "this work must be done posthaste." As a result, hundreds of truck drivers and logistical officers were attached to Dong Hou, and the northeastern military headquarters mustered 260 tractor drivers to tow artillery.[39]

It was still too little, too late, and the problems remained overwhelming. As the combat troops initiated three offensives in a row and advanced about 300 miles south in two-and-a-half months, they left the rear-services units far behind. At the end of the second-phase offensive, the combat forces were already approaching the 38th parallel whereas the first logistical branch was just setting up a depot in Tokchon, more than 190 miles away from the front.

When the supply lines stretched farther south, the distance between depots increased. With no radio communication facilities, the depots were isolated, and when they were notified of a need, the servicemen attached to the depots failed to respond quickly. Transportation was inefficient and cumbersome. Since almost all of the rail tracks in North Korea were destroyed by US/UN air attacks, the Chinese had to rely on trucks to deliver the much-needed supplies. With little air support, the trucks could only move at night, often with headlights off. Though they covered an average of eighteen to twenty miles every night, many supplies and men were lost to US/UN air raids or traffic accidents. Finally, although eight more depots were set up in North Korea, there was not enough personnel to handle transport, storage, finance, and supply matters. Each depot had fewer than 100 people, and most of them did not have any logistical experience. Despite their hard work, the logistical corps only met 25 to 30 percent of the combat troops' needs.[40]

The CPV headquarters now had to urge the combat troops to attend to supplies themselves. In preparing for each offensive, the commanders required the troops to bring with them as much food and munitions as possible. Although each foot soldier could carry an average of 34 pounds of supplies, this amount would sustain him for only one week during combat. It was also impossible for the artillery men to carry the heavy equipment and ammunition. Because of the supply difficulties, the commanders had to ask the troops to rely on captured weapons and materials. Indeed, the U.S. Eighth Army left behind numerous weapons, munitions, trucks, and other military materials as it retreated south from October to December 1950, but this equipment was no boon for the Chinese. The munitions were suitable for American-manufactured weapons only, and many Chinese troops carried Soviet guns. The CPV did not benefit much from captured trucks either. In Samso-ri, for instance, the 113th Division seized more than 1,500 trucks, but the division commanders could not find enough drivers to move the vehicles to safety. The US/UN bombers destroyed all but 200. As for food, the combat troops had to borrow or buy grains and vegetables from the North Koreans, but the local people did not have much to spare. Lack of food remained one of the primary obstacles to CPV combat success. The CPV headquarters complained to Beijing in early January 1951 that the troops "are extremely brave in battle but going through extreme hardships as well."[41]

Insufficient and ineffective logistics became an urgent concern for Beijing authorities. On January 22–30, 1951, the Northeast Military Command, under instructions from the CMC, held a meeting in Shenyang to discuss how to improve the CPV's supply system. Zhou Enlai attended the sessions together with Nie Rongzhen, Yang Lisan, air force commander Liu Yalou, artillery force commander Chen Xilian, transport and engineering corps commander Lu Zhengcao, and deputy political commissar of the Northeast Military Command Li Fuchun. Zhou, Yang, Nie, and Li each made speeches. They all recognized that the old pattern of seizing enemy supplies for replenishment was obsolete and that Dong Hou ought to employ new methods. Having carefully assessed the scope and nature of the problems, the leaders identified transportation as the key issue, since plenty of materials were stored in the rear bases in the Northeast but only a small fraction actually made it to the front. Zhou then directed that "transportation must become the first priority of our rear services." The leaders decided to send immediately a large number of railway and engineering corps into Korea to repair the main railways and bridges and to have the troops on reserve join the rear-service units to construct and guard roads. To strengthen the air defense, they decided to attach more anti-aircraft artillery forces to the logistical corps and to ask the Chinese and Soviet air forces to protect the transportation lines. More important, the leaders requested the logistical personnel to pay closer attention to the management of loading, unloading, storage, and delivery of the supplies, and to find new ways to better coordinate the traffic of trains, trucks, horse-drawn carriages, and handcarts. They also called on each infantry army to share the logistical responsibilities.[42]

The Shenyang meeting seems to have produced significant results. First, the Chinese bolstered the rear-service command communication. In February 1951, the CMC ordered Dong Hou to establish a front command solely responsible for supplying the combat troops. The Northeast Military Command transferred sixty personnel to this new post along with two transceivers and two signal companies. Second, railway and vehicular transportation was improved. In mid-February, the 2d and 3d railway engineering divisions were sent to North Korea to assist the seven engineering regiments already repairing bridges and main roads. The CPV's infantry troops also assumed the responsibility of maintaining the roads within their garrison. By the spring of 1951, railway transportation had extended to the Yangdok area, and vehicular roads to Ichon. The logistical headquarters rearranged transportation into three lines: the first running from Andong through Anju, Pyongyang, and Yonchon to the Seoul area (about 400 miles long); the second from Ji'an through Huichon and Chorwon to Kaepyong (about 500 miles); and the third from Yangdok through Wonsan and Pyongyang to Hongchon (about 200 miles). Altogether, eleven truck, seventeen baggage, and ten laborer regiments were regrouped, and each branch was only responsible for transporting supplies within its designated region. With this change, the transport corps became more familiar with road conditions and more focused on their job.

To boost air defense, four anti-aircraft artillery divisions entered Korea in early February to protect the supply lines. Late in April, the 505th and 513th anti-aircraft artillery regiments moved in to secure the major bridges in North Korea, and four more battalions arrived early in May. Along the main transportation lines, numerous air-defense sentry posts were also set up. When guards heard the approach of the US/UN planes, they would fire on-alert signals. The trucks on the road would turn off their headlights and hide in the nearby shelters. This new air-watch system soon extended along all supply lines. By the middle of 1951, there were more than 1,650 CPV air-sentry posts in North Korea. The trucks were able to cover an average of nearly 100 miles per night, and the damage rate for the supply trucks dropped from 40 percent to less than 1 percent.[43]

As CPV combat troops transformed into a defensive force in the late spring of 1951, the CPV headquarters was able to concentrate on logistics. Since the front line was becoming stabilized, now was the time to fix the supply system. On May 3, Peng Dehuai issued "Instructions on the Problem of Supplies" on behalf of the CPV Party Committee. "War is a contest of manpower and resources," the directive pointed out. "Especially when fighting with the American forces of highly advanced equipment, victory is unlikely if [we] can't guarantee a minimum level of supply." Rear services should be "one of the top priorities of our work at the present time." Peng requested the CPV commanders at all levels to "prioritize the improvement of rear services" in their daily routines. Every army, division, and regiment command should name a deputy commander in charge of logistics. "Since the rear services are extremely difficult and complex," he observed, "it is impossible that the rear-services units could accomplish such a tough task alone without the whole [CPV] armed forces participating." Peng thus ordered all the infantry troops to share such responsibilities as "digging more shelters [for trucks] along the transport lines, sending out more air-watch guards, and building more depots at every major crossroads and along the narrow roads." He called for a "saving-on-materials" campaign that eschewed extravagance and waste, and he went so far as to declare that "any type of extravagant behavior is definitely a suicidal act."[44]

Deeply concerned about the command and communication gap between the logistics and combat troops, the CPV headquarters sought to bring logistics under its direct control. In late April, Peng sent CPV Deputy Commander Hong Xuezhi back to Beijing to brief the central leadership on the lingering problems. Hong explained to Zhou Enlai that "a modern war is three-dimensional which takes place simultaneously in the air, on the ground, and in the sea [as well as in] the front and rear. . . . In order to win on the front, we must win on the rear first." He asserted that the current rear-service system scarcely met the CPV needs in Korea. The most urgent task was to establish a logistical command at the front "to provide a unified leadership responsible for not only organizing rear services but more important, directing the war [against the enemy's strike on our supply lines]." Zhou concurred with Hong and promised to give his suggestions serious thought.[45] Early in May, the CMC sent General Logistical Department Director Yang Lisan, deputy director Zhang Lingbin, air forces commander Liu Yalou, and artillery forces commander Chen Xilian to Korea to inspect the CPV's supply system. Peng Dehuai told these commanders at his headquarters that "the pressing matter of the moment is to establish a frontal logistical command right away." If this issue remained unsettled, he argued, "it will be difficult to take care of the other [logistical] problems." Peng exclaimed, "I already had Hong Xuezhi report to Premier Zhou about this issue in April, and I am repeating my request now!"[46]

The military leaders in Beijing quickly responded to Peng's entreaty. After Yang and Liu reported to Mao and Zhou, the CMC instructed the CPV Command to "establish a CPV Logistical Command and set it somewhere between Andong and the CPV headquarters." It also suggested having one of the CPV's deputy commanders head the new command. On the night of May 14, Peng called the CPV commanders together to discuss this matter. Everyone present wanted Hong Xuezhi to take the assignment because he had already been in charge of logistics. However, many CPV commanders—including Hong—scored rear services as "unheroic, spineless, and sterile." Refusing to accept the job, Hong excused himself on the grounds that he was better at directing battles. When Peng and Deng Hua expressed disappointment at his decision, Hong gave in, but on the condition that he would only be an acting commander and "will not do logistics after the war."[47] The CMC then issued "Decision on Strengthening CPV Rear Services" on May 19, announcing the establishment of the CPV Logistical Command responsible for "administering all the rear services and equipment (including railway transport) within Korea." The CMC directive specified that the new command's tasks involved "receiving, transferring, storing, distributing military materials, taking in wounded soldiers and shipping them home, repairing bridges and vehicular roads, protecting communications, organizing air defense and maintaining stability and safety in the rear." The CMC named Hong Xuezhi as the CPV logistical commander and put all rear-services forces, including engineering, anti-aircraft artillery, communication, railway engineering, truck transport, and security guard corps, under his command.[48]

It took Hong two months to get the logistical command settled in Suwon. The organization consisted of six departments: political work, munitions, transportation, supplies, field medicine, and personnel administration. Attached were three telephone battalions, two guard companies, one truck team, and one medical team, giving Hong more than 3,400 staff members at his headquarters. In August, at the request of the CPV Logistical Command, the CMC decided to replace the civilian laborers in Korea with fourteen impedimenta regiments. Meanwhile, the CPV Command converted the 149th Division of the 50th Army into a logistical division. Hong soon had under his control more than 180,000 rear servicemen, excluding the logistic units belonging to each combat army in the front line.[49] Given these reforms, the CPV commanders believed that their logistical problems would soon be resolved.

The nascent CPV Logistical Command confronted an immediate challenge. In late July 1951, North Korea was subjected to heavy, nonstop rains for several weeks. The rivers flooded, and the tide in some places rose nearly thirty-six feet. Flash floods in the mountains were devastating. The depot near Hoechang, one of the biggest, was completely wiped out, causing the loss of 845 tons of food, 1,184 barrels of gasoline, 142 tons of munitions, and 239 lives, including 167 anti-aircraft personnel. The severe flood also destroyed 205 vehicular bridges and 94 railway bridges. Ninety percent of the storehouses administered by the 1st and 5th logistical branches were inundated. In the midst of this natural disaster, the US/UN air forces intensified their raids on the Chinese supply lines. Beginning in August, American bombers dropped countless bombs on roads, railways, bridges, and warehouses in North Korea day and night with the mission to paralyze the transport of CPV supplies.[50] Indeed, the war was shifting from the front to the rear.

The CPV logistical headquarters had prepared for the flood but had not anticipated its severity or tenacity. Warned by weather assessments, Hong Xuezhi, in late June, had directed all the service branches to store enough materials to meet the troops' needs for two months. In early July, he assigned six regimental engineering corps to consolidate the dikes, dams, roads, and bridges in North Korea and instructed each depot to form a special team to battle the expected flood.[51] Despite the careful preparations, the unprecedented scope of the flood and the subsequent US/UN bombing caught the Chinese logistical commanders off guard. On August 16, Hong called a CPV rear-services meeting at which CPV logistical political commissar Zhou Chunquan spoke first. Acknowledging the adversities caused by the flood and the enemy bombing, Zhou warned that more serious problems were yet to come. Hong then directed the entire rear-service corps to stand at alert to salvage as many materials and vehicles as possible. He ordered each rear-service unit to form an "inspection and report" group with the responsibility of providing the headquarters with accurate information on the situation, and every transport unit to offer its surplus transport capability to help other units. As Hong asserted, the key to winning the battle in the rear was the full participation of the entire CPV forces, combat and logistics alike.[52]

Hong was hopeful that the combat troops could come to his aid. Late in August, he went to Chen Geng, CPV second deputy commander then in charge of combat operations, explaining his desperate need for extra hands. "The road reconstruction proceeds too slowly with the rear-service units doing it alone," Hong contended. "All the [CPV] forces, except those disposed in the first line of defense, must help us." He especially wanted CPV administrative personnel and the North Korean people to share the workload. Chen agreed and asked Hong to design an operational plan that would assign each army and division with specific responsibilities. When Hong submitted his plan, other commanders complained about the "extra burden" the combat troops would have to bear. Chen firmly stood by Hong and instructed each army commander that "this [work] is as important as a combat task and you must be fully devoted to it and work on it day and night." Peng also supported Hong at the September 8 CPV high-ranking command meeting, stating that "all the [combat] troops must participate on [protecting the supplies]. [We] must finish reconstructing the damaged roads as soon as possible and at the same time widen the roads and build a few new roads of strategic value." Shortly afterward, the CPV headquarters directed all eleven infantry armies and nine engineering regiments deployed in the second defense line to take part in the road construction as the CPV Logistical Command had requested.[53]

When the combat troops took over the repair of vehicular roads, the rear-service units were able to concentrate on the railroads. Hong wanted to set up an independent command to direct railway transport and reconstruction, but the leaders in Beijing felt that any such organization would need the consent of the North Koreans. With their concurrence, a Sino-Korean United Railway Transport Command was established in Pakchon in August 1951, with Northeast Military deputy commander He Jinnian as its head. This united command supervised as many as 52,000 personnel, including four divisions and three regiments of railway engineers and several construction brigades.[54]

The military leaders in Beijing regarded railway transportation as essential to winning the battles on the rear. They believed that "the enemy's bombardment of our railways is part of its strategic scheme aiming at frustrating our efforts to fight a protracted war and exerting pressure on our negotiations at Kaesong." In mid-September, the CMC sent PLA transport commander Lu Zhengcao to Shenyang. After meeting with the CPV logistical commanders,

Lu pledged assistance and sent in more personnel, materials, equipment, and anti-aircraft forces. Repairs increased, and railroad transportation began to improve. Between July 1951 and January 1952, despite the terrible flood and the intense US/UN air raids, the amount of freight carried by rail was two-and-a-half times greater than it was in January 1951.[55]

The enhancement of railroad transport capability arose largely from the application of new methods. The rear servicemen were urged by their commanders to be "courageous and creative" in resolving transport problems. One method was the "one-way transport [*pianmian yunshu*]." Most of the railroads in North Korea were single-track lines. Under repeated US/UN air strikes, these rail lines were often open to traffic for just a few hours each day or night. Racing against time, the CPV transport corps soon discovered that one-way transport was more efficient: they would run loaded and unloaded trains in the same direction within the open-traffic period so as to avoid the delays of round-trip transportation. Another solution was "successive carriages [*xuxing xingche*]." For the sake of safety, normally only one train at a time would run on one line. The Chinese railway engineers boldly broke this rule by driving several trains on the same track with the trains separated by only a short distance. This practice was very risky but time-saving. A third method was "combined transportation [*hebing yunzhuan*]." Whenever a railway was open, the transport corps would move as many railcars as possible by combining two or three whole trains and having one or two locomotives pull at the head of the caravan and one or two push at the rear. Such an arrangement was expedient only for short distances. Another practice was "pushing railcars across bridges [*dingniu guojiang*]." During this period, railway bridges were one of the primary US/UN bombing targets. After hasty repairs, many of the damaged bridges were still too weak to bear the weight of a locomotive. The railroad engineers then used one or two locomotives to push the train across the bridge and then had one or two locomotives on the other side pull it away. Finally, the CPV railway corps took advantage of the regular patterns of US/UN air raids. Since the American bombers were more likely to make their runs between 10:00 P.M. and midnight and on nights with a full moon, the transport troops rearranged their working schedule to avoid the enemy air strikes. As a result, they not only improved the CPV transport efficiency but also decreased their losses.[56]

The CPV logistical commanders also developed ways to strengthen air defense. One of their techniques was to consolidate the small anti-aircraft forces and bring them into the areas most frequently raided by the enemy airplanes. On September 2, the CMC decided to assign the Northeast Military Command's 503d, 505th, 508th, and 513th anti-aircraft artillery regiments and six independent anti-aircraft artillery battalions to the CPV Logistical Command. Later that month, eleven anti-aircraft artillery battalions, which had been attached to the infantry troops in the second defense line, were added to the logistical air-defense strength. By December, the CPV logistical headquarters had a total of three anti-aircraft divisions, four anti-aircraft regiments, twenty-three anti-aircraft battalions, one searchlight regiment, and one radar company. Hong Xuezhi divided up these forces into four air-defense zones—Pyongyang-Anju, Sinchang-ri, Yangdok, and Pyongyang–Wokae-li—but he soon realized that the US/UN bombing focused on a triangular area from Sinanju to Sipo to Kaechon, the key junction of the CPV transport network. Hong stationed three anti-aircraft artillery divisions and three battalions in this area in early December. To direct the air defense in the triangle, he established a Railway Anti-aircraft Artillery Command in Anju, equipped with one radar and five searchlight companies. In their tally for the month of December, the Chinese anti-aircraft forces reported that they had downed 55 US/UN aircraft and damaged more than 100. This toughened defensive capability soon eased the intensity of US/UN air raids on the railroads.[57]

Another air-defense action was the organization of an air-watch scout corps, mentioned earlier; eventually every rear-service unit included a group of scouts. In March 1951, the guards of the 1st and 3d logistical branches found it very helpful to post a scout at the top of a nearby hill—someone who could fire warning shots as US/UN planes approached. When a report on this tactic's effectiveness reached the CPV headquarters, Peng immediately ordered all the logistical corps to follow the example of the 21st and 3d branches. Under Peng's instruction, Hong turned seven infantry regiments (two from the 149th Division, two from the 18th Guard Division, three from the guard corps) and two battalions of rear servicemen—altogether, 8,200 troops—into air-watch scouts. Deployed along more than 1,200 miles of main transport lines, 1,568 air-watch scouts were posted at every mile. Each scout was equipped with a rifle, four grenades, and a whistle or trumpet. At first, these scouts were to simply watch the sky and whistle warnings, but their duties gradually extended to directing traffic, repairing roads, evacuating the wounded, guarding the transport trucks, searching South Korean spies, and maintaining communications. Most of the scouts would even supply water to the trucks and troops passing by.[58]

In addition, the logistical corps employed the tactics of deceit to counter the US/UN air raids. The 5th Company of the 4th Vehicle Regiment set the pace when it placed several damaged trucks on a minor road to attract US/UN bombers so that other trucks could safely pass along the major roads. Since this approach seemed to work, other units followed suit: one built a fake bunker to lure the enemy aircraft away from transportation lines. Three US/UN bombers repeatedly raided this decoy and were thus distracted from the vital supply columns. Very pleased at this "smart and creative" method, the CPV logistical commanders instructed the rest of the transport corps to utilize deception. One time, the logistical troops constructed a false warehouse containing bags of dirt and covered it with tree leaves; on other occasions, they placed lamps either on the road or in the hills, or left broken trucks on the road. Throughout the winter of 1951–52, these false targets frequently fooled the US/UN bombers, which delighted the CPV logistical commanders. For every raid, they calculated, the enemy planes had to drop tons of heavy bombs and consume a large amount of gasoline; even if the enemy hit the bogus targets and damaged a truck, the cunning methods were very cost-effective. The commanders hoped that if they could cause the US/UN air forces to waste gasoline and munitions, the enemy would be forced to decrease its bombing in the long run.[59]

Meanwhile, the CPV logistical headquarters planned to build more and better shelters for transport vehicles. The mountainous terrain in North Korea made this task easier. The logistical corps first used the gullies, ravines, and valleys that were mostly camouflaged by dense forest to shelter military materials, the wounded soldiers, trucks, and even trains. Then they discovered that abandoned mines, mountain caves, and railroad tunnels provided better cover. Since these "natural" shelters were often far away from the main transport lines, the truck transport corps dug coverts in the roadsides or at the foot of hills. Whenever the air-watch scouts sent up a warning, they would drive the trucks into these concealed positions. With the shelters nearby and the air-defense scouts in place, the Chinese trucks could now be on the road in the daytime.[60] The railroad transport corps also found the numerous railway tunnels in North Korea very handy. There were as many as 175 such tunnels along the CPV transport lines, some more than one-and-a-half miles long. The CPV railway engineers used these tunnels to shelter their supply trains and even turned them into stations and repair shops. Though surplus steel rails and huge tree trunks hid the exits, the tunnels remained vulnerable to accurate US/UN air strikes, and the Chinese transport corps still had to rely on the support of the CPV anti-aircraft artillery forces.[61]

III

Although the CPV badly needed air protection over its ground troops and, more important, its transportation lines, the PLA Air Force was not in a position to assist. When the Chinese troops entered the war, the CMC had considered sending the newly established People's Air Force to support the ground battles. At their request, the Air Force Command had held a meeting in late October 1950 discussing when to send in the air force and exactly how to do it. The participants, however, concurred that the three infant air force brigades were no match for the US/UN air forces in terms of quantity or quality. Only when the air force numbered 100 to 150 units, in their view, could the command consider "selecting an appropriate time" to engage in the air war. They reported to the CMC that in order to speed up its preparations, the air force should first join the Soviet air forces in northeastern China for combat training. In the second stage, small units, backed by Soviet aircraft, could fly over the Yalu River for combat exercises. Air Force Commander Liu Yalou summarized these points as "accumulating strength, choosing the best timing, and sending out formations [later]." On December 4, Mao approved the Air Force Command's suggestions and agreed that "it is safer to do it this way."[62]

Given the unreadiness of the Chinese air force, Beijing authorities wanted the Soviet air forces to protect the CPV transportation lines. Moscow agreed late in 1950 that the two Soviet air force divisions based in Andong would begin in January 1951 to cover the main transport lines north of the Chongchon River. The Kremlin leaders made it clear that the Soviet aircraft would only protect a zone extending some sixty miles south of the Yalu, and the protection would be very limited. Stalin had told Zhou in Moscow in October 1950 that "although [the Soviet Union] could send some air force units to Korea, our air forces must be confined to the rear area and must never fly deep into the enemy's rear." If a Soviet aircraft was shot down and the pilot was captured, "it would result in an adverse effect on the world [opinion]." Therefore, 200 Soviet planes and their crews were stationed in Andong with instructions from Moscow not to engage in direct air combat with the US/UN air forces. The Russian pilots dressed in Chinese uniforms—blue trousers, orange-red boots, and khaki jackets with badges bearing the profiles of Stalin and Mao—and had to pretend to be of mixed Russian-Chinese ancestry.[63] The Soviets also rendered valuable assistance in equipment and training. Between December 1950 and April 1951, the Soviets helped the Chinese form nine more air force divisions and equipped them with MIG-15s, the best fighter in the Soviet air force. They also sent their best pilots and crews to train the Chinese personnel. It typically required at least 300 hours of flight training to pilot a jet aircraft, but the Soviet instructors were able to adapt the courses to China's urgent needs. With an average of only fifty to sixty hours of flight training, the Chinese students were flying the MIG-15s by themselves.[64]

Late in 1950, the PLA Air Force Command decided to send a small unit to Korea for "real combat practice [*shizhan duanlian*]." With the CMC's approval, some Chinese air units joined the Soviet air units in protecting the CPV transport lines. The air force headquarters assigned the 28th Group of the 4th Air Force Division to its first combat mission. "Since this is the first combat action of our air force," the December 4 order cautioned, "[you] must be very careful."[65] Three weeks later, the 28th Group, led by division commander Fang Ziyi and political commissar Li Shian, shifted from Liaoyang to the Langtou airport in Andong and was attached to the Soviet air force. The division commanders had been cautious and had decided on a three-stage process preliminary to actual combat. First, the pilots would study the U.S. air tactics to become acquainted with their opponents; second, in the absence of enemy air attacks, the group would fly with the Soviet units over the operational theater to get to know the battlefield; third, if there were only small US/UN air units in action, the group would plan to attack the enemy planes. Fang and Li set up a command post with only one transceiver, one telephone, and one flight map. On December 26, the 28th Group's ten aircraft flew for the first time through Anju and Huichon. On the morning of January 21, 1951, this squad had its first encounter with the US/UN air forces when group leader Li Han led six fighters to attack some U.S. F-84 fighter-bombers in the Sinanju area. Catching the enemy by surprise, Li and two other pilots disabled one American aircraft. Afraid of enemy reinforcements, the Chinese planes quickly returned to their base. The PLA Air Force Command was very pleased with the results of the first air combat and congratulated the pilots that "this operation proves that our young air force is capable of air battles with considerable effectiveness." Three days later, Li's group brought down one U.S. F-84 and damaged another in the Anju area with no loss to the Chinese. Encouraged by these operations, the air command soon moved four groups (all from the 4th Air Force Division) to join the 28th Group at Langtou airport. In two months, these units flew 145 sorties in twenty-eight groups, but they only disabled one U.S. F-84 at a loss of two of their own MIG-15s and one pilot.[66]

Becoming more confident, the Chinese air force commanders accelerated the preparations for air combat. On March 15, they formed the CPV Air Force Command with its headquarters in Andong and placed Liu Zhen, PLA Air Force deputy commander, at the helm.[67] Inexperienced and cautious, Liu believed that the Chinese air force was not yet ready to assume actual combat duty. At a division commanders' meeting on April 8, he specifically instructed all the units to focus on coordination between air and ground. He also relieved the 14th Air Force Division from full combat duty. From April 25 to

April 28, Liu organized an exercise on "coordinated attack of air operations" in the suburbs of Shenyang in order to test ground command and air combat communication. The result was not encouraging, and the ground commanders in particular performed very poorly. Liu scheduled another drill on coordination tactics among fighter, attacker, and bomber units in Shenyang, Andong, and Liaoyang between May 28 and June 16. The 3d and 4th fighter divisions, the 5th Attack Division, and the 8th Bomber Division—altogether 180 planes—participated by attacking an "enemy" airfield, intercepting enemy bombing operations, and supporting ground assaults. Despite numerous deficiencies, the air force commanders were satisfied with the considerable improvement the young air force demonstrated during this second drill.[68]

As the air force units intensified their preparations, the CMC dispatched thousands of infantry and engineering troops to construct airfields in North Korea, since constant US/UN air raids had damaged nearly all the existing North Korean sites. Based on an agreement made with the North Koreans in early March 1951, the Chinese were to build four new airfields north of Pyongyang. Late that month, the CMC assigned the 47th Army and more than 1,000 civilian engineers to the task. Bringing with them the necessary materials and equipment from China, the troops worked extremely hard and completed the construction in late July. However, these new airfields could not handle Soviet jet planes, so Beijing decided in mid-August to build three better airfields in the Anju area and sent the 23d Army Corps to do the job. The CMC finally abandoned its attempt to base the CPV air force in North Korea when it realized that the US/UN air forces concentrated on the CPV's rear and had made only minor raids on China's Northeast since the summer of 1951. The Chinese leaders considered it much safer to keep the CPV air force within China's borders. Therefore, late in 1951, Beijing withdrew all the construction personnel from North Korea and reassigned them to work on the airfields in Andong and Shenyang.[69]

As US/UN air strikes on the CPV logistical transport lines increased in August 1951, the CPV headquarters demanded immediate air protection. As approved by the CMC, the 4th Air Force Division, headed by commander Fang Ziyi, moved to Andong on September 12. The division's fifty-six pilots and fifty-five MIG-15 fighters were to guard the Sinanju bridge on the Chongchon River, a key link in the CPV logistical transport network. The first air combat took place on September 25 when 12th Regiment deputy commander Li Wenmu led sixteen MIG-15s against a group of U.S. F-84 bombers. The Chinese pilots, however, did not know that the American bombers were escorted by jet fighters. Surrounded by twenty U.S. F-86s, they had to battle their way out. One pilot and an MIG-15 were lost, one plane was disabled, but the Chinese claimed one downed U.S. F-86. The high-ranking officers commended Li and his pilots. In a telegram to the 4th Division commanders on September 26, the PLA Air Force Command highly praised "the bravery of [your] inexperienced pilots in fighting with more than a hundred of the enemy planes . . . and we still won the battle." On October 2, Mao Zedong also congratulated the 4th Division's "courage and spirit" in confronting the US/UN air superiority.[70]

Believing that they were ready for full participation, the CPV air force commanders decided to fly more interdiction missions. Between September 26 and October 19, the 4th Air Force Division fought seven air battles and reportedly shot down twenty U.S. aircraft and crippled ten, but its own losses remain unknown. The whole division returned to Shenyang for rest and reorganization on October 20.[71] That same day, the 3d Air Force Division, led by acting division commander Yuan Bin, moved into Andong. Although Yuan's fifty MIG-15s were originally supposed to protect the transport lines between Andong and Pyongyang, the PLA Air Force Command directed in early November that they "must determinedly engage in larger-scale air battles." Recognizing that "[we] surely will have some losses in combat," the air force authorities asserted that "we should not worry too much about [losses] and we may avoid [heavy] losses as long as [we] improve our command and combat tactics."[72] Under this mandate, the 3d division actively sought to challenge large enemy formations. From October 21, 1951, to January 14, 1952, the division flew 2,391 sorties in twenty-three groups. According to its own records, it downed fifty-five American planes and damaged eight but only lost sixteen of its own with seven disabled. Mao was extremely satisfied with the division's report on its battle results and noted on February 1, 1952, "I wholeheartedly salute and congratulate the 3d Air Force Division!"[73]

Encouraged by the CPV pilots' bravery and ability to engage U.S. air forces, Chinese air force commanders planned to involve more units in air battles in Korea. In mid-November, the Air Force Command stated that "[we] must dispatch more air units to [North Korea] to gain live combat experiences." It therefore directed that "the twenty formed units must quickly enter the battlefield as soon as they finish basic preparations. Each unit will not stay on the front too long so that other units will have the posts and chance to gain combat experience." Mao thought it was a "wonderful idea." On February 4, 1952, he instructed that "every one must fully understand the significance of obtaining actual combat experience for [our] air force; [because] it will benefit [us] even if each unit would only fight a few air battles."[74]

Between mid-November 1951 and late May 1952, the CPV air force headquarters had at its disposal nine air force divisions (the 3d, 4th, 6th, 12th,

14th, 15th, 17th, and 18th) and one regiment, with as many as 391 MIG-15 fighters. In a total of eight-five dogfights, the Chinese pilots reported that they had crippled 43 US/UN aircraft and downed 123 while only 87 of their MIG-15s were lost with 27 damaged. More important, the Chinese believed that they could eventually win the air war against the superior US/UN air forces. The Soviet air units coordinated the Chinese efforts and always sent the same number of planes as the Chinese did for each major battle, but interestingly, the Soviet pilots were somewhat disdainful of the Chinese. "It was obvious," Col. Y. G. Pepelyayes remarked later, "that the Chinese had many losses and very few victories." In his judgment, the Chinese had no talent for air combat—although another Soviet air force officer acknowledged that "the Chinese were quite capable, especially at night, but tended to become incautious in pursuit." As Jon Holliday observes, there was also resentment at the "Chinese trying to take credit for Soviet 'kills'—including the shooting down of the top U.S. ace, Major George A. Davis, Jr., on February 10, 1952." In June 1952, the CPV air force commanders began sending out air groups in combat missions without Soviet protection. After that, there was virtually no coordination between the Soviet and Chinese air forces.[75]

Though their overall mission had gradually become more offensive, the CPV air units did indeed contribute to the protection of the CPV logistical services. Their presence in North Korea strengthened the CPV air defenses in the rear areas. CPV Logistical Commander Hong happily noticed in June that American air strikes had evidently declined and the enemy had shifted from "intense destruction" to "focused bombing." He was even more pleased to learn that his rear-service corps managed to accomplish their supply and transport tasks for the first half of 1952 one-and-a-half months ahead of schedule.[76]

Early in 1952, no dispatch from Korea received more attention in Beijing than the one on US/UN bacteriological warfare. The CPV headquarters reported on January 28 that enemy planes had spread the smallpox virus in the areas southeast of Ichon. More bulletins from the Korean front in the following month suggested that the US/UN forces dropped insects, rats, shellfish, and chicken feathers with disease-causing germs in the Ichon, Chorwon, Pyongyang, and Kumhwa areas.[77] China's northeastern military headquarters also reported that from February 29 to March 5, the U.S. aircraft "sneaked" into the Northeast and released smallpox and typhus germs. Taken together, the information raised the specter that "the enemy is now trying bacteriological warfare [in Korea]."[78]

The allegations about U.S. bacteriological warfare caused the Chinese troops to panic. Rumors about deadly germs were epidemic, as the rank and file heard that the enemy had already secretly dropped more than a dozen types of germs in North Korea, carrying the plague, cholera, typhoid, bacillary dysentery, meningitis, anthrax, and purpuric fever. The soldiers were warned by field doctors that almost any creature—flies, mosquitoes, fleas, spiders, mice, hare, and birds—could be a carrier. The commander of the 19th Army Corps, Yang Dezhi, even claimed that as four U.S. aircraft flew over his headquarters one day, a piece of white mucus dropped on his sleeve that was found to contain deadly germs.[79] The Chinese troops became more nervous when they learned that in two weeks during late February and early March, thirteen Koreans and sixteen Chinese soldiers contracted cholera and the plague; of forty-five recently deceased, forty-four had been infected with meningitis. Because they were not told how those men caught the diseases, they simply assumed that the enemy was responsible.[80]

Reports about U.S. "germs warfare" brought an immediate response from Beijing. On February 18, 1952, Nie Rongzhen sent an urgent note to Mao and Zhou Enlai briefing them on countermeasures. "Other than sending [bacteriological] specialists [to Korea] for further investigations," Nie stated, "we have asked [the CPV headquarters] to send back to Beijing all insect vectors found [in the battlefield] for laboratory tests so as to verify exactly what disease germs these insects carry. Laboratory reports won't be ready for two days, but our specialists estimate that four disease germs such as cholera, typhoid, the plague, and scarlet fever are the most likely." If the laboratory tests confirmed this supposition, the first priority would be to "strengthen epidemic prevention and treatment [for the CPV]." Nie had already ordered the health division of the PLA General Logistical Department to make preparations, but he suggested that "we must ask the Soviet Union to help us out with their bacteriological specialists and materials."[81] Mao at once authorized Zhou "to pay more attention to this matter and make necessary arrangements."[82] Zhou had previously outlined the following six "urgent measures of anti–bacteriological warfare":

1. Speeding up the laboratory tests of the insect vectors sent back from the front . . . so as to identify all the disease germs
2. Dispatching epidemic prevention groups [to Korea] immediately along with vaccine, powder, and other equipment
3. Issuing a public statement to the world to denounce U.S. bacteriological warfare as war crimes and use news media to pressure the United States to be responsible for the outcomes of its bacteriological warfare
4. Instructing the National Association of Resisting America and Aiding Korea to lodge complaints with the Convention of World Peace and

request that the convention launch a campaign against U.S. bacteriological warfare

5. Sending a cable to the CPV headquarters to request that [the rank and file] be mobilized for epidemic prevention and meanwhile ordering the Northeastern Military Command to get prepared [for possible spread of disease germs in the Northeast] as well
6. Sending a telegram to the Soviet Government asking for its assistance[83]

Interestingly, Beijing authorities were more zealous about a stepped-up propaganda campaign against the United States than epidemic prevention on the front line. Moscow might have coordinated this campaign to discredit Washington or drive a wedge between the US and its allies. The mudslinging began in earnest on February 18 when Moscow radio accused the US of launching bacteriological warfare against North Korea. Four days later, the North Korean foreign minister Pak Hon-yong issued an official statement "exposing and protesting U.S. crimes of spreading smallpox and typhus bacteria in Korea." On February 24, Zhou Enlai declared to the public "on behalf of the Chinese government" that "the Chinese people and government fully support the Korean government's just claim and appeal to all the peace-loving peoples of the world against U.S. bacteriological warfare." Zhou proclaimed that "together with the peoples of the world, the Chinese people will struggle through to the end against this insane crime committed by the U.S. government."[84]

China's germ-warfare propaganda intensified in early March when northeastern CCP authorities announced that they had found "suspicious" disease-carrying insects in the Northeast. Their report indicated that local security forces had discovered a large number of paper bags containing fleas, spiders, and other "unknown insects" in the suburb of Fushun. Since these paper bags "resembled" the ones found in North Korea, they must have been dropped by the U.S. air forces. When Mao read this report, he instructed Zhou to "watch carefully and get fully prepared for" the probable expansion of U.S. bacteriological warfare to Chinese territory.[85] On March 8, Zhou issued another public statement charging the US with "employing bacteriological weapons to slaughter the Chinese people." and he warned that "the Chinese government seriously protests against this U.S. criminal act." On the same day, the Chinese news media released a series of propaganda bulletins appealing to the Chinese people "for an immediate action to meet the new challenge." The CCP authorities in the Northeast also organized a "mass demonstration" in Shenyang on March 13 involving "more than 160,000 civilians who are terribly angry at U.S. criminal acts of spreading disease germs in their homeland."[86] To further mobilize public opinion, the CCP central leadership in mid-March formed a "people's investigation group" composed of seventy "representatives" from various "noncommunist" organizations or "democratic parties." The group was sent to the Northeast and North Korea to "acquire more evidence [of U.S. germ warfare] so as to educate the Chinese people."[87]

Since springtime was usually a period of epidemic in China, in all likelihood the Chinese leaders considered it vital to alert the people to the threat of contagion. Acting Chief of Staff Nie Rongzhen proposed on March 7 that

> (1) the Northeast be regarded as an epidemic prevention zone and northern China, especially Beijing and Tianjin, as a look-out zone; since it is the Waking of Insects season [*jingzhe,* 3d solar term in Chinese calendar], . . . it is very urgent that we set up a central commission to direct the epidemic prevention work and it is appropriate to have Premier Zhou lead this; (2) [we must] mobilize the people in Beijing and Tianjin for prophylactic inoculation and urge them to pay attention to sanitation and hygiene; (3) since epidemic prevention regarding railway transportation is of special importance, [we must] form an ad hoc committee to take over charge of it; (4) [we must] actively make preparations for vaccine and other medicines [for epidemic prevention and treatment].

Mao approved Nie's proposal two days later and urged him to "speed up the preparations."[88]

On March 18, Beijing authorities launched a nationwide "patriotic health and epidemic prevention campaign." The State Council and the People's Revolutionary Military Commission issued a joint directive requesting every citizen to "kill flies, mosquitoes, and fleas and clean cities and major transportation roads." The directive announced the establishment of a central commission for epidemic prevention with Zhou Enlai as director and Guo Moruo and Nie Rongzhen as deputy directors.[89] In the next two weeks, Beijing sent out as many as 129 teams, consisting of more than 20,000 people, to set up sixty-six quarantine stations along China's seaports, border areas, and main transportation routes. A large number of doctors and nurses were also dispatched to the Northeast, and they inoculated nearly five million people against plagues.[90]

Meanwhile, the Chinese leaders tried to galvanize the CPV for epidemic prevention. In a telegram to the CPV headquarters on February 21, the CMC directed that "[you] must make the best use of your time to clean and isolate the contaminated zone, and shall never lower your vigilance and neglect the seriousness of this matter." The CMC stressed that "[you] must take precaution against possible fear or panic among the rank and file."[91] On February 25, the CMC again instructed all CPV commanders to assign top priority to epidemic prevention. "No matter how the U.S. forces might expand the bacteriological warfare," the CMC stated, "you must not hesitate or vacillate but see to it that epidemic prevention be executed quickly and resolutely; otherwise, it would be very likely that we will land ourselves in a disadvantageous position."[92] To ensure that the CPV could defeat the suspected U.S. bacteriological warfare, the CMC organized four anti–bacteriological warfare research centers in Shenyang, Beijing, Tianjin, and Qingdao in early March. It assembled more than forty bacteriologists, parasitologists, entomologists, epidemiologists, and pathologists, many of whom were sent to Korea for "on-the-spot" tests. The CMC also transported as many as 5.8 million doses of vaccines and more than 200,000 gas masks to the front.[93]

With no plan for large-scale offensives, most of the Chinese combat troops were resting and were therefore able to spend more time on disease prevention. At a CPV Party Committee meeting on March 1, Peng Dehuai assigned Deng Hua, Han Xianchu, and Hong Xuezhi to lead the "anti–bacteriological warfare" efforts. The CPV headquarters also issued a number of orders such as "Combat Units' Responsibilities for Epidemic Prevention," "Work Regulations Regarding Health and Anti–bacteriological Warfare," "Rules on Reporting Epidemic Diseases," and "Rules on Sampling and Reporting Epidemic Diseases." Unfortunately, the details of these directives remain classified, but the commanders evidently devoted much time and effort to this matter.[94] As a report by the CPV logistical command indicated, the CPV established one base test center, three front test centers, seven infectious diseases hospitals, and eleven epidemic prevention stations. Through these facilities, 96.1 percent of the combat troops were inoculated against plagues, 92.3 percent against typhoid, and 73.5 percent were given smallpox vaccinations.[95]

The CPV epidemic prevention seems to have been effective. The CPV health department inspected ten infantry armies late in 1952 and found an improvement in the troops' overall health. According to this report, on average only 27 percent of the soldiers carried fleas, and the number of men contracting infectious diseases had been greatly reduced. The CPV health officers then pronounced that "we have smashed the enemy's bacteriological warfare."[96] More important, the Communist propaganda campaign had put the U.S. government on the defensive in its negotiations over the Korean War. In Europe, particularly among the neutral states, there was "stirring worldwide reaction against the United States."[97]

It is noteworthy that Chinese historians who have written about the Korean War seem to have mixed feelings about the alleged U.S. bacteriological warfare. Some who are doubtful about the validity of the charge ignore the subject; some follow the Chinese official line that the US did spread disease germs in Korea and the Northeast and that the Chinese "won the germ warfare." As one Chinese historian argues, the truth about U.S. bacteriological warfare in Korea will remain hidden until the U.S. government declassifies the related documents.[98] In the English literature, however, scholars have not found any hard evidence to support the Communist assertion that the US employed germs to fight the war.[99] Yet Chinese scholars and officials alike remain adamant that Beijing did not overreact to rumors of germ warfare in Korea. In the prevailing atmosphere of preparing for the worst, no CCP leader would have downplayed the danger of a possible bacteriological war in Korea. The available evidence suggests, first, that there was no solid or scientific proof of actual U.S. use of bacteriological weapons; indeed, there is little information about how the Chinese scientists investigated the charges, what conclusions, if any, they reached, and what they reported to the top leadership. Second, given the absence of corroboration, Beijing authorities seemed more interested in exploiting the allegations for propaganda purposes, both domestic and international, as China's anti–germ warfare campaign continued.

The heralded conquest of "U.S. germ warfare" helped to confirm the CCP leaders' romantic disdain of modern technology. It reinforced their belief that human spirit, creativity, and subjective strength would ultimately prevail over all advanced technology, including chemical, bacteriological, or even nuclear weapons. Were the US to employ germs or even an atomic bomb in Korea, it would only prove to the Chinese that Washington was at its wit's end.

IV

The Chinese had reason to be heartened at this point. Since the summer of 1951, the Chinese Communist forces had encountered serious challenges—unprecedented in their military history—including fighting a positional defense, protecting logistics from devastating US/UN air interdiction efforts, and executing anti–bacteriological warfare. Having barely survived these challenges, the CCP leaders were now confident of conducting a stalemated war. As Nie Rongzhen recounted, the CPV troops had displayed their "dauntless and self-sacrificing spirit in their utter disregard of hardship and danger," and there was no obstacle that the troops could not overcome.[100]

The Chinese commanders drew the salutary conclusion that the soldiers had to be creative in dealing with extreme and unexpected difficulties. To them, the troops succeeded in transforming their "subjective world" while also transforming the "objective world." The CPV positional defense capabilities had developed spontaneously when the combat forces learned how to fight tunnel warfare and made the tunnels effective in meeting the requirements of Mao's doctrine: "preserve oneself and destroy the enemy." Hundreds of thousands of rear servicemen demonstrated even more "conscious" abilities. The Chinese Communist forces had never had systemic logistics, and the Korean terrain rendered operations difficult even for an experienced and well-equipped rear-service unit. The CPV logistical units, which had no training or equipment, wracked their brains in the handling of every detail of their daily routines. Given a huge combat army to serve as well as the relentless enemy air raids to guard against, the CPV rear servicemen slowly but surely learned how to collect, transport, store, distribute, and protect military supplies and were amazingly successful in their mission.

The Chinese leaders might have been too creative when they called for anti–bacteriological warfare; however, the troops were able to maintain relatively high morale and evidently improved their health overall. More important, the leaders were encouraged that they had shattered even the enemy's efforts at "germs warfare" and were keen to have their condemnation of the U.S. "criminal act" reverberate around the world.

The Chinese leaders also believed that the CPV was getting stronger as time went on, but this optimism was paid for in blood. The CPV lost as many as 36,000 combat troops during this period of positional defense.[101] Although the CPV forces had replenished their supplies and replaced their casualties by the summer of 1952, they saw no hope for a quick and decisive victory. "Since victory or defeat is determined by many different factors," Nie conceded later, "[in Korea], we could only strive for a better outcome whenever the objective conditions permitted; we could by no means win victory beyond what objective conditions would permit."[102]

8. MOBILIZATION OF MINDS ON THE BATTLEFIELD

CCP military leaders regarded combat morale, or *shiqi*, as one of the most important elements in determining victory or defeat. It was especially essential when a weak army confronted a strong enemy. As long as the weak army maintained a high morale in combat, it would eventually defeat a better equipped opponent. To the Chinese Communist forces, Korea was another battleground to test the validity of this belief.

To evaluate the military *shiqi*, Chinese military commanders often looked for three key elements: bravery and courage [*yongqi*]; benevolence and harmony [*renyi*]; and discipline and justice [*yanji*]. The achievement of these attributes, according to CCP military experience, depended on a highly centralized system of political work in the military [*jundui zhengzhi gongzuo*].

I

"When two adversaries come into unavoidable confrontation," a traditional Chinese military doctrine teaches, "the one with greater courage will win [*xialu xiang feng yongzhe sheng*]."[1] This axiom seems to have dictated the CPV's mobilization efforts. In the early period of China's entry into the war, there was among the rank and file a profound fear and a sense of uncertainty about engaging the American forces and their superior equipment. After the US/UN Inchon landing in mid-September, the overwhelming pessimism of both the North Korean forces and the Soviet advisers in Korea conveyed even stronger negative messages to the Chinese troops, who seemed to believe that, with no air forces or heavy artillery, the Chinese intervention would have the same fate as the North Korean campaign. A survey conducted by the 13th Army Corps Political Department in mid-August suggested that a significant portion of the troops were afraid of coming up against American airplanes, heavy artillery guns, and even atomic bombs.[2]

To overcome the troops' fear, the CCP leadership placed a great emphasis on bravery and courage. Speaking as a figure of authority, Mao Zedong repeatedly asserted that China should not be in awe of American military superiority. "As regard to war [with the United States]," he stated at the CPGC's ninth plenary meeting on September 5, 1950, "we are absolutely not afraid. This is because we have a party and an armed force with twenty-three years experience of armed struggle, [but] the U.S. imperialists have a lot of problems including internal wrangling, disharmony with the allies, and some militarily unmanageable difficulties." He assured his audience that "we are bound to triumph over" the US in the end, even if "we would fight [U.S.] atomic bombs with our grenades."[3] In his October 8 directive on the dispatch of the CPV, Mao appealed to all troops, declaring that "[you] must have a profound understanding of all the possible difficulties we will encounter, and [you] must be prepared to overcome these difficulties with immense zeal, courage, care, and painstaking spirit." Believing that "current international and domestic situations are favoring us, not the aggressors," he pronounced that "as long as you comrades are resolute and brave, as long as you comrades get along well with the local people, as long as you comrades are adept in fighting against the invaders, final victory surely belongs to us!"[4]

Mao selected Peng Dehuai as the field commander in Korea partly because of Peng's reputation as a courageous fighter. As a senior CCP military commander, Peng had assumed the most difficult missions, perhaps more than anyone else in the CCP's military history. He had often survived arduous conditions and won tough battles because of his ability to cope with difficult situations. Shortly before entering Korea, Peng joked with other CPV commanders that "I am decreed by fate to bear hardships." But he was optimistic that "a revolutionary [fighter] with great zeal and courage can always surmount difficulties." Understanding that his troops should be as bold as he was, Peng requested the CPV political officials to focus on convincing the rank and file that as long as they did not flinch from hardship or death, they were bound to be victorious. In early October, he inspected the 13th Army Corps garrisons in Andong and told the troops that "under the leadership of Chairman Mao, we will have no obstacles [that we cannot overcome], and there will be no undefeatable enemy."[5] When he first spoke to the CPV army and division commanders on October 16, Peng went to great lengths to explain why he thought the CPV would win. "Although the United States enjoys air superiority at present time," he asserted, "air force cannot determine the outcome of war." It was more important that "our troops are resolute and brave, adept in hard-fought battles; . . . our troops' political quality is much higher than that of the enemy . . . [because the enemy] is fighting for imperialism, its peoples are opposed to it, and its soldiers are tired of war. We are fighting for a just war and a struggle for national liberation, and we will win over sympathy and support of the peoples from all over the world." To Peng, these were "the fundamental factors that will determine the war's outcome."[6]

As much as military preparations, the CPV commanders took political mobilization very seriously. One of their methods was to instill in the troops' minds the conviction that "we are daring and capable of fighting U.S. aggressive forces." As the 13th Army Corps Political Department instructed in mid-October, it was imperative to spread the word that the U.S. military suffered from vital strategic and tactical weaknesses in Korea, including "fighting an unjust war, lack of sufficient reinforcement, low morale of the soldiers, and overextended supply lines." At the same time, the CPV troops should be told that "our forces are a just and victorious army; . . . we are under the brilliant leadership of Chairman Mao, enjoy the vigorous support of our own peoples, the Korean people, and all the peace-loving peoples all over the world; . . . we have the rich experience of defeating superior enemies, and the Korean terrain is in favor of our tactics of close and night combat."[7] To build up the troops' confidence, Peng considered it essential to compare and contrast CPV strength with that of the enemy. After reviewing the "Political Mobilization Order for the First [Phase] Offensive" drafted by CPV political department director Du Ping, he commented that "for an order of this type, you must start with the reality of the enemy and ourselves, list out favorable and unfavorable conditions [concerning us], and go to full lengths to explain the conditions that will guarantee our victory." He underscored that "[you] should never put about hollow slogans." As vivid and convincing evidence of the "true face" of the U.S. armed forces, CPV political officers organized special presentations by KMT defectors who had received training from American military advisers. These soldiers' accounts left the strong impression that American troops were "spoiled playboys" and altogether inept at close combat and night battles.[8]

Another mobilization program was to arouse the troops' hatred and enmity against "the U.S. aggressors." Early in September 1950, the 13th Army Corps Political Department distributed a handbook on "Historical Facts of U.S. Imperialist Invasions of China." Beginning with the first presence of the U.S. Navy along China's coasts in the 1830s, the publication noted that the US forced the Qing [Ching] government to sign the unequal Sino-American Tianjin Treaty in 1858, that the U.S. military joined seven other foreign nations to suppress China's Boxer Rebellion in 1900, and that the American government supported Chiang Kai-shek's civil war against the Chinese Communists. The propaganda averred that "U.S. imperialists are trying to do the same as Japanese imperialists have done to China, namely, to seize Korea first and invade China second." The handbook also pointed out that "now that American aggressive forces already occupy our territory Taiwan, constantly bomb our towns and villages along the northeastern border with their air force, and send out naval vessels to shell our civilian ships, all these numerous facts prove that U.S. imperialists are the most dangerous enemy of the Chinese people."[9]

As part of the campaign to incite hostility toward "American devils [*meiguo guizi*]," CPV political officers organized various "self-education" activities. One such activity was to encourage the soldiers to pour out the grievances of their personal lives. Those who had endured hardship would be asked to publicly relate how the Japanese devils and the KMT "reactionaries" destroyed their families and ruined their lives. They were strongly urged to blame the U.S. imperialist policy toward China for their sufferings under the Nationalist rule. "It was the U.S. government," the political officers reminded the troops, "who supplied the KMT traitors with weapons and bombs to kill the poor Chinese people." Between September and October 1950, each company's political instructor held several such meetings and asked the soldiers to exchange memories of their personal experiences. These vivid stories told by comrades, often with great emotion, seldom failed to move the troops. The seeds of hatred, in the judgment of the CPV political officers, were thus deeply sown in the minds of the soldiers.[10] Another self-education technique was to invite the Korean people to tell how the US/UN aggressors brought about the calamities in Korea. An old Korean man would be invited to recall how all of his family members were killed during U.S. air raids; a young Korean woman would tell "true" stories about how many Korean girls were raped and abused by the enemy troops (without specifying exactly whether they were American or South Korean troops); or a local Korean leader would make a presentation on how many Korean children were orphaned. Company political instructors would also take the soldiers to view burned-down houses and unburied dead bodies. The Chinese soldiers were led to believe that "should we allow U.S. imperialists to invade China, they would inflict the same sufferings on our people as on the Korean people."[11]

A primary objective of these activities was to convince the Chinese troops that they were fighting for their own interests. By such means, the CPV political officers expected to mold valiant souls willing to sacrifice their lives in combat. Before taking the first offensive in late October, company political instructors required every soldier to hand in a written pledge stating his determination to fight the enemy to death. "Don't leave the front line on account of minor wounds" and "as long as I am alive I will hold up my position" became the most popular slogans of those pledges.[12] These instructors also arranged group meetings in which each soldier would swear an oath drafted and printed by the CPV political department:

> We are Chinese People's Volunteers. For the purposes of opposing U.S. imperialist brutal aggression, assisting the national liberation movement of the Korean brothers, and defending the interests of the Chinese, Korean, and Asian peoples, we enter the Korean War on our own free will to fight shoulder to shoulder with the Korean people against the common enemy and for shared victory. To accomplish this great and glorious mission, we are determined to fight a brave and indomitable struggle; we will follow orders without any conditions and advance to wherever we are directed to; we will never be afraid of nor waiver before death and hardship; we will keep up our staunch spirit in enduring hardship and danger and carry forward the revolutionary heroism to render outstanding services in battles; we will respect the leadership of [North] Korean people's leader General Kim Il-sung and learn from the brave and prudent spirit of the [North] Korean People's Army in combat; we will never offend the Korean peoples' customs or life styles and value every piece of property in Korea; we shall unite with the Korean people and armed forces to destroy U.S. imperialist forces of aggression resolutely and completely.[13]

After the CPV entered Korea, political work focused on exhorting the troops to contend for the title of hero. The CPV political department sent military and civilian correspondents to each infantry army and some divisions to track down and report heroic deeds. During the second-phase offensive, the 112th Division of the 38th Army fought a fierce battle in Samso-ri in late November 1950. The 3d Company of the 335th Regiment, under company leader Dai Yuyi, stood firmly against the severe assaults of the units of U.S. 2d Division. Dai and some of his soldiers were killed during the first few waves of the U.S. attack. The company's political instructor immediately called on the men to avenge Dai's death. The rest of the company then responded by hurling themselves into the U.S. attacking forces with only bayonets, grenades, rocks, and even fists. When reinforcements arrived, only six wounded soldiers led by the deputy political instructor were left in the company's position. A senior CCP propaganda official, Wei Wei, who had been with the 38th Army, immediately wrote a field report entitled "Who Are the Most Lovable Men?" that gave a detailed and vivid description of how the whole company sacrificed themselves in combat. When this report was passed among the troops, it fostered a strong sentiment that "we must seek revenge for the 3d Company and to learn from the 3d Company in order to become a most lovable man."[14]

Another heroic deed that the CPV political department highly publicized was the suicidal charge made by Yang Gensi. Yang was a company leader in the 50th Division and had been well-known as a courageous hero during the CCP-KMT civil war. His company joined a blocking action against the U.S. 1st Marine Division in Yudam-ri during the second-phase offensive. On the morning of November 29, Yang led one platoon to build a defense post on a hill. Shortly afterward, U.S. Marines attacked Yang's position but failed to seize it after nine attempts. When the enemy's tenth assault began, Yang only had two wounded soldiers at his disposal. Expecting no reinforcements and seeing no hope of holding the hill, he grabbed an explosive charge and waited for the enemy troops to close in. As more than forty American marines climbed up the slope, Yang dashed toward them and detonated the charge. His suicidal attack scared the marines into an immediate retreat. Witnessing this astonishing event, the two surviving wounded soldiers asked their superiors to promise that their beloved company leader would be avenged. The CPV political department took Yang as an excellent role model of bravery and courage and launched a publicity campaign to "learn from Yang Gensi." The CPV headquarters named the company after Yang and printed a series of tracts on his poor family, difficult childhood, heroic deeds during the civil war, and, most of all, his willingness to give his life to defend a position in Korea. These materials were widely circulated among the CPV troops.[15]

While urging the rank and file not to fear death or hardship, Peng Dehuai believed that the high-ranking commanders should be exemplars. Before each battle or campaign, he would request the army and division commanders to move their command posts as close to the front as possible. Peng himself demanded on several occasions that the CPV headquarters be established near the front line. He would frequently inspect the combat troops in the bunkers and trenches to convey the idea that he, the supreme commander, was always with his troops on the front, facing the same danger and bearing the same hardship.[16]

To that end, Peng made the tough decision to inter Mao Anying, Mao's eldest son, in Korea. Mao Anying had had a very hard life when he was a child because his father was considered a most-wanted man by the Nationalists. In the late 1930s, he was sent to the Soviet Union to study military science. When he returned a decade later, his father urged him to experience other occupations, and the young Anying had thus become a farmer and then a worker. Before the Korean War, he had served as a deputy party secretary of the Beijing Machinery Plant. The twenty-eight-year-old Mao Anying volunteered to join the CPV, a decision his father supported. Concerned about Anying's safety, Peng declined his request to command an infantry regiment and appointed him as his secretary and Russian language interpreter at the headquarters. On the morning of November 24, 1950, a US/UN air raid hit the CPV headquarters. While Peng and other command personnel took shelter in a nearby tunnel, Mao Anying and staff officer Gao Ruixin were trapped inside of Peng's office, which was actually an abandoned cabin in an open field. An incendiary bomb hit the timber structure and killed Mao and Gao. Everyone at the headquarters was shocked. Peng immediately asked CPV Chief of Staff Xie Fang to inform Mao of his son's death. When the CPV's deputy political commissar, Lai Chuanzhu, suggested shipping Mao Anying's body home, Peng rejected the idea and insisted that Mao Anying should be buried in Korea like any other dead CPV soldier. That night, he cabled Zhou Enlai, advocating that "in my opinion, [Mao Anying's body] ought to be buried in North Korea. I, on behalf of the CPV Command, will inscribe a tombstone tablet indicating that he joined the CPV on his free will and died in the battlefield, and he has proven himself as a fine son of Mao Zedong." Peng added that "to bury Mao Anying together with staff officer Gao Ruixin [in North Korea] will be of a great significance as regard to the Korean people and will serve to comfort others who lost their sons and daughters [in Korea]." After consulting with Liu Shaoqi and Deng Xiaoping, Zhou agreed with Peng but decided not to inform Mao of his son's death.[17] Mao was greatly surprised when several months later Peng told him about Mao Anying's death and apologized for failing to protect him. The CCP chairman was deeply grieved but absolved Peng because "Anying has done just his duty." Mao told the CPV commander to inform the troops that "Anying was merely one of those many ordinary CPV soldiers who died in the war to resist the US, aid Korea, and defend our own country." He also agreed with Peng that Mao Anying should be buried in Korea because "that represents the characteristic of our revolutionary spirit to share weal and woe."[18]

Nevertheless, the Chinese troops were unprepared for the demands of the war in Korea. From the first- to the third-phase offensives, the CPV forces advanced an average of 300 miles. Most of the infantrymen marched on foot and had to carry their rations and ammunition. The mountainous terrain and the harsh winter rendered combat life almost unbearable. From October to December the troops hardly rested. Taking offensive actions at night, they had to watch for US/UN air raids during the day. Complaints that "we would never fear the enemy's brutality but we are so afraid of running short of munitions and having nothing to eat" rose from the rank and file.[19] To solve these problems, CPV political department head Du Ping called a meeting in late November of each army's political director. These high-ranking officers conceded that "in stimulating the troops' bravery and courage, we talked too much about our advantages and too little about difficulties, and consequently we misled our troops into underestimating problems in real life." The CPV political work, they suggested, should be more realistic. "We should give an objective analysis of our weaknesses and the enemy's advantages," they asserted, "[and] we should assist the troops in building up confidence for victory [so that they will be able to] endure severe hardships in a protracted war." Moreover, they discovered that their routine political programs did not function at all. Company instructors, in particular, were only good at giving mobilization talks and organizing oath-taking and pledge-making ceremonies, which had only short-term effect. To sustain the troops' courage to bear and overcome difficulties required the constant and systematic attention of the political officers.[20]

To improve the political work, the CPV political officers gave CCP organizations a crucial role. Following the military tradition of the Chinese Communists, the CPV had established a close-knit party network. At the very top was the CPV Party Committee with Peng as the chief. Every army, division, regiment, and battalion had its own party committee, generally headed by political commissars or battalion instructors. The committees at these levels would frequently meet to make decisions on both military and political matters. However, the most important party instrument was the party branch at the company level [*lian dui dangzhibu*]. In most cases, the company political instructor was the branch secretary, and the company leader was deputy secretary. Other branch offices included deputy company leader, deputy political instructor, and two or three platoon leaders, and there were also party groups formed by the soldiers. The company party branch controlled the Communist Youth League branch [*tuanzhibu*], composed of those who expected to join the party. This youth league was also divided into several groups. Indoctrination at the company level operated through meetings of these two branches—the youth league and the company party—and the individual membership.[21]

Regarding company party branch members as the backbone of political work, the CPV political department requested each army political department to provide instruction. The trainees would assemble for a week-long session on how to function more effectively. According to the CPV political department's statistics, an average of six to seven people from each company had undergone this training in 1951, seven to eight in 1952, and eight to nine in 1953. During the sessions, the party and youth league members were taught how to be role models. Mao's teaching that "our party members must be the first to bear hardships and the last to enjoy comforts" became their motto. Specifically, the party members were to assume the most dangerous combat tasks and perform difficult jobs such as carrying food and ammunition and standing guard while others slept. The trainees also learned one-on-one methods of indoctrination. Formal meetings, for example, were less effective than informal conversations. Party and league members should make friends with nonmember soldiers by listening to their problems and offering help. Closely watching the words and actions of members and nonmembers, the party branch leaders would be able to control the mind and behavior of every soldier. Finally, the trainees were taught how to organize themselves as a party branch even in the most severe situations. In combat, if the deaths of party branch members rendered the branch inoperative, the remnant members should either form a temporary branch or join another unit's branch. Party branches, the CPV political officials insisted, should exist everywhere and at all times.[22]

However, the losses of the 180th Division during the fifth-phase offensive in late May 1951 generated enormous pessimism among the rank and file. In explaining what had gone wrong, the CPV political department concluded that the blame fell on the weak political control the division had long exercised. "First, the division commanders paid no attention to the construction of company party branches," the department's report pointed out; "second, the party members were not encouraged to keep up with our revolutionary heroism, and they were poorly prepared for tough battles and lacked confidence in overcoming difficulties; third, many military and political officers were not qualified as a role model in commanding the troops, . . . fourth, the whole division suffered from poor disciplines and the tradition of criticism and self-criticism was abandoned." This clearly demonstrated that political work in the military was a life-and-death matter, and the CPV political department directed commanders at all levels to learn the lessons of the 180th division experience.[23]

II

As much as bravery and courage, Chinese military leaders believed, benevolence and harmony were elements of morale. China's traditional military teachings stress the importance of amity and the unity of armed forces, or *shi he*. An amiable and harmonious army, Sun Tzu asserts, would enjoy a high combat spirit [*qi sheng*] and would "be ever-victorious wherever it advances." Wu Tzu also warns that "without domestic harmony [*he yu guo*], one should not enter a war; without military unity [*he yu jun*], one should not engage in combat operations; without frontal concord [*he yu zhen*], one should not take offensive actions." According to these ancient strategists, commanders should exercise tremendous care, love, trust, and encouragement in order to build a benevolent and harmonious army.[24] Such teachings had a great impact on the political work of the CCP armed forces, especially in dealing with relationships between political authorities and military commanders, civilians and servicemen, and officers and soldiers. There can be little doubt that CPV political officers observed these traditions fully in the Korean War.

An important program to promote unity was the CPV's "outstanding service" award. At a CPV party meeting in late April 1951, political director Du Ping stated that a central task of each party organization was to turn the minds of the troops wholly toward the war. A traditional way, he asserted, was a political campaign identifying and rewarding model services so as to encourage the rank and file to learn by example. As a resolution of this meeting, the CPV political department issued "Chinese People's Volunteers' Regulations Regarding Rendering Meritorious Service," a twenty-five-page document detailing standards and procedures for selecting, approving, and recognizing remarkable deeds. "An outstanding service campaign," the guide's first paragraph read, "is one of the fine traditions of the Chinese people's army. . . . It mainly aims at boosting morale, encouraging contribution-making, and stimulating everyone's enthusiasm and creativity. It embodies tremendous effectiveness in keeping up the people's army to always march forward, triumph over the enemies all the time, and accomplish every difficult mission." As a "best method" to spread "revolutionary heroism," this document exhorted that "we Chinese People's Volunteers must carry on this fine tradition by popularizing the outstanding service campaign in the entire [CPV] armed forces, and establishing it as an important routine of [our] political work."[25]

A key element of the campaign was to get every serviceman involved. The regulations stressed that "we must make sure that everyone render meritorious service in carrying out every task." However, those who have done a deed of merit that goes beyond an average standard are qualified for an outstanding service medal; and those who have made one or several extraordinary contributions, demonstrated fine political qualities, and enjoyed popular esteem and respect are to be named hero or model." The CPV political department set up four categories of outstanding service—third, second, first, and special class—and three for heroes and models—second, first, and special grades. Although company deputy political instructors were responsible for nominating candidates, the regulations enjoined "every ordinary soldier to take notes or record his and others' achievement." To collect sufficient evidence about potential nominees, each squad was required to meet at least once a month to record the "meritorious deeds" of every squad member and, more important, to let each person know how much he would need to accomplish in order to own an outstanding service medal or to earn the title of hero of model. There would be a general nomination every six months or immediately after a battle or campaign. Supervised by the Revolutionary Servicemen Committee and the Communist Youth League, each company would meet to select candidates, and deputy instructors would report the names to regiment or division political departments for approval. The CPV political department requested that these procedures be incorporated into each company's routines.[26]

The CPV's political department also set up brief and concrete standards for the award. Broadly, what was required was a demonstration of "bravery and skills in battles, acting in friendly, unified, alert, earnest, lively way, and [of] willingness to help others in noncombat situations." A meritorious service award would be given to "those who destroy enemy obstacles, one bunker, one tank, or supply storage with explosive packages or grenades or bring down one enemy airplane with anti-aircraft guns; those who are good at annihilating the enemy forces with light infantry weapons at no or small costs; those who sneak into enemy positions and capture an enemy officer, or a scout or guard; and those who do not leave the front line on account of minor wounds or are always in the van to advance and in the rear to evacuate." In a noncombat situation, honors would go to those who "play a role model in helping others to overcome difficulties such as caring about the wounded and the new recruits," those who "are active in thinking to improve combat tactics or technique, . . . and have excellent outcomes in training or mutual learning activities," and those who "strictly observe disciplines, always respect local people and authorities, take good care of weapons and equipment, and are good at criticism and self-criticism." CPV political authorities further stipulated that those "who have owned two medals of third or second class or one of the first-grade award, who are mostly outstanding at an army or army corps level, and whose remarkable contributions are also recognized by friendly units" would be named heroes or models.[27]

CPV political leaders intended to make the outstanding service awards impressively staged events. With regard to the prize-giving ceremony, they specified that

> a third-class award owner is to be announced and presented with the medal at a celebration meeting, his name is to be listed on the [CPV] newspapers, and a report on his outstanding service is to be sent to his family or hometown; a second- or first-class award owner is to be praised by a [CPV] order of commendation, to have a picture taken in front of

> the [CPV] army flag, and to be listed on the newspapers, and a report on his outstanding service is to be sent to his family or hometown; a special-grade award owner is to have an order of commendation, a picture taken in front of the army flag, and a report on his prize sent home, and moreover, his deeds are to be compiled and broadcast nationwide [in China].

As for posthumous awards, the recipient's heroic service would be recorded in the army's history book, and his tombstone would bear a tablet describing his meritorious deeds. The CPV political department made it very clear that every award winner should be treated to a serious yet grand celebration. Each company, battalion, and regiment would have its own ceremony involving every man of the unit. Every six months there would be a commemoration at the division level, and once a year at the army level. Moreover, all celebrative activities should "aim at encouraging and educating the troops by giving publicity to these heroic and meritorious deeds so as to promote the outstanding service campaign."[28]

The North Korean authorities complemented the CPV's outstanding service campaign by issuing military exploits medals to CPV soldiers in June 1951. Using it as a vehicle to promote its own campaign, the CPV political department announced that all those who had earned one first-class or two second-class citations were eligible to receive the Korean awards. It proclaimed that "it is more glorious to win honors in the Korean War than in any other wars. [Because] we are making contributions not only for the Chinese people but for the Korean people and the peoples all over the world. It is an international honor."[29] One of North Korea's top officials presided over the first ceremony at the CPV headquarters in early July. Awarding Peng Dehuai and seventeen other CPV outstanding servicemen with the first-class flag medals, the North Korean leader proclaimed that "the [North] Korean people will never forget the heroic contributions that you have made." Throughout the war, the North Korean government held five ceremonies to honor the CPV, granted the Chinese as many as 526,354 medals, and named twelve CPV heroes (including Peng) as the "Republic Heroes of North Korea." To win an international honor was exalted as an important incentive for the Chinese troops to fight heroically in Korea.[30]

The CPV's outstanding service campaign also found tremendous support in China. As early as December 1950, Beijing authorities made it compulsory to "support the army [in Korea] and give preferential treatment to families [of the CPV] [*yongjun youshu*]." The Ministry of Internal Affairs and the PLA General Political Department cosponsored a directive on December 22 that the favorable treatment of CPV families should a be central task of local governments during 1951. On November 9, 1951, the CPGC approved a report by Minister of Internal Affairs Xie Juezhai that led off with the statement, "We must take seriously the work of offering special care to the families of [CPV] servicemen." "This work," Xie pointed out, "is a long-term political task . . . to show our support to the people's army as Chairman Mao has instructed." He proposed that "every county's people council must prioritize this work in its routines; every county, district, and village must assign special persons to supervise this work; and all the local authorities must regularly meet with the families of servicemen to listen to their problems so as to resolve them promptly." The single objective, Xie concluded, was to assure the military servicemen that their families were respected and cared for.[31]

The CCP local authorities did their best to look after the CPV families. In the countryside, they would assign these families the best land in the land reform, and village leaders would arrange help for the needy families. Some county authorities even adopted a policy of "four guarantees" (guaranteeing thorough ploughing, prompt weeding, careful cultivation, and a 10 percent increase in crop yield) and "five priorities" (priority to ploughing, weeding, hoeing, harvesting, and storing) in succoring the CPV families. Officials also called on local people to donate money, food, and clothing to the soldiers' kin. In cities and towns, the focus was on "assisting the CPV family members in finding jobs and providing material help." Some cities opened new factories or shops exclusively for the CPV family members. Statistics indicated that in October 1951, the municipal government of Chongqing created 61 production units and 1,977 jobs for the CPV families; in 1952, Wuhan and Guangzhou provided employment for 3,734 CPV family members. In most cities and towns, the CPV families were assured of sufficient food, clothing, and medical care. During festivals and holidays, the local CCP leaders paid special visits to these families, and neighbors and schoolmates were enjoined to offer extra hospitality. In January 1951, a central government notice on "showing support and appreciation to the CPV families during the spring festival" charged that "we must make sure that the CPV families spend a joyful spring festival . . . and that every member [of the CPV families] has a comfortable and satisfactory holiday."[32]

The local authorities directly coordinated with the CPV's outstanding service campaign by organizing jubilant celebrations whenever a report on military exploits arrived from Korea. They would honor the recipient's family with a letter of thanks or a *jin bian*—a horizontal board inscribed with words of praise that was traditionally considered a high honor for patriotism. The leaders would personally present a board emblazoned with "A CPV Hero's Family" or "A Glorious Family" and hang it in the family's living room. The authorities would then ask CPV family members, especially parents, wife, or fiancée, to write to the soldier not only to express pride but also to relate how well they were cared for (especially the elderly and the children) and how other people respected them. Most of all, the family letters would exhort the servicemen to strive for more honors. CPV soldiers who had not yet earned medals would receive letters from their families filled with anxiety about their failure to achieve a military exploit. When these family letters reached the front, they put great pressure on the troops. Honor and pride drove the CPV soldiers to aim for heroic contributions in battle.[33]

The CCP leaders tried to make the campaign to support the CPV a nationwide effort. On December 1, 1950, the CPPCC called on the Chinese people to send gift bags containing gloves, underwear, pens, notebooks, and letters of appreciation to the CPV troops. It also encouraged the donation of money to finance the CPV's fight in Korea.[34] College students were the first to respond with enthusiasm. Three days after the CPPCC's announcement, the students of Yanjing University in Beijing mailed out more than 300 thank-you letters and 600 gift bags. Although many students donated merely a bar of soap, toothbrush or toothpaste, and towel, all of them enclosed notes praising the CPV. Residents in the big cities soon followed suit. In Nanjing, more than 20,000 letters of appreciation and 5,000 gift bags were sent out within a few days. Between December 1950 and January 1951, as many as 450,000 letters of thanks, 360,000 gift bags, and 1,140,000 renminbi reached the Korean front. Some letters were especially touching. One read, "As a teacher, I will encourage my students to join the volunteer army to become your reinforcement." Another stated, "I saved this cake of soap for you so that you can clean off the enemy's blood sprinkled on your clothes and prepare for another battle." Exchanging these letters soon became a daily activity among the CPV troops.[35]

The practice of sending gifts escalated into a large-scale movement to raise money, especially to purchase Soviet weaponry for the CPV. On June 1, 1951, the Federation of Chinese People to Resist U.S. Aggression and Aid Korea appealed to the whole nation to donate funds to "buy aircraft and artillery for the volunteer army to enhance their combat effectiveness." The appeal stated that "the biggest difficulty [the CPV suffers] is the lack of powerful weapons such as airplanes and artillery guns; . . . in order to support them and to win a final victory, we must supply them with more aircraft, heavy cannons, tanks, anti-aircraft artillery, and antitank guns." Five days later, the federation listed the cost of different weapons in China's major newspapers: 150,000 renminbi for a MIG fighter, 250,000 for a Soviet tank, and 90,000 for a piece of long-range artillery. It also detailed the procedures for making contributions.[36] Given the nation's poor economy at this time, however, collecting money was a rather formidable task for the CCP local authorities. Although donations were to be voluntary, they became a contractual obligation in many places. In numerous private businesses, workers had to sign a "contract of patriotism [*aiguo gongyue*]" to "donate" a certain portion of their salary to the CPV. Factory workers and farmers had to pledge to produce more and to donate the increase of their production yields. Government officials signed agreements to reduce expenses and save for the CPV weapons. The outcome of this campaign, which formally ended on June 24, 1952, seemed very impressive. By the end of May 1952, the federation had collected a total of 556.5 million renminbi—enough to purchase 3,710 MIG fighters. More important than the amount raised, the weapons bought with the donated money would be inscribed with the names of donors, and when they were shipped to the front, the troops would be deeply inspired by the knowledge that the motherland was truly behind them.[37]

The leaders in Beijing were closely involved in promoting the political campaign. In 1951, they decided to invite some CPV heroes to celebrate National Day in Beijing. When the CMC invitation arrived on September 26, Peng Dehuai was very pleased and instructed Du Ping to let the troops know how much "the central leadership cares about our political well-being."[38] The next day, Du and ninety-eight CPV heroes set out for Beijing. At the railway station, they were welcomed by more than 3,000 government officials and well-wishers in a splendid ceremony. The Chinese soldiers were greeted by large crowds wherever they went. On the evening of September 30, Mao, Zhu De, and Zhou Enlai hosted a huge banquet in the heroes' honor at Zhongnanhai. Mao gave a toast to the CPV representatives: "I congratulate your victories. Let's drink to the health of Comrade Peng Dehuai and all the CPV servicemen who are fighting bloody battles in Korea!" Other leaders, including Zhu, Zhou, Liu Shaoqi, Dong Biwu, Luo Ronghuan, and Nie Rongzhen, followed Mao in hailing the CPV heroes. These honorees were overwhelmed because they had never imagined that "an ordinary soldier can dine together with the country's top leaders."[39] The next morning, all the CPV heroes were invited to stand with Mao and other leaders on the rostrum at Tiananmen Square to inspect the parades celebrating National Day. Du Ping was asked by the central leadership to report to the CPPCC's third plenary meeting on the afternoon of October 29. Mao and other top officials attended and applauded Du's speech. Meanwhile, other CPV representatives recounted their heroic exploits at numerous mass meetings. When they returned to Korea, their stories about the visit to Beijing excited enthusiasm among the troops and held out the hope of similar rewards. Peng thus decided to send another CPV delegation of 170 soldiers back home on January 18,

1952. These propaganda missions promoted the outstanding service campaign by inspiring the troops to make great military contributions and thereby earn a chance to meet Chairman Mao in Beijing.[40]

At the same time, the PLA political department sent mass delegations to inspect the troops in Korea in what was called the "coming-and-going" program. In early April 1951, Liao Chengzhi, president of the Chinese Youth Union, led the first group to Korea. Saluting the CPV on behalf of the Chinese people, Liao and 174 other visitors brought with them more than 2,000 boxes of gifts, 1,093 silk banners printed with words of appreciation, and thousands of thank-you letters. This contingent of farmers, workers, scientists, professors, artists, writers, singers, and dancers was divided into eight groups and toured the CPV front positions. Wherever they went, they would talk to the servicemen and encourage them to win honors for their parents and loved ones. The artists and musicians also performed for the troops. The one-month visit comforted many servicemen and lifted their spirits. "I no longer feel home-sick," one soldier claimed; "I feel just like my friends and folks are visiting me." Others wrote that "when I am with the delegation, [I feel] I am with Chairman Mao and my parents."[41] Since this visit was successful, Beijing authorities sent another delegation, this time consisting of 1,097 people, in September 1952. For more than forty days, the group inspected CPV combat units and held more than 3,100 meetings with the troops. As tribute, each serviceman recieved a tea cup inscribed with the words, "This Is for the Most Lovable People." Several famous Peking opera singers came with this delegation and put on numerous shows for the troops as an expression of their gratitude.[42]

The CPV song-and-dance ensembles also played an important role in boosting the troops' morale. The CCP armed forces had a long tradition of maintaining propaganda troupes at army and division levels, charged with the task of arousing the troops through entertainment. When the Chinese forces entered Korea, several companies of actors came with them. During the different phases of the CPV's offensives, these troupes had difficulty keeping up with the armies' rapid advance. Divided into smaller groups, they would merely perform on the roadside to encourage the combat units passing by. The CPV headquarters often assigned them to other tasks such as evacuating the wounded, burying the dead, guarding the captives, and helping those who dropped out of the march. The entertainers were mostly young girls, and they performed in less than ideal conditions. In a joint show with a North Korean song-and-dance ensemble in late January 1951, the Chinese performers were embarrassed by their shabby uniforms.[43] As the CPV shifted to an overall defensive position that summer, the PLA General Political Department sent more and more propaganda teams into Korea, and Peng Dehuai urged Du Ping to improve the troops' entertainment. "Propaganda troupes in the military are a fine tradition," he declared, "[and] we must always uphold the banner of the CPV song-and-dance ensembles." Du directed Xue Li, head of the CPV music ensemble subdivision, to focus all programs on the glorification of outstanding servicemen and meritorious deeds. He required the playwrights and musicians to live with the troops and so share their experiences. Since the frequent US/UN air raids made big, open shows impossible, the troupes had to perform before small groups and make their appearances brief. Hundreds of young entertainers, men and women, blanketed the CPV positions, often performing in bunkers, trenches, and tunnels. Their repertoire generally involved putting on a short play, singing a few songs, or playing some Chinese music, and they successfully enlivened the hard and often dull life of the troops. The girls were held in special regard by the rank and file and eased their hardship cleaning and patching their clothes and repairing their gloves and shoes.[44]

To show a paternal concern for the CPV soldiers was a prominent goal of the CCP leaders. Mao was especially solicitous toward both CPV commanders and rank and file. The deputy director of the PLA General Political Department, Xiao Hua, recalled that during the Korean War, Mao would always find time to meet personally with CPV commanders (above the army rank) whenever they came to Beijing. After hearing about the situation on the front, the CCP chairman would ask about their health. Several times, Mao urged the CPV commanders to look after Peng Dehuai and guarantee Peng's safety.[45] At a meeting with Hong Xuezhi in Beijing in late 1951, Mao displayed great concern when he heard that the health of the troops had declined because of poor nutrition. "We must take care of this problem right away," he urged. "We shall at least make sure that each soldier will have one egg every day." Since it was hard to transport eggs, Mao directed Zhou Enlai to ship egg powder to the front and see to it that the troops had the powder added to their regular diet.[46] Zhou also did what he could to improve the CPV's living conditions. Since preparing a hot meal in Korea was almost impossible, the CPV's primary food was a mixture of parched wheat, soybean, and peanut flour flavored with salt. The CPV troops preferred this type of field ration because it was convenient to carry and simple to eat. In early November 1951, Zhou told the CCP authorities in the Northeast to mobilize every family to prepare parched flour and cooked meat for the troops. Though he asked all staff members at the State Council to contribute, Zhou personally took part in the work. When the news about Premier Zhou's participation in the flour parching on behalf of the CPV reached Korea, many troops felt honored. "Since our leaders care about us so much," some stated in their pledges of determination, "we shall win more battles to repay the party leaders' kindness."[47] The demonstration of concern on the part of the high-ranking leaders no doubt affected the CPV soldiers, as honor, pride, and gratitude made them feel duty-bound to perform outstanding service on the battlefield.

III

Traditional Chinese military strategists believe that a weak army, as long as it is a righteous army—as long as it is *yi shi*—could defeat any strong enemy. To build such an army, Wu Tzu points out, "one must assign priority to instructions and disciplines [*jiaojie wei xian*]." In his view, a commander should "teach his troops with rites, impel them with justice, and control them with discipline."[48] CPV political work followed these lines, not only trying to convince the troops that they were fighting a just war in Korea but also doing everything possible to discipline the troops and make them respect the Korean people.

An important aim of CPV political work was to maintain good relations with the Korean people and authorities. This was truly an arduous task given the linguistic and cultural differences separating the two nations. Korea's historic suspicion of China's dominance in East Asia could have easily developed into an open hostility. Moreover, China's intervention to salvage North Korea was a point of such overwhelming pride to the Chinese troops that it proved difficult to keep them from offending the North Korean authorities or soldiers. Without native civilian support, however, military operations would be handicapped. "After our Chinese People's Volunteers enter Korea," Mao ordered on October 8, 1950, "[we] must respect and support the Korean people, [North] Korean People's Army, [North] Korean government and the Korean Labor Party; [our troops] must strictly observe military and political disciplines." These two requirements were "extremely important political elements that would guarantee the accomplishment of our military mission [on the battlefield]."[49] On January 1, 1951, Mao cabled the CPV headquarters, again instructing commanders and soldiers alike to build a friendly relationship with the North Korean authorities and people. "The Chinese and Korean comrades," his telegram read, "must be united as brothers, share weal and woe, live and die together, and fight against the common enemy through to the end." In particular, he directed the CPV soldiers to "treat the [North] Korean problems as ours and care about everything in Korea and never touch Korean people's [property]." In his view, "just as what we have experienced at home, this is a political safeguard for victory. As long as we can observe [these regulations], we are bound to win a final victory."[50]

The CPV headquarters took Mao's instructions very seriously. In December 1950, the CPV political department drafted "The CPV Regulations of Political Work" as a general guide regarding CPV relations with the Korean people. Both Peng and Deng Hua approved this document and signed it into effect on December 14. The regulations emphasized obedience to certain behavioral norms.

1. [We] must continue to educate [the troops] to observe [our] disciplines regarding treatment of the [Korean] masses, and to require [them] to abide by our policies of caring about everything in Korea.
2. [We] shall organize a mass campaign within the troops calling for the observance of disciplines through joint pledges and mutual encouragement and surveillance.
3. [We] shall teach the [Korean] masses how to prepare for air defense and assist them in disguising food and other properties so as to minimize losses to [US/UN] air raids; if our troops need to borrow grains from the local people, we shall always leave them enough for their own need; if we need to borrow things from those who are absent, we must always leave a receipt.
4. As soon as we find out whoever has violated these disciplines, we must immediately investigate and punish [them] and circulate a notice of criticism among all the units.
5. Each company must form a group in charge of [Korean] mass work, which, supervised by each company's political instructor, is responsible for discipline examination and mass mobilization.

The CPV headquarters also required all the army, division, and regiment commanders to come up with detailed plans to implement these "political regulations." Each unit was to thoroughly and regularly evaluate how the troops observed the disciplines.[51]

The 19th Army Corps provides one example of how the CPV put the regulations into effect. In late December 1950, the corp's political department set up eight rules as specific guidelines: "caring about everything in Korea, complying with all the rules and policies of the [North] Korean government, respecting the Korean people's customs and lifestyles, guarding schools and cultural and educational resorts, protecting factories and all the public facilities, never breaking into private houses or confiscating people's property, never interfering with churches, temples, or any religious organizations, and never dealing with [the Korean people or authorities] without superiors' permission in advance." The document also stressed the necessity of observing "the Three Main Rules of Discipline and Eight Points for Attention of the PLA [*san da jilu ba xiang zhuyi*]." The three rules were "(1) obey orders in all your actions, (2) don't take a single needle or piece of thread from the masses, (3) turn in everything captured. The eight points followed: "(1) speak politely, (2) pay fairly for what you buy, (3) return everything you borrow, (4) pay for anything you damage, (5) don't hit or swear at people, (6) don't damage crops, (7) don't take liberties with women, and (8) don't ill-treat captives." In dealing with the Korean authorities and troops, the guidelines admonished that "[we] must guard against arrogance and conceit and, instead, we shall be honest, polite, modest and respectful." Whenever disputes occurred, "we must have a self-criticism first, and we shall never criticize [the Koreans] behind their backs. We shall always promptly and carefully treat the wounded of the [North] Korean troops and see to it that they return to their own units safe and well. We shall actively coordinate with the NKPA troops in battles and should never fight with them over captives."[52]

As the CPV moved south during the five offensive campaigns, the commanders paid closer attention to discipline surveillance. In early December 1950, as the US/UN forces evacuated Pyongyang, the Chinese troops prepared to seize the North Korean capital. Keenly concerned about a possible conflict of interest between the Chinese forces and the North Korean authorities, Peng directed Du Ping to "make detailed rules to guide our occupation [of Pyongyang]." Du then dispatched explicit orders to the units of the 39th Army that upon entering the city, "no one is permitted to talk with the [Korean] residents except the special political work teams; no one is allowed to confiscate or utilize any materials [there] without permission; no one has the authority to arrest any person unless he [or she] is armed and refuses to give in; and no one should violate the Three Major Rules and Eight Points of Attention."[53] One week after the CPV occupied the North Korean capital, the CPV political department sent a group of political personnel to check on the troops. They were pleased to find that the soldiers strictly observed the rules. In "Number One Political Notice," dated December 26, the CPV headquarters highly commended the division because its troops "help repair roads, electricity lines, water pipes, clean the streets, and prepare firewood for the local residents." There were, however, some reported violations; some units used the local people's firewood to cook meals without leaving a receipt, and others ate captured U.S. canned food without permission. When the North Korean officials complained about these "bad behaviors," the CPV political department ordered immediate corrections.[54]

When the CPV was advancing on Seoul in early January 1951, the CPV commanders were as concerned about a potential dispute with the North

Koreans over the occupation of South Korea's capital as they were about the military operation. Having carefully studied the North Korean laws and regulations, the political department drafted "Working Regulations Regarding [Occupation of] Seoul," enjoining that "[we] strictly forbid careless arrest and execution [of the South Koreans]; . . . no one shall enter foreign embassies without permission; [we] strictly forbid occupying civilian houses and casual walk in the streets; all the troops must bring with them enough grains and vegetables for three to five days, and no one is allowed to fight [with the North Koreans] over any [captured] materials."[55] On January 5, the political department issued a supplementary notice, "On Some Policy Issues Regarding Seoul Occupation." This instruction specified that "South Korean currency is allowed to circulate in Seoul; all the troops are permitted to take over [the enemy's] arms and equipment and only the NKPA 1st Corps is authorized to guard these military materials and transport them back [to North Korea]; [and] only North Korean authorities are authorized to expropriate nonmilitary materials and civilian properties." These rules satisfied Kim Il-sung and other North Korean leaders, who then agreed to compensate the CPV by allowing the Chinese troops to expropriate a certain amount of grain. Chinese troops seem to have observed the regulations well, and there were hardly any recorded complaints from the North Koreans during the Seoul occupation.[56]

Even so, CPV food acquisition caused serious conflicts with the North Koreans. Although the Chinese troops mainly relied on food supplies transported from China, they often had to obtain provisions from the surrounding countryside. Given the heavy demands of supporting the North Korean forces, the local people could scarcely spare anything for the Chinese. During the first- and second-phase offensives, the North Koreans vigorously objected when some CPV units obtained food without a permit from the local authorities. When the CPV moved south of the 38th parallel in early 1951, the CPV commanders consulted the North Korean leaders and set up criteria for borrowing food from the Korean people. The first was "to have the local people share the burden at a reasonable portion." Landlords would "loan" no less than 50 percent of their stored grain to the troops, rich and middle-class peasants would spare 20 to 30 percent, and poor peasants would surrender no more than 5 percent. Second, CPV grain collection should be completely supervised by local Korean authorities. Each village or *ni* government would survey the availability of surplus food within its boundaries and collect it for the Chinese troops. If no local authority was available, the rule specified that only the CPV food acquisition personnel were authorized to collect grains directly from the local people. Third, "all the loans must be paid off appropriately." The Chinese troops had to provide a triplicate receipt: one copy would go to

Korean lenders, one copy to the local Korean authorities, and one copy to the CPV unit. It was clearly stated that both the North Korean government and the CPV logistical services were responsible for repaying loans "whenever they can."[57]

In practice, these rules constricted CPV food sources, since the Chinese troops had to depend on the largess of the local authorities. On September 18, 1951, the CPV's logistical commander, Hong Xuezhi, went to see Kim Il-sung about more food supplies. Hong pointed out that the US/UN air raids made CPV food transport so difficult that the troops on the front line were running out of food, yet they were forbidden to acquire any provisions from the local residents. Although Kim agreed to spare some grains, vegetables, and firewood to the frontline CPV units, he suggested that the CPV rear-service units open supply cooperatives to sell household necessities to the Korean people. This, Kim explained, would not only help deflate the North Korean currency but facilitate the CPV's ability to purchase food directly from the local people. Moreover, if the CPV transport units helped evacuate the Korean civilians, "the local governments can spare more food and other materials for the combat troops." Hong accepted all of Kim's conditions. Soon the CPV rear-service units set up a number of cooperatives in Pyongyang, Yangdok, Songchon, Anju, Huichon, Tokchon, and Ichon to sell badly needed goods, including clothing, shoes, toothbrushes, toothpaste, towels, all shipped in from China. Meanwhile, the CPV trucks carried Korean refugees and their belongings back to safety. The North Koreans welcomed the Chinese assistance and responded with increased liberality. Beginning in November, the local Korean authorities supplied the frontline CPV troops with 54,000 tons of grains, 3,000 tons of vegetables, and enough firewood for two months.[58]

Faced with the ravages of war, the North Koreans wanted the Chinese troops to participate fully in their economic recovery. US/UN air bombing and constant ground battles had rendered farming impossible in many places and had destroyed factories, schools, and hospitals. The unprecedented flood in North Korea in the summer of 1951 had so devastated the country's agriculture that thousands of North Koreans suffered from starvation the following spring. The North Korean authorities informed the CPV headquarters in May that 50 to 60 percent of their people had nothing to eat. Regarding it as essential to their goal of good relations with the North Koreans, the CPV commanders called on the troops of the second defense line to help the local people survive the famine. Everyone was required to set aside a portion every day for the starving Koreans; altogether the Chinese relief effort netted 10,000 tons of grains, 133.7 tons of cotton, 336,000 pieces of clothing, 16,000 pairs of shoes, and more than 221,748 renminbi for the North Koreans. The

CPV commanders also organized the troops to assist the North Korean farmers in cultivating land and growing vegetables. Since most of the Chinese soldiers were peasants, they proved very valuable. That spring, the CPV troops tilled more than 70,000 acres, seeded 6,900 acres, and transplanted rice seedlings in 25,000 acres of rice field. They constructed 2,226 dikes and dams, and dug 200 miles of irrigation canals and 1,167 wells. Soldiers worked alongside the local people building houses, schools, and hospitals and repairing bridges. They even planted more than five million trees in North Korea. Most of the CPV units dispatched medical teams to treat the Korean locals at no charge, and many military hospitals were opened to them. The CPV political department recorded that Chinese doctors cared for more than 641,400 Korean civilians. For example, the 20th Army Corps' hospital admitted more than 210 Korean patients and performed 200 surgical operations in 1951.[59]

The CPV political department spotlighted a number of role models in its campaign to foster an "internationalist spirit" in Korea, and one of the most distinguished was Luo Shengjiao. Luo was a scout in the 141st Division of the 47th Army. On the morning of January 2, 1952, he dived into an icy river three times to rescue a drowning Korean boy. Luo struggled to push the boy on shore but was himself drowned. The political department cited Luo as a hero, posthumously awarded him a first-grade medal for his sacrifice for the Korean child, and widely publicized his glorious deed.[60] Other soldiers won acclaim by following Luo's example. Wang Yongwei, a nurse in the 148th Division's hospital, died while rescuing an old Korean woman from a US/UN air raid on the evening of November 20, 1952. Two stretcher-bearers of the 187th Division, Lu Yujiu and Zhang Minlu, were trapped in a burning house but managed to save eight Korean women before they themselves succumbed to the fire. Shi Yuanhou, a guard of the CPV railway corps, drowned after rescuing a Korean child in the river near the Anju railway station. All these soldiers were awarded special medals by the CPV political department. The CPV newspapers highly commended their "sacrificing spirit" for the Korean people and named them as "great fighters of internationalism."[61]

At the same time, CPV political authorities adopted a tough stance against those who offended the Koreans. When the CPV first entered North Korea, most of the lower-ranking officers took a lax attitude toward infractions against civilians. They contended that as long as the troops did well in battles, discipline should be light. The North Korean authorities lodged increasing complaints about the Chinese troops: many paid no attention to Korean customs, some searched local families and forcibly removed valuables, others abused and struck Korean civilians, and some even raped Korean women. Even worse, the Chinese troops would not tolerate any criticism from the local authorities. The CPV commanders regarded these actions as "shameful" and detrimental to the CPV's military actions. In mid-December, they instituted a military court and named Du Ping as the chief judge. Du immediately drafted a legal code and distributed it to all units. He also sent organization division director Ren Rong with a group of political personnel to investigate alleged violations and execute summary judgment.[62] In January 1951, the political department issued a special instruction requesting each company's commanding officers to "take discipline surveillance and examination into serious consideration." Whoever violated the "Three Major Rules and Eight Points of Attention" or disregarded Korean customs, the directive ordered, "must be brought to compensation, apology, and punishment with no exception."[63]

Aside from civilian/military relations, the CPV political authorities had to adjudicate military misconduct, and they were especially harsh with the officers. Peng in particular was strict with high-ranking commanders. In late May 1951, the 180th Division of the 60th Army was destroyed by the US/UN forces, and Peng accused the division commanders of deserting the troops in the middle of a crisis. When division commander Zheng Qigui returned to safety, Peng not only ordered his court-martial but took disciplinary action against Zheng's superior, 60th Army Commander Wei Jie. Although Wei was finally excused from punishment, Zheng and division deputy commander Duan Longzhang were demoted.[64] In early 1953, the CPV political department publicly punished 16th Army Commander Yin Xianbing because of his notorious sexual misconduct. Yin had long been known as a capable commander among CCP military leaders, but his habitual violation of the young female nurses under his authority raised protests. At length the CPV commanders relieved Yin from command and reduced him in rank. Desertion had also become a serious problem by the end of 1952. In October, an infantry company leader deserted near Kumhwa and wounded himself, hoping to be shipped back home. After a doctor reported his deception, he was court-martialed and sentenced to death. Generally, however, for those soldiers attempting to flee, the political authorities would organize "criticism and self-criticism" meetings and have them sign a pledge that they would not desert again. Most of them would then be sent back to their original units.[65]

In dealing with the desertion problem, CPV political officers discovered that former KMT defectors were key troublemakers. Some would desert on the front, others would agitate fellow soldiers to surrender, and still others would conspire to kill their commanding officers. What happened to the 180th Division was an astonishing example. Soon after the troops were surrounded by the US/UN forces, a number of former KMT officers and soldiers began to press the division and regimental commanders to surrender and forced other soldiers to lay down their arms.[66] Shaken by this episode, Beijing ordered an immediate purge of the disloyal. In a notice to the CPV headquarters on September 10, 1951, the CMC authorized a full investigation to "ferret out [these] bad elements." Beijing sent Minister of Public Security Luo Ruiqing and deputy political director Xiao Hua to supervise a "CPV internal security meeting" in Shenyang. Du Ping, CPV internal security department director Yang Lin, and the heads of each army's internal security bureau attended the meeting on September 22. Luo and Xiao passed on Mao's instructions that "the whole [CPV] forces should seize the noncombat opportunity to conduct a thorough check to uncover those disguised counterrevolutionaries." The primary targets of scrutiny should be "those defected [KMT] elements, new recruits, and those of unclear political history or with no personal records."[67]

Peng Dehuai, however, had some reservations on this internal check. Talking with Du before he left for Shenyang, Peng warned that "we must be very careful in handling this examination and we should mainly rely on persuasion and education." He pointed out that it would be better to encourage the rank and file to monitor themselves than to have internal security personnel investigate secretly. In his view, it was more important to look at a person's performance in combat than judge him by his family background or prior history. Peng thus urged that "we must strictly control the scale of this check, and [we] shall begin with staff members first and combat troops second, commanding officers first and ordinary soldiers second." This campaign, he stressed, "shall be carried out like a gentle breeze and a mild rain rather than in a stormy way."[68]

As the CPV political department began its check on October 15, 1951, Du took Peng's warning very seriously. Without disturbing the troops along the front line, the CPV political officials focused on the commanding staff at the CPV headquarters. Every member was asked to make a clean breast of his personal background and encouraged to provide information about others' past experience as well as their actual behavior in Korea. The results shocked the CPV high command. They discovered that one person in the CPV political department was a prison escapee from Sichuan province who had fabricated his identification to join the CPV. Allegedly preparing to defect to the US/UN forces, he was arrested and sent back to prison in China. A CPV headquarters' driver was identified as a former KMT battalion leader; now considered a potential threat to the Chinese commanders, he was immediately removed. One of Peng Dehuai's personal aides was also discharged, simply because his father had been executed as a "counterrevolutionary" and his past record was incomplete.[69] The security check was extended to the rear servicemen in the spring of 1952, and the internal security personnel conducted numerous covert investigations. On June 28, they arrested thirty-eight former KMT members who were accused of committing murder, robbery, and rape before they joined the CCP forces. All these people were sent back to their hometowns to be tried and executed by the local authorities. A dozen CPV deserters were also court-martialed, and four of them who were supposedly planning to defect were given life sentences. The editor of the CPV newspaper *Shengli* [Triumph] hailed on September 16 that "the arrest and execution of these counterrevolutionaries will prove essential to [our effort to] purify our troops and consolidate our internal unity."[70] It is not known how many were mistreated during this purge or what type of impact it had on the KMT defectors within the CPV ranks.

Though Peng was skeptical of the security check, he was wholeheartedly behind the "campaign against corruption, waste and bureaucracy [*sanfan yundong*]." As the movement unfolded in China in late 1951, Peng was zealous to eliminate these evils so as to enhance CPV combat effectiveness. "Should we allow serious corruption and waste to happen," he declared before CPV headquarters' staff members on January 1, 1952, "it would not only be harmful to our nation's economic construction but affect [our efforts] to win the War to Resist U.S. Aggression and Aid Korea." In his view, this was a life-and-death struggle because corruption, waste of materials, and bureaucracy would erode "our troops' morale and combat strength." He thus requested each unit's commanding officers to "look at yourselves in a mirror and make criticism and self-criticism [first] in order to arouse the rank and file's enthusiasm to oppose these bourgeois ideas and make sure that those who have committed corruption and waste will have no place to hide." He asserted that "we must take strict discipline punishment against, court-martial, and even execute those who have repeatedly committed corruption and refused to turn over a new leaf."[71] It is important to note that Peng took the lead by holding his own "mutual criticism meeting among comrades," in which he asked his two guards for their evaluation of him. The guard pointed out that he wasted a lot of "people's money" by smoking tinned cigarette, for this type of smoking "costs 12 yuan a month, 144 a year and 2,000 to 3,000 in next twenty years." In response, Peng quit smoking immediately, and he also accepted the guards' suggestion that he keep his torn cotton-padded clothes for another year. Peng reasoned that "Chairman Mao has always led a simple and frugal life . . . by cutting his guards to one and reducing his personal expenses in half," and every high-ranking officer should follow Mao's example.[72]

The strongest challenge to the political control of the CPV troop was US/UN psychological warfare. As the war had reached a stalemate in late

1951, the enemy's propaganda campaign had become wider and more intense. American planes dropped a large number of leaflets, propaganda cartoons, and "security passes." These materials used simple and vivid language to encourage the Chinese soldiers not to fight for the Russians or the North Koreans, promising to reward them with money and women if they defected. American military personnel set up amplifiers on tanks about 2,000 feet away from the CPV's outposts and broadcast messages about how little the CPV commanders cared about the soldiers' lives. These propaganda measures had a great effect on the Chinese troops. CPV political personnel found out that many soldiers kept the US/UN "security passes" in case they were captured and that there were more and more complaints about the hard life in Korea. Consequently, friction between formerly friendly units and disputes between officers and the troops increased. Maintaining high morale among the CPV rank and file became a serious challenge.[73]

The CPV political officers did not know how to deal with this problem at first because it was entirely new. Realizing that psychological warfare was an important part of modern war, they soon organized a massive campaign to counter the enemy's propaganda. The CPV political department publicized the alleged US/UN abuses of Chinese captives and charged that under the U.S. command, a large number of KMT special agents from Taiwan committed atrocities against CPV prisoners, such as live burials, gang rapes, executions, and using them for biological tests. Later, CPV political officers distributed materials stating that the US/UN forces employed gas and other biological weapons against not only Korean civilians but also Chinese troops. They repeated that it was the U.S. aggressors who were cruel and ruthless. As part of this "anti–psychological warfare," the CPV political authorities also anticipated that the public execution of deserters would deter others who were considering defection. These methods seemed persuasive: some confessed or turned in their U.S. security passes and propaganda materials, and most pledged to resist with determination the enemy's psychological assaults. It soon became a generally accepted rule among the troops that no one should "pick up, look at, listen to, or keep the enemy's evil leaflets."[74]

IV

In retrospect, the Chinese "volunteers" fought an extremely difficult war in Korea—a "people's war" against the US/UN high-technology war. One American military historian vividly describes the gap between the US/UN and CPV forces:

> One was 6,000 miles from home, the other in its own backyard; one was boisterous and issued daily communiqués to the world, the other was taciturn; one had armor, artillery, and air cover, the other had men . . . ; one had trucks of every size and shape, the other carried only what a man could pack on his back; one competed with itself for road space, the other glided overland from valley to valley, hilltop to hilltop; one left a trail whenever it went, the other left no trail at all.[75]

Though offering only grudging respect for the CPV, this comparison has captured the essence of China's "people's war."

The CPV performance in the Korean War, another American military historian finds, equaled "the best of antiquity."[76] However, the romanticism embedded in China's warfare was not at all dysfunctional. The Chinese Communists inherited the nation's classic traditions on maintaining troop morale. They executed it through the disciplined leadership of the Communist Party's vigorous political indoctrination and the cultivation of group solidarity and unity among the rank and file. More important, their belief in the "subjective strength" of a highly politicized and mobilized army inspired the CCP leaders' daring attempts to battle the American forces in Korea.

Nevertheless, one should not exaggerate the party's success in mobilizing the minds of the troops. The CPV soldiers were largely the sons of poor peasants, and the rate of illiteracy was very high. Raised in a culture that strongly emphasized obedience, loyalty, and sacrifice, these peasant soldiers were born to "bear hardship and fear no death." Even so, the CPV's political indoctrination faltered in the face of poor logistics, resulting in inadequate clothing and poor food, repeated military setbacks, and an effective US/UN propaganda war. Indeed, the Chinese forces were not well-prepared for the war, and their low morale suggested that political training had not caught up with the fast-moving events.[77]

9. NEGOTIATING WHILE FIGHTING

"Our [traditional] strategist Sun Tzu says it correctly," Peng Dehuai pointed out in an interview with Ba Jin [Pa King], a famous Chinese writer, on March 22, 1952: "Knowing the enemy and knowing yourself, you can fight a hundred battles with no danger of defeat." In his view, U.S. policymakers had not accurately appraised Chinese strength and resolve and thus "now face a dilemma [in Korea]." Peng explained that "if they continue advancing [northward], they see no possibility of total victory or any way out [of the Korean conflict] quickly; if [they] make concessions [regarding peace terms], the big capitalists would no longer be able to reap staggering profits [from the war] and economic crisis would take place again." But the Chinese forces, he believed, had no difficulty advancing or retreating in Korea. "Since we are here to fight for peace," he asserted, "we will welcome peace [at any time]; but we are not afraid of continuing the fight because the longer we fight, the stronger we will be."[1]

I

The military situation in Korea came to a standstill in the first half of 1952, as both sides maintained a defensive posture. The US/UN first line of defense was composed of six U.S. and six ROK divisions, and one British brigade; its second line was formed by one U.S. and two ROK divisions and one Turkish brigade. The Chinese deployed eight CPV infantry armies and three NKPA corps on its front line, ten divisions (nine CPV and one NKPA) in a second echelon formation, and six CPV armies and three NKPA corps along the western and eastern coasts of North Korea. Confronting each other across a line approximately 120 miles in length along the 38th parallel, neither belligerent attempted large-scale offensives. While continuing the strategic bombing of the Chinese logistical network, the US/UN ground forces were in the process of reorganization. At the same time, the CPV marshalled the troops to improve the supply system and fortify outposts and tunnels. Clearly, the two sides were locked in a military stalemate.[2]

Interestingly, both sides changed field commanders during this period of stagnation. In April, Washington named General Matthew B. Ridgway as the new commander-in-chief of the NATO armed forces and appointed General Mark Clark to command the US/UN forces in Korea. Beijing recalled Peng Dehuai, for medical reasons. Though he continued to act as the CPV commander, Peng remained in Beijing and in charge of the CMC's daily operations for the duration of the war. The 3d Army Corps commander Chen Geng assumed the helm of the CPV but departed in June for a new assignment—to build a PLA Military Academy of Engineering and Technology. Deng Hua became the CPV's acting commander and political commissar, but more changes occurred in July. Nineteenth Army Corps Commander Yang Dezhi was named the second deputy commander of the CPV and was given responsibility for combat operations; Han Xianchu was made head of the 19th Army Corps, 19th Army Corps Deputy Commander Zheng Weishan replaced Yang Chengwu as the commander of the 20th Army Corps, and 3d Army Corps Deputy Commander Wang Jianan took Song Shilun's position over the 9th Army Corps. After that, Chen Geng, Yang Chengwu, and Song never returned to the front line.[3]

The Chinese refrained from an offensive campaign for several reasons. Beijing's war objective was limited. As Mao Zedong had stated it in late 1950, this objective was twofold. First, Korea's physical status quo must be restored, meaning that there should be no U.S. or ROK troops north of the 38th parallel. "We would never agree to start an armistice negotiation," Mao explained in his December 4, 1950, instructions to Peng Dehuai, "unless the U.S. imperialists withdraw back south of the 38th parallel." He stressed that the Chinese forces would continue to fight until this goal was obtained. Second, Korea's political status quo must also be restored. In the same instructions, Mao insisted that China would accept a final settlement of the war only when "the Korean people are allowed to elect their own government under UN supervision with as much Chinese and Soviet participation as possible." To achieve these goals, Mao envisioned that the Chinese forces would "prepare to fight for at least one or a few [more] years."[4]

After the CPV secured their foothold around the 38th parallel, a peace agreement for the restoration of the status quo seemed advisable to Beijing. As acting Chief of Staff Nie Rongzhen asserted, "now that we have accomplished the political objective of driving the enemy out of North Korea, [we] should not cross the 38th parallel, [because] restoration of the status quo prior to the outbreak of the war would be acceptable to all [the governments] that are involved [in the conflict]." Most of the military strategists in Beijing, Nie recalled later, supported his idea, and Mao also concurred. A policy of "keeping on fighting while negotiating on peace [*biantan bianda*]" was thus agreed upon by the central leadership.[5] During Kim Il-sung's visit to Beijing in early June 1951, Mao and Zhou Enlai persuaded Kim to accept "the restoration of the 38th parallel [as a short-term objective] and phased withdrawal of all foreign troops [from Korea] through negotiations and a political settlement of Korea's future by peaceful means [as long-term goals]."[6]

The field commanders supported Beijing's blueprint. In a telegram to Mao on July 16, 1951, Peng Dehuai pointed out that "withdrawal of all the foreign troops from Korea within a limited time period should be the most fundamental objective; a second goal is to restore the status quo prior to June 25, 1950, with a demarcation at the 38th parallel." In his estimation, "issues other than these two (for instance, the repatriation of POWs) are only of minor significance and merely concern technical questions." Peng further explained that "it is reasonable [*you li*] for us to request the withdrawal of all foreign troops from Korea; it is appropriate [*you jie*] to set up the demarcation at the 38th parallel; and it serves both the Chinese and the Korean interests [*you li*] to end the war as soon as possible."[7]

As part of the policy of "keeping on fighting while negotiating peace," the Chinese leadership acquiesced to the Soviet proposal of June 23, 1951, calling for cease-fire tanks. Beijing announced on July 1 that China would send a delegation to Kaesong to meet with US/UN representatives on July 10. Meanwhile, the CCP Central Committee issued a directive explaining why China decided to participate in the negotiations. "[We] have fought for eight months in Korea and forced the enemy to recognize our strength and give up its original plans for [further] aggression so that [we] have safeguarded the security of both the People's Democratic Republic of Korea and the People's Republic of China. These are the direct outcomes of our war to resist America and aid Korea." Now that the US/UN forces "are encountered with grave difficulties on the battlefield," the CCP document asserted, "they have to ask for an immediate cease-fire. Therefore, it will benefit both sides to achieve a cessation of hostilities right now."[8]

The CCP authorities took the parley very seriously. In his telegram to Peng Dehuai and Kim Il-sung on June 29, Mao requested that "while actively preparing for combat operations . . . you must begin to consider possible issues concerning the truce talks and select appropriate negotiators." On July 2, he suggested that Deng Hua and Chief of Staff Xie Fang represent the Chinese forces. He also instructed that Deng and Xie be assisted by a group of handpicked diplomatic specialists led by Li Kenong, first deputy foreign minister and CMC intelligence director, and Qiao Guanhua, director of the press bureau of the Ministry of Foreign Affairs—two of Zhou Enlai's best aides. Mao himself directed the CPV headquarters to "arrange a special working resort for Li and Qiao which should be one or two kilometers [about a half to one mile] away from where the actual meetings take place" so that Li and Qiao could closely monitor the negotiations. He stressed that "everything must be prepared appropriately and [you should see to it that] nothing would go wrong."[9] Before Li and Qiao left for Pyongyang, Mao had a long discussion with them and urged them to "carefully form a working team" in order to produce a positive outcome to the talks.[10]

Mao regarded the armistice talks as the peace negotiations that would settle the Korean conflict. After the talks started on July 10, he supervised every step taken by the Chinese and the Korean representatives. Every night Deng and Xie would meet with Li and Qiao, briefing them on the US/UN propositions. Li and Qiao would report to Zhou Enlai, who would then immediately relay the information to Mao. Mao's instructions for the next step would go back through Zhou, Li, and Qiao to Deng and Xie.[11] Mao firmly maintained that the withdrawal of all foreign troops from Korea should be given priority in these negotiations. In his telegram at 7:00 A.M. on July 11 to Li Kenong, he ordered that "[we] must hold on to [our] position requesting all [foreign] forces to withdraw." When the US/UN representatives refused to put the issue on the agenda, Mao urged the Chinese delegates to press for its inclusion. "We have sufficient reason to insist on this demand," he wired Li on July 17. "Since all the foreign troops came to Korea to fight, not to visit, why is it that a cease-fire negotiation is only authorized to discuss the cessation of hostilities but with no authority to talk about withdrawal of all the troops?" In his view, there was no reason to exclude this issue in the truce talks. He directed the Chinese negotiators to keep requesting that "the meeting be authorized not only to discuss a cease-fire but negotiate on withdrawing [foreign] troops." Simply achieving an armistice agreement was not what Mao had in mind. While editing a proposed response from Kim and Peng to Ridgway, Mao made it very clear that "all misunderstandings over minor issues should be avoided . . . [so as] to guarantee carrying out this negotiation on a peace treaty [*heping tanpan*] smoothly."[12]

The talks, however, did not proceed as Mao had hoped, and he came to believe that Washington was not yet ready for a peaceful settlement. He was then determined to stand firm. On July 26, 1951, Mao directed Peng to immediately activate the troops "for combat operations" because it was doubtful "whether the enemy truly intends to talk about peace."[13] More important,

China should never lay down its arms because of US/UN military pressure. On November 14, he cabled the Chinese negotiators that "[although] we must apply flexible tactics [in the negotiation], we shall never show any [sign] of anxiety to achieve peace." He declared that "even if achieving peace now is in our favor, we are not afraid of letting the war drag on."[14] When he learned that the truce talks might come to a halt in late December, Mao reiterated his position that "we are not afraid that the war will protract, and we must be prepared for the possibility that [the conflict] will drag on for a considerable length of time before it is resolved. As long as we are not anxious to end the war, the enemy will be at its wit's end."[15]

Though seeking more than a cease-fire, Mao would not accept any settlement that smacked of Chinese concessions. When the US/UN negotiators proposed a number for the repatriation of captives in July 1952, Mao ordered the Chinese negotiators to reject it. He explained in his July 14 telegram to Li Kenong that "you comrades would be too naive [if you accept the enemy's proposal]. We must agree upon a cease-fire only when political and military situations are favorable to us. To accept the enemy's proposal under pressure means to sign a peace treaty under coercion [*jie chengxia zhi meng*] which is detrimental to us." After the talks broke off indefinitely in early October, the Chinese negotiators consulted Beijing in February 1953 about whether they should broach the reopening of the sessions. In his response of February 19, Mao repeated that "if we initiate the resumption of the negotiation, . . . it would leave the opponents with an impression that we are anxious to achieve peace thus suggesting a sign of weakness." He argued that "action is not as good as inaction; [we] shall let the war drag on until the United States is willing to make compromises."[16]

Beijing authorities believed that only when Washington could no longer afford the war in Korea would it be ready to make peace. In their views, China could not expect to win a complete victory, but it could coerce the US/UN allies into accepting China's terms by denying them final victory. The most effective way to accomplish this was to prolong the war in Korea. Peng had proposed this strategy as early as June 25, 1951, at an enlarged CPV high command meeting. First, he argued, the U.S. strategic front was too long to sustain an action in Korea for any length of time. Peng quoted a statement made by Warren R. Austin, U.S. ambassador to the United Nations, on June 1 that with its main forces tied down in Korea and Western Europe, the US "can no longer reinforce the U.N. collective security forces." Second, Peng believed that Washington could no longer finance a war of attrition in Korea. He noted Senator Robert Taft's remarks that the US would go bankrupt if its military budget exceeded $70 billion, yet U.S. newspapers reported on June 8 that American military expenditures had already reached $60 billion a year, excluding $15–20 billion for the Korean War. Peng thus contended that the U.S. government was already "on the edge of an economic crisis." Third, he perceived the spread of American domestic opposition to the war. "The peace movement in America," he told the CPV commanders, "has recently become better organized; the states on the eastern coast will hold 500 mass rallies, and New York City alone will have 100 between June 15–20." Washington's military crusade, in Peng's view, would never have popular support in America. With all these difficulties, he concluded that the Americans could not long continue a war in Korea. In a telegram to Mao in mid-July, Peng expressed his confidence that a protracted war strategy would "compel the enemy to yield to peace while facing difficulties [*zhi nan er tui*]."[17]

Mao completely agreed. Addressing the standing committee of the First National Committee of the CPPCC on August 4, 1952, he stated that "[i]t is unlikely [that] there will be a 'Thirty Years' war or a 'Hundred Year War' [in Korea], because a protracted war there is very unfavorable to the United States." The chairman offered the following reasons for his analysis.

1. It costs them lives. In their struggle to detain 10,000 or so prisoners of war, more than 30,000 of their peoples have been killed. After all, they have many fewer people than we do.
2. It costs money. They use up more than $10 billion each year. We spend much less money than they do, and we have cut down our cost this year to half of what we spent last year. . . .
3. They have insurmountable contradictions both in the international and domestic arenas.
4. There is a strategic problem [for the United States]. The strategic focus of the United States is Europe. They dispatched forces to invade Korea without anticipating that we would dispatch forces to aid Korea.[18]

On the other hand, Mao was optimistic that China's military position was getting stronger. "Originally we had three questions regarding this war," he reminded the committee in the August 4 address. "First, could we fight it at all? Second, could we defend [our positions]? Third, would we have enough to eat?" The first question, in his view, "was answered within two or three months. The enemy had more cannons than we did, but their morale was low. They had a lot of iron but little spirit." The CPV's response to the second question, Mao pointed out, "was to dig holes. We dug two levels of [defense] works, and whenever the enemy attacked we went into the tunnels. . . . Then when the enemy entered our positions, we would counterattack and inflict on them extremely heavy casualties. We just use this indigenous method to pick up Western cannons, and there was little the enemy could do to us." On the question of sufficient provisions, he asserted that "[a]t the time, we didn't know to dig holes to store the grain. Now we know. Each division has three months' provisions, and each has a storage granary. We even have an auditorium, and [the troops] live very well." Of greater significance was the fact that "[w]e had been fighting wars for more than twenty years but never had any air force; it was always the other people who bombarded us. Now we have an air force, also anti-aircraft guns, cannon, and tanks." In short, Mao predicted that "as far as the U.S. government is concerned, the general tendency is that the US will be in trouble if peace does not come soon." Therefore, China "must stand firm to the end . . . [and] the talks must go on, and the fighting must continue."[19] The logic of Mao's calculation was simple: Only when the enemy was badly hurt would it accept peace.

Despite Mao's sanguine tone, Beijing was clearly aware of the difficulties in sustaining its war in Korea. One grave problem was reluctant and shoddy Soviet military assistance. Most of the Soviet munitions arriving in Korea were either too old or too inferior in quality to be useful to the CPV. In the early summer of 1951, Mao had to send Xu Xiangqian, the PLA chief of staff, to Moscow to appeal for urgently needed munitions and military technology. But Xu's bargaining with the Soviets turned out to be a marathon session, dragging on for four months without substantial results. Mao then sent Gao Gang, the party secretary of the Northeast, and Kim Il-sung to reinforce Xu's efforts. In conference with them, Soviet party secretary Nikolai A. Bulganin insisted that the previous agreement to provide enough military equipment to equip sixteen divisions annually had to be reduced to a ten-division level. Neither Gao nor Kim could alter Bulganin's position. When Xu came back later that year, he told Mao that Soviet hesitancy was due to Stalin's twin fears of fighting a world war with the United States and of China's becoming too strong.[20]

This perception was confirmed when another military mission to Moscow in April 1952 ended in even greater disappointment. The purpose of the mission, led by Xiao Jinguang, the commander of the People's Navy, was to acquire Soviet naval vessels and aircraft, but the Soviets demanded that Beijing pay for the equipment with hard currency. "There is no possibility," Xiao reported home, "that the Soviets would provide us any new weapons and advanced military technology even if they continue supplying us with conventional munitions."[21] China had been relying mainly on Soviet military supplies for their operations in Korea, and when that support was curtailed, the Chinese had to adjust their ambitions in Korea accordingly.

Domestic problems also made the Chinese leaders cautious in Korea. Beijing authorities were trying all possible means to finance the war but found the task increasingly onerous. When China intervened in Korea, the new regime had accomplished little in its economic rehabilitation. The Chinese leaders had to adopt wartime economic measures in order to fully—and sometimes forcibly—mobilize national revenue and war-related materials, such as medicine, clothes, and food. Late in 1951, Beijing called for a nationwide campaign of "increasing production and strictly practising economy," but serious problems remained. Mao noted in August 1952 that "the prices of commodities cannot be stabilized yet and that revenue and expenditure have not yet been balanced. Revenue is limited and expenses are in excess [of revenue]." Given that in 1951 "the cost of the War to Resist America and Aid Korea was approximately equivalent to the cost of domestic construction," the domestic economy would surely collapse unless China cut its war expense by "half of what it was last year."[22] Chen Yun, vice-premier and then in charge of national economy, even warned that "we will, one day, fail to provide what we need in Korea."[23]

China's domestic political situation concerned the CCP leaders as well. Shortly after the Chinese forces entered the war, Beijing started a nationwide campaign of "love-the-country commitment." The party's call to the people for patriotism "to defend China" and internationalism "to aid the Korean people" had almost become compulsory. However, the CCP leaders were worried about the factors that could undermine such a patriotic fever: KMT remnants were not yet eliminated, the control of Tibet was uncertain, and pro-American elements both within and outside the party were not totally suppressed. The campaigns of the "three-antis" (opposing corruption, waste, and bureaucratism) and the "five-antis" (opposing bribery, tax evasion, theft of state property, cheating on government contracts, and stealing economic information), launched by the CCP in December 1951, clearly reflected the CCP's concerns about internal disorder.[24] In his directive of December 8, 1951, Mao gave notice that "although those who have committed corruption, waste, and bureaucratism are not antirevolutionaries (some of them may be), their sins of corruption, waste, and bureaucratism are causing serious problems now; therefore, [we] must treat them the same way as [we deal with] antirevolutionaries, including arousing the masses to struggle against them on a grand scale and punishing them with death and imprisonment sentences." In his view, "perhaps only after [we] execute a few tens of thousands of those guilty of corruption throughout the entire nation can [we] resolve these problems."[25] Mao evidently shifted his attention to domestic affairs after 1951 and devoted most of his time to the two "anti" campaigns.[26]

In the late spring of 1952, the CCP central leadership assigned priority to economic reconstruction. As announced in its "Outlines of the Main Issues Concerning China's Domestic Affairs in Last Three Years and Reconstruction Policies for Next Five Years," the leadership decided to begin a "First Five-Year Plan" in 1953. Seeking more economic assistance from the Soviet Union, Zhou Enlai visited Moscow in August 1952 and presented this outline to Stalin. Zhou explained Mao's policy of "continuing fighting [in Korea] while seeking [domestic] stability, and conducting [economic] construction [*bianda bianwen bianjian*]." He emphasized that Mao had decided "to begin a five-year state [economic] construction in 1953 so as to assure that China will steadily advance toward a socialist country [even if the Korean War prolongs]."[27]

Determined to fight a protracted war in Korea, Beijing authorities resolved to rotate forces on the front. As early as April 16, 1951, Deng Hua wrote to the CMC suggesting that "given the protracted nature of the war, our forces adhere to the principles of rotation and replacement in [carrying out] combat duties." Under Mao's instructions, Zhou Enlai directed Nie and Deputy Chief of Staff Su Yu to confer with Peng on this matter. Their discussions in May led to a decision that the forces in Korea should be completely replaced by troops newly equipped with Soviet weaponry. Accordingly, the General Staff Department planned for the 23d, 24th, and 46th armies to relieve the 20th, 27th, and 42d armies by September 1952. However, Deng Hua wanted all the troops, including artillery, tank, and engineering personnel, to be rotated out by the end of 1953. Mao endorsed Deng's request, and the General Staff Department revised its plan accordingly. In December, the CMC also decided to recall the CPV high-ranking (division and above) commanders and assign to Korean duty officers who had finished command training at PLA military academies.[28]

To fight by turns, Mao believed, was an extremely innovative idea. "The War to Resist America and Aid Korea has been a great school," he observed in August 1952, "in which we conducted large-scale maneuvers; these exercises are better than running a military academy. If we continue the fight for another year, next year we can send all our army troops in turn to experience the war." Approving the General Staff Department's report on the dispatch of army and division commanders to Korea, Mao stressed that "all those army and division commanders must go, and only those who are ill can be excused."[29]

II

To fight a protracted war, the field commanders understood that their responsibility was to hold on to their main line of resistance along the 38th parallel.

At a command meeting on June 6–9, 1952, they all agreed that "whether the war would end soon or drag on, the [CPV] forces must be prepared to carry on the fight" and the rank and file must be urged not to entertain any dreams of a quick peace. The commanders believed that the best way to sustain a protracted war was "an active positional defense," which required "[us] to stand fast to the present positions, especially along [our] main line of resistance." In their view, any loss of CPV positions would be militarily detrimental because "the enemy could use [our] fortified outposts against us." The commanders were also convinced of the need to augment reserves. Should the enemy "assault one [CPV] army's positions with one or two divisions," they asserted, "[we] must counterattack with our reserves resolutely." The combat troops had to be prepared to fight seesaw battles. Therefore, "tactically, [we] must be active in battling [the enemy]," the commanders reasoned, and "each unit must seize every opportunity to assault the enemy line of defense in order to squeeze the enemy positions" or decimate US/UN effectiveness piecemeal. In this way, they calculated, the CPV could achieve an offensive momentum and roll small victories into a big one.[30]

The CPV headquarters thus adjusted its force dispositions into a "zone defense" with the emphasis on strengthening the western and eastern coastal areas against a possible US/UN amphibious attack. The primary line of defense now consisted of the 19th Army Corps (the 39th, 40th, 63d, and 65th armies), the 3d Army Corps (the 38th, 15th, and 60th armies), and the 20th Army Corps (the 12th, 67th, and 68th armies). The eastern coast was guarded by the 20th and 27th CPV armies and the 5th and 7th NKPA Corps, with the NKPA troops forming the first line of defense and the two CPV armies holding position directly behind them. Along the western coast, the 42d, 64th, and 50th CPV armies and the 4th NKPA Corps built an in-depth defense. The 47th Army was positioned as reserves to the entire CPV infantry.[31]

Since autumn was the most favorable season for the motorized US/UN forces, the Chinese anticipated they would choose those months to step up their assaults. In mid-July, the CPV intelligence noted that U.S. Army Chief of Staff Joseph Lawton Collins inspected the western coast; on July 30, US/UN Commander in Chief Clark visited ROK army headquarters in Taegu and examined the U.S. 7th Division's positions west of Kumhwa; and shortly afterward, U.S. Eighth Army Commander James Van Fleet accompanied Syngman Rhee on a tour of the positions of the U.S. 7th Division and the ROK 2d and 9th divisions. Meanwhile, U.S. naval and marine forces conducted coordination exercises for an amphibious operation. Three U.S. aircraft carriers, including the flagship *Iowa*, approached North Korea's western coast from the Yellow Sea.[32] In assessing US/UN intentions, Deng Hua and

CPV Deputy Commander Yang Dezhi concluded that the enemy was planning to launch an amphibious assault on the western coast. In their analysis, it was most likely that the U.S. 1st Cavalry Division, then in Japan, would land on the Yonan peninsula and roll east to seize Kukchon and join the U.S. 1st Marine Division advancing from Munsan to Kaesong. At the same time, other US/UN forces, in a diversionary maneuver, would engage the CPV main line of defense. In late August, the CPV headquarters informed each army command of its evaluation and urged all troops to "watch closely the changes of the enemy situation." The CPV directive in particular instructed the 68th and 15th armies to increase their reconnaissance to keep track of the movements of the U.S. 1st Marine and 7th Infantry divisions. On August 28, Deng Hua formally ordered the 19th Army Corps to get combat-ready for a US/UN amphibious attack in the Kukchon-Kaesong areas.[33]

The expected US/UN drive, however, did not occur. A CPV intelligence report in mid-September indicated that the U.S. 1st Cavalry Division remained in Japan and the U.S. 1st Marine Division had not been activated. Yet US/UN planes had dropped a number of smoke bombs in the Kumhwa area to cover the gathering of ground forces and materials there.[34] The CPV commanders concluded that "the enemy is deterred by our military preparedness from launching an amphibious attack and might plan to assault the Kumhwa area." Yang Dezhi then proposed an immediate attack on the US/UN forces and cited a traditional Chinese military maxim that "he who strikes first prevails, he who strikes late fails." Deng Hua supported Yang and, on September 10, he informed the CMC of his plan to "set out the 39th, 12th, and 68th armies for a series of tactical strikes [at the enemy's outpost] . . . with each army to select three or five targets." The main goal of this operation, he explained, was "to annihilate a large number of the enemy troops through seesaw battles." Deng recommended beginning these assaults on September 20, breaking off one month later, and then sending the three armies home.[35] Having won CMC approval, Deng issued a formal order of action two days later.[36]

The army commanders were eager to attack, desiring, in Yang Dezhi's words, "to teach the new US/UN commander in chief Clark a lesson." However, the CPV headquarters cautioned that full preparations were absolutely essential. In its directive to each attacking unit, the headquarters set strict guidelines: first, "taking action only when fully prepared and avoiding hasty engagement," and to that end, the CPV commanders let each army commander decide when to act; second, "conducting constant reconnaissance to probe the enemy situation and carefully designing plans to coordinate infantry, tank, and artillery forces in battle"; third, "organizing combat exercises before actual actions and deploying troops secretly near the enemy positions so as to catch the enemy off guard"; and fourth, "concentrating sufficient attaching forces [on selected targets] and disposing strong reserves to reinforce resistance against the enemy counterattack." In short, the CPV stressed that "we must ensure certainty of success before taking action; otherwise, we need not attack."[37] From September 15 to September 18, the CPV headquarters telephoned each army corps and army commander several times, underscoring the doctrine of "fighting no battle unprepared [and] fighting no battle that you are not sure of winning."[38]

The 39th Army reported combat-ready two days ahead of schedule. As it began its attack on September 18, the 65th, 40th, 38th, 12th, and 68th armies and the NKPA 3d and 1st corps followed suit. The entire operation was focused on seven outposts of the U.S. 2d and 7th divisions and eleven of the ROK 2d Corps's positions, most manned at company strength. Taking the US/UN forces by surprise and outnumbering them, the attacking troops succeeded in breaking through the enemy lines. After two weeks of fighting, the CPV troops seized six US/UN outposts. The field commanders reported 2,000 CPV casualties and more than 8,300 enemy losses, including 2,000 Americans.[39] In the judgment of the CPV commanders, the most significant outcome of the operation was that the Chinese forces learned how to conduct tactical offensives. The lower-level commanders, granted more freedom of action, were able to act more effectively. Zheng Weishan, 20th Army Corps acting commander, held back his troops for ten days after the 39th Army opened fire. Zheng explained later that he had gained three advantages during those ten days: "(1) in terms of logistics, the troops prepared more materials; (2) spiritually, the troops, getting increasingly anxious at seeing friendly units winning, were bursting with energy; and (3) tactically, our inaction fooled the enemy forces in front of us and once they became relaxed, we caught them off guard." With this leverage, the 12th and 68th armies, under Zheng's command, seized most of the ROK outposts minutes after they finally entered the battle.[40]

This tactical offensive boosted the CPV commanders' overall confidence in small-scale attacks. Drawing lessons from the operation, they realized that it was crucial to obtain the backing of artillery and engineering forces. To attack one fortified US/UN outpost manned at company strength, they calculated, the CPV needed to deploy at least forty artillery pieces to support two infantry companies' assault. Sufficient engineers were also needed to extend tunnels close to the enemy position so that the infantry could hide there on the eve of the attack. Moreover, the CPV troops felt that it was more effective and safer to fight a quick battle for a quick decision [*suzhan sujue*]. Understanding that the US/UN forces would counterattack with superior firepower, the CPV assault units would retire north to stay out of US/UN artillery range and then rush back to charge the enemy forces before they consolidated their positions. In doing so, the CPV commanders believed that they could avoid heavy casualties and at the same time decimate the enemy troops through seesaw actions. The 68th Army noted its success in inflicting more than 3,000 ROK casualties after wrestling back and forth more than sixty-five times over two CPV hilltop positions.[41]

Lured by the unexpected success of positional defense, the CPV commanders decided to make a larger-scale tactical offensive in which all seven armies would move simultaneously. As the CPV headquarters' directive of October 3 asserted, an all-out attack would "force the enemy to disperse their forces and firepower so that we can overrun the targeted [US/UN] positions one by one."[42] Supported by 760 artillery pieces, thirty CPV infantry companies stormed twenty-three US/UN outposts along 120 miles of the front line at dusk on October 6. The next day, the Chinese troops broke through sixteen of the targeted positions. The 38th Army, however, met vigorous resistance in assaulting Hill 394.8 near Chorwon. After nine days and nights of fierce fighting, the 38th Army lost more than 6,700 men and had to withdraw. The 65th, 39th, 15th, 12th, and 68th armies continued the drive and attacked eleven more targets on October 8–21, but with no substantial gains.[43]

The Chinese commanders had been overly optimistic. In his report on "Major Lessons of the Tactical Offensives in September and October," 20th Army Corps Acting Commander Zheng Weishan observed that "all of [our] assaults on positions defended by one ROK company prevailed and all of [our] assaults on ROK outposts manned at platoon strength had quick results." When attacking U.S. positions manned at battalion strength, however, Zheng noted that "we had to throw in more troops and ended up with more casualties." Furthermore, "the U.S. forces have built an in-depth defense which forced [us] to fight arduous and tedious battles," and as soon as the enemy had time to reorganize its troops and firepower, the CPV assaults were shattered. Therefore, in Zheng's view, the CPV should only attack enemy positions defended by units no larger than one company and strictly one at a time.[44]

The CPV headquarters had originally planned to end the tactical offensive on October 22, but the sudden onset of the US/UN "Kumhwa offensive" in mid-October prolonged the operation. The Chinese commanders had expected that the US/UN forces would launch a counteroffensive, but they thought that it would center in the Pyongyang area where the flatlands favored motorized US/UN forces. Instead, the US/UN forces engaged the CPV 15th Army in the Osong-san region, a mountainous terrain well-suited to defense. The U.S. 7th and ROK 2d divisions began the intensive shelling of the Chinese positions there on October 12, which confirmed a defected South Korean officer's report on the US/UN plan. Before the Chinese commanders could thoroughly assess the situation, the US/UN troops occupied hills 597.9 and 537.7 on October 14 and forced the Chinese troops off the ridge and into their tunnels. At the CPV headquarters' luncheon the next day, Deng Hua and Yang Dezhi pointed out that Osong-san was the main target of the US/UN attack because of its geographic importance. Osong-san guarded the Kumsong-Tongchon road to the east and the Pyongyang flatland to the west. The two key heights (hills 597.9 and 537.7) rose like two fists threatening Kumhwa. Deng and Yang believed that the enemy's occupation of the hills was a first step toward control of the entire Osong-san area so as to establish an advance base for a future attack on Pyongyang and Kumsong. Recognizing the grave danger posed by the loss of the Osong-san outposts, they decided to defend these sites regardless of cost. In a telephone conversation with the 3d Army Corps's chief of staff, Wang Yunrui, Yang warned that "the enemy attack is getting increasingly fierce and may become the most fierce attack of the past two years. You must see to it that the 15th Army is prepared for a huge cost in order to hold fast to [our positions]."[45]

The US/UN attack on the Osong-san area soon turned into one of the severest battles of the war. The U.S. 7th Division, the ROK 2d and 9th divisions, the U.S. 187th Airborne regiment, and the Ethiopian and Colombian battalions (altogether, 60,000 men) were supported by 170 tanks, 300 artillery pieces, and a number of airplanes as they combated the CPV's four infantry and two artillery divisions. For forty days and nights, the two sides fought a seesaw action mainly over hills 597.9 and 537.7—a battlefield less than three square miles. From October 14 to October 20, the 15th Army deployed as many as twenty-one infantry companies to defend the two heights. The battle fell into a pattern: the US/UN troops would force the CPV into tunnels during the day, then the Chinese would counterattack at night and recover their surface positions, only to lose them again in the daytime. The situation became acute on the night of October 20 when the 45th Division's casualties totaled 3,200 and the division had only remnant forces left—hiding in the tunnels, extremely exhausted, and with little remaining food, water, or munitions. Receiving 15th Army Commander Qin Jiwei's report, Deng and Yang immediately arranged for reinforcements. They directed the 29th Division of the 15th Army to join the 45th Division, filled the 45th Division with 1,200 new recruits, and placed the 12th Army on reserve. Yang also attached one artillery battalion plus four individual artillery companies and one anti-aircraft regiment to the 15th Army.[46]

Determined to defend those positions, the CPV commanders also viewed the battle as a chance to deplete the enemy strength. On the night of October 21, Deng Hua telephoned the commanders of the 15th and 12th armies and declared that "the enemy is making a serious mistake by storming our fortified positions in battalion and regiment formation; it presents us a good opportunity of decimating the enemy troops in a large number." He urged the commanders to "firmly seize this opportunity to inflict heavy casualties on the enemy forces . . . so that we can nail the enemy by the throat [*zhidi yu siming*]."[47] It was, however, a very costly "opportunity" for the CPV. Since it took time for the reinforcements to move to the front, the troops hidden in the tunnels had to keep on fighting. The 45th Division's remnants reorganized themselves and, with CPV long-range artillery support, not only survived the constant US/UN assaults but launched several counterstrikes from the tunnels from October 21 to October 29. Meanwhile, at the 15th Army Command meeting on October 25, Qin Jiwei proposed to attack Hill 597.9 first and then Hill 537.7 using the entire 29th Division. The army corps headquarters approved Qin's plan but warned that the CPV forces must expect a seesaw battle, "attack with small (platoon or squad) units, and pay attention to coordination with artillery fire support."[48]

The 15th Army carefully prepared for the counterattack. To make sure that the troops would have sufficient munitions, food, and water, Qin dispatched all staff personnel and three infantry battalions to assist in the transport of supplies to the front line. On October 27, he ordered all artillery pieces at his disposal to shell Hill 597.9 for two days. At the same time, five companies of the 45th Division and two companies of the 29th Division secretly entered the tunnels at the foot of the hill. At 11:00 P.M., October 30, the CPV opened the attack on Hill 597.9. Supported by fifty field guns and howitzers and twenty-four rocket guns, the infantry captured the hill within five hours. The combat grew fiercer on November 1 when six US/UN infantry battalions struck back with the substantial support of aircraft, tanks, and artillery. Having already blocked fourteen US/UN onslaughts, however, the CPV ran out of men and munitions. That night, the 3d Army Corps Command had to send in the 91st Regiment of the 31st Division (12th Army) to replenish supplies and replace the 29th Division's casualties. The reinforcements arrived in time to meet another wave of US/UN attacks on the afternoon of November 2. After a brutal battle lasting three more days, the CPV managed to stop the US/UN forces and held fast to Hill 597.9.[49]

Though the 15th Army had no men left to attack Hill 537.7, the 3d Army Corps commanders were emboldened to try to seize that ground as well. On November 5, they assigned two divisions of the 12th Army for the operation.

The 12th Army's deputy commander, Li Desheng, set up a frontal command, assisted by 7th Artillery Division commander Yan Fu, who was responsible for coordinating the artillery forces. Anticipating a fierce fight, the 3d Army Corps Command cautioned that "if we succeed in seizing [Hill 537.7], we shall hold firm to the main positions, and only defend those positions that are important to us; . . . should our positions be lost to the enemy, we shall take action to recover them only when we are fully prepared . . . [and] only when there is a chance of assured success."[50] The CMC approved the operational plan in its telegrams on November 4 and November 7 but set high expectations for the attack: "since the battle of Osong-san has expanded into a campaign, you must see to it that the troops fight bravely to win complete victory."[51]

With the direct fire support of seventy field guns and howitzers and twenty-four rocket guns, two companies of the 92d Regiment (31st Division) launched a two-pronged assault on Hill 537.7 at 4:25 P.M. on November 11. The troops reported that they destroyed the US/UN defending forces and controlled the height in less than an hour but lost two positions at the foot of the hill the next day. Repeatedly attempting to regain that ground, the companies became combat-ineffective after three days. The 93d Regiment came to their aid and fought ferociously for another three days. When they too were unable to carry on, the regiment was replaced by the 106th Regiment of the 34th Division. After beating back repeated US/UN assaults over the next seven days, the CPV finally compelled the US/UN forces to break off action on November 28 and withdraw to safety.[52]

The CPV headquarters was very pleased with the outcome of the battle. With 11,500 casualties of their own, the CPV stated that it had killed more than 25,000 US/UN troops, shot down 270 airplanes, and destroyed 61 artillery pieces and 14 tanks.[53] This great victory, Deng Hua believed, was the result of prudent tactics of positional defense. In his report "On Some Tactical Issues Concerning Active Defense," dated November 30, 1952, he defined an active defense strategy: "when the enemy comes to attack us, [we] will hold fast to our positions and decimate [the enemy troops] as much as possible; when the enemy ceases assaulting us, [we] will attack the enemy from our positions to wipe out a whole [US/UN] platoon or company one at a time." In Deng's view, an active defense should consist of three stages: first, "storm and capture the enemy's positions and prepare for the enemy's counterattack"; second, "fight a seesaw battle"; third, "fight a quick combat for a quick decision and evacuate quickly." There were four tactical maneuvers integral to the success of this strategy: first, to employ small units to resist larger enemy formations, "such as two fighters against one enemy squad, a combat group against one platoon, or a squad against one company"; second, to engage the enemy in "close combat" and open fire only when the enemy was twenty to thirty meters away; third, to "strike relentlessly" for the purpose of wiping out the enemy's attacking units in each assault so as to strike terror into the minds of enemy troops; and fourth, to take "quick action" to strike and then withdraw and to avoid advancing too far from the defensive positions.[54]

These active defense tactics excited Mao. In his October 24 telegram to the CPV headquarters, he restated the concept:

> This way of fighting involves concentrating superior forces and firepower at certain chosen key tactical points and employing sudden maneuvers in order to strike at entire enemy platoons, companies, battalions so as to annihilate all or a large part of them. When the enemy launches a counteroffensive against us, we inflict massive casualties upon the enemy through repeated assaults. After that, according to the circumstances of the positions that fall into our hands, we staunchly defend those positions that can be defended, and abandon those that cannot be defended so as to maintain our initiative and to prepare for further counteroffensive operations.

The CCP chairman was optimistic that "if we continue to employ such methods of fighting, we will surely bring our enemies to their knees and force them to come to terms so as to end the war in Korea." On November 8, Mao directed all the PLA high-ranking commanders to study carefully the lessons of the Osong-san operation.[55] Basking in the successes on the battlefield, Beijing's authorities seemed complacent about bringing the war to a quick end.

III

The Chinese leaders never believed that the military stalemate in Korea would last long. In the prevailing atmosphere of distrust, they remained alert to unexpected developments. The tortuous and ineffectual armistice talks at Panmunjom seemed unlikely to progress since neither side was willing to make concessions on the outstanding issues, especially on how the prisoners of war should be repatriated. More significant was the strong conviction held by the Chinese leaders in late 1952 that the US/UN forces would mount a large-scale offensive for the purpose of pressing Beijing and Pyongyang to accept U.S. peace terms. In his December 16 analysis of the Korean situation, Mao pointedly argued that "now that the armistice negotiations have come to a halt, and the difficulties that American forces are facing in Korea have not reached the extent to which the United States would be compelled to cease fighting, therefore the Korean war situation will intensify in the coming period (assuming one year). [Dwight D.] Eisenhower [the president-elect] is probably preparing a larger military action in Korea after he takes office." What, then, would Eisenhower be most likely to do? Mao contended that "the possibility of amphibious attack on both sides of our rear [in North Korea] is much greater than an enemy attack on our in-depth defense line on the front."[56]

Chinese leaders believed that their expectation of U.S. amphibious operations was not chimerical because they had been closely watching the statements made about the war during the American presidential campaign of 1952. As early as the summer of 1952, Zhou Enlai directed the Ministry of Foreign Affairs to collect and scrutinize every public speech given by Eisenhower as the Republican presidential candidate in relation to the Korean War. Chinese foreign affairs analysts soon concluded that Eisenhower would adopt a more aggressive stance in Korea. They noted that Eisenhower promised on July 11 that he would lead an American crusade against communism in the world; he also announced on August 24 that he would build a stronger military force to contain the communists and that his administration would be prepared to "roll back" communist expansion.[57] Eisenhower's pledge to achieve an "honorable" peace in Korea through "deeds," not "words," especially alarmed Beijing. The CCP leaders understood that "the peace honorable to the U.S. imperialists will never be honorable to the Chinese or the Korean peoples." To accomplish such an "honorable" peace, the Chinese leaders predicted, Eisenhower would definitely "intensify the [Korean] war." Since Eisenhower seemed to win the election on the basis of his Korean plank, the Chinese press concluded that the new president would doubtless treat the Korean problem as his first priority.[58]

In estimating how Eisenhower would execute his "deeds," the military leaders in Beijing decided that he might prefer an amphibious operation to other options. The Eisenhower administration, they calculated, had four alternatives if it chose to escalate the fighting: (a) a large-scale offensive on the front; (b) intensive air raids on the areas of strategic importance in North Korea and even China's Northeast, combined with a naval blockade of China's coastline; (c) the use of atomic weapons; and (d) amphibious attacks on both sides of the CPV rear in North Korea. The first two options were unlikely because the US had been bombing strategic targets in North Korea and imposing a naval blockade since the fall of 1952, but with little effect. As for the possibility of nuclear attack, Nie Rongzhen recognized that "the US might want to test its tactical atomic weapons in Korea," but he believed that "the enemy won't use the weapon on a large scale." Furthermore, the military leaders argued, "the United States is under great pressure of world opinion and is also deterred by possible Soviet nuclear retaliation from doing this in the Far East."[59]

Therefore, amphibious attack seemed to be the most likely course of action the US/UN forces might undertake. In his report to the CMC dated December 4, 1952, on the possible development of the war for 1953, Deng Hua predicted that the US/UN forces would launch an amphibious assault on the western coast of North Korea for the purpose of cutting off the CPV's retreat and supply lines. "As the war drags on," Deng asserted, "the enemy will organize a landing operation sooner or later. We must be clearly aware of this possibility while we prepare for our countermeasures." Other CPV commanders concurred with Deng, because "both Mark Clark and [U.S. Eighth Army Commander] Van Fleet have demonstrated great interest in this kind of action." Yang Dezhi even "carefully studied records [edited by the CMC] of Eisenhower's personal experience" and told other commanders that "we should never forget that Eisenhower was the person who commanded the Normandy landing during the Second World War."[60]

Chinese intelligence reported that the US/UN forces had already been activated for an amphibious operation. The CMC passed the information on Eisenhower's visit to South Korea to the CPV headquarters on December 2, warning that "the visit of Eisenhower with his top military advisors, including the new secretary of defense, the chairman of the Joint Chiefs of Staff, the commander of the U.S. Pacific Fleet, could be a prelude to a full-scale offensive."[61] One intelligence study suggested that the enemy's maneuvers for amphibious attack had intensified toward the end of 1952, as the US/UN had dispatched more agents to the eastern and western coasts of North Korea to collect weather and hydrographic information. Moreover, the ROK forces had recently been strengthened with two newly created divisions, six regiments, and twenty-eight artillery battalions now deployed on the front. Another report even guessed that the enemy would take the anticipated action no later than February 1953.[62]

Increasingly alert to the possibility of a US/UN attack, Beijing pressed the CPV to get fully prepared. On December 9, Mao cabled Deng Hua that "we must [plan our actions on] the assumption that the enemy has already decided and is actively preparing to take amphibious attack [along the coast between] the Han and Chongchon rivers, and our troops must treat the preparations against the enemy's landing plan as the most urgent task."[63] A few days later, reading Deng's December 4 report on US/UN military intentions for 1953, he added his assessment that "the enemy will launch a major amphibious attack with five or seven divisions along the line of the Han, Chongchon, and Yalu rivers, perhaps assisted by airborne operations in our rear, either in spring or even earlier." Consequently, the CPV had to "consolidate bunkers and tunnels and deploy five armies including four of the most experienced to defend this line." In order to "resolutely prevent the enemy," Mao stressed that he "won't tolerate a tiny error [in preparations]." The CCP chairman also pointed out that "a second dangerous landing area is between Tongchon and Wonsan [in the east], and a third dangerous place is the area between Nampo and the Chongchon River." Given its strategic significance, however, Mao was determined that the CPV "shall never allow the enemy to land in the western coast, especially between the Han and Yalu rivers."

Zhou Enlai warned the CPV headquarters on December 16 that "it is likely that, to support the landing operation in Korea, the enemy might take diversionary assaults against China's mainland including bombing our airfields in Andong, supporting the KMT remnants to harass our coastal areas, and coordinating the KMT forces in Burma to attack the Sino-Burmese border."[64] At the same time, Mao called Deng Hua back to Beijing and instructed Deng "in person" that nothing should shake the CPV resolve to encounter "the enemy landing action in the western coast and in spring."[65] In Mao's view, the anticipated US/UN attack embodied both danger and opportunity. "If we can smash the enemy's landing plan," he pointed out in his instruction of December 16, "and in the meantime, annihilate a larger number of the enemy forces with our tactical offensive on the front, the military situation in Korea would become more stable and more favorable to us."[66]

On December 20, Mao penned a CCP Central Committee document entitled "Instructions on Preparing All Possible Conditions to Smash the Enemy's Risky Amphibious Operations and Strive for a Bigger Victory in Korea" as a formal order to the CPV headquarters. He confirmed that the enemy "will land at our rear coastal lines, particularly along the western coast between . . . the Han and the Yalu [rivers]." He wanted the CPV headquarters to establish an ad hoc command to direct the antilanding campaign. He also requested all rear-service units, "especially those who are responsible for supply transportation, maintaining communication lines, and storing munitions and other materials," to try their best to support the combat troops' defensive efforts. He named "April 1953" (without specifying a date) as the deadline for both combat and logistical forces to complete the necessary preparations. Finally, it was his belief that "the [US/UN] landing attack is the only, probably the last, action the enemy will take in Korea." If the CPV could successfully smash it, "the final fate of enemy's defeat will so be destined." In one last warning, Mao reiterated that "the key to our success is how much we can get prepared."[67]

To implement Mao's instructions, the CPV headquarters drafted the "Operational Plan for Smashing the Enemy's Landing Offensive" at a four-day meeting beginning December 17. The first part of the plan redeployed the forces. To strengthen the defense of both eastern and western coasts, the CPV Command decided to dispatch more experienced forces—those who had previously fought on the front—to the two flanks. The 38th and the 40th armies would move to the western coast, and the 15th and 12th armies to the eastern coast. Altogether seven infantry armies (twenty-two CPV divisions, two independent regiments, and one NKPA corps), fourteen artillery regiments plus nine battalions, two anti-aircraft artillery regiments plus thirteen battalions, and six tank regiments would gather on the western coast. Four infantry armies (thirteen CPV divisions and two regiments), two artillery regiments plus three battalions, five anti-aircraft battalions, and one tank regiment would be sent to the eastern coast. Anticipating a costly struggle, the second part of the CPV order emphasized the allocation of sufficient reinforcements. The 1st, 16th, 21st armies, the 33d Division, and the 1st Tank Division stationed in North Korea were to form the first group of reinforcements, and the 54th Army, which had just assembled in the Northeast, was to serve as the second source of reserves. In addition, the CPV headquarters wanted all fourteen CPV air force divisions and one naval team to assist the ground forces. The third part contained requirements to strengthen rear services. The 5th, 6th, 7th, 9th, and 10th CPV railway divisions and 5,000 laborers would be assigned at once to guard the three main North Korean railroads. Finally, the CPV order directed the mobilization of all forces in Korea to construct more and larger defensive works and to dig longer tunnels and urged the combat forces to intensively practice antilanding maneuvers.[68]

Table 9. 1. CPV Command: December 18, 1952–July 27, 1953

CPV Commander	Peng Dehuai
Political Commissar	Peng Dehuai
1st Deputy Commander	Deng Hua (acting CPV commander when Peng Dehuai left Korea)
2d Deputy Commander	Yang Dezhi
Chief of Staff	Xie Fang
	Li Da (replacing Xie in May 1953)
Director of Political Department	Gan Siqi
	Li Zhimin (replacing Gan in May 1953)
West Coast Commander	Deng Hua
Deputy Commander	Liang Xingchu

(continued)

Table 9. 1. (continued)

Chief of Staff	Wang Zhengzhu
Director of Political Department	Du Ping
East Coast Commander	Xu Shiyou
Deputy Commander	Wang Jinshan
Chief of Staff	Wang Yunrui
Director of Political Department	Liu Youguang
9th Army Corps Commander	Wang Jianan
Political Commissar	Wang Jianan
Deputy Commander	Tao Yong
	Wang Bicheng (replacing Tao in May 1953)
Chief of Staff	Tan Jian
Director of Political Department	Xie Youfa
19th Army Corps Commander	Han Xianchu
	Huang Yongsheng (replacing Han in May 1953)
Deputy Commander	Ceng Siyu
Chief of Staff	Ceng Siyu
Director of Political Department	Chen Xianrui
20th Army Corps Commander	Zheng Weishan (Acting)
	Yang Yong (replacing Zheng in May 1953)
Political Commissar	Zhang Nansheng
	Wang Ping (replacing Zhang in May 1953)
Chief of Staff	Xiao Wenjiu
Artillery Force Commander	Gao Cunxin
Political Commissar	Liu He
Chief of Staff	Zhu Guang
Air Force Commander	Nie Fengzhi (acting)
Deputy Commander	Wang Nian (NKPA)
	Duan Suquan
Chief of Staff	Wu Su
Director of Political Department	Wang Xuewu
Logistics Commander	Hong Xuezhi
Deputy Commander	Zhang Mingyuan
Director of Political Department	Li Xuesan
Deputy Chief of Staff	Luo Wen

Despite the belief that the US would not use tactical nuclear weapons in Korea, Nie Rongzhen personally studied confiscated U.S. pamphlets on "the destructiveness of atomic bombs and appropriate protective measures." He also asked one of China's nuclear scientists, Qian Sanqiang, to verify the information contained in the materials. On February 28, 1952, Nie proposed to Zhou Enlai that "200 copies of these materials be made and sent to the [CPV] headquarters for the commanders [eyes] only." He informed Zhou of his plan to dispatch a group of nuclear "specialists" to the Korean front with the mission to help the troops prepare "for possible nuclear strikes." Both Mao and Zhou approved Nie's proposal.[69]

Chinese preparations were soon in full swing, and the CPV headquarters pronounced the readiness of the forces in April 1953. The troops, it reported to the CMC, had consolidated defense works not only on the main line of resistance but along the coasts. Thousands of combat troops and rear servicemen participated, with sometimes more than 500,000 working on defense projects day and night, and their output was impressive. More than 8,090 new tunnels totaling 430 miles in length and 2,000 miles of trenches were built. As many as 605 new bunkers and shelters made of reinforced concrete were constructed. The artillery forces set up a tight network of fire cover for these new outposts. The troops also secured adequate provisions. Each infantry army stored 3,100 tons of ammunition, and each artillery division had more than 1,000 tons at its disposal. More than 248,000 tons of food supplies were stockpiled, sufficient to feed the entire CPV force for eight-and-a-half months. Moreover, the combat troops were restored to full strength, as 90,000 new recruits arrived in North Korea to replace the casualties. All combat units conducted anti-amphibious exercises. Each army command in particular organized training seminars for all their commanders above the rank of platoon leader, focusing on antilanding, anti-airborne, and antitank tactics. With no previous experience against modern amphibious welfare, the Chinese troops demonstrated considerable facility with these preparations.[70]

During these months, the Chinese leaders reflected on the implications of a US/UN offensive. As Mao pointed out in an instruction to the CPV Command on January 16, the anticipated US/UN amphibious attack would be the enemy's biggest operation of the war. Should it succeed, he believed, "not only the Korean situation would take a turn for the worse, but our grand cause of [economic] reconstruction [at home] would be devastated." But if the CPV succeeded in smashing the enemy landing attack, "American aggression in Korea would invariably meet its final doom." Mao wanted the CPV commanders to understand that the future of China's military intervention in Korea would hinge on the outcome of this campaign.[71] Beijing authorities became more certain that Eisenhower would mount an immediate offensive in Korea after the new president's announcement that he was "unleashing Chiang" in early February 1953. They believed that a Chinese Nationalist attack on the southern and eastern China coasts was part of Eisenhower's Korean scheme. Mao pointedly told the CPPCC audience on February 7 that

> we desire peace, but as long as U.S. imperialism does not discard its barbaric and unreasonable demands, and its plots to expand its aggression, the resolution of the Chinese people can only be to continue to fight together with the Korean people to the end. This is not because we like war, we would like to stop the war immediately and wait to resolve the remaining problems in the future; but the U.S. imperialism does not want to do things this way. . . . If that is the case, that's all right; we will continue to fight. No matter how many years U.S. imperialism is willing to fight, we are prepared to fight with them for as many years, right up to the time when U.S. imperialism is willing to stop.[72]

Mao's speech appeared in *Renmin Ribao* the next day, and Beijing obviously expected that its warning would be imparted to Washington.

The feared U.S. amphibious action, however, did not occur. On the contrary, the CPV headquarters received a proposal from US/UN Commander in Chief Mark Clark on February 22 that the two sides should exchange their sick and wounded prisoners of war pending any agreement on an armistice. Regarding Clark's offer as a good opportunity to scale down tensions in Korea, Mao judged that "after taking office, Eisenhower . . . is trying to seize the initiative, and this proposal of exchanging the sick and wounded POWs indicates [Washington's] intention to sound [us] out about the negotiations at Panmunjom." On March 23, he directed Ding Guoyu, the new head of the Chinese delegation at the truce talks, that "[we] shall lodge no protest to the other side in the next week . . . and let it be known that we are prepared to accept [Clark's] proposal of February 22."[73] Zhou Enlai formally announced China's acceptance of Clark's offer on March 28 and also suggested that the negotiations be reopened at Panmunjom. Two days later, Zhou declared over Radio Peking that China was willing to have all POWs who refused repatriation turned over to a neutral state "so as to ensure a just solution to the question of their repatriation."[74]

These announcements reflected, not the CCP's newfound trust that the Eisenhower administration would be willing to end the war on China's terms, but rather their expectation that China's moderate response to the U.S. proposal would have a favorable impact on world opinion. In his telegram to the CPV headquarters on April 20, Deng Hua relayed Mao's instruction that "[diplomatically] we will try to reopen the truce talks and, at the same time, to prepare for protracted negotiations; but militarily, our forces should only prepare for protracted fighting." Mao continued to urge that "[the troops] should always be alert and do what has already been planned." Even when he was considering accepting Clark's February offer, Mao did not want the CPV to be informed of Beijing's new diplomatic move because the troops who were already mobilized to counter the enemy attack might relax their vigilance. Yang Dezhi later noted that "Chairman Mao still wanted us to follow the plan to counter possible U.S. amphibious operations."[75]

By late spring of 1953, there was still no sign of the expected enemy attack, which puzzled the military leaders in Beijing. Reassessing the situation, they came up with three explanations. First, the United States might be encountering great difficulties in reaching a consensus internally and with its allies on how to end the conflict. The Chinese leaders particularly noted that Britain and France were afraid that another full-scale offensive in Korea might provoke a general war. Second, the Eisenhower administration, because of "U.S. strategic and military problems," might need more time to prepare for a sizable amphibious offensive. The Chinese believed that Eisenhower was playing to world opinion by agreeing to reopen the truce talks and at the same time intensifying U.S. military preparations. Thus the American willingness to resume negotiations, in the eyes of the Chinese leaders, was a smoke screen intended to gain more time for military actions. Third, despite their readiness to parley, the US might still hope to obtain favorable terms in the peace talks by exerting military pressure on the battlefield. In his report to Mao dated April 20, Deng Hua repeated that the enemy would never willingly come to terms unless it faced military difficulties it could no longer afford. To compel the enemy to accept peace, he believed that "a policy of tit for tat [*zhenfeng xiangdui*] must be adopted."[76]

The CPV's tit-for-tat strategy was to initiate offensive actions instead of waiting to defend positions. The idea of striking out greatly appealed to the field commanders, whose patience for playing a waiting game seems to have worn thin. On March 31, Wang Jianan, the commander of the 9th Army Corps, suggested to the CPV headquarters that an all-out counteroffensive be launched in early May, concentrating on ten outposts of the enemy's main line of resistance so as "to deal the enemy a fatal blow." Supporting Wang's suggestion, the CPV commanders immediately relayed it to Beijing for approval. On April 3, the CMC gave its endorsement. Confirming that "this suggested action will certainly strengthen our position in the truce talks," the CMC instructed that "the planned offensive actions should be based on full preparedness and should start in middle or late May." Mao in particular was cautious and thought that this offensive might be premature. In his letter to Peng on April 23, he directed that "you may let them [field commanders] begin preparations, but we shall wait until some time in May to decide whether we open this offensive or give it up for the sake of [maintaining] the truce talks."[77]

Though anxious to take action, the field commanders had to incorporate Mao's caution into their plans. The CPV headquarters called a five-day meeting beginning April 30, which resulted in the "Supplementary Instructions on Preparing for the Summer Counteroffensive," issued on May 5. The order affirmed that the main objective of this counteroffensive was "to reinforce our diplomatic efforts at Panmunjom with military actions in the battlefield," as well as "to stretch out our line of defense southward as much as possible so that we will be in a more favorable strategic position even after the war is over." Regarding military plans, the CPV headquarters instructed the attacking units to target the ROK forces in the east and the U.S. troops in the west. To avoid any precipitate moves, the whole campaign was divided into three phases; within each phase, there would be ten days of actual fighting and five days of resting to gauge the enemy response. In this way, "we will always firmly hold the initiative and the freedom of action regarding escalation [of the offensive]." The CPV headquarters then set the end of May as the deadline for completing all the preparations, "so that those troops that are assigned to take this action would begin the attack in early June and end the entire campaign by early July."[78] Yang Dezhi recalls that "[we] just wanted to impress the enemy with the 'iron' facts that we were capable—not afraid—of fighting the war [through to the end]."[79]

Acknowledging that such an operation might trigger large-scale US/UN counteroffensives, the CPV headquarters planned to deploy sufficient combat troops to meet this possibility. The western and eastern coastal commands spared nine infantry divisions, eight howitzer battalions, four rocket-gun regiments, one anti-aircraft artillery division plus two regiments, and six engineering battalions to join the six infantry armies along the front for this operation. The 16th and 54th armies, the 1st Howitzer Division, two regiments of the 2d Howitzer Division, and two regiments of 21st Rocket Division were positioned as reserves. Moreover, a large number of new recruits were sent to the front line on stand-by for the purpose of replacing casualties once the offensive started. The CPV commanders also gave detailed instructions on how to select targets and assault them effectively. The primary targets, in their view, should be those US/UN outposts with strong defense works and favorable defensive ground so that after they were seized, the CPV troops could hold off the enemy's counterattack and decimate its forces in the process. For US/UN positions that had no strong defense works or were unsuitable for defense, the commanders directed the troops to storm and capture them, quickly withdraw to safety, and then prepare to storm them again before the enemy forces reestablished a firm foothold. The main goal was still to annihilate the enemy strength through seesaw battles.[80] In line with these instructions, the attacking units selected fifty-six US/UN positions mostly manned at platoon or company strength. Each CPV unit conducted reconnaissance to learn the specific conditions at these US/UN outposts. Some units secretly dug tunnels that extended close to the enemy positions and served as an advance base for the attack.[81]

In mid-May, CPV Chief of Staff Xie Fang came back to the headquarters from Panmunjom with the news that the armistice negotiations had once again stalemated because of a "rigid U.S. insistence on its counterinitiative on the POW issue." Upset by this development, the top four CPV commanders—Deng, Yang, Xie, and Li Zhimin (the new director of the CPV political department)—agreed that since one could negotiate only from strength, they should start the first phase of their counteroffensive right away. In order to show unanimity of opinion, they all signed on the order directing the CPV to begin the campaign on May 11. The lower-level commanders welcomed this decision. The acting commander of the 20th Army Corps, Zheng Weishan, telephoned Yang the next morning to congratulate him: "This is a remarkable decision. If you did not decide to do this now, I would have started to attack by myself."[82] Without even obtaining Beijing's approval, the CPV launched its offensive on May 13—far ahead of the CMC's original schedule. When the Beijing authorities learned of the CPV operation, they were concerned that it might be premature both militarily and politically. On May 16, the CMC cabled the CPV headquarters, insisting that all actions should be kept small scale so as to "avoid unfavorable effects upon world opinion." The CMC also instructed that any major offensive should strictly follow the original plan and that all commanders should take "operational difficulties into more careful consideration."[83]

In early June, a dramatic change in the Panmunjom negotiations made the CPV commanders alter their offensive plans. They were informed by the CMC that the U.S. negotiators had offered concessions on the POW repatriation issue on May 25 and that the long-expected armistice agreement would be signed soon. However, the commanders were also told that South Korean leader Rhee had bluntly rejected the accord and declared that his forces would continue fighting toward the Yalu.[84] "If a disease changes ten thousand times," Yang Dezhi pointed out, "so should medical treatment." To compel Rhee to accept peace, the CPV commanders decided that they should now concentrate on the ROK forces. On June 1, they significantly revised the original plan: instead of attacking the American and British forces, the primary target of the offensive would be the South Koreans. "We mean to kill the chicken so as to scare the monkey [*shaji xia hou*]," Deng Hua commented; "whoever makes trouble, we are surely to punish him."[85]

With Beijing's concurrence, another all-out offensive against the South

Korean troops on both sides of the Pukhan River commenced as a surprise attack on June 10. The CPV 20th Army Corps rapidly smashed Rhee's troops at several points along the front line, and the 19th Army Corps followed suit in the west. The onslaught did not stop until Peng Dehuai's cease-fire order arrived at CPV headquarters to inform them that "the agreement on the settlement of a military dividing line is reached and we should cease fighting on June 16." The Chinese recorded that the offensive had eliminated 41,000 South Korean soldiers at a cost of 19,000 CPV casualties. Moreover, the commanders were convinced that this military victory had played a key role in finally bringing the enemy to terms.[86]

Peng Dehuai was on his way to Panmunjom to sign the armistice agreement when an unexpected development halted his journey in Pyongyang. The North Korean leaders informed Peng that the South Koreans had "forcibly seized 27,000 North Korean POWs and dispatched them to the front line" on June 17 and 18. Given this sudden provocation, Mao directed on June 19 that "we must take another major [military] action to pressure the enemy side to assure that this type of incident won't happen again."[87] Peng was furious at Rhee's "unfaithful act." After talking with Kim Il-sung in Pyongyang, he decided not to go to Panmunjom. At 10:00 P.M. on June 20, he telegraphed Mao, "to put off the [truce] signing until after [we] wipe out 15,000 more South Koreans so as to intensify the contradictions among the enemies." With no hesitation, Mao agreed. "When [we will] sign it all depends," he declared, "but it is quite necessary to eliminate ten thousand more South Koreans before going to sign the truce agreement." Peng then directed Deng Hua to prepare for an immediate attack against the ROK forces.[88]

The bellicose CPV headquarters was again happy to comply. After two weeks of preliminary arrangements—including secretly moving troops through tunnels to advance bases and luring the ROK troops' attention toward other parts of the front line—the CPV 20th Army Corps's five infantry armies (the 67th, 68th, 60th, 54th, and 21st) embarked on another surprise attack on July 13 on the outposts of the ROK 3d, 6th, and 8th divisions in the area south of Kumsong. Within twenty-four hours, the CPV troops had devastated the ROK Capital, 6th, 8th, and 3d divisions. On July 16, generals Clark and Maxwell B. Taylor, who had replaced Van Fleet in February 1953 as commander of the U.S. Eighth Army, flew to the front to direct the resistance. They sent the ROK 11th and 7th divisions to reinforce the troops under CPV attack, even though they understood that the main reason for the Communist offensive "was to give the ROKs a 'bloody nose' and [to] show them and the world that 'puk chin'—'go north'—was easier said than done." Also on July 16, the CPV headquarters, concerned about the enemy reinforcements and the difficulties caused by rainy weather, ordered all attacking troops to break off contact. In their next day's instruction, the CPV commanders directed the troops to "repair newly captured defense works, organize fire support, and improve transport conditions" because a US/UN counteroffensive seemed imminent.[89] Though fighting did resume, it soon stalemated, as neither China nor the US were inclined to continue the war.

The Chinese noted that General William K. Harrison, Jr., the new U.S. negotiator at Panmunjom, had twice stated between July 11 and July 16 that the United States would not let Rhee disrupt the armistice again.[90] Perhaps to signify his own determination, Mao ordered the CPV on July 23 to evacuate the newly occupied areas south of the 38th parallel and instructed Peng to sign the armistice. The US/UN command welcomed the Chinese initiative and agreed to end the hostilities. In response, the CPV Command issued its final cease-fire order on July 26.[91] The armistice agreement was signed into effect the next day.

Map of Korean Demilitarized Zone (Source: *Central Intelligence Agency. Reproduced courtesy of the University of Chicago Libraries)*

IV

Although the Chinese leaders welcomed the armistice, they failed to recognize that had they managed the truce talks more realistically after negotiations began in July 1951, a settlement might have been reached much earlier—long before Eisenhower took office in January 1953 or before Stalin's death on March 5, 1953. They blamed American arrogance, stubbornness, and egotism for dragging out the war, but in retrospect, their misperception of the diplomatic process and their overrated confidence in CPV defensive capabilities were at least equally responsible.

Beijing wanted China's intervention to achieve two key objectives: militarily, to push the US/UN forces back to the 38th parallel, and politically, to press the US to settle the conflict on terms favorable to China and North Korea by withdrawing all "foreign" troops from Korea and holding a "UN supervised" general election in Korea as a whole. Unfortunately, they expected to obtain their political goal through the truce talks at Kaesong and Panmunjom. They could not understand why negotiations on an armistice agreement were not the time to deal with peace settlements. At one point in 1951, even Stalin had to ask the Chinese and the North Korean leaders to clarify for him what they really hoped to achieve through the talks. When he discovered their confused goals, he gave them a lecture on the differences among "conventional diplomatic norms" regarding cease-fires, truces, armistices, and peace agreements.[92]

Nevertheless, even when the Chinese had grasped more clearly the purposes of an armistice agreement, they still let the negotiations drag on. Consistently emphasizing the importance of such "major issues" as the withdrawal of foreign troops and the demarcation line, the Chinese leaders paid little attention to "minor issues" such as the POW repatriation. As Peng Dehuai believed, this point was irrelevant to a final peace settlement. When the US/UN negotiators insisted on dealing first with the military questions, including POW repatriation, the Chinese jumped to the conclusion that the US lacked "good will" and was only interested in making "ungrounded excuses."

More important, a hidden goal of China's intervention—namely to send a message to the world that China had finally stood up against foreign invasion and humiliation—became a powerful inducement for the Chinese to stand firm and play tough during the talks. The sensitive and proud Chinese leaders interpreted the US/UN refusal to compromise on "minor issues," such as the repatriation of POWs, as confirmation that the Americans still looked down on the Chinese people. Therefore, Mao regarded as "naive" the belief that any Chinese concession would instigate reciprocal concessions on the part of the US. To him, military action would invariably speak louder than diplomatic talks.[93]

Militarily, the Chinese were optimistic that the longer the war continued, the stronger China would become and the weaker the enemy would be. In fact, as the war prolonged, the more hazardous major CPV offensives became. The CCP leaders were as yet only dimly aware that a war of attrition not only hurt the US/UN forces but devastated China's economy and society and the troops' strength as well.

10. CONCLUSION: THE LESSONS OF KOREA

July 27, 1953, was set as the date for the signing of the Korean armistice at Panmunjom. The chief negotiators, General William K. Harrison, Jr., for the US/UN forces and Nam Il for the Communists, were the signatories. As the commanders in chief countersigned at their respective headquarters—Clark at Munsan, Kim Il-sung at Pyongyang, and Peng Dehuai at Kaesong—the Korean cease-fire went into effect at 10:00 P.M. that day.[1] Even so, China did not withdraw its forces from Korea until 1958.

In the end, the Chinese People's Volunteers were in Korea for eight years after their first entry in October 1950: two years and nine months of actual combat and five years and three months of garrison duties. How did Beijing authorities evaluate China's intervention in Korea? What lessons did they learn? And finally, how can the experience of Chinese intervention illuminate future studies of international conflict resolution?

China had paid a huge price for its Korean campaign. As many as twenty-five infantry armies (73 percent of the PLA forces), sixteen artillery (67 percent), ten armored (100 percent), twelve air force (52 percent), and six guard divisions fought in Korea along with hundreds of thousands of logistical personnel and laborers. More than two million combatant and noncombatant Chinese were engaged in battlefield operations. According to Chinese statistics, the CPV had lost a total of 390,000 troops—148,400 dead, 21,000 captured, 4,000 missing in action, and the remainder wounded. The CPV consumed approximately 5.6 million tons of war materials including 399 airplanes and 12,916 vehicles. The People's Republic spent more than 6.2 billion renminbi on the intervention.[2]

From a military point of view, the Chinese and the US/UN forces merely fought to a draw in Korea. Yet in China, instead of popular dissatisfaction, a widespread celebration of victory followed the announcement of the Korean armistice. Speaking at the Twenty-fourth Session of the CPGC on September 12, 1953, Mao Zedong proclaimed that the Chinese had undoubtedly defeated the US/UN forces and won "a great victory."[3] In his report to the council that same day, Peng Dehuai also stated that "[China's] great victory . . . would have a grave and profound impact on the situation in the Far East as well as in the world."[4]

Chinese leaders were convinced that the intervention strengthened the security of a new China. "We fought our way back to the 38th parallel and held firmly at that parallel." Mao explained. "If . . . [our] front lines had remained along the Yalu and Tammen rivers, it would have been impossible for the people in Shenyang, Anshan, and Fushun to carry on production free of worry."[5] Chinese leaders also believed that the CPV had so devastated American military strength that a general war between China and the US was delayed. According to Peng's report to the CPGC, the US had dispatched 1.2 million troops to Korea: a third of its army, a fifth of its air force, and one half of its navy. By Peng's estimates, after three years of fighting, the US had suffered 390,000 casualties and deaths, South Korea and other countries had lost 700,000 men, and more than 12,000 airplanes and 257 naval vessels had been destroyed. Washington had spent $83 billion and expended more than 7.3 million tons of war materials in Korea. Considering the drain on manpower and material resources, Peng was certain that the U.S. aspiration "for another world war is thus smashed."[6] Concurring in Peng's assertion that "a new imperialist war of aggression against China and a third world war have been put off," Mao stated unequivocally that "the imperialist aggressors ought to bear this in mind: the Chinese people are now organized, they are not to be trifled with. Once they are provoked to anger, things can get very tough."[7]

There was palpable euphoria among Chinese leaders. For the first time in its history, China could claim that it stood up to a dominant Western power. Only five decades ago, CCP propaganda reminded the Chinese people, a small contingent of a "united army of eight Western countries" had subdued China (referring to the international intervention of 1900); even more recently, 700,000 Japanese troops had conquered most of the country (in the Japanese invasion of 1937). But in Korea "after three years of fierce fighting," Peng maintained, "the first-rate armed forces of the greatest industrial power of the capitalist world were forced [by the Chinese troops] to stop at where they began [their invasion of North Korea]." To him, this result had indisputably proved that "gone for ever is the time when the western powers have been able to conquer a country in the [Far] East merely by mounting several cannons along the coast [as they had] in the past hundred years."[8]

Moreover, Beijing authorities felt that China's participation in the Korean War had won Moscow's trust. Sensitive to the Kremlin's suspicions about their political stand, the CCP had been anxious to demonstrate their internationalist—not nationalist—communist identity. In the mid-1960s, Marshall Chen Yi, then minister of foreign affairs, recalled that Chinese intervention had altered Stalin's perception that China was a potential Yugoslavia. After China entered the war, Stalin several times expressed his "admiration" for the CCP's courage and determination. Chinese leaders also noticed that in the immediate post–Korean War years, the Soviet Union amended its cautious policy of aid for China and offered to construct 156 large industrial and scientific enterprises in China.[9] Mao was especially pleased with the change in the Soviet attitude toward his regime. In his telegram to the Kremlin on September 15, 1953, he praised it as "a historically great undertaking" that the two governments had achieved this agreement on long-term Soviet assistance after only one round of negotiations. With Soviet technological economic aid, Mao assured Moscow, "we will industrialize China . . . so that China will play an important role in enhancing the strength of the socialist camp."[10]

In addition, the CCP leaders believed that the Korean victory helped China to reclaim its long-lost status and respect in Asia. On November 12, 1953, Kim Il-sung brought a large group of high-ranking officials to Beijing to sign agreements on long-term military, economic, and cultural cooperation. Kim publicly commended the Chinese for their "magnificent contributions to the Korean War, which will remain as immortal as Korea's beautiful mountains and rivers."[11] In return, Beijing proclaimed on November 23 that China would regard all materials that China had provided to Pyongyang during the war as "gifts to the North Korean Government." Furthermore, China would contribute another 800 million renminbi for North Korea's reconstruction in 1954–1957. Chinese leaders also made it clear in 1958 that the CPV would return to Korea if and when they were needed.[12] It is interesting that the old pattern of tribute relations between the two countries was now restored after it had been disrupted—mainly by Japan—for more than half a century.

In Beijing's view, China's success in halting U.S. expansion in Asia would encourage the anticolonialism movement in the region. "Undoubtedly," Peng pointed out in September 1953, "[our] Korean experience will stimulate the confidence and aspiration of those peoples under colonial and semicolonial rule in their struggle against imperialism."[13] Indeed, Ho Chi Minh's movement against the French rule in Indochina intensified right after the Korean armistice. Chinese military aid and advisers flooded into Vietnam during the fall of 1953 and the spring of 1954. With China's assistance, the Vietminh scored a big victory at Dienbienphu in March 1954.[14] Vietnamese military leader General Vo Nguyen Giap, who had commanded the Dienbienphu offensive, observed in 1964 that "Mao Zedong's military thought greatly contributed to our war against [the French]. . . . As our troops and people had a better opportunity of studying Mao Zedong's military thought, [we] succeeded in applying it in the practice of our armed struggle." In his judgment, this was "the key to the rapid growth and constant successes of our military forces and especially of the Dienbienphu victory in 1953–1954."[15]

Chinese leaders calculated that the impact of the Korean victory at home was no less important than it was abroad. A signal achievement of China's involvement in Korea, Mao argued, was that "the people of the whole country have heightened their political awareness."[16] Zhou Enlai declared in October 1958 that the Korean victory had fostered a profound and widespread "spirit [*jingshen*]" among the Chinese people. As another CCP leader put it in 1958, such a spirit of "fearing no hardship or death and daring to struggle against brutal forces" certainly mobilized full domestic support of the postwar reconstruction.[17] Indeed, Beijing authorities attributed the great success in economic reconstruction to the Korean War spirit. The CCP inherited a badly disrupted economy in 1949, and the Korean War stalled the nation's industrial and agricultural production. After the war ended, Beijing concentrated on the development of heavy and defense industries. The First Five-Year Plan created a spectacular advance in industrial output. In 1957, steel production reached 5.35 million tons; iron, 5.8 million tons; electric power, 19.3 billion kwh; coal, 131 million tons; and crude oil, 1.46 million tons.[18]

The industrial growth fed the CCP leadership's ambition for quick modernization. Addressing the CPCG's thirtieth session on June 14, 1954, Mao laid out a timetable for China to become an industrial power: it would take China "fifteen years" to "lay down a foundation" and "approximately fifty years" to "build a powerful socialist country."[19] Mao reiterated this goal in 1955. Proudly proclaiming that China would soon catch up with the US, he noted that "America only has a history of 180 years. Sixty years ago, it produced 4 million tons of steel. We are [therefore] only sixty years behind . . . [and] we will surely overtake it."[20] During his visit to Moscow on November 2–21, 1957, the CCP chairman boasted at a meeting with other leaders of communist countries that China would first surpass Britain in iron, steel, and other heavy industries within the next fifteen years and would then beat the US in these areas as well.[21]

After he returned home, Mao became engrossed with the idea that China could win a contest of industrial strength against the West. In April 1958, he vociferously argued that "it probably will not take us as long as we have anticipated to overtake the capitalist powers in industrial and agricultural production." His illusion pushed the central leadership to include in its planning the goals of surpassing Britain in seven years and catching up with the US in eight or ten years. One month later, Mao told the high-ranking PLA commanders that "we are quite sure that we will exceed Britain in seven years and overtake the US in ten years."[22] The result of Mao's specious aspiration was the "Great Leap Forward" movement, calling for a 19 percent increase in steel production, 18 percent in electricity, and 17 percent in coal output for 1958. Buoyed by groundless optimism, the CCP leaders kept raising the production goals in hopes of achieving an unprecedented rate of growth. These fanciful ideas, however, led to economic disaster in the following years.[23]

Perhaps most important, the victorious mentality that the Korean experience had fostered within the CCP greatly reinforced the party's military romanticism. In the reasoning of the Chinese leaders, having gained combat experience in fighting the U.S. troops, there was no need to fear American military power. "This time we have taken the measure of the U.S. armed forces," Mao asserted in September 1953. "If you have never taken them on, you are liable to be scared of them. We have fought them for thirty-three months and got to know them for what they are worth. U.S. imperialism is not terrifying, nothing to make a fuss about."[24] Almost every high-ranking commander thought that China's success in Korea shattered the myth of U.S. invincibility and proved that a weak nation could defeat a strong one. Even though Chinese troops were inferior to the US/UN military in technology, equipment, and firepower, Mao argued, China's "glorious people's war" smashed doubts about "(1) whether we are capable of fighting [the war]; (2) whether we are able to defend [our positions]; (3) whether we could assure logistic supplies; and (4) whether we could [even] beat the enemy's bacteriological warfare."[25] Peng was even more extravagant, contending that the CPV accomplishment in Korea "has completely exposed the lie about advanced weapons' 'omnipotence' with which U.S. imperialists have attempted to bluff, threaten, and scare people since the end of World War II, and totally uncovered the weakness and impotence of the military thoughts of imperialist camp and the true inside story about the debility of its so-called 'powerful war machinery.'" Regarding the U.S. military as "outwardly strong but inwardly weak [*waiqiang zhonggan*]," he maintained that any U.S. aggression attempts in the future "can be completely smashed."[26]

Chinese military commanders believed that the Korean War offered invaluable lessons on how a weak army could defeat a strong enemy in modern wars. During the PLA's high-ranking command meetings from December 7, 1953, to January 26, 1954, Peng called on the commanders to "summarize every aspect of our lessons" from the war and use the knowledge to educate officers and train troops.[27] Concurring with Peng, Deng Hua added that, "since we beat the highly modernized invading forces led by U.S. imperialists with [our] inferior equipment, [our] experience in the Korean War is real and evidently invaluable."[28] To the Chinese military leaders, a review of the war simply validated their belief that human strength would ultimately prevail over material power. "My general observation," Deng Hua wrote in early 1954, "is that in modern warfare, nature of war and army's political quality will still play a decisive role, no matter how important material and technological conditions may be." As the Korean War had proved, he continued, "victory in modern wars largely hinges upon a correct military line including correct strategic decision making, [shrewd] execution of campaign or battle plans."[29] In the July 1954 report entitled "Summary of Basic Lessons of CPV Political Work in the War to Resist U.S. Aggression and Aid Korea," the CPV political department pointed out that in "fighting a modern war, political work remains the lifeline of our army, given that the role of political work was not reduced but greatly heightened [in Korea]." A supplementary report drafted by former CPV political commissars Gan Siqi and Li Zhimin in March 1956 stated even more positively that "a decisive factor of our victory over the enemy [in Korea] was our political advantage, not equipment or technology." To them, political work in the army "has been, and will be, our *magic weapon* to defeat the enemy."[30]

In early August 1953, the Air Force Command also formed a commission to draw lessons from the CPV air combat experience, especially the way in which the novice CPV air force dared to engage the much-more-experienced American pilots during Korea's air battles. This commission collected as many as 3,653 individual papers by the end of 1955 and compiled 119 of them into "Collected Reflections on the Air Force's Combat Experience in the War to Resist U.S. Aggression and Aid Korea" in September 1956. As the report declared, "The fact that our young air force was capable of fighting both small- and large-scale air battles against the U.S. air force and scoring several victories brings to light one truth: human factor still is decisive in determining victory and defeat in modern warfare."[31]

For years after the end of the Korean War, the CCP's romantic attitude toward threat and use of force shaped Beijing's foreign and defense policies. Despite its chronic inferiority in technology and resources, the PRC emerged from the Korean War with a powerful *image* that China had resumed "her rightful place among the nations—the first place."[32] As a result, Beijing viewed itself as the champion of the sentiments and causes of the oppressed people and nations in Asia, Africa, and Latin America. If China could defeat the mightiest power in the world, Chinese leaders believed, other nations or forces could achieve the same result. An immediate consequence of this belief was China's involvement in Ho Chi Minh's struggle against the French, which precipitated the first Indochina crisis in 1954. The massive amount of support, both in materiel and manpower, provided by the Chinese for the Vietminh's national liberation eventually culminated in the Vietnam War (1964–1972).[33]

With hindsight, however, what can one infer from the Chinese intervention in Korea to better understand Beijing's conflict-resolution behavior during the Cold War? There is ample evidence in the available Chinese materials that China felt threatened when the US intervened in Korea and decided to counter the American threat at the time of the US/UN advance toward the Yalu River. But the *cultural elements* that propelled China into Korea should not be overlooked or downplayed. The Chinese leaders' historical consciousness, images, and sense of moral and political superiority played at least as important a role as their security concerns. Notwithstanding China's inferiority in modern technology, economic strength, and military capabilities, Beijing authorities decided to confront the US in Korea. They did so partly because they believed certain things about themselves. To understand their historical mindset, we must examine the images the Chinese Communist leaders held about China and the outside world.

The necessary text for understanding the outlook of the Chinese leadership is a single sentence in Mao's proclamation at the Tiananmen Square on October 1, 1949, that "*the Chinese people have finally stood up!*" This short but well-celebrated statement had a dual implication. First and foremost, it projected the image of a China that had long been subject to oppression and victimization at the hands of foreign evil forces invading China. During the previous century (1839–1949), often referred to by the Chinese as the century of humiliation, China had suffered a great deal as the unwilling prize of Western and Japanese power struggles. Indemnities, territorial cessions, expansion of international settlements, and extraterritorialities all became the rhetoric of "China's humiliation." Compounded by the political, economic, and cultural disintegration within, these diplomatic chains fostered, in the words of John K. Fairbank, "self-pity, resentment, and the need for an explanation of history in terms of evil and justice."[34]

Growing up in the heyday of imperialism in China, Mao and his comrades had deplored the humiliations inflicted on China by foreigners, and exhorted his fellow citizens to strengthen their bodies so that they could stand up against the foreigners.[35] As much as the modern Chinese elites, Mao and his followers saw themselves as the restorers of China's traditional pride and the redressers of the wrongs inflicted on the country by the West. Ultimately, the Chinese Communists created an *image* of "national liberation" and viewed themselves as a generation of liberators with the historical mission to completely rid China of foreign bullies, interference, or invasion. To accomplish that mission remained a central goal of the CCP's foreign policy on the eve of its nationwide victory.[36]

The CCP's portrait of an external threat was an equally important factor in Beijing's decision to intervene in Korea. Deeply concerned about their vulnerability to foreign intervention in the late 1940s, the CCP leaders maintained the suspicion that the US would not concede the "loss of China" and would do whatever it could to "make troubles" against a new China. This perception of American intentions was largely assumed rather than based on any realistic understanding of how nations related to one another along the spectrum of amity and enmity. With little attempt to identify whether this adversarial image was real or fanciful, Chinese leaders fed their sense of danger when they interpreted all American aggression as directed toward them. It was hardly surprising that Mao had justified his call for precautions against American intervention within his conceptual frameworks of "two camps," "intermediate zone," and "three dangerous spots."

Mao's images of national liberation and of American threat were closely linked to his belief in China's long-standing moral superiority. This notion was in a corollary of the firm conviction held by the Chinese people that China was a superior civilization, especially in comparison with the "foreign barbarians." Rather than fearing "foreign devils [*yangguizi*]," Mao called on the Chinese people to condemn them, curse them, and more important, despise them. Commenting on the fate of Japan's invasion of China in the mid-1930s, he had asserted that Japan would eventually be defeated because the Chinese people had "the spirit to fight the enemy to the last drop of our blood, the determination to recover our lost territory by our own efforts, and the ability to stand on our own feet in the family of nations."[37]

Throughout the 1940s, Mao had persistently portrayed "imperialism and all reactionaries" as "paper tigers." In his view, U.S. imperialists, even with the atomic bomb, appeared "terrifying, but in reality they are not so powerful" because "from a long-term point of view, it is not the reactionaries but the people who are powerful."[38] So confident was Mao in the final victory of Chinese intervention in Korea that he proclaimed in October 1950: "You [the United States] can use the atomic bomb, I will respond with my hand grenade. I will catch the weak point on your part and defeat you."[39]

China's moral superiority, Mao believed, was rooted in the basic fact that the outcome of war depended on the masses of people, not weapons. Mao had automatically equated a people's war with a war of the masses. Therefore, he argued that "the mobilization of the common people throughout the country will create a vast sea in which to drown the enemy, create the conditions that will make up for our inferiority in arms and other things, and create the prerequisites for overcoming every difficulty in the war."[40] Mao stressed the key function of what he termed "man's conscious dynamic role" in warfare. Although the objective conditions set the stage for victory or defeat, yet they hardly determined the outcome of war. To him, it was the subjective factors that proved decisive. How to explore the subjective elements in a war thus remained a primary concern of Mao's. One of the basic principles he formulated was that the party must command the gun, not the other way around. From the very beginning, he had fought fiercely for the establishment of the rule that the party, and only the party, would lead the armed forces and the armed struggle, and the army must never be allowed to become independent of the political leadership of the party. To him, political work in the military was the most effective way to mobilize the subjective strength of the rank and file.

Furthermore, Mao thought it was impossible to defeat a stronger enemy without strictly applying the correct military line. As a self-educated strategist, he studied and absorbed the rich lessons of warfare, some foreign but mostly Chinese. Regarding war as possessing its own particular features and laws, Mao contended that warfare should not merely be subsumed under politics in general but must be carefully studied, codified, acted on, developed, and tested through actual combat. Respected by his comrades-in-arms as a leading innovator in strategic thought, Mao brilliantly applied materialist *dialectics* to the question of how a weak army could triumph: first proceed from the strategic defensive, then wage the war in such a way as to prepare for and finally go over to the strategic offensive, thereby carrying the war through to victory.

Against a technologically superior enemy, he also advocated prudent military tactics. They included always knowing your enemy and yourself; adhering to the principle of flexibility; concentrating a superior force to eliminate the enemy forces one by one; fighting quick battles with a quick decision; attacking dispersed, isolated enemy forces first and attacking concentrated, strong enemy forces later; fighting no battles unprepared and fighting no battles you are not sure of winning; and striving to wipe out the enemy when he is on the move. Having won the civil war, the Chinese Communists entertained the belief that Mao's thought on warfare constituted their most formidable military weapon against the imperialist West. Indeed, it was hardly surprising that the CPV's high-ranking commanders—Peng Dehuai, Deng Hua, Hong Xuezhi, and Yang Dezhi—never doubted that Mao's military thought would work in Korea.

Clearly, cultural thoughtways—myth as well as reason, and image as well as reality—formed the core of Chinese Communist military thought. However, it is evident that Chinese leaders held an *ethnocentric* view of modern warfare. They demonstrated a strong tendency to see the whole objective world through the prism of their own subjective experience, images, memories, and, sometimes, aspirations. Moreover, they were as likely to mold the enemy to fit their own strategy as to adapt their strategy to the behavior of the enemy.[41]

Indeed, Chinese leaders found the Korean experience at odds with their understanding of war. Both Beijing and Washington wanted to confine the conflict to the Korean peninsula; the US resorted to conventional weaponry only; and neither side sought a total destruction of the opponent. As the world entered the nuclear age at the end of World War II, limited wars—namely, wars of "limited time, space, means and objectives"—emerged as a tool of international conflict resolution. The Korean War was the very first instance of a limited war in the nuclear era. Unfortunately, Chinese military leaders failed to see this challenge to their traditional thinking, and they made little attempt to correct the crude images they had of themselves and the enemy.

First, limited warfare makes a protracted war strategy unrealistic and disadvantageous to the protractor. Since political considerations often require wars of limited and sometimes flexible objectives, including punishment, compulsion, or restoration of a status quo, military actions will be constrained within the predetermined time and space. Given this change in warfare, China's strategy of "gaining mastery by striking only after the enemy has struck [*hou fa zhi ren*]" was not viable, because once the initiative is lost in a limited war, there is no time to gain it back. Recent studies have convincingly demonstrated that given the advantage of a blitzkreig strategy over a war of attrition, conventional deterrence based on a defensive posture becomes very vulnerable.[42]

Moreover, offense and defense switch so frequently and rapidly in a limited war that a nation focused on defense will be at a disadvantage in the conflict. When the CPV first entered the war, the Chinese planned to fight a defensive action, and they did not allow for the possibility of an immediate engagement with the US/UN forces. Though they quickly changed from the defensive to the offensive, their military unpreparedness caused the Chinese troops to suffer greatly. The 9th Army Corps was rendered combat-ineffective primarily because the troops were not equipped to combat cold weather. The same type of mistake was repeated in the spring of 1951. After three offensives in a row, the CPV headquarters wanted the forces to rest and reorganize, never expecting that the motorized US/UN troops would open an immediate counteroffensive. Underestimation of the enemy's options again resulted in CPV setbacks in the battlefield.

Second, a limited war makes numerical advantage less crucial to the outcome of war than technological advantage. In a war of limited space and time, one has to fight a quick battle to force quick decisions. The main requirement is to maximize the destruction of the adversary in minimum time and space; new weapons and advanced technologies will play the key role in achieving these ends. Therefore, technological superiority is far more important than numerical superiority—as the Korean experience proved. The Chinese understood that they were technically inferior to the US/UN forces, yet they strongly believed in their numerical advantage. However, they were soon rudely awakened by combat reality. Mao, for instance, had initially expected to eliminate one US/UN army with three or four CPV armies, but the CPV never wiped out a single enemy division in one battle. Later during the war, the CPV headquarters several times had to employ one whole army in an attack on a US/UN position manned at battalion strength, yet their assault often ended in vain. The Chinese discovered that numerical superiority became a liability, not an asset, given the logistical needs of a large army. Also, since mobilization takes time, a limited war might end well before enough troops gather on the battlefield to constitute a numerical advantage. Peng Dehuai became cautious about sweeping offensives in 1951–1952 mainly because of his deep concerns about manpower and supply shortage. In the summer of 1953, he finally gathered fifty-nine infantry, fifteen artillery, nine air force, ten engineering, and one guard divisions, a total of 1.35 million troops in Korea. Before he could open another large-scale offensive, however, a cease-fire agreement was reached. Many years after the war, Peng was still bitter about "the carefully prepared but never implemented offensive [in Korea]."[43]

Third, assistance and support from an ally becomes extraneous and unreliable in a limited war of the nuclear age. According to Mao, the rationale for a weak nation to fight a protracted war was to recruit international sympathy and backing during the period of its strategic defensive. But China's experience in the Korean War suggested that the process of acquiring international support was both complicated and complicating. Before China decided to intervene, Beijing expected unconditional support from its ally, the Soviet Union. In reality, Russian assistance was often too little and too late because of the Kremlin's fear of direct involvement in an unwanted—possibly nuclear—war. After the Korean War, the Chinese thought they could count on Moscow more, but they soon discovered that the Soviet Union was still an unreliable ally. The Chinese leaders were increasingly suspicious of the Kremlin's moves to restrict Beijing's freedom of action in foreign affairs, while the Soviet authorities became increasingly troubled by the reckless desire of the Chinese leadership to confront the US. During China's massive bombardment of the offshore islands Jinmen and Mazu in late August 1958, Khrushchev was shocked by Beijing's "relentless and irresponsible action." As a result, he sent foreign minister Andrei A. Gromyko to Beijing for a "peaceful resolution" of the crisis. Gromyko "was flabbergasted" when he heard Mao suggesting that

> if the USA attacks China with nuclear weapons, the Chinese armies must retreat from the border regions into the depths of the country. They must draw the enemy in deep so as to grip US forces in a pincer inside China. . . . In the event of war, the Soviet Union should not take any military measures against the Americans in the first stage. Instead, you should let them penetrate deep inside the territory of the Chinese giant. Only when the Americans are right in the central provinces should you give them everything you've got.[44]

The subsequent Soviet rejection of Mao's proposal invariably signaled the beginning of the end of the Sino-Soviet military alliance. It is, however, interesting that from 1950 through the first Indochina crisis in 1954 to the end of the Vietnam War in 1973, Beijing consistently honored an informal alliance with the Vietnamese Communists, only to regret in the late 1970s that their long-time friends turned against them.

Fourth, domestic support can hardly be taken for granted in fighting a limited war in the nuclear age. A country's strategic resources, both human and material, compensate for a country's weakness in weaponry and technology, but rapid technological development of offensive capabilities makes that remedy increasingly difficult. It is true that a nation such as China with a long tradition of total political control may encounter less difficulty in mobilizing its people's support, yet it becomes harder to sustain popular enthusiasm for a war that drags on and incurs huge human and material losses. Indeed, the Chinese people were highly mobilized by the CCP's call for patriotism during the Korean War, but as a result of the war fatigue, the popular anxiety for peace and stability increased so rapidly in 1952–1953 that the CCP leadership had to tighten up political control by executing the "three-antis" and "five-antis" campaigns. In Shanghai, for instance, a large number of private factories and manufacturers refused to produce military supplies because too high taxes and too low prices were forcing them out of business. As the "antis" campaign started, the CCP arrested hundreds of businessmen and confiscated their properties. Since then, state-society relations in China have changed dramatically.[45] The fact remains that China was largely free from US/UN air attack through the Korean War yet it still could not sustain unilateral support for its military action. Today, offensive technology is so inconceivably sophisticated that the front and the rear hardly differ from one another. Strategic bombing, either for "countervalue" or "counterforce" purposes, makes mobilization of popular support for a war of attrition extremely difficult, if not impossible. Probably because of this concern, China never openly intervened in Vietnam as they had in Korea.

Fifth, it is an oversimplification to base an army's morale on political indoctrination alone. Certainly a just cause, such as defending one's own country or punishing aggressors, may motivate the troops, but it is dangerous to assume that spiritual power will ultimately prevail over technological strength. The Chinese Communists successfully indoctrinated the rank and file during the Korean War, partly because the Chinese soldiers were relatively manipulable. Statistics show that in 1951, 67 percent of the Chinese troops were illiterate and only 16 percent had received formal education at the elementary level or above. With little reading and writing skills, they barely grasped the political and military situations of the war. Moreover, raised in the Chinese traditions, the CPV soldiers were generally obedient and respectful to their commanding officers and would follow orders almost blindly. Coming from a peasant background, most of them had borne hardships or made sacrifices since their childhood. Even so, a large number of soldiers were affected by US/UN psychological warfare and resisted CCP political indoctrination. Some asked to be sent home, some deserted on the eve of a battle, and others surrendered to the enemy. The CPV political department had to admit that Korea was by far the most severe challenge to the CCP's political work in the army, and the political officers faced many new problems with no easy solution.[46] After the war was over, Peng, among other military leaders, conceded the seriousness of ineffective political control in the army. During his tenure as defense minister between 1954–1959, he vigorously devoted himself to improving the troops' combat effectiveness by professionalizing the command and control system. Peng adopted advanced managerial strategies to standardize military training, hoping thereby to eventually minimize the military's reliance on political indoctrination. Severely criticized by Mao and Lin Biao as putting military professionalism above political work, Peng and his followers were purged in 1959. Political control has remained an indispensable element of the Chinese armed forces.[47]

The highly dubious lessons that Beijing drew from Korea can lead in a very dangerous direction. For those nations who suffer from an inferiority complex after long years as a weak power, it would be detrimental to romanticize warfare in the nuclear age because short-term belligerency might slip into a total disaster. It is pernicious to assume that human power is unlimited because the exaggeration of spiritual force may well block a decision maker's vision and render military actions reckless and harmful. It is also hazardous to believe that a protracted war strategy could lead to ultimate victory, because in trying to deplete the enemy's strength, one's own strength is depleted, possibly resulting in self-destruction. For better or worse, China's strategic planners continue to theorize on how a weak nation can forestall invasion by a stronger enemy.[48] At the same time, China is determined to dispel its image as a victim; as Jonathan Pollack notes, "China is now embarked on an ambitious effort to move to the front ranks of the world's powers by the year of 2000."[49]

On the American side, an equally interesting lesson of the Korean War is that *ethnocentrism* assumed a vital role in U.S. strategic thinking on Korea. American officials demonstrated a strong tendency to see "the others" through their own myths and values. While the Chinese took special pride in their moral superiority, American strategists emphasized U.S. technological superiority. American history itself had fostered the perception of military invincibility. As the nation of farmers began to industrialize in the nineteenth century, so the outcome of its wars increasingly came to depend on superior ways to kill. Victory, in the minds of Americans, largely depended on technology, which was itself the product of "Yankee ingenuity" and "American know-how." The technological mentality culminated in the mushroom cloud that ended World War II, a memory still fresh at the time of the Korean War. It was as if Americans *were* technology. Advanced technology created an American faith that the United States could not be beaten in war—not by any nation or by any combination of nations. The US could fight where, when, and how it wished, without risking failure.

The conviction of U.S. invincibility on the basis of American technological superiority misled American strategists. After all, the US had already beaten the Indians, French, British (twice), Mexicans, Spanish, Germans (twice), Italians, Japanese, and Koreans—why worry about the Chinese? Indeed, the Joint Intelligence Committee had asserted in early July 1950 that the combat experience of Communist Chinese forces had been mostly "hit-and-run" guerrilla tactics, and their peasant soldiers had never met a "well-trained force with high morale equipped with modern weapons." Even in November, MacArthur bluntly scorned the importance of Chinese intervention. "If the Chinese tried to get down to Pyongyang," he boasted, "there would be the greatest slaughter."[50] Given the Chinese inferiority in equipment and supply support, Major General Oliver P. Smith, commander of the 1st Marine Division, remarked that "even Genghis Khan wouldn't have tried Korea in the winter."[51] When the Chinese troops appeared unintimidated by US/UN firepower, the Americans found it hard to believe. Major General Hobart Gay, commander of the 1st Cavalry Division, heard a pilot of an observation plane radio in his report on November 1, 1950: "This is the strangest sight I have ever seen. There are two large columns of enemy infantry moving southeast over the trails. . . . Our shells are landing right in their columns and they keep coming."[52]

Trapped by its own self-image, the U.S. military hardly paid attention to the strategy and tactics of the Chinese Communist force. Gene Z. Hanrahan and Edward L. Katzenbach, Jr., both specialists in "irregular warfare," discovered in 1954 that little of Mao's military philosophy had been known to the American military or intelligence community. Although translations of Mao's works on warfare had a "Communist-worldwide circulation," they had been disregarded by American military intelligence. Until Mao's works were published in London in 1954 and later that year by International Publishers in New York, they were "virtually unobtainable in the United States." The Library of Congress did not have them, nor did any libraries of U.S. military branches.[53] It is unfortunate, to say the least, that the lack of interest in understanding a "non-Western" military philosophy or the tactics of "an irregular army" may have contributed to the much more tragic error of U.S. intervention in Vietnam.

Today Beijing authorities have finally learned their bloody lessons. However, there has been little study of how Mao's military romanticism affected the leaders of the small and/or weak states and to what extent it shaped their behavior in international conflict resolution. In addition to the Korean hostilities, the Cuban Missile Crisis, and the Vietnam War, the recent Gulf War may serve as an important illustration of how military romanticism—this time, on the part of Saddam Hussein—can entail grave risks to global security. In the final analysis, as Akira Iriye correctly points out, "military power and economic performance may ebb and flow, but historical consciousness will linger."[54] There is thus a need to devote more academic effort to the study of international security through the examination of cultural factors intrinsic to different nation-states or ethnic groups.

APPENDIX
CPV Forces in Korea

Table A.1. CPV Forces in Korea: October 19–November 5, 1950

Army Corps	Army	Division	Regiment
13th	38th	112th	334th, 335th, 336th
		113th	337th, 338th, 339th
		114th	340th, 341st, 342d
	39th	115th	343d, 344th, 345th
		116th	346th, 347th, 348th
		117th	349th, 350th, 351st
	40th	118th	352d, 353d, 354th
		119th	355th, 356th, 357th
		120th	358th, 359th, 360th
	42d	124th	370th, 371st, 372d
		125th	373d, 374th, 375th
		126th	376th, 377th, 378th
	50th	148th	442d, 443d, 444th
		149th	445th, 446th, 447th
		150th	448th, 449th, 450th
	60th	196th	586th, 587th, 588th
		197th	589th, 590th, 591st
		198th	592d, 593d, 594th
CPV Artillery Force		1st	25th, 26th, 27th
		2d	28th, 29th, 30th
		8th	42d, 44th, 45th, 46th

Total: 6 infantry armies (18 divisions), 3 artillery divisions

Table A.2. CPV Forces in Korea: November 25, 1950–January 8, 1951

Army Corps	Army	Division	Regiment
13th	38th	112th	334th, 335th, 336th
		113th	337th, 338th, 339th
		114th	340th, 341st, 342d
	39th	115th	343d, 344th, 345th
		116th	346th, 347th, 348th
		117th	349th, 350th, 351st
	40th	118th	352d, 353d, 354th
		119th	355th, 356th, 357th
		120th	358th, 359th, 360th
	42d	124th	370th, 371st, 372d
		125th	373d, 374th, 375th
		126th	376th, 377th, 378th
	50th	148th	442d, 443d, 444th
		149th	445th, 446th, 447th
		150th	448th, 449th, 450th
	60th	196th	586th, 587th, 588th
		197th	589th, 590th, 591st
		198th	592d, 593d, 594th
9th	20th	58th	172d, 173d, 174th
		59th	175th, 176th, 177th
		60th	178th, 179th, 180th
		89th	265th, 266th, 270th
	26th	76th	226th, 227th, 228th
		77th	229th, 230th, 231st
		78th	232d, 233d, 234th
		88th	262d, 263d, 264th
	27th	79th	235th, 236th, 237th
		80th	238th, 239th, 240th
		81st	241st, 242d, 243d
		94th	280th, 281st, 282d
CPV Artillery Force		1st	25th, 26th, 27th
		2d	28th, 29th, 30th
		8th	42d, 44th, 45th, 46th
Engineer Corps			4th, 5th, 6th, 8th
Railway Engineer Corps		1st	1st, 11th, 21st

Total: 9 infantry armies (30 divisions), 3 artillery divisions

Table A.3. CPV Order of Battle: January 27–April 21, 1951

Army Corps	Army	Division
3d	12th	31st, 34th, 35th
	15th	29th, 44th, 45th
	60th	179th, 180th, 181st
9th	20th	58th, 59th, 60th, 89th
	26th	76th, 77th, 78th, 88th
	27th	79th, 80th, 81st, 94th
13th	38th	112th, 113th, 114th
	39th	115th, 116th, 117th
	40th	118th, 119th, 120th
	42d	124th, 125th, 126th
	50th	148th, 149th, 150th
	60th	196th, 197th, 198th
19th	63d	187th, 188th, 189th
	64th	190th, 191st, 192d
	65th	193d, 194th, 195th
Artillery Force		1st, 2d, 8th
		21st, 31st (Rocket)
		61st, 62d, 63d, 64th (Anti-aircraft)

Total: 15 infantry armies (48 divisions), 9 artillery divisions

Table A.4. CPV Order of Battle: April 22–June 10, 1951

Army Corps	Army	Division
3d	12th	31st, 34th, 35th
	15th	29th, 44th, 45th
	60th	179th, 180th, 181st
9th	20th	58th, 59th, 60th
	26th	76th, 77th, 78th
	27th	79th, 80th, 81st
13th	38th	112th, 113th, 114th
	39th	115th, 116th, 117th
	40th	118th, 119th, 120th
	42d	124th, 125th, 126th
	47th	139th, 140th, 141st
19th	63d	187th, 188th, 189th
	64th	190th, 191st, 192d
	65th	193d, 194th, 195th
Artillery Force		1st, 3d, 7th, 8th
		21st, 31st, and 32d (Rocket)
		61st, 62d, 63d, 64th (Anti-aircraft)
Air Force		3d, 4th, 5th, 6th, 7th, 8th, 9th, 15th

Total: 14 infantry armies (42 divisions), 11 artillery divisions plus 4 tank regiments, 8 air force divisions

Table A.5. CPV Order of Battle: June 11, 1951–August 1952

	Army Corps	Army	Division
Under CPV Command		38th	112th, 113th, 114th
		39th	115th, 116th, 117th
		40th	118th, 119th, 120th
		42d	124th, 125th, 126th
		47th	139th, 140th, 141st
		50th	148th, 149th, 150th
West Coast Command	3d	12th	31st, 34th, 35th
		15th	29th, 44th, 45th
		60th	179th, 180th, 181st
	19th	63d	187th, 188th, 189th
		64th	190th, 191st, 192d
		65th	193d, 194th, 195th
	20th	67th	199th, 200th, 201st
		68th	202d, 203d, 204th
	23d	36th	106th, 107th, 108th
		37th	109th, 110th, 111th
East Coast Command	9th	20th	58th, 59th, 60th, 89th
		26th	76th, 77th, 78th, 88th
		27th	79th, 80th, 81st, 94th
Artillery Force			2d, 7th, 8th
			21st, 31st (Rocket)
			61st, 62d, 63d, 64th (Anti-aircraft)
Air Force			2d, 3d, 4th, 5th, 6th, 7th, 8th, 9th, 10th, 11th, 14th, 15th

Total: 19 infantry armies (50 divisions), 9 artillery divisions plus 5 tank regiments, 12 air force divisions

Table A.6. CPV Forces in Korea: September 18–November 25, 1952

	Army Corps	Army	Division
Under CPV Command		38th	112th, 113th, 114th
		39th	115th, 116th, 117th
		40th	118th, 119th, 120th
		46th	133d, 136th, 137th
		47th	139th, 140th, 141st
	3d	12th	31st, 34th, 35th
		15th	29th, 44th, 45th
		60th	179th, 180th, 181st
West Coast Command		42d[a]	124th, 125th, 126th
		50th	148th, 149th, 150th
	19th	63d	187th, 188th, 189th
		64th	190th, 191st, 192d
		65th	193d, 194th, 195th
	20th	67th	199th, 200th, 201st
		68th	202d, 203d, 204th
East Coast Command	9th	20th[b]	58th, 59th, 60th, 89th
		23d[c]	67th, 69th, 73d
		26th[d]	76th, 77th, 78th, 88th
		27th[e]	79th, 80th, 81st, 94th
		24th[f]	70th, 72d, 74th
Artillery Force			1st, 2d, 7th, 8th
			21st, 31st (Rocket)
			61st, 62d, 63d, 64th (Anti-aircraft)
Air Force			3d, 4th, 5th, 6th, 8th, 9th, 12th, 15th, 17th, 18th

Total: 20 infantry armies (63 divisions), 10 artillery divisions, 10 air force divisions

[a] Returned to China in September 1952
[b] Returned to China in October 1952
[c] Entered Korea in September 1952
[d] Returned to China in June 1952
[e] Returned to China in October 1952
[f] Entered Korea in September 1952

Table A.7. CPV Forces in Korea: December 18, 1952–July 27, 1953

	Army Corps	Army	Division
CPV Reserves		21st	61st, 62d, 63d[a]
		47th[b]	139th, 140th, 141st
West Coast Command		16th[c]	32d, 46th, 47th
		38th	112th, 113th, 114th
		39th	115th, 116th, 117th
		40th	118th, 119th, 120th
		50th	148th, 149th, 150th
		54th[d]	130th, 134th, 135th
East Coast Command	3d	12th	31st, 34th, 35th
		15th	29th, 44th, 45th
	9th	23d	67th, 69th, 73d
		24th	70th, 72d, 74th
	19th	1st[e]	1st, 2d, 7th
		46th	133d, 136th, 137th
		63d	187th, 188th, 189th
		64th	190th, 191st, 192d
		65th	193d, 194th, 195th
	20th	60th	179th, 180th, 181st
		67th	199th, 200th, 201st
		68th	202d, 203d, 204th
Artillery Force			1st, 2d, 7th, 8th
			21st, 31st (Rocket)
			61st, 62d, 63d, 64th (Anti-aircraft)
Air Force			3d, 4th, 5th, 6th, 8th, 9th, 12th, 15th, 17th, 18th

Total: 20 infantry armies (60 divisions), 10 artillery divisions plus 4 tank regiments, 10 air force divisions

[a]Attached to the 20th Army Corps in May 1953
[b]Attached to the 9th Army Corps in May 1953
[c]Entered Korea in January 1953 and attached to the 9th Army Corps in May 1953
[d]Attached to the 20th Army Corps in May 1952
[e]Entered Korea in February 1953

Table A.8. CPV Order of Withdrawal from Korea

Year	Month	Army
1953	May	39th Army
	July	38th Army
	July	40th Army
	August	64th Army
	September	63d Army
	September	7th Artillery Div.
	October	65th Army
	October	60th Army
	October	2d Artillery Div.
	October	61st Anti-air. Artillery Div.
	October	21st Rocket Artillery Div.
1954	April	12th Army
	April	50th Army
	May	15th Army
	August	64th Anti-air. Artillery Div.
	September	47th Army
	September	67th Army
	September	65th Anti-air. Artillery Div.
	December	22d Rocket Artillery Div.
1955	March	3d Artillery Div.
	April	68th Army
	September	63d Anti-air Artillery Div.
	October	24th Army
	October	46th Army
1957	February	1st Artillery Division
	February	8th Artillery Division
1958	March	23d Army
	April	16th Army
	August	21st Army
	August	54th Army
	October	1st Army

NOTES

CHAPTER 1. INTRODUCTION

1. William Whitney Stueck, Jr., *The Road to Confrontation: American Policy Toward China and Korea, 1947–1950* (Chapel Hill: University of North Carolina Press, 1981), 3.

2. Ellis Joffe, *Party and Army: Professionalism and Political Control in the Chinese Officer Corps, 1948–1964* (Cambridge, Mass: Harvard University Press, 1967), ix.

3. Jonathan D. Pollack, "The Korean War and Sino-American Relations," in Harry Harding and Yuan Ming, eds., *Sino-American Relations, 1945–1955: A Joint Reassessment of a Critical Decade* (Wilmington, Del.: Scholarly Resources, 1989), 214.

4. William Whitney Stueck, Jr., "The Korean War as International History," *Diplomatic History* 10 (Fall 1986): 294.

5. For this point see, in particular, Gerald Segal, *Defending China* (New York: Oxford University Press, 1985), 92.

6. For an excellent review of the studies of the American intervention, see Rosemary Foot, "Making Known the Unknown War: Policy Analysis of the Korean Conflict in the Last Decade," *Diplomatic History* (Summer 1991): 412–15. Typical traditional views are found in Robert T. Oliver, *Why War Came in Korea* (New York: Fordham University Press, 1950); Richard E. Lauterback, *Danger from the East* (New York: Harper and Brothers, 1947); Frank Moraes, *Report on Mao's China* (New York: Macmillan, 1954); Courtney Whitney, *MacArthur: His Rendezvous with History* (New York: Alfred Knopf, 1956); Leon Gordenker, *The United States and the Peaceful Unification of Korea: The Politics of Field Operation* (The Hague: Nijhoff, 1959); Tang Tsou, *America's Failure in China, 1941–1950* (Chicago: University of Chicago Press, 1963); David Rees, *Korea: The Limited War* (New York: St. Martin's, 1964); and Denna F. Fleming, *The Cold War and Its Origins, 1917–1960* (Garden City, N.Y.: Doubleday, 1961). For other, more balanced views, see Robert R. Simmons, *The Strained Alliance: Peking, Pyongyang, Moscow and the Politics of the Korean Civil War* (New York: Free Press, 1975); Stueck, *Road to Confrontation;* Bruce Cumings, *The Origins of the Korean War*, Vol. 1, *Liberation and the Emergence of Separate Regimes, 1945–1947* (Princeton: Princeton University Press, 1981), and Vol. 2, *The Roaring of the Cataract, 1947–1950* (Princeton: Princeton University Press, 1990); Rosemary Foot, *The Wrong War: American Policy and the Dimensions of the Korean Conflict, 1950–1953* (Ithaca: Cornell University Press, 1985), and *A Substitute for Victory: The Politics of Peacemaking at the Korean Armistice Talks* (Ithaca: Cornell University Press, 1990); Nancy Bernkopf Tucker, *Patterns in the Dust: Chinese-American Relations and the Recognition Controversy, 1949–1950* (New York: Columbia University Press, 1983); Gordon H. Chang, *Friends and Enemies: The United States, China, and the Soviet Union, 1948–1972* (Stanford: Stanford University Press, 1990); and John Lewis Gaddis, *The Long Peace: Inquiries into the History of the Cold War* (New York: Oxford University Press, 1987). Contributions by political scientists include Alexander L. George

and Richard Smoke, *Deterrence in American Foreign Policy: Theory and Practice* (New York: Columbia University Press, 1974); Richard Ned Lebow, *Between Peace and War: The Nature of International Crisis* (Baltimore: Johns Hopkins University Press, 1981); Richard K. Betts, *Nuclear Blackmail and Nuclear Balance* (Washington D.C.: Brookings, 1987); J. H. Kalicki, *The Pattern of Sino-American Crises: Political-Military Interactions in the 1950s* (New York: Cambridge University Press, 1975); and John G. Stoessinger, *Nations in the Darkness: China, Russia, and America*, 4th ed. (New York: Random House, 1986).

7. Foot, "Making Known the Unknown War," 417.

8. Allen S. Whiting, *China Crosses the Yalu: The Decision to Enter the Korean War* (New York: Macmillan, 1960).

9. J. H. Kalicki, *The Pattern of Sino-American Crises*, part 1; Melvin Gurtov and Byong-Moo Hwang, *China Under Threat: The Politics of Strategy and Diplomacy* (Baltimore: Johns Hopkins University Press, 1980), 16–19; Segal, *Defending China*, 92–99.

10. Anthony Farrar-Hockley, "A Reminiscence of the Chinese People's Volunteers in the Korean War," *China Quarterly* 98 (June 1984): 287–304.

11. Warren I. Cohen, "Conversations with Chinese Friends: Zhou Enlai's Associates Reflect on Chinese-American Relations in the 1940s and the Korean War," *Diplomatic History* 11 (Summer 1987): 288.

12. See Russell Spurr, *Enter the Dragon: China's Undeclared War Against the U.S. in Korea* (New York: New Market, 1988). Also see Foot, "Making Known the Unknown War," 418 n. 25.

13. Zhai Zhihai and Hao Yufan, "China's Decision to Enter the Korean War: History Revisited," *China Quarterly* 121 (March 1990): 106–11.

14. When I was in Beijing in July 1992, one of the compilers of Mao's manuscripts verified that little has been sanitized from the original documents. For more detailed discussions on new Chinese materials, see Michael Hunt and Odd Arne Westad, "The Chinese Communist Party and International Affairs: A Field Report on New Historical Sources and Old Research Problems," *China Quarterly* 122 (June 1990): 258–72; and Steven M. Goldstein and He Di, "New Chinese Sources on the History of the Cold War," *Cold War International History Bulletin*, Woodrow Wilson International Center for Scholars, no. 1 (Spring 1992): 4–6.

15. Most of these aides are historians of the party or the army. Once they obtain special permission from the Secretariat of the CCP Central Committee, they can "borrow" records from the central archives.

16. When I interviewed Yao Xu in Beijing in October 1988, he confirmed that much of his information was based on conversations with some senior PLA commanders.

17. Xu Yan, *Diyici Jiaoliang: Kangmei Yuanchao Zhanzheng de Lishi Huigu yu Fansi* [The first encounter: Historical retrospection and review of the War to Resist U.S. Aggression and Aid Korea] (Beijing: Chinese Radio and Television Press, 1990), 334–46.

18. Ye Yumeng, *Heixue: Chubing Chaoxian Kangmei Yuanchao Lishi Jishi* [The black snow: Historical records of Chinese military intervention in Korea] (Beijing: Writer's Press, 1989), 49–51. The long telegram from Kim to Mao is now exhibited at the Dandong (Andong) Korean War Museum, Dandong, Liaoning.

19. Qi Dexue, *Chaoxian Zhanzheng Juece Neimu* [Inside stories of decision makings in the Korean War] (Shenyang: Liaoning University Press, 1991), 286–87.

20. Pollack, "The Korean War and Sino-American Relations," 31; also see Jonathan D. Pollack, "Into the Vortex: China, the Sino-Soviet Alliance, and the Korean War," Rand Corporation, R-3910-RC, Stanford, 1990.

21. Thomas Christensen, "Threats, Assurances, and the Last Chance for Peace: The Lessons of Mao's Korean War Telegrams," *International Security* 17 (Summer 1992): 144–46. See also Michael Hunt, "Beijing and the Korean Crisis, June 1950–June 1951," *Political Science Quarterly* 107 (Fall 1992): 453–78.

22. Chen Jian, *China's Road to the Korean War: The Making of the Sino-American Confrontation* (New York: Columbia University Press, 1994), 1–30; see also Chen Jian, "China's Changing Aims During the Korean War," *Journal of American–East Asian Relations* 1 (Spring 1992): 8–41.

23. Sergei N. Goncharov, John W. Lewis, and Xue Litai, *Uncertain Partners: Stalin, Mao, and the Korean War* (Stanford: Stanford University Press, 1993), 203–25.

24. Alexander L. George, *The Chinese Communist Army in Action: The Korean War and Its Aftermath* (New York: Columbia University Press, 1967), 7.

25. See Roy E. Appleman, *East of Chosin: Entrapment and Breakout in Korea, 1950* (College Station: Texas A&M University Press, 1987); idem, *Disaster in Korea: The Chinese Confront MacArthur* (College Station: Texas A&M University Press, 1989), 3–12, 77–85, 154–88; idem, *Ridgway Duels for Korea* (College Station: Texas A&M University Press, 1990), 38–58, 218–54, 449–552; idem, *Escaping the Trap: The US Army X Corps in Northeast Korea* (College Station: Texas A&M University Press, 1990), 75–154 and 204–8; James A. Huston, *Guns and Butter, Power and Rice: United States Logistics in the Korean War* (London: Associate University Press, 1989), 350–64; D. M. Giangreco, *War in Korea: 1950–1953* (Novato, Calif.: Presidio, 1990), 128–30, 137–39, 313–16; and John Toland, *In Mortal Combat: Korea, 1950–1953* (New York: William Morrow, 1991), 198–201, 235–39, 270–75, 280–81, 288–91, 411–65. For an official history of U.S. military-strategic decision making regarding Korea, see U.S. Joint Chiefs of Staff, *The History of the Joint Chiefs of Staff*, vol. 3, *The Joint Chiefs of Staff and National Policy—The Korean War*, by James F. Schnabel and Robert J. Watson (Wilmington, Del.: Michael Glazier, 1979); U.S. Office of the Secretary of Defense, *History of the Office of the Secretary of Defense*, vol. 2, *The Test of War, 1950–53* (Washington, D.C., 1988). For an official history of U.S. military experience in Korea, see U.S. Department of the Army, *United States Army in the Korean War*, vol. 1, *South to the Naktong, North to the Yalu*, by Roy Appleman; vol. 2, *Truce Tent and Fighting Front*, by Walter Hermes; vol. 3, *Policy and Direction: The First Year*, by James F. Schnabel (Washington, D.C.: Government Printing Office, 1961–1972).

26. Mark A. Ryan, *Chinese Attitudes Toward Nuclear Weapons: China and the United States During the Korean War* (New York: M. E. Sharpe, 1989).

27. Pollack, "The Korean War and Sino-American Relations," 215.

28. Foot, "Making Known the Unknown War," 418–19.

29. Akira Iriye, "Culture and International History," in Michael Hogan and Thomas Paterson, eds., *Explaining the History of American Foreign Policy* (New York: Cambridge University Press, 1991), 214–15.

30. John Mueller, *Retreat from Doomsday: The Obsolescence of Major War* (New York: Basic Books, 1980), 7.

31. Stuart Schram, *The Thought of Mao Tse-tung* (New York: Cambridge University Press, 1989), 55.

32. Mao Zedong, "On Protracted War," May 1938, *Selected Military Writings of Mao Tsetung* (Beijing: Foreign Languages Press, 1967), 217; "Speech at the Moscow Communist and Workers' Parties," November 18, 1958, *Quotations from Chairman Mao Tsetung* (Peking: Foreign Languages Press, 1966), 79.

33. Max Hastings, *The Korean War* (New York: Simon and Schuster, 1987), 329.

CHAPTER 2. MAO'S MILITARY ROMANTICISM

1. Mao Zedong, "Our Great Victory in the War to Resist U.S. Aggression and Aid Korea, and Our Future Tasks," September 12, 1953, *Selected Works of Mao Tsetung* (Beijing: Foreign Languages Press, 1977), 5:115 (hereafter *SW*).

2. Ibid.

3. Ibid., 115–18.

4. Xia Zhennan, "On the Relationship Between War and Politics," *Mao Zedong Sixiang Yanjiu* [Studies of Mao Zedong thought] 3 (1987): 48–49. Also see Bob Avakian, *Mao Tsetung's Immortal Contributions* (Chicago: RCP Publications, 1979), 39–40.

5. Mao, "Problems of Strategy in China's Revolutionary War," December 1936, *SMW*, 78.

6. Mao, "On Protracted War," May 1938, ibid., 226.

7. Ibid., 227.

8. Ibid.

9. "Problems of Strategy in China's Revolutionary War," ibid., 81.

10. "On Protracted War," ibid., 228.

11. Ibid., 228–29.

12. Ibid., 228.

13. For the CCP leadership's emphasis on political mobilization and indoctrination, see Jiang Siyi, ed., *Zhongguo Renmin Jiefangjun Zhengzhi Gongzuo Shi: 1924–1950* [History of the Chinese People's Liberation Army's political work] (Beijing: PLA Political Institute Press, 1984), 1–94.

14. Mao's report to the CCP Central Committee, "The Struggle in the Chingkang [Jinggang] Mountains," November 25, 1928, *SMW*, 29–30.

15. Mao, "On Correcting Mistaken Ideas in the Party," December 1929, ibid., 53–56. For a good Western study of the CCP's military and political command structure, see William W. Whitson, *The Chinese High Command: A History of Communist Military Politics, 1927–1971* (New York: Praeger, 1973).

16. Mao's instructions on the political work in the army is cited in Jiang, *Zhongguo Renmin Jiefangjun Zhengzhi Gongzuo Shi*, 90–95.

17. Ibid., 314.

18. Telegram, CCP Central Military Commission to CCP military authorities in Shandong, February 5, 1994, ibid., 302.

19. Department of Political Affairs of the CCP Central Military Commission, "Report on the Issues of Political Work in the Army," April 11, 1944, ibid., 302–13.

20. Telegram, CCP Central Military Commission to all local CCP military authorities, April 20, 1944, ibid., 314.

21. Xia, "On the Relationship Between War and Politics," 48–49.

22. University of National Defense, *Junshi Bianzhengfa Xintan* [A new look of military dialectics] (Beijing: National Defense University Press, 1987), 208–312.

23. "Problems of Strategy in China's Revolutionary War," *SMW*, 78,

24. "On Protracted War," ibid., 238.

25. Ibid., 227–28.

26. "Problems of Strategy in China's Revolutionary War," ibid., 81.

27. Ibid., 83–84.

28. Liu Huajing and Shan Xufa, *Mao Zedong Junshi Bianzhengfa Yanjiu* [A study of Mao Zedong's military dialectics] (Wuhan: Hubei Peopel's Press, 1984), 4–5.

29. Mao's speech at the "August 7th Meeting," August 7, 1927, *Mao Zedong Junshi Wenxuan—neibuban* [Selected military works of Mao Zedong—internal edition] (Beijing: PLA Soldiers' Press, 1981), 4.

30. Liu and Shan, *Mao Zedong Junshi Bianzhengfa Yanjiu*, 53.

31. "Problems of Strategy in China's Revolutionary War," *SMW*, 88.

32. Ibid., 95–96.

33. Mao, "Pay Attention to Economic Work," August 20, 1933, cited in Lin Boye, *Xuexi Mao Zedong Junshi Zhuzuo Zhong De Zhexue Sixiang* [The philosophical points contained in Mao Zedong's military writings] (Tianjin: People's Press, 1982), 37.

34. Ibid., 38.

35. "Problems of Strategy in China's Revolutionary War," *SMW*, 96.

36. "The Struggle in the Chingkang Mountains," ibid., 31. Also see Liu and Shan, *Mao Zedong Junshi Bianzhengfa Yanjiu*, 59–60.

37. Mao, "On Protracted War," *SMW*, 260.

38. Liu and Shan, *Mao Zedong Junshi Bianzhengfa Yanjiu*, 68–69.

39. "On Protracted War," SMW, 217. Also see Liu and Shan, *Mao Zedong Junshi Bianzhengfa Yanjiu*, 68–71.

40. "Problems of Strategy in China's Revolutionary War," *SMW*, 88–89.

41. "On Protracted War," ibid., 225–26.

42. Ibid., 225.

43. Ibid., 235; emphasis added.

44. Ibid., 238–39, 264–65.

45. Guo Huaruo, ed., *Sun Zi Jinyi* [A new interpretation of Sun Tzu's *Arts of War*] (Shanghai: People's Press, 1977), 9.

46. "Problems of Strategy in China's Revolutionary War," *SMW*, 85.

47. Ibid., 85–86.

48. Ibid., 86.

49. "On Protracted War," ibid., 441–43.

50. "Problems of Strategy in China's Revolutionary War," ibid., 87.

51. "On Protracted War," ibid., 242.

52. Ibid., 235–37.

53. Ibid., 239.

54. Ibid., 239–40.

55. Ibid., 240.

56. Ibid., 210–14.

57. "Problems of Strategy in China's Revolutionary War," ibid., 131–32.

58. Ibid., 134–35.

59. Ibid., 137.

60. Ibid., 139.

61. Ibid., 139–40; "On Protracted War," ibid., 233.

62. "Problems of Strategy in China's Revolutionary War," ibid., 144.

63. Ibid., 142–43; "On Protracted War," ibid., 233.

64. "Problems of Strategy in China's Revolutionary War," ibid., 146–47.

65. "On Protracted War," ibid., 251.

66. Mao, "A Study of Physical Education," *Xin Qingnian* [New youth], April 1917, cited in Stuart Schram, *The Thought of Mao Tse-tung* (New York: Cambridge University Press, 1989), 15.

67. Ibid., 17.

68. Liu and Shan, *Mao Zedong Junshi Bianzhengfa Yanjiu*, 23–26. For the Long March, see chap. 3, n. 1, below.

69. Ibid., 30. For a short summary of Mao's military thought, see Avakian, *Mao Tsetung's Immortal Contributions*, 39–81.

70. Mao, "Talk with American Correspondent Anna Louise Strong," August 1946, *SW*, 4:100–101.

71. Mao, "The Current Situation and Our Tasks," December 25, 1947, *Mao Zedong Junshi Wenxuan*, 343–50.

72. Zhu De, "On Several Basic Principles of Tactics," [undated] 1933, *Zhu De Xuanji* [Selected works of Zhu De] (Anhui: People's Press, 1983), 15.

73. *Zhou Enlai Xuanji* [Selected works of Zhou Enlai] (Beijing: Central Archives and Manuscripts Press, 1984), 2:62.

74. Liu and Shan, *Mao Zedong Junshi Bianzhengfa Yanjiu*, 22.

75. Schram, *The Thought of Mao Tse-tung*, 14.

76. Han Qiufeng and Li Qinyang, "Mao Zedong Inherited and Developed the Traditional Strategists' Thoughts On Military Spirit," *Mao Zedong Sixiang Yanjiu*, [Study of Mao Zedong Thought] 4 (1989): 73–74.

77. *Junshi Bianzhengfa Xintan* 283–85.

78. "Problems of Strategy in China's Revolutionary War," SMW, 110–11; "On Protracted War," ibid., 238–39.

79. Ibid., 51 nn. 24–26.

80. Ibid., 51 nn. 27–29.

81. Schram, *The Thought of Mao Tse-tung*, 55.

82. Loren Baritz, "God's Country and American Know-How," in *The American Experience in Vietnam: A Reader*, ed. Grace Sevy (Norman: University of Oklahoma Press, 1989), 13.

CHAPTER 3. PREPAREDNESS ELIMINATES MISHAPS

1. Bo Yibo, *Ruogan Zhongda Juece yu Shijian de Huigu* [My recollections of decision making on several important policies and events] (Beijing: CCP Central Archives Press, 1991), 1:155 (hereafter cited as *Bo Yibo Memoirs*). The Long March refers to the CCP's "strategic retreat," which officially began on October 15, 1934, from southeastern China to the northwestern part where the Communists reestablished themselves. The epic Long March covering some 6,000 miles is still considered a celebrated event in CCP history.

2. Instruction, the CCP Central Committee, "Our Diplomatic Policy Toward the United States," September 1, 1945, *Zhonggong Zhongyang Wenjian Xuanji* [Selected documents of the CCP Central Committee] (Beijing: CCP Central Archives, 1989–1992), 15:262 (hereafter *Wenjian Xuanji*); instruction, the CCP Central Committee, "Our Policy Toward the U.S. Armed Forces After Their Landing [in China]," September 29, 1945, ibid., 15:302; telegram, Liu Shaoqi to Zhang Aiping, "Current Situation and Our Policy Toward the United States," ibid., 15:308; instruction, the CCP Central Committee, "Firmly Resist the Landing [Operations of] the U.S. Armed Forces," October 6, 1945, ibid., 13:161.

3. Telegram, Zhou Enlai to the CCP Central Committee, August 6, 1946, Division of Central Archives and Manuscripts, *Zhou Enlai Nianpu: 1898–1949* [The chronicle of Zhou Enlai: 1898–1949] (Beijing: Central Archives and Manuscripts Press, 1989), 685.

4. Telegram, Zhou Enlai to the CCP Central Committee, Ye Jianying, and Li Kenong, August 31, 1946, *Zhonggong Zhongyang Nanjingju* [The Nanjing bureau of the CCP Central Committee] (Beijing: CCP History Press, 1990), 138–39. For Zhou's analysis of the Marshall mission, see also telegram, Zhou to Mao, August 10, 1946, ibid., 117–18.

5. Mao Zedong, "The Truths about U.S. 'Mediation' and the Future Civil War in China," September 29, 1946, *SM*, 4:109. It is interesting that the Soviet Union had the same assessment of U.S. intentions regarding China. "China," the Soviet foreign ministry concluded in September 1946, "is gradually turning into a bridgehead for American military forces." Nikolai V. Novikov, "The Foreign Policy of the USA During the Postwar Period," September 27, 1946, AVPSSSR [Archives of foreign policy of the USSR], file 06, entry 08, folder 45, case 759, in Sergei N. Goncharov, John W. Lewis, and Xue Litai, *Uncertain Partners: Stalin, Mao, and the Korean War* (Stanford: Stanford University Press, 1993), app., 229–30.

6. Telegram, CCP Central Committee to Zhou Enlai and the CCP delegation in Nanjing, September 16, 1946, *Zhou Enlai Nianpu*, 690–91; instruction, the CCP Central Committee, "A Weekly Campaign to Call for Withdrawal of the U.S. Armed Forces in China," September 29, 1946, *Wenjian Xuanji*, 13:492.

7. Lu Dingyi, "Explanations of Several Basic Problems Concerning the Postwar International Situation," *Jiefang Ribao* [Liberation daily], January 4, 1947, 1.

8. Telegram, the CCP Central Committee (drafted by Zhou Enlai) to Dong Biwu and Wang Bingnan, February 17, 1947, *Zhou Enlai Nianpu*, 720.

9. Telegram, the CCP Central Committee to Liu Xiao and Qian Ying, August 21, 1947, ibid., 745.

10. Instruction, the CCP Central Committee, "Several Points on Current International Situation," December 26, 1947, partly cited in ibid., 756–57.

11. Instruction, the CCP Central Committee, "On Our Diplomatic Policy Lines Toward the United States," March 14, 1948, cited in telegram, Zhou Enlai to Rao Shushi and Chen Yi, March 24, 1948, ibid., 767.

12. Ren Bishi's speech, September 13, 1948, cited in Xinghuo Liaoyuan Editorial Division, *Jiefangjun Jiangling Zhuan* [The chronicle of PLA senior generals] (Beijing: PLA Press, 1988), 7:152.

13. Zhou Enlai's speech at the staff meeting of the CCP headquarters, September 28, 1947, Chinese Academy of Military Sciences, *Zhongguo Renmin Jiefangjun Liushinian Dashiji: 1927–1987* [Records of important events of the People's Liberation Army from 1927 to 1982] (Beijing: Military Sciences Press, 1988), 407–8.

14. Zhu De's speech at the briefing of CCP Bureau of Combat Operations, October 16, 1948, *Zhu De Xuanji* [Selected works of Zhu De] (Anhui: People's Press, 1983), 244.

15. Instruction, the CCP Central Committee (drafted by Mao Zedong), "The Current Situation and Our Party's Tasks in 1949," January 8, 1949, *Wenjian Xuanji*, 14:489–90.

16. Zhou Enlai, "Report on the Current Situation," January 16, 1949, *Zhou Enlai Nianpu*, 808.

17. Instruction, the CCP Central Committee, "The Current Situation and Our Party's Tasks in 1949," *Wenjian Xuanji*, 14:490.

18. Ye Fei, *Ye Fei Huiyilu* [Ye Fei memoirs] (Beijing: PLA Press, 1988), 534–38 (hereafter *Ye Fei Memoirs*).

19. Instructions, the Central Military Commission, February 3–March 20, 1949, are cited in Chinese Academy of Military Sciences, *Zhongguo Renmin Jiefangjun Zhan Shi* [The war history of the People's Liberation Army] (Beijing: Military Sciences Press, 1987), 3:322.

20. Telegram, the Central Military Commission, May 23, 1949, ibid., 320.

21. Ibid., 335; *Ye Fei Memoirs*, 536–38.

22. CMC directive, "Instructions on How to Prepare for Imperialist Intervention Against the Chinese Revolution," May 28, 1949, *Wenjian Xuanji*, 18:308–9 (emphasis added); see also He Di, "The Evolution of the CCP's Policy Toward the United States, 1945–1949," *Lishi Yanjiu* [Historical studies] 3 (1987): 21.

23. Telegram, Zhou Enlai to Deng Xiaoping, "On How to Deal with Diplomatic Affairs," April 25, 1949, *Wenjian Xuanji*, 18:233–34. Chen Xiaolu, "China's U.S. Policy, 1949–1955," in Harry Harding and Yuan Ming, eds., *Sino-American Relations, 1945–1955: A Joint Reassessment of a Critical Decade* (Wilmington, Del.: Scholarly Resources, 1989), 186. For CCP's policy toward the American consulates in China, see CCP Central Committee's supplementary instruction of diplomatic guidelines, January 25, 1949, *Wenjian Xuanji*, 14:531–32; CMC instruction, "Every Action Concerning Diplomatic Affairs Must Be Reported [to the Central Committee] in Advance," April 26, 1949, ibid., 18:246–47.

24. He Di, "Evolution of the CCP's Policy," 44. When I interviewed Wang Bingnan, who then worked in the Foreign Affairs Commission, on October 14, 1988, Wang confirmed the instructions to Huang Hua. For more on CCP policy regarding the Huang-Stuart talks, see the CCP Central Committee to the Nanjing Bureau, June 3, 1949, *Wenjian Xuanji*, 18:324–25. Stalin recommended in April 1949 that the CCP "must not

reject establishing official relations with some of the capitalist countries, including the United States, if these states officially abandon [their] military, trade, and political support of Chiang Kai-shek's Nationalist government"; telegram, Stalin to Mao, April [undated], 1949, in Goncharov, Lewis, and Xue, *Uncertain Partners*, app., 231.

25. Instruction, the CCP Central Committee (drafted by Mao Zedong), "On Our Diplomatic Policies," January 19, 1949, *Wenjian Xuanji*, 14:514–18; instruction, the CCP Central Committee, "Our Foreign Trade Policy," February 26, 1949, ibid., 14:559; Mao Zedong, "Report to the Second Plenary Session of the Seventh Central Committee of the CCP," March 5, 1949, *SW*, 4:370–71. Also see Warren I. Cohen, "Conversations with Chinese Friends: Zhou Enlai's Associates Reflect on Chinese-American Relations in the 1940s and the Korean War," *Diplomatic History* 11 (Summer 1987): 287–88. Cohen found out in his interview with Huang that the CCP leaders "were not looking for friendly relations. They had at best one concern: to forestall a major American intervention which might rescue the Guomindang [Kuomintang] at the eleventh hour, cheating them of their impending victory" (ibid., 288). See also Ivan V. Kovalev, "Stalin's Dialogue with Mao Zedong," *Problemy Dal'nego Vostoka* [Problems of the Far East] (Moscow) 6 (1991): 89. Also see Goncharov, Lewis, and Xue, *Uncertain Partners*, app., 231. It is not known how seriously the CCP leaders took Stalin's suggestion.

26. Instruction, the Central Military Commission, "Prepare to Take Over the Control of Shanghai," August 27, 1949, *Wenjian Xuanji*, 18:248–49; telegram, CMC to the General Front Command, April 22, 1949, *Dang de Wenxian* [CCP documents and materials] 4 (1989): 43. See also Chen Xiaolu, "China's U.S. Policy, 1949–1955," in Harding and Yuan, *Sino-American Relations*, 186; Zhang Baijia, "Comments on the Seminar on the History of Sino-American Relations, 1945–1955," *Lishi Yanjiu* [Historical studies] 3 (1987): 40–41.

27. Mao Zedong, "Address to the Preparatory Meeting of the New Political Consultative Council," June 15, 1949, *SW*, 4:407.

28. Ibid.

29. Steven Goldstein, "Communist Chinese Perceptions, 1945–1950," in Dorothy Borg and Waldo Heinrichs, eds., *Uncertain Years: Chinese-American Relations, 1947–1950* (New York: Columbia University Press, 1980), 253. Evidence of Stalin's doubt about Mao's reliability can be seen in the Soviet leader's cultivation of a special relationship with Gao Gang, the Communist leader in northeastern China. In July 1947, Gao made a secret trip to Khabarovsk in the Far East for talks with Marshall R. Ia. Malinovskii, commander of the Soviet Far Eastern military district. There Gao "confidentially reported on the 'nationalistic and anti-Soviet' attitudes within the Chinese Communist leadership." Goncharov, Lewis, and Xue, *Uncertain Partners*, 26–28.

30. Shi Zhe, *Zai Lishi Juren Shengbian: Shi Zhe Huiyilu* [Together with historical giants: Shi Zhe Memoirs] (Beijing: Central Archives and Manuscripts Press, 1991), 397–414 (hereafter *Shi Zhe Memoirs*); *Bo Yibo Memoirs*, 35–38. Also see Kovalev's notes on Stalin's conversation with Liu in July 1949. "I am saying," Stalin stressed, "that you are already playing a significant role now, and you, of course, must not be arrogant. But at the same time, I assert that the responsibility that has been laid on you has grown ever greater. You must fulfill your duty toward the revolutions in the countries of East Asia." Ivan V. Kovalev, "Stalin's Dialogue with Mao Zedong," 78. However, in light of Ivan V. Kovalev's unpublished memoirs, Goncharov, Lewis, and Xue argue that Stalin stood firm against Liu's request for the withdrawal of Soviet forces from the Chinese ports of Dalian or Lushun; *Uncertain Partners*, 61–70. Mao had in fact planned a trip to Moscow in late 1948, but the Kremlin suggested that he postpone. Yang Chengwu, "A Call on Chairman Mao," *Dangshi Yanjiu yu Jiaoxue* [Study and teaching on the party's history] 5 (1990): 51.

31. China Today series, *Dangdai Zhongguo Jundui de Junshi Gongzuo* [China today: The military affairs of the Chinese army] (Beijing: Chinese Social Sciences Press, 1989),

2:108–9; Zhu Tunshi, "Liu Shaoqi's Secret Visit to the Soviet Union in 1949," *Dang de Wenxian* [CCP documents and materials] 3 (1989):75.

32. Telegram, Mao to Wang Jiaxiang, "On Chairman Mao's Visit to the Soviet Union," November 9, 1949, in Mao Zedong, *Jianguo Yilai Mao Zedong Wengao* [Mao Zedong's manuscripts since the founding of the PRC], vols. 1–4 (Beijing: Central Archives and Manuscripts Press, 1987–1990), 1:31 (hereafter cited as *Mao's Manuscripts*). Stalin evidently failed to understand the implications of Zhou's accompanying Mao to Moscow and thus did not respond. Goncharov, Lewis, and Xue, *Uncertain Partners*, 83–84.

33. *Shi Zhe Memoirs*, 431–35.

34. Ibid., 436–37.

35. Ibid. However, there is another explanation: Mao was upset because the Soviet leader "did not take the initiative to propose" aid to China; *Bo Yibo Memoirs*, 40–41. Kovalev went to talk to Mao on December 20, 1949. He reported to Stalin Mao's insistence that Zhou Enlai should be summoned to Moscow should the Soviet Union consent to sign agreements with the People's Republic of China regarding Sino-Soviet relations, loans, trade, and the establishment of air transport lines. Kovalev to Stalin, December 20, 1949, in Goncharov, Lewis, and Xue, *Uncertain Partners*, app., 238–39.

36. "Chairman Mao in Moscow," *Xinhua Yuebao* [New China's monthly] 3 (1950): 579.

37. Telegram, Mao to the CCP Central Committee, "On Zhou's Participation in Moscow Negotiations," January 2, 3, 1950, *Mao's Manuscripts*, 1:211.

38. Mao's telegram to the CCP Central Committee, January 5, 1950, ibid., 215.

39. Telegram, Mao to the CCP Central Committee, January 3, 1950, ibid., 213.

40. Wu Xiuquan, *Huiyi yu Huainian* [Remembering and cherishing the memory] (Beijing: Central University of the Party Press, 1991), 237–39 (hereafter *Wu Xiuquan Memoirs*).

41. Telegrams, Mao to the CCP Central Committee, January 2 and 3, 1950, *Mao's Manuscripts*, 1:213. Regarding Soviet policy toward establishing trade relations with Communist China, see telegrams from Stalin to Kovalev, March 15, 1949, and Stalin to Mao, April [undated] 1949, in Goncharov, Lewis, and Xue, *Uncertain Partners*, app., 230–31.

42. *Shi Zhe Memoirs*, 17; *Bo Yibo Memoirs*, 41.

43. Mao Zedong's speech at the sixth meeting of the Central People's Government Council, April 11, 1950, *Mao's Manuscripts*, 1:291.

44. Zhou Enlai, "International Situation and Our Diplomatic Work After the Signing of the Sino-Soviet Alliance Treaty," March 20, 1950, *Zhou Enlai Waijiao Wenxuan* [Selected diplomatic works of Zhou Enlai] (Beijing: People's Press, 1990), 11; Song Qingling, "Talks with *Jiefang Ribao* Correspondences," February 22, 1950, and April 12, 1950, in Division of Central Archives and Manuscripts, *Song Qingling Nianpu* [The chronicle of Song Qingling] (Beijing: Central Archives and Manuscripts Press, 1986), 166–67.

45. Telegram, Mao to Liu Shaoqi, January 17, 1950, *Mao's Manuscripts*, 1:238–39. For the origins of the Vietminh's revolution, see George C. Herring, *America's Longest War: The United States and Vietnam, 1950–1975*, 2d edition (New York: Alfred Knopf, 1986), 3–7.

46. Mao Zedong's reply to the Vietminh, January 19, 1950, *Renmin Ribao* [People's daily], January 19, 1950, 1. In Mao and Zhou Enlai's telegram to Liu Shaoqi, February 1, 1950, *Mao's Manuscripts*, 1:254, they told Liu that the Soviet Union had agreed to recognize the Vietminh and that Mao had already sent his request to the embassies of Eastern European countries in Moscow. Mao stated, "I am so glad to see that the Vietminh will join the anti-imperialist and democratic big family."

47. Huang Zheng, *Ho Chi Minh yu Zhongguo* [Ho Chih Minh and China] (Beijing: PLA Press, 1987), 124–25.

48. Hoang Van Hoan, *Changhai Yishu: Huang Wenhuan Geming Huiyilu* [A drop in the ocean: Hoang Van Hoan's revolutionary reminiscences] (Beijing: PLA Press, 1987), 259 (hereafter Hoang, *Revolutionary Reminiscences*].

49. Huang, *Ho Chi Minh yu Zhongguo*, 125.

50. Ibid., 126.

51. Telegram, Mao to Ho Chi Minh, May 20, 1950, *Renmin Ribao* [People's daily], May 20, 1950, 1. Also see *Xinhua Yuebao* [New China's monthly] 2 (1950): 290.

52. Hoang, *Revolutionary Reminiscences*, 263.

53. Xu Peilan and Zheng Pengfei, *Chen Geng Jiangjun Zhuan* [Biography of General Chen Geng] (Beijing: PLA Press, 1988), 573–74.

54. *Dangdai Zhongguo Jundui de Junshi Gongzuo*, 1:520 and 576.

55. Ibid., 520–22.

56. Li Ke, "The Chinese Military Advisory Group in the Struggle of Aiding Vietnam and Resisting France," *Junshi Lishi* [Military history] 3 (1989): 27.

57. Huang, *Ho Chi Minh yu Zhongguo*, 126; *Dangdai Zhongguo Jundui de Junshi Gongzuo*, 1:519.

58. Li Ke, "Chinese Military Advisory Group," 28.

59. *Dangdai Zhongguo Jundui de Junshi Gongzuo*, 1:522–27. For Chen's direction of the border campaign, see Zhou Yizhi and Qu Aiguo, "Chen Geng and the Vietnamese Border Campaign of 1950," *Ren Wu* [Biographical studies] 3 (1993): 42–55.

60. Hu Sheng, "How Did American Imperalists Attempt to Invade China in History," originally printed in *Shishi Shouce* [Current affairs handbook] 3 (1949), reprinted in *Xinhua Yuebao* [New China's monthly] 2 (1949): 275–76.

61. Zhou Enlai, "To Refute Acheson's Speech," March 18, 1950, *Xinhua Yuebao* [New China's monthly] 6 (1950): 1360.

62. Kathryn Weathersby, "Soviet Aim in Korea and the Origins of the Korean War, 1949–1950: New Evidence from Russian Archives," Working Paper No. 8, Cold War International History Project (Woodrow Wilson Center for Scholars, Washington, D.C., November 1933), 20 n. 55.

63. Pak Toufu, *Zhonggong Canjia Hanzhan Yuanying Zhi Yanjiu* [An examination of why the CCP decided to participate in the Korean War] (Taipei: Nimin Cultural Service, 1975), 30, 32–33.

64. Huang Daoxia, ed., *Zhonghua Renmin Gongheguo Sishi Nian Dashiji: 1949–1989* [The chronicle of important events in PRC's forty-year history] (Beijing: Guangming Ribao Press, 1989), 6.

65. Nie Rongzhen, *Nie Rongzhen Huiyilu* [Nie Rongzhen memoirs] (Beijing: PLA Press, 1984], 2:748 (hereafter *Nie Rongzhen Memoirs*). For a detailed discussion of the relationships between the North Korean Communists and the CCP before the outbreak of the conflict, see Bruce Cumings, *The Origins of the Korean War*: Vol. 2, *The Roaring of the Cataract, 1947–1950* (Princeton: Princeton University Press, 1990), chap. 11. These Korean soldiers had been affiliated with the PLA's 156th Division and the 164th and 166th divisions of the Fourth Field Army. Returning to North Korea in the fall of 1949, they would eventually form the 5th, 6th, and 7th divisions of the NKPA, becoming the backbone of North Korea's attacking forces in June 1950.

66. Division of Central Archives and Manuscripts, *Zhu De Nianpu* [The chronicle of Zhu De] (Beijing: Renmin Press, 1986), 343.

67. China Today series, *Dangdai Zhongguo Haijun* [China today: The People's Navy] (Beijing: Chinese Social Sciences Press, 1987), 4–5.

68. Nie Rongzhen's report on the PLA force dispositions, June 6, 1950, cited in Tang Qun, "The Third Plenary Session of CCP's Seventh Congress, June 6–9, 1950," *Dangshi Yanjiu Ziliao*, [Studies and materials of the party's history] 3 (1982): 672.

69. *Dangdai Zhongguo Haijun*, 12–13.

70. China Today series, *Dangdai Zhongguo Jundui de Qunzhong Gongzuo* [China today: Mass work of the military] (Beijing: Chinese Academy of Social Sciences Press, 1988), 63–64.

71. Telegram, Mao to Lin Biao, "Instructions on Rearrangements of the Force Deployment," October 31, 1949, *Mao's Manuscripts*, 1:106–7.

72. Ibid., 107.

73. Telegram, Mao to Peng Dehuai, "On Combat Planning in China's Southeast and Northwest," October 13, 1949, ibid., 54.

74. CMC decision to establish Central South China Military Command, December 26, 1949, cited in Yan Wei, ed., *Zhongguo Renmin Jiefangjun Wu Da Yezhan Budui Fazhan Shilue* [A short history of the development of PLA's five field armies] (Beijing: PLA Press, 1987), 232–39.

75. CMC decision to establish East China Military Command, January [undated] 1950, ibid., 164–69.

76. CMC instruction on PLA's participation in economic production and construction, December 5, 1949, *Zhongguo Renmin Jiefangjun Liushinian Dashiji*, 479.

77. *Dangdai Zhongguo Jundui de Qunzhong Gongzuo*, 74–75.

78. Instruction, the CCP Politburo, "Current Situation and Our Party's Task in 1949," January 8, 1949, cited in *Jiefangjun Jiangling Zhuan*, 7:180.

79. Memorandum, Zhu De to Mao Zedong, July [undated] 1949, *Zhu De Nianpu*, 330.

80. Memorandum, Mao to Zhou Enlai, July 10, 1949, China Today series, *Dangdai Zhongguo Kongjun* [China today: The air force] (Beijing: Chinese Social Sciences Press, 1989), 35.

81. Telegram, the CCP's Secretariat to Liu Shaoqi, July 26, 1949, cited in *Jiefangjun Jiangling Zhuan*, 7:180–81.

82. Ibid., 181; Lu Liping, *Tongtian Zhilu* [The path to the sky] (Beijing: PLA Press, 1989), 137.

83. Yi Yun, "When Was the People's Air Force Established," *Junshi Lishi* [Military history] 1 (1990): 55. Also see *Dangdai Zhongguo Kongjun*, 39–40.

84. *Jiefangjun Jiangling Zhuan*, 7:180–81.

85. Ibid., 182–83; Lu Liping, *Tongtian Zhilu*, 156–69.

86. Yi Yun, "When Was the People's Air Force Established," 55; also see *Zhongguo Renmin Jiefangjun Liushinian Dashiji*, 478; *Dangdai Zhongguo Kongjun*, 41–42.

87. *Jiefangjun Jiangling Zhuan*, 7:181.

88. Minutes of Liu–Zhu De, Liu–Zhou Enlai, and Liu-Mao talks are cited in ibid., 181–82.

89. Ibid., 184.

90. Ibid., 184–85. Also see *Dangdai Zhongguo Kongjun*, 49.

91. Ibid., 76.

92. Ibid., 79.

93. *Dangdai Zhongguo Haijun*, 10.

94. Mao's speech at the Chinese People's Political Consultative Conference, September 21, 1949, *SW*, 5:6.

95. Mao's ascription to the East China Navy Command, October 10, 1949, cited in *Dangdai Zhongguo Haijun*, 38–39.

96. Ibid., 15–16, 28–30.

97. *Dangdai Zhongguo Jundui de Junshi Gongzuo*, 2:26.

98. *Dangdai Zhongguo Haijun*, 58–59.

99. Ibid., 57–61.

100. *Dangdai Zhongguo Jundui de Junshi Gongzuo*, 2:155.

101. *Dangdai Zhongguo Haijun*, 71.

102. Ibid., 48–49.

103. Ibid., 86.

104. Ibid., 85–86. Also see Zhang Aiping's speech at the first meeting concerning naval training, March [undated] 1950, *Dangdai Zhongguo Jundui de Junshi Gongzuo*, 2:306–7.

105. *Dangdai Zhongguo Haijun*, 106.

106. Ibid., 113.

107. *Dangdai Zhongguo Jundui de Junshi Gongzuo*, 1:250–51.

108. *Dangdai Zhongguo Haijun*, 236–37.

109. Ibid., 155–56.

110. Ibid., 157.

111. Ibid., 158–62.

112. Shang Jinsuo, *Luelun yi Lie Sheng You* [On how a weak nation can defeat a strong enemy] (Beijing: PLA Press, 1990), 97–99.

CHAPTER 4. "WE CAN'T SIT STILL WITH FOLDED HANDS"

1. Zhou Enlai's aide on military affairs, Lei Yingfu, recalls that everyone at Zhou's staff office was surprised when they learned of the outbreak of the Korean War on the morning of June 25, 1950. Lei Yingfu, "My Recollection of the Decision Making on Several Crucial Issues During the War to Resist U.S. Aggression and Aid Korea," *Dang de Wenxian* [CCP documents and materials] 6 (1993): 76. Based on his 1992 interview with Shi Zhe, Mao's Russian-language interpreter, Chen Jian reports that Kim did not fully inform Mao of his war plans before North Korea's invasion. Only by June 27, when its army already occupied Seoul, did Pyongyang formally notify Beijing of its military action. "This made Mao unhappy," wrote Chen Jian, *China's Road to the Korean War: The Making of the Sino-American Confrontation* (New York: Columbia University Press, 1994), 134. Most Western scholars have concluded that Kim took the decision to attack South Korea largely alone, although Stalin and Mao were probably consulted. See Callum A. MacDonald, *Korea: The War Before Vietnam* (New York: Free Press, 1986), 28; William Whitney Stueck. Jr., "The Korean War as International History," *Diplomatic History* 10 (Fall 1986): 293; and Geoffrey Wamer, "The Korean War," *International Affairs* 56 (January 1980): 99–100. Chinese historians, however, insisted that "only Stalin [and not Mao] was informed of Kim's detailed plan and the possible date for action, since, in Kim's mind, the Soviet Union was the only patron capable of helping to carry out his reunification plan." Zhai Zhihai and Hao Yufan, "China's Decision to Enter the Korean War: History Revisited," *China Quarterly* 121 (March 1990): 100. For an excellent study of the Soviet role in shaping Pyongyang's decision for war on the basis of recently available Soviet materials, see Sergei N. Goncharov, John W. Lewis, and Xue Litai, *Uncertain Partners: Stalin, Mao, and the Korean War* (Stanford: Stanford University Press, 1993), 131–67.

Recently declassified Soviet documents suggests that Kim Il-sung informed Mao and the Chinese leaders during his visit to Beijing in mid-May 1950 of Stalin's endorsement of his plan to attack South Korea. Kim relayed to Mao Stalin's directives that "the present situation has changed from the situation in the past and that North Korea can move toward actions; however, this question should be discussed with China and personally with comrade Mao Tse-tung." Seemingly puzzled by this directive, Mao sent Zhou Enlai to see N. V. Roshchin, Soviet ambassador to Beijing, on May 13, with instructions that Mao "would like to have personal clarification of comrade Filippov [Stalin] on this question." Telegram, Roshchin to Stalin, May 13, 1950, Archive of the President of the Russian Federation (APRF), "Documentation," *Cold War International History Bulletin*, Woodrow Wilson International Center for Scholars, 4 (Fall 1994): 61. Stalin replied on the next day that "in light of the changed international situation, [I] agree with the proposal of the

Koreans to move toward reunification. In this regard a qualification was made [*pri etom bilo ogovoreno*] that the question should be decided finally by the Chinese and Korean comrades together, and in case of disagreement by the Chinese comrades the decision on the question should be postponed until a new discussion." Telegram, Stalin to Mao Zedong, May 14, 1950, ibid. There is no Chinese evidence on this correspondence. It is still difficult to determine if or how much Mao knew about Kim's action plan.

2. Mao Zedong, "Speech at the Eighth Session of the CPGC," June 28, 1950, *Mao's Manuscripts*, 1:43. An English version is in Michael Y. M. Kau and John K. Leung, eds., *The Writings of Mao Zedong, 1949–1976* (Armonk, N.Y.: M. E. Sharpe, 1986), 1:118.

3. Zhou Enlai's statement on the Chinese government's stand on the outbreak of the Korean War, *Renmin Ribao* [People's daily], June 28, 1950, 1.

4. Mao's conversation with other CCP leaders, early July 1950, cited in China Today series, *Kangmei Yuanchao Zhanzheng* [China today: The War to Resist U.S. Aggression and Aid Korea] (Beijing: Chinese Social Sciences Press, 1990), 17 (hereafter *Kangmei Yuanchao Zhanzheng*).

5. Ibid., 17–18.

6. China Today series, *Dangdai Zhongguo Jundui de Junshi Gongzuo* [China today: The military affairs of the Chinese army] (Beijing: Chinese Social Sciences Press, 1989), 1:449–50.

7. Nie Rongzhen to Mao, July 7, 1950, cited in *Mao's Manuscripts*, 1:428 n. 2; also see Hong Xuezhi, *Kangmei Yuanchao Zhanzheng Huiyi* [Recollections of the War to Resist U.S. Aggression and Aid Korea] (Beijing: PLA Art Press, 1990), 1–2 (hereafter *Hong Xuezhi Memoirs*); Du Ping, *Zai Zhiyuanjun Zhongbu* [My years at the CPV headquarters] (Nanjing: PLA Press, 1989), 13–14 (hereafter *Du Ping Memoirs*); and Qi Dexue, *Chaoxian Zhanzheng Juece Neimu* [Inside stories of decision makings in the Korean War] (Shenyang: Liaoning University Press, 1991), 30.

8. Mao to Nie Rongzhen, July 7, 1950, *Mao's Manuscripts*, 1:428.

9. *Du Ping Memoirs*, 14. Minutes of this meeting have yet to be released.

10. The CMC resolution on defending China's northeastern border, July 13, 1950, summarized in Chinese Academy of Military Sciences, *Zhongguo Renmin Zhiyuanjun Kangmei Yuanchao Zhan Shi* [The war history of the Chinese People's Volunteers in the War to Resist U.S. Aggression and Aid Korea] (Beijing: Military Sciences Press, 1988), 7–8.

11. Memoranda, Nie and Zhou to Mao, and Mao to Nie and Zhou, July 22, 1950, cited in *Du Ping Memoirs*, 14–15.

12. Memorandum, Du Ping to Luo Ronghuan, June 1950, *Du Ping Memoirs*, 11, 15. For the difficulties in deploying the NBDA forces, see also Jiang Yonghui, *Sanshibajun Zai Chaoxian* [The 38th Army in Korea] (Shenyang: Liaoning People's Press, 1989), 1–8 (hereafter *Jiang Yonghui Memoirs*); also see Yang Chengwu, "The Entry of the 66th Army into the Korean War," *Dangshi Yanjiu yu Jiaoxue* [Study and teaching on the party's history] 2 (1990): 55–58.

13. *Du Ping Memoirs*, 16.

14. Ibid., 12–14.

15. Telegram, the CMC to Du Ping, July 19, 1950, ibid., 15.

16. *Zhongguo Renmin Zhiyuanjun Kangmei Yuanchao Zhan Shi*, 8; *Kangmei Yuanchao Zhanzheng*, 450.

17. Telegram, Mao to Gao Gang, August 5, 1950, *Mao's Manuscripts*, 1:454.

18. *Hong Xuezhi Memoirs*, 2–6.

19. Memorandum, Lin Biao to Nie Rongzhen, August 9, 1950, ibid., 6–7.

20. Ibid., 7.

21. Deng Hua's speech at the NBDA command meeting, August 13, 1950, cited in Xinhuo Liaoyuan Editioral Division, *Jiefang Jiangling Zhuan* [The chronicle of PLA senior generals] (Beijing: PLA Press, 1988), 7:29.

22. Telegram, Mao to Gao Gang, August 18, 1950, *Mao's Manuscripts*, 1:469.

23. *Hong Xuezhi Memoirs*, 7–8, 12; *Du Ping Memoirs*, 20–21.

24. Mao and Zhou Enlai's speeches at the CCP Politburo meeting, August 4, 1950, cited in *Bo Yibo Memoirs*, 43; see also minutes of the Politburo meeting, cited in Qi Dexue, *Chaoxian Zhanzheng Juece Neimu*, 30.

25. *Zhongguo Renmin Zhiyuanjun Kangmei Yuanchao Zhan Shi*, 8; Qi Dexue, "Zhou Enlai's Important Contribution to the Command of the War to Resist U.S. Aggression and Aid Korea," *Junshi Lishi* [Military history] 1 (1992): 5.

26. Telegram, Mao to Peng Dehuai, August 27, 1950, *Mao's Manuscripts*, 1:485.

27. Mao's instruction on the deployment of the 9th Army Corps, September 8, 1950, ibid., 498.

28. The CMC's statistics on PLA weaponry, May 1950, *Dangdai Zhongguo Jundui de Junshi Gongzuo*, 2:49, 127, 141; minutes of the national security meeting, August 26, 1950, cited in Qi Dexue, *Chaoxian Zhanzheng Juece Neimu*, 31; also see Qi, "Zhou Enlai's Important Contribution," 4.

29. Chinese Academy of Military Sciences, *Zhongguo Renmin Jiefangjun Liushinian Dashiji; 1927–1987* [Records of important events of the People's Liberation Army from 1927 to 1987] (Beijing: Military Sciences Press, 1988), 492; *Zhongguo Renmin Zhiyuanjun Kangmei Yuanchao Zhan Shi*, 8.

30. *Dangdai Zhongguo Jundui de Junshi Gongzuo*, 2:141–42.

31. Ibid., 74–75. The PLA had first established an anti-aircraft corps in November 1945. On August 10, 1949, the acting chief of staff Nie Rongzhen, CCP's secretary-in-general Yang Shangkun, and the minister of the PLA logistical department Yang Lishan jointly proposed construction of ten more anti-aircraft artillery and ten anti-aircraft machine-gun regiments to strengthen China's coastal defense. Zhou Enlai approved the proposal on August 11. By May 1950, the PLA had formed three anti-aircraft artillery divisions: the 1st Division was deployed in the Northeast, 2d Division in Guangdong, and the 3d Division in Shanghai. ibid., 75.

32. *Jiefangjun Jiangling Zhuan*, 7:289–90; *Zhongguo Renmin Jiefangjun Liushinian Dashiji*, 492; *Dangdai Zhongguo Jundui de Junshi Gongzuo*, 2:53, 147, and 263.

33. China Today series, *Dangdai Zhongguo Kongjun* [China today: The air force] (Beijing: Chinese Social Sciences Press, 1989), 78.

34. PLA Air Force Command, "An Outline of Plans for Constructing the People's Air Force: 1950–1953," August 1950, cited in ibid., 49.

35. Memorandum, Zhou Enlai to the Air Force Command, September 2, 1950, and Air Force Command's response, September 29, 1950, ibid., 68.

36. Ibid., 79–81.

37. Third Field Army Deputy Commander Su Yu's speech, mid-July 1950, cited in China Today series, *Dangdai Zhongguo Haijun* [China today: The People's Navy] (Beijing: Chinese Social Sciences Press, 1987), 41.

38. Telegram, Mao to Deng Zihui, July 27, 1950, *Mao's Manuscripts*, 1:444.

39. Telegram, Mao to Deng Zihui and the Central South China Military Command, August 25, 1950, ibid., 480–81.

40. Su Yu's talks with the People's Navy commanders, mid-July 1950, *Dangdai Zhongguo Haijun*, 41 and 166.

41. Resolution of the People's Navy Command meeting, August 1950, ibid., 41–42.

42. Ibid., 51–52.

43. Ibid., 53.

44. Ibid., 56.

45. Ibid., 166–70.

46. Ibid., 171–82.

47. *Dangdai Zhongguo Jundui de Junshi Gongzuo*, 1:521–22.

48. Chen Geng, *Chen Geng Riji (Xu)* [Chen Geng's diary (continued)] (Beijing: PLA Soldiers' Press, 1984), 7.

49. Ibid., 9.

50. Telegram. Mao to Chen Geng, July 28, 1950, ibid., 13; see also *Dangdai Zhongguo Jundui de Junshi Gongzuo*, 1:523.

51. Ibid., 523–26.

52. Telegram, Mao to the Central South China Military Command, September 16, 1950, *Mao's Manuscripts*, 1:519–20; 521.

53. Telegram, Mao to Chen Geng, October 16, 1950, *Chen Geng Riji*, 35; and *Dangdai Zhongguo Jundui de Junshi Gongzuo*, 1:526.

54. Chai Chengwen, *Banmendian Tanpan* [The Panmunjom negotiations] (Beijing: PLA Press, 1989), 35–37 (hereafter cited as *Chai Chengwen Memoirs*). The five intelligence officers were Ni Weitin, Xu Zhonghua, Zhang Hengya, Zhu Guang, Wang Daguang, and Liu Xiangwen.

55. Ibid., 39–40.

56. Ibid., 41–45. It is interesting that Rear Admiral R. H. Hillenkoetter, the director of U.S. central intelligence, sent President Truman a report on August 1, 1950, that "a 'Supreme Military Committee' consisting of forty Russians, twenty Chinese, and fifty North Korean Army personnel was established in Seoul on 1 July 1950." The report also indicated that "a Chinese Communist Army liaison office has existed in North Korea since 1946." Memorandum, Hillenkoetter to Truman, August 1, 1950, cited in Joseph C. Goulden, *Korea: The Untold Story of the War* (New York: Times Books, 1982), 275.

57. *Chai Chengwen Memoirs*, 66–67; Lei Yingfu, "My Recollection," 79–80. Lei recalls that when he reported his assessment to Mao, the CCP chairman questioned him about MacArthur's leadership style. When Lei told him that MacArthur was "a stubborn, warlike old warrior," Mao commented, "That's fine, because the more stubborn and more warlike he is, the more advantages we would have." Ibid., 80. See also Zhang Ding and Zhang Bing, *Lingxiu Shenbian de Junshi Gaocan* [The senior staff by the leaders' side] (Chengdu: University of Electronic Science Press, 1993), 90–97.

58. *Hong Xuezhi Memoirs*, 4 and 8.

59. Telegram, Deng Hua to Lin Biao, August 31, 1950, cited in *Jiefangjun Jiangling Zhuan*, 7:30; also see Luo Yinwen, "Realistically Putting Forward New Ideas: Two or Three Facts About General Deng Hua," *Ren Wu* [Biographical Studies] 5 (1985): 63. Deng's report consisted of six parts: (1) Korea's geographical conditions; (2) contrast our forces with the enemy's; (3) our supply problems; (4) the enemy war objectives; (5) our military doctrines; (6) our military equipment and training situation. This report was first addressed to Lin Biao, then CMC vice-chairman, and relayed to Mao on September 8, 1950. See Qi Dexue, "On *Heixue*," *Junshi Lishi* [Military history] 6 (1989): 40.

60. *Chai Chengwen Memoirs*, 77–78.

61. Sun Baoshen, "Mao Zedong Had Predicted that the US/UN Would Land at Inchon," *Junshi Shilin* [Studies of military history] 5 (1990): 13.

62. *Hong Xuezhi Memoirs*, 8–9; *Chai Chengwen Memoirs*, 77. One questionable source contends that, shocked by MacArthur's landing attack, Stalin wired Mao "bluntly stating that China had to save Kim Il-sung. Stalin added, somewhat gratuitously, that if the PLA were defeated, he would intervene himself." Wang Ming, *Polveka KPK i Predatelstvo Mao Zedong* [Half a century of the CCP and the treachery of Mao Zedong] (Moscow: Politizdat [Party publishing house], 1975), 206–7. Wang, who had been ousted as Mao's rival for party leadership in 1938, claimed that Liu Shaoqi had told him this in Moscow during his visit in November 1952. Also see Goncharov, Lewis, and Xue, *Uncertain Partners*, 174.

63. *Chai Chengwen Memoirs*, 79.

64. Ibid., 80.

65. Letter, Kim Il-sung and Pak Hon-yong to Mao Zedong, October 1, 1950, in Ye Yumeng, *Heixue: Chubing Chaoxian Kangmei Yuanchao Lishi Jishi* [The black snow: Historical records of Chinese military intervention in Korea] (Beijing: Writers' Press, 1989), 49–51. Pak Hon-yong traveled to Beijing and hand-delivered the letter to the Beijing leaders.

66. Minutes of the 13th Army Corps Command meeting, August 13, 1950, *Du Ping Memoirs*, 18–20.

67. Telegram, Deng Hua to the CMC, August 31, 1950, *Jiefangjun Jiangling Zhuan*, 7:31.

68. Minutes of the 13th Army Corps Command meeting September 1950, *Hong Xuezhi Memoirs*, 9–10; see also *Du Ping Memoirs*, 19–20.

69. *Hong Xuezhi Memoirs*, 11.

70. Instruction by the CMC, "On Our Combat Principles," drafted by Zhou Enlai, September 29, 1950, *Chai Chengwen Memoirs*, 79–80.

71. A Statement by Ministry of Foreign Affairs, September 22, 1950, *Renmin Ribao*, [People's daily], September 23, 1950, 1. Also see Allen S. Whiting, *China Crosses the Yalu: The Decision to Enter the Korean War* (New York: Macmillan, 1960), 104–9.

72. Telegram, Mao to Stalin, "On Our Decision to Dispatch Troops to Fight in Korea," October 2, 1950, *Mao's Manuscripts*, 1:539–41.

73. Telegram, Mao to Gao Gang and Deng Hua, October 2, 1950, ibid., 538.

74. Division of Diplomatic History, Ministry of Foreign Affairs, *Xinzhongguo Waijiao Fengyun* [Winds and clouds of New China's diplomacy] (Beijing: World Knowledge Press, 1990), 97.

75. Zhou-Panikkar meeting, 1:00 A.M., October 3, 1950, is cited in *Chai Chengwen Memoirs*, 81. Panikkar, however, recalled that Zhou Enlai explicitly stated that "we will intervene." K. M. Panikkar, *In Two Chinas: Memoirs of a Diplomat* (London: Allen and Unwin, 1955), 108–10.

76. Telegram, Mao to Gao Gang and Deng Hua, October 2, 1950, *Mao's Manuscripts*, 1:538; *Jiefangjun Jiangling Zhuan*, 7:157–58. About the Secretariat meeting, see China Today series, *Peng Dehuai Zhuan* [The biography of Peng Dehuai] (Beijing: Dangdai Zhongguo Press, 1993), 400. Goncharov, Lewis, and Xue wrongly cite the October 2 meeting as the first Politburo meeting; *Uncertain Years*, 176.

77. Miao Changqing, "A Reappraisal of the Gao-Rao Affair," *Lilun Xuekan* [Theoretical bulletin] 6 (1990): 50–51. Zhou Enlai recalled the dissenting opinions in 1965; see China Today series, *Dangdai Zhongguo Waijiao* [China today: Diplomacy] (Beijing: Chinese Social Sciences Press, 1987), 38. Also see *Peng Dehuai Zhuan*, 401–2. For a study in English of Gao Gang's opposition to China's entry into the war, see Frederick C. Teiwes, *Politics at Mao's Court: Gao Gang and Party Factionalism in the Early 1950s* (Armonk, N.Y.: M. E. Sharpe, 1990).

78. Lin Biao had expressed his worry in early September. See *Chai Chengwen Memoirs*, 78–79; *Hong Xuezhi Memoirs*, 17; and *Nie Rongzhen Memoirs*, 736. Mao had personally preferred Lin because, he commented, "Lin Biao is only forty-four years old and well-known for his artful, ferocious, and tricky direction of war." Zhang and Zhang, *Lingxiu Shenbian de Junshi Gaocan*, 99. Because Lin was ostracized during the Cultural Revolution, most CCP high-ranking officials still condemn his refusal to direct the Chinese forces in Korea. However, Lin truly was suffering from serious neurasthenia, and Dr. Fu Lianzhang, who was then in charge of CCP leaders' health, forbade him to go.

79. Ye Yumeng, *Heixue*, 51–54 (emphasis added); see also CCP Central Committee document, "A Guide to Interpretations of the Current Situation," October 26, 1950, cited in Yao Xu, *Cong Yalujiang dao Banmendian* [From the Yalu River to Panmunjom] (Beijing: People's Press, 1985), 23–24; Hu Guangzheng, "On the Decision to Send Troops Participating in the War to Resist American and Aid Korea," *Dangshi Yanjiu* [Studies of the CCP history] 1 (1983): 33–38; and *Peng Dehuai Zhuan*, 402.

80. Minutes of Mao-Peng meeting, October 5, 1950, cited in *Peng Dehuai Zhuan*, 402; Museum of the Chinese Military Revolutions, *Peng Dehuai Yuanshuai Fengbei Yongcun* [The remarkable achievement of Marshall Peng Dehuai will be remembered forever] (Shanghai: People's Press, 1985), 423; Xiao Jianning, "An Analysis of the U.S. Policy Toward China on the Eve of the Outbreak of the Korean War," *Dangshi Yanjiu* [Studies of CCP history] 6 (1987): 173. Also see Zhang and Zhang, *Lingxiu Shenbian de Junshi Gaocan*, 100–101.

81. CMC instruction, drafted by Mao Zedong, "An Order to Establish the Chinese People's Volunteer Army," October 9, 1950, *Mao's Manuscripts*, 1:543–44.

82. Telegram, Mao to Kim Il-sung, October 8, 1950, ibid., 545.

83. *Chai Chengwen Memoirs*, 83–84.

84. Xiong Huayuan, "Zhou Enlai's Secret Visit to the Soviet Union Right Before China's Entry in the War to Resist U.S. Aggression and Aid Korea," *Dang de Wenxian* [CCP documents and materials] 3 (1994): 83–86; Kang Yimin's recollections, cited in Qi Dexue, *Chaoxian Zhangzheng Juece Neimu*, 62–63, and Qi Dexue, "On Some Key Issues Concerning the Decision Making of Entering the Korean War," *Junshi Lishi* [Military history] 2 (1993): 52–53. Shi Zhe recalls the Stalin-Zhou talks; see Zhao Yongtian and Zhang Xi, "The Book *Heixue* Is Seriously Faulty," *Junshi Lishi* 6 (1989): 42, and *Shi Zhe Memoirs*, 495–503. There exists another version in the Chinese literature: Mao had asked for Soviet air support in his October 2 telegram to Stalin, but Moscow informed the CCP leaders through its embassy to Beijing of its refusal to dispatch the Soviet air force. Very upset at the Soviets' breaking their promise, Mao sent Zhou to Moscow to persuade Stalin to change his mind. See *Shi Zhe Memoirs*, 495–99; Ye Yumeng, *Heixue*, 106–7; *Hong Xuezhi Memoirs*, 25–26; Chen Jian, *China's Road to the Korean War*, 196–200. See also Khrushchev's account of Zhou's visit to Stalin in Nikita Khrushchev, *Khruschchev Remembers: The Last Testament*, and ed. Strobe Talbott (Boston: Little, Brown 1970), 371–72. A recent study on the basis of new Soviet materials points out that Stalin had second thoughts on supporting Chinese intervention because he was concerned that Mao might have tried to push Stalin to war eventually. See Goncharov, Lewis, and Xue, *Uncertain Partners*, 188–92; the authors base their argument on a previously classified book, A. M. Ledovskii, *Delo Gao Gana-Rao Shushi* [The case of Gao Gang and Rao Shushi] (Moscow, 1990), 72–73. Ledovskii was the Soviet consul general in Shenyang during the Korean War. For details of Soviet military assistance to China, see Mineo Nakajima, "The Sino-Soviet Confrontation: Its Roots in the International Background of the Korean War," *Australian Journal of Chinese Affairs* (January 1979): 19–47. Soviet materials on this matter have yet to be declassified.

85. Telegram. Mao to Peng Dehuai and Gao Gang, October 12, 1950, *Mao's Manuscripts*, 1:552.

86. Telegram, Mao to Rao Shushi and Chen Yi, October 12, 1950, ibid., 553.

87. Telegram. Mao to Zhou Enlai, October 13, 1950, ibid., 556. Mao's instructions on Zhou's stay did not appear on *Mao's Manuscripts* but are cited in Xiong Huayuan, "Zhou Enlai's Secret Visit to the Soviet Union," 86. Right after the meeting, Peng wired the 13th Army Corps headquarters that "the troops should resume preparations for entering the war according to the original plan." Wang Yazhi, "Peng Dehuai and Nie Rongzhen During the War to Resist U.S. Aggression and Aid Korea: A Recollection of a Staff Member," *Junshi Shilin* [Studies of military history] 1 (1994): 10.

88. *Shi Zhe Memoirs*, 502; *Hong Xuezhi Memoirs*, 27; *Nie Rongzhen Memoirs*, 758.

89. *Dangdai Zhongguo Kongjun*, 78–79. For a Soviet account, see Steven J. Zaloga, "The Russians in MIG Alley," *Air Force Magazine* 74 (February 1991): 76; see also Jon Holliday, "Air Operations in Korea: The Soviet Side of the Story," in *A Revolutionary War: Korea and the Transformation of the Postwar World*, ed. William J. Williams (Chicago: Imprint, 1993), 149.

90. William Whitney Stueck, Jr., *The Road to Confrontation: American Policy Toward China and Korea, 1947–1950* (Chapel Hill: University of North Carolina Press, 1981), 254–55; Stueck, *The Korean War: An International History* (Princeton University Press, forthcoming). See also Rosemary Foot, *The Wrong War: American Policy and the Dimensions of the Korean Conflict, 1950–1953* (Ithaca: Cornell University Press, 1985), 67–74.

91. Memorandum, untitled, Walter Bedell Smith to Truman, October 12, 1950 (emphasis added); "Situation Summary," CIA, October 27, 1950, cited in Goulden, *Korea*, 276–77, 284.

CHAPTER 5. LURING THE ENEMY IN DEEP

1. Mao Zedong, "On Protracted War," *SMW*, 235.

2. Ibid., 210–11.

3. Ibid., 215.

4. Ibid., 232.

5. Telegram, Mao to Zhou Enlai, 3:00 A.M., October 14, 1950, *Mao's Manuscripts*, 1:558–59.

6. Telegram, Mao to Zhou Enlai, October 14, 1950, ibid., 560–61.

7. Telegram, Mao to Ni Zhiliang, Beijing's ambassador to Pyongyang, October 9, 1950, ibid., 546. The idea of gathering the remnant NKPA troops in China's Northeast had been proposed by General M. V. Zakharov, the deputy chief of the Soviet general staff, who was in Pyongyang as head of a special mission to North Korea in October 1950. Stalin pushed Beijing to accept the idea when he met with Zhou Enlai on October 8 at Sochi. Sergei N. Goncharov, John W. Lewis, and Xue Litai, *Uncertain Partners: Stalin, Mao, and the Korean War* (Stanford: Stanford University Press, 1993), 174–75, 189.

8. Telegram, Mao to Kim Il-sung and Peng Dehaui, October 19, 1950, *Mao's Manuscripts*, 1:547. By U.S. estimate, only 20,000 North Korean troops, the remnants of seven NKPA divisions, continued in combat. An additional 15,000 were north of the 38th parallel but cut off behind US/UN lines. Some 10,000 others remained in the South as guerrillas. "Situation Summary," CIA, October 27, 1950, cited in Joseph C. Goulden, *Korea: The Untold Story of the War* (New York: Times Books, 1982), 287.

9. Gao Gang's speech at the CPV Command meeting, October 9, 1950, cited in *Hong Xuezhi Memoirs*, 19–20.

10. Peng Dehuai's speech at the CPV Command meeting, October 9, 1950, ibid., 20–21. For a detailed description of the command meeting, see Da Wan, "Miraculous Forces from the Sky: The First Battle After Chief Peng Entered Korea," *Ren Wu* [Biographical studies] 5 (1990): 7–9.

11. Minutes of Peng–Deng Hua–Hong Xuezhi conversation, October 9, 1950, *Hong Xuezhi Memoirs*, 21.

12. Telegram, Mao to Peng Dehuai, October 11, 1950, *Mao's Manuscripts*, 1:548.

13. *Hong Xuezhi Memoirs*, 22–23; telegram, Mao to Chen Yi, the East China Military commander, October 12, 1950, *Mao's Manuscripts*, 1:551.

14. Peng Dehuai's speech at the CPV Command meeting, October 14, 1950, Peng Dehuai, *Peng Dehuai Junshi Wenxuan* [Selected military writings of Peng Dehuai] (Beijing: Central Archives and Manuscripts Press, 1988), 320–22. Peng made this speech on October 16, 1950, at the 13th Army Corps headquarters in Andong, Chinese Academy of Military Sciences, *Zhongguo Renmin Zhiyuanjun Kangmei Yuanchao Zhan Shi* [The war history of the Chinese People's Volunteers in the War to Resist U.S. Aggression and Aid Korea] (Beijing: Military Sciences Press, 1988), 15.

15. *Kangmei Yuanchao Zhanzheng*, 321 and 323.

16. Ibid., 323 and 325.

17. Telegram, Mao to Gao Gang and Deng Hua, October 15, 1950, *Mao's Manuscripts*, 1:563.

18. Telegram, Mao to Gao Gang, Peng Dehuai, and Deng Hua, October 15, 1950, ibid., 564–65.

19. Telegram, Mao to Peng, Gao, and Deng, October 17, 1950, ibid., 567.

20. Telegram, Mao to Deng, Hong Xuezhi, Han Xianchu, and Xie Fang, October 18, 1950, ibid., 568. Also see Qi Dexue, *Chaoxian Zhanzheng Juece Neimu* [Inside stories of decision makings in the Korean War] (Shenyang: Liaoning University Press, 1991), 63.

21. Zhang Xi, *Peng Dehuai Shouming Shuaishi Kangmei Yuanchao de Qianqian Houhou* [On the eve and after Peng Dehuai's appointment to direct the war of resisting America and aiding Korea] (Beijing: CCP Historical Materials Press, 1989), 155; Telegram, Mao to Deng Zihui, Tan Zheng, Rao Shushi, Chen Yi, Liu Bocheng, Deng Xiaoping, Xi Zhongqin, October 19, 1950, *Mao's Manuscripts*, 1:571.

22. Telegram, Mao to Peng, Deng, Hong, and Xie and each CPV army commander, October 19, 1950, cited in *Zhongguo Renmin Zhiyuanjun Kangmei Yuanchao Zhan Shi*, 20–21; see also *Hong Xuezhi Memoirs*, 31–33.

23. *Zhongguo Renmin Zhiyuanjun Kangmei Yuanchao Zhan Shi*, 20; *Hong Xuezhi Memoirs*, 30–31. Also see Roy E. Appleman, *Disaster in Korea: The Chinese Confront MacArthur* (College Station: Texas A&M University Press, 1989), 12–13.

24. Telegram, Mao to Peng, October 21, 1950, *Mao's Manuscripts*, 1:575; *Zhongguo Renmin Zhiyuanjun Kangmei Yuanchao Zhan Shi*, 29; and *Kangmei Yuanchao Zhanzheng*, 21.

25. Telegram, Mao to Peng Dehuai and the 13th Army Corps Command, October 21, 1950, *Mao's Manuscripts*, 1:575–76.

26. Ibid.

27. Telegram, Mao to Deng Hua, October 21, 1950, ibid., 577.

28. Cui Lun, "Recall the Days Working as Chief Peng's Communication Officer in the Initial Stage of the War to Resist U.S. Aggression and Aid Korea," *Junshi Lishi* [Military history] 4 (1989): 43; Peng Dehuai to Deng Hua, October 21, 1950, cited in *Hong Xuezhi Memoirs*, 37. For more details on Peng's loss of contact with the troops, see China Today series, *Peng Dehuai Zhuan* [The biography of Peng Dehuai] (Beijing: Dangdai Zhongguo Press, 1993), 411–14.

29. *Chai Chengwen Memoirs*, 95–98; *Hong Xuezhi Memoirs*, 44–45.

30. Telegram, Peng Dehuai to the CMC, 4:00 P.M., October 21, 1950, *Peng Dehuai Junshi Wenxuan*, 328–29.

31. Telegram, Mao to Peng Dehuai, 7:00 A.M., October 22, 1950, *Mao's Manuscripts*, 1:582–83.

32. Telegram, Mao to Deng Hua, Hong Xuezhi, Han Xianchu, Xie Fang, October 22, 1950, ibid., 584.

33. Telegram, Peng to Deng Hua, Hong Xuezhi, Han Xianchu, 10:00 A.M., October 22, 1950, Mao Zedong, *Mao Zedong Junshi Wenxuan—neibuban* [Selected military works of Mao Zedong—internal edition] (Beijing: PLA Soldiers' Press, 1981), 686 n. 3.

34. Telegram, Peng to Deng Hua, Hong Xuezhi, Han Xianchu, and Xie Fang, 3:00 P.M., October 22, 1950, *Peng Dehuai Junshi Wenxuan*, 329.

35. Telegram, Peng Dehuai to Mao, 7:00 P.M., October 22, 1950, *Mao Zedong Junshi Wenxuan—neibuban*, 686 n. 4.

36. Telegram, Mao to Peng and Gao Gang, October 23, 1950, *Mao's Manuscripts*, 1:588–89. Mao directed Peng to destroy the telegram after he read it; ibid., 589.

37. *Hong Xuezhi Memoirs*, 46; telegrams, Mao to Peng and Deng Hua, October 23, 1950, *Mao's Manuscripts*, 1:592; Mao to Gao Gang, October 24, 1950, ibid., 598; Mao to Chen Yi and Tan Zheng, October 23, 1950, ibid., 597.

38. *Hong Xuezhi Memoirs*, 46–47.

39. Minutes of the 13th Army Corps Command meeting, October 24, 1950, ibid., 48–49; telegram, Mao to the 13th Army Corps Command, October 25, 1950, *Mao's*

Manuscripts, 1:600; also see Sun Yaoshen, "General Xie Fang in the War to Resist U.S. Aggression and Aid Korea," *Junshi Lishi* [Military history] 4 (1990): 42–43.

40. *Hong Xuezhi Memoirs*, 51.

41. Ibid., 52–53; *Kangmei Yuanchao Zhanzheng*, 34–35; Liu Hansheng, "A Glorious Beginning," *Zhiyuanjun Yingxiong Zhuan* [The chronicle of the CPV Heroes] (Beijing: People's Literature Press, 1956), 1:30–31 (hereafter ZYZ); Dai Baocheng's diary, October 25, 1950, ibid., 18–21. Dai was deputy battalion leader of the 354th Regiment. For the US/UN side of the story, see Appleman, *Disaster in Korea*, 19–20, and Korean War Enemy Materials series, *Chaoxian Zhanzheng: Zhonggongjun Canzhan ji Lianhejun Congxin Fangong* [The Korean War: Intervention of the Chinese Communist forces and counteroffensive of the US/UN forces], internal ed. (Henongjiang: Korean Minority Press, n.d.) 1:141–45.

42. Telegram, Mao to Peng Dehuai and Deng Hua, October 25, 1950, *Mao's Manuscripts*, 1:605.

43. Telegram, Peng Dehuai to Mao, October 25, 1950, *Peng Dehuai Junshi Wenxuan*, 329–30.

44. Telegrams, Mao to Peng and Deng, 5:00 A.M., October 26, 1950, *Mao's Manuscripts*, 1:609; Mao to Peng, 2:00 P.M., October 26, 1950, ibid., 610–11; Mao to Peng, Deng, Hong, and Han, 4:00 P.M., October 26, 1950, ibid., 612–13; Mao to Peng and Deng, 11:00 P.M., October 26, 1950, ibid., 614–15.

45. Telegram, Peng to each CPV army command, October 27, 1950, *Peng Dehuai Junshi Wenxuan*, 322–23.

46. Mao to Peng, 10:00 P.M., October 27, 1950, *Mao's Manuscripts*, 1:619.

47. Telegram, minutes of CPV Command meeting, October 27, 1950, *Hong Xuezhi Memoirs*, 53; see also *Kangmei Yuanchao Zhanzheng*, 36.

48. Telegrams, Mao to Peng and Deng, 11:00 A.M., October 28, 1950, *Mao's Manuscripts*, 1:622; Mao to Peng and Deng, 4:30 P.M., October 28, 1950, ibid., 623.

49. Telegram, Peng to each CPV army command, October 28, 1950, cited in *Hong Xuezhi Memoirs*, 54; see also *Zhongguo Renmin Zhiyuanjun Kangmei Yuanchao Zhan Shi*, 29. Mao approved the requested change; see his telegram to Peng, 11:00 P.M., October 28, 1950, *Mao's Manuscripts*, 1:624.

50. *Hong Xuezhi Memoirs*, 54–55; *Zhongguo Renmin Zhiyuanjun Kangmei Yuanchao Zhan Shi*, 37–38; Xinhuo Liaoyuan Editorial Division, *Jiefangjun Jiangling Zhuan* [The chronicle of PLA senior generals] (Beijing: PLA Press, 1988), 7:380–81; *Jiang Yonghui Memoirs*, 38–39.

51. Telegrams, Peng to the CMC and each CPV army commander, 9:00 A.M., October 30, 1950, *Peng Dehuai Junshi Wenxuan*, 333; *Hong Xuezhi Memoirs*, 56; Mao to Peng and Deng Hua, October 30, 1950, *Mao's Manuscripts*, 1:632.

52. *Zhongguo Renmin Zhiyuanjun Kangmei Yuanchao Zhan Shi*, 32; *Kangmei Yuanchao Zhanzheng*, 39–41; Wang Yang, "The Military Prowess of the First Battle," ZYZ, 34–40. Wang was then the 114th Division commander. Also see Appleman, *Disaster in Korea*, 20; without giving an exact figure, Appleman stated, "The 8th Cavalry Regiment was destroyed."

53. Telegrams, Mao to Peng and Deng Hua, 3:00 A.M., November 2, 1950, *Mao's Manuscripts*, 1:639; Mao to Peng and Deng, 7:00 P.M., November 2, 1950, ibid., 640; Mao to Peng and Deng, 10:00 A.M., November 2, 1950, ibid., 642.

54. Telegram, Peng Dehuai to each CPV army command, November 3, 1950, cited in *Zhongguo Renmin Zhiyuanjun Kangmei Yuanchao Zhan Shi*, 33–34; for CPV pursuing operations, see *Kangmei Yuanchao Zhanzheng*, 42; Mao to Peng and Deng, 10:00 P.M., November 3, 1950, *Mao's Manuscripts*, 1:645.

55. Telegram, Peng to Mao, November 4, 1950, *Mao Zedong Junshi Wenxuan—neibuban*, 687–88 n. 9.

56. Telegram, Mao to Peng, 1:00 A.M., November 5, 1950, *Mao's Manuscripts*, 1:647.

57. For the combat experience of the 42d Army in the Chosin Reservoir area, see *Zhongguo Renmin Zhiyuanjun Kangmei Yuanchao Zhan Shi*, 35–37, and *Kangmei Yuanchao Zhanzheng*, 43–46. According to Appleman, 4,157 of the U.S. Eighth Army had been killed in action, 391 more had died of wounds, and 4,834 were missing in action. Appleman, *Disaster in Korea*, 22.

58. Telegrams, Mao to the 19th Army Corps and all regional military commands, October 30, 1950, *Mao's Manuscripts*, 1:630; Peng to Mao, November 4, 1950, *Mao Zedong Junshi Wenxuan—neibuban*, 687–88 n. 9.

59. Peng's assessment proved right. In late October 1950, there still existed a view at MacArthur's headquarters that even if the Chinese entered the war, they should not be taken seriously. As General Charles Willoughby, chief of intelligence at MacArthur's headquarters, explained: "It is to be recognized that most of the CCF [Chinese Communist Force] troops have had no significant experience in combat operations against a major combat power. In addition, their training, like that of the original North Korean forces, has been greatly handicapped by the lack of uniform equipment and assured stocks of munitions." "Daily Intelligence Summary," Far Eastern Command, October 28 and 29, 1950, cited in Goulden, *Korea*, 287–88. Also, in a talk with John J. Muccio, U.S. ambassador to South Korea, on November 17, MacArthur insisted that no more than 30,000 Chinese could have been infiltrated into North Korea; ibid., 317.

60. Telegram, the CPV Command to the CMC, November 8, 1950; part of the telegram is in *Peng Dehuai Junshi Wenxuan*, 344–45, and another part is cited in *Zhongguo Renmin Zhiyuanjun Kangmei Yuanchao Zhan Shi*, 44–45.

61. Telegram, Mao to Peng, Deng, and Pak, November 9, 1950, *Mao's Manuscripts*, 1:653.

62. Peng's speech at the first CPV Party Committee meeting, November 13, 1950, *Peng Dehuai Junshi Wenxuan*, 335–37. For Peng's criticism of the 38th Army, see *Hong Xuezhi Memoirs*, 67, and *Jiang Yonghui Memoirs*, 75.

63. Peng's speech at the first CPV Party Committee meeting, November 13, 1950, *Mao Zedong Junshi Wenxuan—neibuban*, 337–42.

64. *Zhongguo Renmin Zhiyuanjun Kangmei Yuanchao Zhan Shi*, 46. For the combat tasks of the 9th Army Corps, see telegram, Mao to Peng and Deng, November 5, 1950, *Mao's Manuscripts*, 1:650; Mao to Li Tao, director of CMC Combat Operations Department, November 5, 1950; ibid., 651; Peng to Song Shilun, November 6, 1950, *Peng Dehuai Junshi Wenxuan*, 343–44; Mao to the 9th Army Corps Command, October 30, 1950, *Mao's Manuscripts*, 1:630–31; Mao to Peng, November 12, 1950, ibid., 657.

65. Peng talked about this special force at the November 13 CPV Party Committee meeting; see *Peng Dehuai Junshi Wenxuan*, 338.

66. *Zhongguo Renmin Zhiyuanjun Kangmei Yuanchao Zhan Shi*, 46; *Hong Xuezhi Memoirs*, 70.

67. Minutes of the CPV Command meeting, November 16, 1950, cited in *Hong Xuezhi Memoirs*, 71–73; also see *Peng Dehuai Zhuan*, 423–27; *Kangmei Yuanchao Zhanzheng*, 58–60.

68. Telegram, Mao to Peng, November 5, 1950, *Mao's Manuscripts*, 1:648.

69. Telegram, Mao to Peng, Deng, and Pak, November 18, 1950, ibid., 672.

70. Telegram, Peng to the CMC, 6:00 P.M., November 21, 1950, *Peng Dehuai Junshi Wenxuan*, 345–46.

71. Telegram, Mao to the CPV Command, 7:00 P.M., November 24, 1950, *Zhongguo Renmin Zhiyuanjun Kangmei Yuanchao Zhan Shi*, 50–51.

72. Ibid., 51–52; *Hong Xuezhi Memoirs*, 73.

73. *Kangmei Yuanchao Zhanzheng*, 62; *Hong Xuezhi Memoirs*, 82. The mission of scout deputy director Zhang was very successful, and the Chinese government produced a fic-

tionalized account in the film *Qi Xi* [An unexpected attack], which was shown in China through the 1970s; see Ye Yumeng, *Heixue: Chubing Chaoxian Kangmei Yuanchao Lishi Jishi* [The black snow: Historical records of Chinese military intervention in Korea] (Beijing: Writers' Press, 1989), 285. Also see Appleman, *Diaster in Korea*, 76–81.

74. *Zhongguo Renmin Zhiyuanjun Kangmei Yuanchao Zhan Shi*, 54; *Kangmei Yuanchao Zhanzheng*, 62–63.

75. Telegram, the CPV Command to each CPV army command, November 26, 1950, cited in *Kangmei Yuanchao Zhanzheng*, 63.

76. Telegram, the CPV Command to each CPV army command, 12:00 A.M., November 27, 1950, cited in ibid., 64; see also *Zhongguo Renmin Zhiyuanjun Kangmei Yuanchao Zhan Shi*, 55–56.

77. *Hong Xuezhi Memoirs*, 82–85; regimental commander Zhu Yuehua, "The Most Valuable Five Minutes," ZYZ, 153–57. See also Appleman, *Disaster in Korea*, 88–89.

78. Telegram, Mao to Peng, Deng, Pak, and Hong, November 28, 1950, *Mao's Manuscripts*, 1:687.

79. Telegram, Peng to each CPV army command, 1:00 P.M., November 28, 1950, *Peng Dehuai Junshi Wenxuan*, 347–48.

80. Telegram, Mao to Peng, Deng, Pak, and Hong, 12:00 P.M., November 28, 1950, *Mao's Manuscripts*, 1:689.

81. *Kangmei Yuanchao Zhanzheng*, 68–69; *Jiang Yonghui Memoirs*, 174–202; Appleman, *Disaster in Korea*, 93.

82. Telegram, Peng to each CPV army command, November 29, 1950, cited in *Zhongguo Renmin Zhiyuanjun Kangmei Yuanchao Zhan Shi*, 51. Fo the details of the 42d Army's enveloping operations, see ibid., 58. For an account of the US/UN combat effort at Sinchang-ri, see Appleman, *Disaster in Korea*, 98–99.

83. Telegram, the CPV Command to each army commander, 5:00 A.M., December 2, 1950, cited in *Zhongguo Renmin Zhiyuanjun Kangmei Yuanchao Zhan Shi*, 59; also see Mao to Peng, Deng, Pak, and Han, 5:00 A.M., December 2, 1950, *Mao's Manuscripts*, 1:696.

84. Telegram, Peng, Deng Hua, and Hong Xuezhi to the 9th Army Corps Command, 7:00 A.M., November 24, 1950, *Mao Zedong Junshi Wenxuan—neibuban*, 690 n. 13.

85. *Hong Xuezhi Memoirs*, 90–91.

86. Telegrams, Peng, Deng, and Hong to the 9th Army Corps Command, 3:00 P.M., November 28, 1950, *Mao Zedong Junshi Wenxuan—neibuban*, 690–91 n. 15; Mao to Peng, Deng, Song Shilun, and Tao Yong, December 2, 1950, *Mao's Manuscripts*, 1:698; Mao to Peng, Deng, Pak, Song, and Tao, 1:00 A.M., December 3, 1950, ibid., 705; and Mao to Peng, Deng, Pak, Song, and Tao, 1:00 P.M., December 4, 1950, ibid., 708.

87. Telegram, Mao to Peng, December 12, 1950, *Mao's Manuscripts*, 1:699.

88. Telegram, Peng to Mao, 12:00 P.M., December 4, 1950, *Mao Zedong Junshi ,Wenxuan—neibuban*, 691 n. 16.

89. Telegrams, Mao to Peng, Deng, Pak, Song, and Hong, 11:30 P.M., December 4, 1950, *Mao's Manuscripts*, 1:709; Mao to Peng and Song Shilun, 7:00 A.M., December 5, 1950, ibid., 712.

90. For the CPV casualties report, see *Kangmei Yuanchao Zhanzheng*, 81. Mao was so pleased with the battle result that he personally edited the news release on the CPV capture of Pyongyang; *Mao's Manuscripts*, 1:710–11 and 715. As for the U.S. casualties, I cannot find a total number from any source, but according to Appleman, the U.S. 2d Division alone lost 5,295 as of November 30, 1950; Appleman, *Disaster in Korea*, 286.

91. Telegram, Peng to Mao, 6:00 P.M., December 4, 1950, *Peng Dehuai Junshi Wenxuan*, 349.

92. *Jiang Yonghui Memoirs*, 221–23.

CHAPTER 6. BETWEEN THE OFFENSIVE AND THE DEFENSIVE

1. Mao Zedong, "On Protracted War," *SMW*, 241–42.

2. On the meeting between Kim, Mao, Zhou, and Gao Gang, December 3, 1950, see Ye Yumeng, *Hanjiang Xue* [The blood of the Han River] (Beijing: Daily Economy Press, 1990), 6–11; Mao also mentioned his talks with Kim in his telegram to Peng Dehuai and Song Shilun, December 5, 1950, *Mao's Manuscripts*, 1:712.

3. Telegram, the CMC to Peng, December 4, 1950, cited in Chinese Academy of Military Sciences, *Zhongguo Renmin Zhiyuanjun Kangmei Yuanchao Zhan Shi* [The war history of the Chinese People's Volunteers in the War to Resist U.S. Aggression and Aid Korea] (Beijing: Military Sciences Press, 1988), 76–77. It is interesting that this telegram is not included in *Mao's Manuscripts*. Since it might contain Mao's critical view of the North Korean leaders, it remains classified.

4. Telegram, Peng to Mao and Gao Gang, December 8, 1950, cited in Ye Yumeng, *Hanjiang Xue*, 14–16.

5. Telegram, Mao to Peng, Gao Gang, and Song Shilun, 10:00 A.M., December 11, 1950, *Mao's Manuscripts*, 1:719–20.

6. Minutes of Zhang Hanfu–Panikkar conversation, December 7, 1950, cited in *Chai Chengwen Memoirs*, 113; minutes of Zhou Enlai–Panikkar conversation, December 11, 1950, ibid., 113–14.

7. Telegram, Mao to Peng and Gao Gang, December 13, 1950, *Mao's Manuscripts*, 1:722–25.

8. Telegram, Mao to Peng, Gao, and Song Shilun, December 17, 1950, ibid., 724–25.

9. Ye Yumeng, *Hanjiang Xue*, 7; see also telegram, Mao to each regional military command, December 18, 1950, *Mao's Manuscripts*, 1:726.

10. Minutes of the CPV Command meeting, December 15, 1950, cited in *Hong Xuezhi Memoirs*, 98–100, and *Du Ping Memoirs*, 151–52; telegram, the CPV Command to each army commander, December 15, 1950, in Peng Dehuai, *Peng Dehuai Junshi Wenxuan*, [Selected military writings of Peng Dehuai] (Beijing: Central Archives and Manuscripts Press, 1988), 355–56.

11. Telegram, Peng Dehuai to the CMC, 12:00 P.M., December 19, 1950, Mao Zedong, *Mao Zedong Junshi Wenxuan—neibuban* [Selected military works of Mao Zedong—internal edition] (Beijing: PLA Soldiers' Press, 1981), 691–92. n. 18.

12. Telegram, Mao to Peng and Gao Gang, December 21, 1950, *Mao's Manuscripts*, 1:731–32.

13. Telegrams, Mao to Peng, December 24, 1950, ibid., 733; Mao to Peng and Pak and Kim Il-sung, December 26, 1950, ibid., 734–35.

14. Telegram, Peng to Han Xianchu, 12:00 A.M., December 12, 1950, *Peng Dehuai Junshi Wenxuan*, 357–58.

15. *Hong Xuezhi Memoirs*, 103–4.

16. Ibid., 103; also see *Zhongguo Renmin Zhiyuanjun Kangmei Yuanchao Zhan Shi*, 82; Xu Yan, *Diyici Jiaoliang: Kangmei Yuanchao Zhanzheng de Lishi Huigu yu Fansi* [The first encounter: Historical retrospection and review of the War to Resist U.S. Aggression and Aid Korea] (Beijing: Chinese Radio and Television Press, 1990), 64.

17. Telegram, Peng to Han Xianchu, December 22, 1950, *Peng Dehuai Junshi Wenxuan*, 358.

18. Telegram, Peng to Mao and Gao Gang, 8:00 P.M., December 28, 1950, ibid., 359–60.

19. Telegram, Mao to Peng and Gao Gang, December 29, 1950, *Mao's Manuscripts*, 1:741–42.

20. Telegrams, Kim Ung to Peng Dehuai, December 29, 1950, cited in Ye Yumeng, *Hanjiang Xue*, 51; Peng to Han Xianchu, December 29, 1950, ibid., Han Xianchu to Peng,

10:00 A.M., December 30, 1950, ibid., 54–55. For the losses of the 1st Artillery Division, see ibid., 56–57.

21. *Kangmei Yuanchao Zhanzheng*, 93–97; *Zhongguo Renmin Zhiyuanjun Kangmei Yuanchao Zhan Shi*, 83–86; *Hong Xuezhi Memoirs*, 105–6; Zhang Feng, deputy commander of the 116th Division, "The New Year Eve Offensive," *ZYZ*, 188–89; Li Guangzhi, regimental commander, "A Three-minute Breakthrough," ibid., 192–95. See also Roy E. Appleman, *Ridgway Duels for Korea* (College Station: Texas A&M University Press, 1990), 38–51.

22. Telegram, Peng Dehuai to each army command, 12:00 P.M., January 4, 1951, *Peng Dehuai Junshi Wenxuan*, 360–61. For the antitank efforts of the 149th Division, see *Kangmei Yuanchao Zhanzheng*, 98.

23. Telegram, Han Xianchu to Peng, Hong Xuezhi, and Xie Fang, January 5, 1951, cited in Ye Yumeng, *Hanjiang Xue*, 79–80; also see *Hong Xuezhi Memoirs*, 111; Zhang Feng, "The New Year Eve Offensive," 189.

24. CPV intelligence department's report to Peng, January 8, 1951, cited in Ye Yumeng, *Hanjiang Xue*, 80.

25. Telegram, Peng to each army commander, January 8, 1951, ibid., 80; see also *Zhongguo Renmin Zhiyuanjun Kangmei Yuanchao Zhan Shi*, 87.

26. *Zhongguo Renmin Zhiyuanjun Kangmei Yuanchao Zhan Shi*, 88, and Xu Yan, *Diyici Jiaoliang*, 67.

27. On the Peng-Kim-Pak talks, January 10, 1951, see Ye Yumeng, *Hanjiang Xue*, 80–84; also see *Hong Xuezhi Memoirs*, 110 and 113. The head of the Soviet military advisory group to China also expressed his discontent at Peng's order to call off the pursuit. Wang Yazhi, "Peng Dehuai and Nie Rongzhen During the War to Resist U.S. Aggression and Aid Korea: A Recollection of a Staff Member," *Junshi Shilin* [Studies of military history] 1 (1994):11.

28. *Hong Xuezhi Memoirs*, 111–12; Yao Xu, "A Wise Decision Making in the War to Resist the US and Assist Korea," *Dangshi Yanjiu* [Studies of CCP history] 5 (1980): 12; Steven J. Zaloga, "The Russians in MIG Alley," *Air Force Magazine* 74 (February 1991): 76.

29. Editorial, "Celebrating the Recovery of Seoul," *Renmin Ribao* [People's daily], January 3, 1951, 1; Xinhua News Agency report, "The People's Parade in the Capital to Celebrate the Recovery of Seoul," ibid., 1.

30. China Today series, *Peng Dehuai Zhuan* [The biography of Peng Dehuai] (Beijing: Dangdai Zhongguo Press, 1993), 443; Ye Yumeng, *Hanjiang Xue*, 86–87; Deng Hua, "On Initial Experience in Fighting the U.S. Army," June 8, 1951, in Deng Hua, *Lun Kangmei Yuanchao Zhanzheng Zuozhan Zhidao* [On combat organization and operations in the War to Resist U.S. Aggression and Aid Korea], internal ed. (Beijing: Military Sciences Press, 1989), 1–24.

31. Telegram, Peng to Mao, January 10, 1951, cited in Ye Yumeng, *Hanjiang Xue*, 85 and 89. For Peng's concerns of the front, see *Du Ping Memoirs*, 68–69.

32. Telegram, Mao to Peng, January 14, 1951, cited in *Zhongguo Renmin Zhiyuanjun Kangmei Yuanchao Zhan Shi*, 92–93, and Qi Dexue, *Chaoxian Zhanzheng Juece Neimu* [Inside stories of decision makings in the Korean War] (Shenyang: Liaoning University Press, 1991), see also Xu Yan, *Diyici Jiaoliang*, 69.

33. Ye Yumeng, *Hanjiang Xue*, 91–92.

34. On the CPV Command meeting, January 22, 1951, see ibid., 97–100.

35. Peng's report at the CPV-NKPA Joint Command meeting, January 25, 1951, *Peng Dehuai Junshi Wenxuan*, 364–70.

36. Mao edited Peng's draft and had Cheng Pu, CPV deputy director of daily work division, bring it to Peng on January 16, 1951; *Du Ping Memoirs*, 187.

37. Summary of Gao Gang's speech at the CPV-NKPA Joint Command meeting, January 28, 1951, cited in *Hong Xuezhi Memoirs*, 115–16; Kim Il-sung's speech of January 29, 1951, at the joint command meeting cited in *Du Ping Memoirs*, 192.

38. Ye Yumeng, *Hanjiang Xue*, 119–20.

39. *Zhongguo Renmin Zhiyuanjun Kangmei Yuanchao Zhan Shi*, 99–100. For the US/UN attack, see Appleman, *Ridgway Duels for Korea*, 157–65.

40. Telegram, Peng to Mao, 12:00 P.M., January 27, 1951, cited in *Peng Dehuai Zhuan*, 446; see also Ye Yumeng, *Hanjiang Xue*, 124–25.

41. Telegram, Mao to Peng, 7:00 P.M., January 28, 1951, Ye Yumeng, *Hanjiang Xue*, 126–28; also see *Du Ping Memoirs*, 192.

42. Telegram, Peng to Mao, January 31, 1951, *Peng Dehuai Junshi Wenxuan*, 372.

43. Ibid., 272–73.

44. Telegram, Peng to Mao, February 5, 1951, cited in *Zhongguo Renmin Zhiyuanjun Kangmei Yuanchao Zhan Shi*, 101.

45. The CMC decision, February 7, 1951, ibid., 94; telegram, Mao to the CCP headquarters, February 9, 1951, cited in Qi Dexue, *Chaoxian Zhanzheng Juece Neimu*, 132–33.

46. Telegram, the CPV Command to each army and division command, January 31, 1951, *Zhongguo Renmin Zhiyuanjun Kangmei Yuanchao Zhan Shi*, 103; for the vigorous resistance of the 50th Army, see *Kangmei Yuanchao Zhanzheng*, 113–14.

47. *Zhongguo Renmin Zhiyuanjun Kangmei Yuanchao Zhan Shi*, 104; also see *Kangmei Yuanchao Zhanzheng*, 114.

48. On the 38th Army Command meeting, February 8, 1951, see Ye Yumeng, *Hanjiang Xue*, 157–59; see also *Kangmei Yuanchao Zhanzheng*, 114–16.

49. Telegram, the CMC to Peng, February 4, 1951, Ye Yumeng, *Hanjiang Xue*, 146–47; the CPV Command to each army command, February 5, 1951, ibid., 147.

50. Summary of Peng's correspondences with Deng Hua and Han Xianchu is cited in ibid., 173–74; see also *Zhongguo Renmin Zhiyuanjun Kangmei Yuanchao Zhan Shi*, 106–7.

51. *Zhongguo Renmin Zhiyuanjun Kangmei Yuanchao Zhan Shi*, 108–9; see also *Kangmei Yanchao Zhanzheng*, 118–20, and *Hong Xuezhi Memoirs*, 125–26. For the US/UN side of the story, see Appleman, *Ridgway Duels for Korea*, 293–300. According to Appleman, the US/UN lost 18,360 men at Hoengsong, ibid., 249.

52. Ye Yumeng, *Hanjiang Xue*, 175–80; telegram, the CPV Command to each army command, February 15, 1951, cited in *Zhongguo Renmin Zhiyuanjun Kangmei Yuanchao Zhan Shi*, 110–11. Appleman states that the US/UN had a total of 404 casualties at Chipyong-ni; *Ridgway Duels for Korea*, 287.

53. Telegram, Peng to the CMC and each army command, February 17, 1951, *Peng Dehuai Junshi Wenxuan*, 373–74.

54. *Hong Xuezhi Memoirs*, 129; telegram, Peng to each army command and the CMC, February 17, 1951, *Peng Dehuai Junshi Wenxuan*, 378–79.

55. Peng Dehuai, *Memoirs of a Chinese Marshall: The Autobiographical Notes of Peng Dehuai, 1898–1974*, trans. Zheng Longpu (Beijing: Foreign Languages Press, 1984), 479–80. *Peng Dehuai Zhuan*, 451–54, gives a rather vivid description of how anxious Peng was to see Mao. Arriving in Beijing early on the afternoon of February 21, Peng went directly to Mao's "resting house" in Beijing's western suburb. While Mao was taking a nap, Peng "broke into" the chairman's bedroom.

56. Telegram, Mao to Peng, March 1, 1951, *Mao Zedong Junshi Wenxuan—neibuban*, 349–51.

57. CPV-NKPA Joint Command's instructions on tactics, 12:00 A.M., March 8, 1951, cited in *Zhongguo Renmin Zhiyuanjun Kangmei Yuanchao Zhan Shi*, 114–15; telegram, the CPV Command to each army command, March 10, 1951, ibid., 115.

58. Ibid., 115–19; see also *Hong Xuezhi Memoirs*, 131–33.

59. Telegram, Mao to Peng, March 7, 1951, cited in *Zhongguo Renmin Zhiyuanjun Kangmei Yuanchao Zhan Shi*, 125–26.

60. Telegram, Peng to each army command, 5:00 P.M., March 17, 1951, *Peng Dehuai Junshi Wenxuan*, 378–80.

61. Minutes of the CPV headquarters meeting, March [undated] 1951, cited in *Hong Xuezhi Memoirs*, 136–38; also see *Du Ping Memoirs*, 218–19.

62. Peng Dehuai, "Speech at the Fifth Enlarged CPV Party Committee," August 4, 1951, *Peng Dehuai Junshi Wenxuan*, 384–86.

63. Ibid., 386–87.

64. Ibid., 387–89.

65. Telegram, Mao to Peng, April 13, 1951, cited in *Hong Xuezhi Memoirs*, 140.

66. Telegram, the CPV Command to each army and division command, April 11, 1951, cited in *Zhongguo Renmin Zhiyuanjun Kangmei Yuanchao Zhan Shi*, 128 (emphasis added).

67. Telegram, the CPV Command to each army command, April 15, 1951, ibid., 129–30.

68. The CMC's order to establish the CPV logistical command, April 16, 1951, ibid, 129. For CPV force buildup for the fifth-phase offensive, see Hu Guangzheng and Ma Shanying, eds., *Zhongguo Renmin Zhiyuanjun Xu Lie: October 1950–July 1953* [The CPV order of battles: October 1950–July 1953] (Beijing: PLA Press 1987), 43–61.

69. Telegrams, Peng to each army command and the CMC, April 18, 1951, *Peng Dehuai Junshi Wenxuan*, 390–92; Peng to each army command and Kim Il-sung, April 21, 1951, cited in *Du Ping Memoirs*, 238.

70. *Hong Xuezhi Memoirs*, 153–54; *Yang Dezhi Memoirs*, 53–57; see also *Zhongguo Renmin Zhiyuanjun Kangmei Yuanchao Zhan Shi*, 132–33.

71. Telegram, Peng to Mao, April 26, 1951, ibid., 135–36.

72. Telegram, Mao to Peng, April [undated] 1951, ibid., 136–37.

73. Ibid., 137; also *Hong Xuezhi Memoirs*, 155–56.

74. Ibid., 156; Peng to 19th Army Corps Commander Yang Dezhi, late April 1951, *Yang Dezhi Memoirs*, 58–59.

75. Telegram, the CPV Command to each army command, April 28, 1951, cited in *Zhongguo Renmin Zhiyuanjun Kangmei Yuanchao Zhan Shi*, 138.

76. Telegrams, Peng to each army command and the CMC, 10:00 P.M., May 6, 1951, *Peng Dehuai Junshi Wenxuan*, 392–95; the CPV Command to each army commander, May 8, 1951, cited in *Zhongguo Renmin Zhiyuanjun Kangmei Yuanchao Zhan Shi*, 139.

77. Minutes of the joint command in the east front, May 8–9, 1951, cited in *Zhongguo Renmin Zhiyuanjun Kangmei Yuanchao Zhan Shi*, 139–41.

78. Ibid., 141–45; Xu Yan, *Diyici Jiaoliang*, 88–91; *Hong Xuezhi Memoirs*, 157–58; *Yang Dezhi Memoirs*, 60.

79. Telegram, Peng to each army command, May 21, 1951, *Peng Dehuai Junshi Wenxuan*, 395–401.

80. Telegram, the CPV Command to the 19th Army Corps Command, May 22, 1951, cited in *Zhongguo Renmin Zhiyuanjun Kangmei Yuanchao Zhan Shi*, 146.

81. *Hong Xuezhi Memoirs*, 158–66; Xu Yan, *Diyici Jiaoliang*, 91–95; *Du Ping Memoirs*, 247–49. The U.S. 24th Division captured between 3,098 and 3,295 Chinese prisoners from the CPV 180th Division; Appleman, *Ridgway Duels for Korea*, 542.

82. Telegram, the CPV Command to each army command, May 27, 1951, cited in *Zhongguo Renmin Zhiyuanjun Kangmei Yuanchao Zhan Shi*, 151. For the resisting operations of the 19th Army Corps, see *Yang Dezhi Memoirs*, 61–68; four of the CPV Command's orders to each army command between May 27–31, 1951, are cited in *Kangmei Yuanchao Zhanzheng*, 155; for the number of CPV casualties, see *Zhongguo Renmin Zhiyuanjun Kangmei Yuanchao Zhan Shi*, 152.

CHAPTER 7. FIGHTING A STALEMATED WAR

1. Telegram, Mao to Peng, May 26, 1951, Mao Zedong, *Mao Zedong Junshi Wenxuan—neibuban* [Selected military works of Mao Zedong—internal edition] (Beijing: PLA Soldiers' Press, 1981), 352–53.

2. Ibid., 353.

3. Minutes of Mao–Chen Geng–Xie Fang talks, May 27, 1951, contained in Xie Fang to Peng, May 27, 1951, *Du Ping Memoirs*, 262–63; also see Mu Xin, *Chen Geng Dajiang* [Senior general Chen Geng] (Beijing: New China Press, 1985), 699.

4. Minutes of Mao–Deng Hua conversations, June 4, 1951, cited in Qi Dexue, *Chaoxian Zhanzheng Juece Neimu* [Inside stories of decision makings in the Korean War] (Shenyang: Liaonying University Press, 1991), 176; telegram, Mao to Peng Dehuai, June 13, 1951, ibid., 177. Also see *Du Ping Memoirs*, 263.

5. Peng's speech at the enlarged CPV Party Committee meeting, June 25, 1951, Peng Dehuai, *Peng Dehuai Junshi Wenxuan* [Selected military writings of Peng Dehuai] (Beijing: Central Archives and Manuscripts Press, 1988), 403–5; also see Deng Hua's speech, June 25, 1951, in Deng Hua, *Lun Kangmei Yuanchao Zhanzheng Zuozhan Zhidao* [On combat organization and operations in the War to Resist U.S. Aggression and Aid Korea], internal ed. (Beijing: Military Sciences Press, 1989), 25–34.

6. Summary of Mao–Zhou Enlai–Kim Il-sung talks, June 3, 1951, cited in *Chai Chengwen Memoirs*, 125; telegram, Kim Il-sung to Mao, June 30, 1951, *Du Ping Memoirs*, 268–69.

7. Xu Yan, *Diyici Jiaoliang: Kangmei Yuanchao Zhonzheng de Lishi Huigu yu Fansi* [The first encounter: Historical retrospection and review of the War to Resist U.S. Aggression and Aid Korea] (Beijing: Chinese Radio and Television Press, 1990), 106; *Du Ping Memoirs*, 265–66. Du recalls that the 60th Army's political commissar Yan Ziqin was anxious to fight "an upswing battle."

8. Xu Yan, *Diyici Jiaoliang*, 107; telegram, Peng to Mao, July 1, 1951, *Peng Dehuai Junshi Wenxuan*, 411–12. Peng also urged his headquarters staff to work harder on the preparations for the sixth-phase offensive; *Du Ping Memoirs*, 272.

9. Deng Hua, "On the Protracted War in Korea," July 8, 1951, cited in Xu Yan, *Diyici Jiaoliang*, 107; also see Xinhuo Liaoyuan Editoral Division, *Jiefangjun Jiangling Zhuan* [The chronicle of PLA senior generals] (Beijing: PLA Press, 1988), 7:34–35.

10. Telegram, Peng to Mao, July 24, 1951, cited in Xu Yan, *Diyici Jiaoliang*, 107, and Qi Dexue, *Chaoxian Zhanzheng Juece Neimu, 179*; Mao to Peng, July 26, 1951, ibid., 204.

11. Telegram, the CPV Command to each army corps command, August 8, 1951, Xu Yan, *Diyici Jiaoliang*, 107; minutes of the CPV Command meeting, mid-August 1951, cited in *Du Ping Memoirs*, 271.

12. Telegram, the CPV Command to each army commander, August 17, 1951, cited in Xu Yan, *Diyici Jiaoliang*, 107; see also *Du Ping Memoirs*, 277–78.

13. Telegram, Deng Hua to Peng Dehuai and Mao Zedong, August 18, 1951, cited in *Jiefangjun Jiangling Zhuan*, 7:36–37.

14. Telegram, Mao to Peng, August 19, 1951, cited in Qi Dexue, *Chaoxian Zhanzheng Juece Neimu*, 204–6; Chinese Academy of Military Sciences, *Zhongguo Renmin Zhiyuanjun Kangmei Yuanchao Zhan Shi* [The war history of the Chinese People's Volunteers in the War to Resist U.S. Aggression and Aid Korea] (Beijing: Military Sciences Press, 1988), 171.

15. Telegram, Deng Hua to Mao and Peng, August 26, 1951, cited in *Jiefangjun Jiangling Zhuan*, 7:35.

16. Minutes of the enlarged CPV Party Committee meeting, September 4–10, 1951, cited in *Zhongguo Renmin Zhiyuanjun Kangmei Yuanchao Zhan Shi*, 175–77.

17. Ibid., 178–79; *Kangmei Yuanchao Zhanzheng*, 182–83.

18. Telegram, the CPV Command to each army corps command, October 2, 1951, cited in *Zhongguo Renmin Zhiyuanjun Kangmei Yuanchao Zhan Shi*, 179.

19. Yang Dezhi, *Weile Heping* [For the sake of peace] (Beijing: Long March Press, 1987), 84–87 (hereafter *Yang Dezhi Memoirs*); *Hong Xuezhi Memoirs*, 201–2.

20. *Zhongguo Renmin Zhiyuanjun Kangmei Yuanchao Zhan Shi*, 181–83; *Kangmei Yuanchao Zhanzheng*, 186–89.

21. Yang Chengwu's report, late October 1951, cited in Xu Yan, *Diyici Jiaoliang*, 116–17.

22. The CPV Command, "Instructions on the Tactics of Small-Scale Battles," September 16, 1951, cited in *Zhongguo Renmin Zhiyuanjun Kangmei Yuanchao Zhanzheng Zhan Shi*, 177; *Kangmei Yuanchao Zhanzheng*, 227.

23. Xu Yan, *Diyici Jiaoliang*, 113; *Yang Dezhi Memoirs*, 93–94.

24. Telegrams, Nie Rongzhen to Mao and Zhou Enlai, October 9, 1951, *Nie Rongzhen Junshi Wenxuan* [Selected military writings of Nie Rongzhen] (Beijing: CCP Central Archives, 1992), 359–61; also see Qi Dexue, *Chaoxian Zhanzheng Juece Neimu*, 255–56; Mao to Peng, November 14, 1951, and Mao to Peng and Kim Il-sung, November 23, 1951, ibid., 256.

25. Telegram, the CPV Command to each army commander, December 29, 1951, *Kangmei Yuanchao Zhanzheng*, 121 and 118.

26. Ibid., 192–94; also see *Zhongguo Renmin Zhiyuanjun Kangmei Yuanchao Zhan Shi*, 184–85.

27. The CPV Command instructions on the construction of tunnels, April 17, 1952, cited in *Kangmei Yuanchao Zhanzheng*, 229.

28. Minutes of the CPV staff meetings, April 26–May 1, 1952, ibid.

29. Ibid., 229–30.

30. Minutes of the CPV Command meeting, June 6–9, 1952, ibid., 230–31; Deng Hua, "Adjusting Force Dispositions and Strenghtening Our In-depth Defense to Smash the Enemy Attack Resolutely," June 6, 1951, *Lun Kangmei Yuanchao Zhanzheng Zuozhan Zhidao*, 48–88.

31. *Hong Xuezhi Memoirs*, 196–97; *Du Ping Memoirs*, 279–81.

32. *Nie Rongzhen Memoirs*, 2:747.

33. Li Jukui, *Li Jukui Huiyilu* [Memoirs of Li Jukui] (Beijing: PLA Press, 1986), 263–64 (hereafter *Li Jukui Memoirs*).

34. Telegram, the CMC to the Northeast Military Command, late July 1950, cited in *Kangmei Yuanchao Zhanzheng Houqin Jingyan Zongjie—Jiben Jingyan* [A summary of the CPV rear services experiences in the War to Resist U.S. Aggression and Aid Korea—basic lessons] (Beijing: Golden Shield Press, 1987), 11.

35. Ibid., 12.

36. *Li Jukui Memoirs*, 264–65.

37. Ibid., 265–66; *Kangmei Yuanchao Zhanzheng Houqin Jingyan Zongjie—Jiben Jingyan*, 16–17. Also see Nie Rongzhen's speech at Dong Hou's first meeting on January 30, 1951, *Nie Rongzhen Junshi Wenxuan*, 350.

38. Minutes of Peng–Li Jukui talk, October 17, 1950, *Li Jukui Memoirs*, 266.

39. *Kangmei Yuanchao Zhanzheng Houqin Jingyan Zongjie—Jiben Jingyan*, 16–17.

40. Ibid., 22–28; *Li Jukui Memoirs*, 268–69; Xu Yan, *Diyici Jiaoliang*, 161–63.

41. *Kangmei Yuanchao Zhanzheng Houqin Jingyan Zongjie—Jiben Jingyan*, 34–37; see also telegrams, Mao to Peng and Gao Gang, December 3, 1950, *Mao's Manuscripts*, 1:707; Mao to Kim Il-sung, December 31, 1950, ibid., 759; Peng to Mao, December 4, 1950, *Mao Zedong Junshi Wenxuan—neibuban*, 691 n. 17; Zhou Chunquan to the CMC, January [undated] 1951, cited in *Nie Rongzhen Junshi Wenxuan*, 350; also see Roy E. Appleman, *Ridgway Duels for Korea* (College Station: Texas A&M University Press, 1990), 249 and 487–88.

42. Minutes of the first CPV logistics meeting, January 22–30, 1951, cited in *Kangmei Yuanchao Zhanzheng Houqin Jingyan Zongjie—Jiben Jingyan*, 41–44; see also *Li Jukui Memoirs*, 269; *Nie Rongzhen Memoirs*, 749–50; Nie Rongzhen's speech at the meeting, January 30, 1951, *Nie Rongzhen Junshi Wenxuan*, 350.

43. *Kangmei Yuanchao Zhanzheng Houqin Jingyan Zongjie—Jiben Jingyan*, 51–57.

44. CPV Party Committee, "Instruction on the Problems of Supply," May 3, 1951, ibid., 59–61; also see *Hong Xuezhi Memoirs*, 181.

45. Minutes of Zhou Enlai–Hong Xuezhi talks, late April 1951, *Hong Xuezhi Memoirs*, 172–77.

46. Ibid., 178.

47. Ibid., 180–83. It is interesting that because of his remarkable achievements as the CPV logistics commander, Hong worked as head of the General Logistics Department until his retirement in 1987, when he was replaced by Zhao Nanqi, who had served as one of his aides in Korea.

48. CMC, "Decision on Strengthening the CPV Rear Services," May 19, 1951, *Kangmei Yuanchao Zhanzheng Houqin Jingyan Zongjie—Jiben Jingyan*, 61–62.

49. Ibid., 63–65; see also *Hong Xuezhi Memoirs*, 184.

50. Ibid., *Hong Xuezhi Memoirs*, 196–97; *Kangmei Yuanchao Zhanzheng Houqin Jingyan Zongjie—Jiben Jingyan*, 67–68.

51. *Kangmei Yuanchao Zhanzheng Houqin Jingyan Zongjie—Jiben Jingyan*, 68–69.

52. Minutes of the second CPC logistics meeting, August 16, 1951, ibid., 87.

53. *Hong Xuezhi Memoirs*, 197–98.

54. Xu Yan, *Diyici Jiaoliang*, 176; *Kangmei Yuanchao Zhanzheng Houqin Jingyan Zongjie—Jiben Jingyan*, 66; see also telegram, Nie Rongzhen to Peng Dehuai, September 27, 1951, *Nie Rongzhen Junshi Wenxuan*, 356–57.

55. Telegram, Nie Rongzhen to the CPV headquarters, September 26, 1951, cited in Qi Dexue, *Chaoxian Zhanzheng Juece Neimu*, 228–29; see also *Kangmei Yuanchao Zhanzheng Houqin Jingyan Zongjie—Zhuan Ye Qinwu* [A summary of the CPV rear service experiences in the War to Resist U.S. Aggression and Aid Korea–special work] (Beijing: Golden Shield Press, 1987), 2:23–24.

56. Ibid., 52–63. In late September 1951, Nie Rongzhen wrote specific instructions on how to apply "creative methods" to the improvement of railway transportation; see telegram, Nie to Peng, September 27, 1951, *Nie Rongzhen Junshi Wenxuan*, 357–58. Mao also expressed his "great enthusiasm" over how "creative" the logistical corps were in resolving the supply problems. See Wu Ruilin, "Report to Chairman Mao on the Accomplishment of the Engineering Corps [During the Korean War]," *Junshi Shilin* [Studies of the military history] 6 (1993); 25–27.

57. Telegram, He Jinnian to the CPV headquarters, November 25, 1951, cited in Qi Dexue, *Chaoxian Zhanzheng Juece Neimu*, 235–36; see also *Kangmei Yuanchao Zhanzheng Houqin Jingyan Zongjie—Jiben Jingyan*, 73–74; *Hong Xuezhi Memoirs*, 221–22.

58. Ibid., 219.

59. Ibid., 218–19.

60. Ibid., 217–18.

61. *Kangmei Yuanchao Zhanzheng Houqin Jingyan Zongjie—Zhuan Ye Qinwu*, 2:71–73.

62. Minutes of the PLA Air Force Command meeting, late October 1950, China Today series, *Dangdai Zhongguo Kongjun* [China today: The air force] (Beijing: Chinese Social Sciences Press, 1989), 127–28; telegram, Liu Yalou to Mao, December 3, 1950, and Mao to Liu Yalou, December 4, 1950, ibid., 129.

63. Stalin-Zhou talks, October 9, 1950, cited in *Shi Zhe Memoirs*, 498; also Xu Yan, *Diyici Jiaoliang*, 199. For Soviet accounts, see Jon Holliday, "Air Operations in Korea: The Soviet Side of the Story," in *A Revolutionary War: Korea and the Transformation of the Postwar World*, ed. William J. Williams (Chicago: Imprint, 1993), 151–52.

64. Xu Yan, *Diyici Jiaoliang*, 201; see also *Dangdai Zhongguo Kongjun*, 87–88. The Soviet Union had equipped altogether nine fighter divisions (the 6th, 7th, 12th, 14th, 15th, 16th, 17th, and 18th), two attacker divisions (the 5th and 11th), two bomber divisions (the 8th and 10th) and one transport division (13th); ibid., 88. However, there is still no Soviet evidence on this issue.

65. Telegrams, the PLA Air Force Command to the CMC, January [undated] 1951, cited in Qi Dexue, *Chaoxian Zhanzheng Juece Neimu*, 232–33; telegram, the PLA Air

Force Command to the 4th Air Force Division Command, December 4, 1950, *Dangdai Zhongguo Kongjun*, 129. One Soviet air force division commander, Lt. Gen. Georgi Ageyevich Lobov, recalls that he reluctantly allowed the Chinese air units to join his force; Holliday, "Air Operations in Korea," 152.

66. *Dangdai Zhongguo Kongjun*, 130–31; see also *Kongjun Shi* [History of the People's Air Force] (Beijing: PLA Press, 1987), 64–65.

67. *Dangdai Zhongguo Kongjun*, 133–35.

68. Minutes of the PLA Air Force Command meeting, April 8, 1951, ibid., 136; for the air-combat exercise, see ibid., 137–38.

69. Ibid., 138–41; also see Dong Qiwu, *Rongma Chunqiu* [Years of my military career] Beijing: Central Literature and History Press, 1986), 364–76 (hereafter *Dong Qiwu Memoirs*). On the deployment of the 23d Army Corps, see memorandum, Nie Rongzhen to Mao, Liu Shaoqi, and Zhou Enlai, August 29, 1951, *Nie Rongzhen Junshi Wenxuan*, 354–55.

70. *Dangdai Zhongguo Kongjun*, 143–47.

71. Ibid., 146–47.

72. *Kongjun Shi*, 67–68; *Hong Xuezhi Memoirs*, 223–24.

73. *Dangdai Zhongguo Kongjun*, 150.

74. The PLA Air Force Command's instruction, mid-November 1951, ibid., 155; telegram, Mao to the PLA Air Force Command, February 4, 1952, ibid., 158.

75. Ibid., 155–59; Xu Yan, *Diyici Jiaoliang*, 202–3 and 207; Holliday, "Air Operations in Korea," 154.

76. *Hong Xuezhi Memoirs*, 233.

77. Telegram, the CPV headquarters to the CMC, January 28, 1952, cited in *Yang Dezhi Memoirs*, 101; see also *Jiang Yonghui Memoirs*, 465.

78. *Kangmei Yuanchao Zhanzheng*, 215.

79. *Yang Dezhi Memoirs*, 101–2.

80. *Kangmei Yuanchao Zhanzheng*, 316.

81. Memorandum, Nie Rongzhen to Mao and Zhou, February 18, 1952, cited in Qi Dexue, *Chaoxian Zhanzheng Juece Neimu*, 280–81.

82. Memorandum, Mao to Nie Rongzhen, February 19, 1952, *Mao's Manuscripts*, 3:239.

83. Memorandum, Zhou Enlai to Mao, January 20, 1952, cited in Qi Dexue, *Chaoxian Zhanzheng Juece Neimu*, 282.

84. Burton I. Kaufman, *The Korean War: Changes in Crisis, Credibility, and Command* (New York: Alfred Knopf, 1986), 265.

85. Memoranda, the Northeast Military Command to the CMC, March 3, 1952, and Mao to Zhou, March 4, 1952, *Mao's Manuscripts*, 3:303.

86. *Renmin Ribao* [People's daily], March 8, 1952, 1.

87. *Kangmei Yuanchao Zhanzheng*, 218.

88. Memorandum, Nie Rongzhen to Mao and Zhou Enlai, Mao's Manuscripts, 3:328; Mao's instruction, March 9, 1952, ibid.

89. *Kangmei Yuanchao Zhanzheng*, 220–21.

90. Ibid., 221.

91. Telegram, the CMC to the CPV headquarters, February 21, 1952, cited in ibid., 220.

92. Telegram, the CMC to the CPV headquarters, February 25, 1952, ibid.

93. *Yang Dezhi Memoirs*, 103; memorandum, Nie Rongzhen to Mao, Zhou Enlai, Zhu De, Liu Shaoqi, and Lin Biao, February 28, 1952, *Nie Rongzhen Junshi Wenxuan*, 365.

94. *Kangmei Yuanchao Zhanzheng Houqin Jingyan Zongjie—Jiben Jingyan*, 85.

95. Ibid.; see also CPV new branch's report, March 15, 1952, *Mao's Manuscripts*, 3:239.

96. *Kangmei Yuanchao Zhanzheng Houqin Jingyan Zongjie—Jiben Jingyan*, 86; and *Kangmei Yuanchao Zhanzheng*, 222.

97. Kaufman, *Korean War*, 268–69.

98. Qi Dexue, *Chaoxian Zhanzheng Juece Neimu*, 286–87. For an excellent account of Chinese allegation of U.S. bacteriological warfare, see Mark A. Ryan, *Chinese Attitude Toward Nuclear Weapons: China and the United States During the Korean War* (New York: M. E. Sharpe, 1989), 83–104. Ryan argues that evidence found in internal military documents in China suggests "the seriousness with which the Chinese military treat this subject and perhaps reflects the continuing credence given to the BW [biological warfare] charges by the Chinese"; ibid., 104.

99. Rosemary Foot, "Making Known the Unknown War: Policy Analysis of the Korean Conflict in the Last Decade," *Diplomatic History* (Summer 1991): 425.

100. *Nie Rongzhen Memoirs*, 759.

101. *Zhongguo Renmin Zhiyuanjun Kangmei Yuanchao Zhan Shi*, 223.

102. *Nie Rongzhen Memoirs*, 760.

CHAPTER 8. MOBILIZATION OF MINDS ON THE BATTLEFIELD

1. Lin Boye, *Xuexi Mao Zedong Junshi Zhuzuo Zhong de Zhexue Sixiang* [The philosophical points contained in Mao Zedong's military writings] (Tianjin: People's Press, 1982), 55.

2. Gan Siqi and Li Zhimin, eds., *Zhongguo Renmin Zhiyuanjun Kangmei Yuanchao Zhanzheng Zhengzhi Gongzuo Zongjie* [A summary of the CPV political work in the War to Resist U.S. Aggression and Aid Korea] (Beijing: PLA Press, 1985), 22; see also *Du Ping Memoirs*, 23–24.

3. Mao's speech at the Ninth Plenary Meeting of the Central People's Government Council, September 5, 1950, cited in Chinese Academy of Military Sciences, *Zhongguo Renmin Zhiyuanjun Kangmei Yuanchao Zhan Shi* [The war history of the Chinese People's Volunteers in the War to Resist U.S. Aggression and Aid Korea] (Beijing: Military Sciences Press, 1988), 7.

4. CMC directive, October 8, 1950, *Mao's Manuscripts*, 1:544.

5. Deng Hua, Li Zhimin, and Hong Xuezhi, "We Remember Comrade Peng Dehuai's Brilliant Leadership of the CPV," in *Hengdao Lima Peng Jiangjun* [Senior general Peng is on the battle steed] (Beijing: People's Press, 1979), 123–24; *Du Ping Memoirs*, 36.

6. Peng's speech at the meeting of the CPV high-ranking commanders, October 16, 1950, Peng Dehuai, *Peng Dehuai Junshi Wenxuan* [Selected military writings of Peng Dehuai] (Beijing: Central Archives and Manuscripts Press, 1988), 323–24. The speech is dated October 14, but it was delivered on October 16.

7. 13th Army Corps political department, "How to Implement the Directive on Entering the Korean War," October 12, 1950, *Du Ping Memoirs*, 25 and 43.

8. Ibid., 55–56.

9. 13th Army Corps political department, "Historical Facts of U.S. Imperialist Invasions of China," September 1950, ibid., 24–25. See also University of National Defense, *Zhongguo Renmin Jiefangjun Zhengzhi Gongzuo Shi* [History of the PLA's political work] (Beijing: National Defense University Press, 1989), 29–30.

10. CPV Political Department, *Zhongguo Renmin Zhiyuanjun Kangmei Yuanchao Zhanzheng Zhengzhi Gongzuo Zongjie* [A summary of the CPV political work in the War to Resist U.S. Aggression and Aid Korea] (Beijing: PLA Press, 1989; orig. publ. for internal circulation, 1955), 16–17.

11. Gan and Li, *Kangmei Yuanchao Zhengzhi Gongzuo Zongjie*, 25–26; *Du Ping Memoirs*, 145–46.

12. *Kangmei Yuanchao Zhanzheng*, 23–24.

13. A complete version of the CPV oath appears in ibid., 24; also see two pictures of a CPV unit taking an oath before entering Korea, ibid., 24 and 56.

14. Ibid., 68–69; Wei Wei, "Who Is the Most Lovable?" *Renmin Ribao* [People's daily], April 11, 1951, 1.

15. *Kangmei Yuanchao Zhanzheng*, 74–75.

16. *Hong Xuezhi Memoirs*, 75–76; *Du Ping Memoirs*, 91–93; Deng, Li, and Hong, "We Remember Comrade Peng Dehuai," 133–34.

17. Sun Jingli, "Mao Anying Was Buried in Korea," *Renmin Ribao—Haiwaiban* [People's daily—overseas edition], December 17, 1990, 8.

18. *Du Ping Memoirs*, 97–98.

19. Gan and Li, *Kangmei Yuanchao Zhengzhi Gongzuo Zongjie*, 36–38.

20. Minutes of the CPV political work meeting, late November 1950, *Du Ping Memoirs*, 73–74.

21. Liu Zhiquan, *Zhidaoyuan Gongzuo Yishu* [The art of political work of company political instructors] (Beijing: PLA Press, 1990), 11–18. Also see William W. Whitson, *The Chinese High Command: A History of Communist Military Politics, 1927–1971* (New York: Praeger, 1973), 527.

22. CPV Political Department, *Zhiyuanjun Zhengzhi Gongzuo Zongjie*, 20–21. See also Gan and Li, *Kangmei Yuanchao Zhengzhi Gongzuo Zongjie*, 38–40.

23. CPV Political Department, "Report on the Loss of the 180th Division," late May 1951, *Du Ping Memoirs*, 251–53.

24. Wang Shijun and Li Shuozhi, *Wu Zi Qian Shuo* [An introduction to Wu Tzu's *Art of War*] (Beijing: PLA Press, 1986), 40.

25. CPV Political Department, "The Chinese People's Volunteers Regulations Regarding Rendering Meritorious Services," June 1951, in CPV Political Department, *Zhiyuanjun Zhengzhi Gongzuo Zongjie*, app., 332–33.

26. Ibid., 332, 350–53.

27. Ibid., 343–49.

28. Ibid., 353–55.

29. CPV Political Department, "A Note on Korean Military Exploits Medals," July 1951, cited in *Du Ping Memoirs*, 256–57.

30. Ibid., 257–59.

31. Instruction of the Ministry of Internal Affairs and the PLA General Political Department, December 22, 1950, in *Weida de Kangmei Yuanchao Yundong* [The great movement of resisting America and aiding Korea] (Beijing: People's Press, 1950), 3:711–13; Minister of Internal Affairs Xie Juezhai's report, September 20, 1950, approved by the CPGC, November 9, 1950, ibid., 818–22. For a Western scholar's account of China's popular mobilization for the Korean War, see John Gittings, *The Role of the Chinese Army* (New York: Oxford University Press, 1967), 83–98.

32. *Kangmei Yuanchao Zhanzheng*, 358–59.

33. Gan and Li, *Kangmei Yuanchao Zhengzhi Gongzuo Zongjie*, 210–12.

34. Instruction of the CPPCC, December 1, 1950, in *Weida de Kangmei Yuanchao Yundong*, 710–11.

35. *Kangmei Yuanchao Zhanzheng*, 361.

36. The Federation of the Chinese People to Resist U.S. Aggression and Aid Korea, "Instruction on How to Donate Weapons for the CPV," June 7, 1951, in *Weida de Kangmei Yuanchao Yundong*, 835–36.

37. *Kangmei Yuanchao Zhanzheng*, 350–53; also see Xu Yan, *Diyici Jiaoliang:Kangmei Yuanchao Zhanzheng de Lishi Huigu yu Fansi* [The first encounter: Historical retrospection and review of the War to Resist U.S. Aggression and Aid Korea] (Beijing: Chinese Radio and Television Press, 1990), 243.

38. Telegram, the CMC to the CPV Command, September 26, 1951, cited in *Du Ping Memoirs*, 300–301.

39. Ibid., 302–7.

40. Ibid., 313–29. See also Gan and Li, *Kangmei Yuanchao Zhengzhi Gongzuo Zongjie*, 210–11.

41. Wang Yongnian, "Glory Belongs to the Motherland," in Li Zhimin, ed., *Zhadan yu Xianhua* [Bombs and flowers] (Beijing: PLA Press, 1985), 297–98; Gan and Li, *Kangmei Yuanchao Zhengzhi Gongzuo Zongjie*, 193–95.

42. Li Zhimin, *Zhadan yu Xianhua*, 297–98.

43. Ibid., 15–16; see also *Du Ping Memoirs*, 194.

44. Ibid., 193–95; Li Zhimin, *Zhadan yu Xianhua*, 1–9, 15–31, 37–41, and 102–9.

45. *Du Ping Memoirs*, 130–31; Sun Yaoshen, "General Xie Fang in the War to Resist U.S. Aggression and Aid Korea," *Junshi Lishi* [Military history] 4 (1990): 43–44.

46. *Hong Xuezhi Memoirs*, 212–13.

47. Ibid., 94–96.

48. *Wu Zi Qian Shuo*, 43–47.

49. The CMC decision on dispatch of military forces into Korea, October 8, 1950, *Mao's Manuscripts*, 1:543–44. Also see Yan Shixin, "A Glorious Example of Patriotism and Internationalism: New Development of Political Work in the War to Resist U.S. Aggression and Aid Korea," *Dangshi Yanjiu* [Studies of CCP history] 6 (1984): 37.

50. Telegram, Mao to Peng, January 19, 1951, cited in *Du Ping Memoirs*, 176–77; also see Gan and Li, *Kangmei Yuanchao Zhengzhi Gongzuo Zongjie*, 164.

51. CPV Political Department, "The CPV Regulations of Political Work," December 14, 1950, cited in *Du Ping Memoirs*, 128–29.

52. 19th Army Corps Political Department, "Rules to Guide Our Combat in Korea," December [undated] 1950, CPV Political Department, *Zhiyuanjun Zhengzhi Gongzuo Zongjie*, app. 4, 360–61. Also see *Zhongguo Renmin Jiefangjun Zhengzhi Gongzuo Shi*, 38–40.

53. CPV Political Department, "Rules to Guide the Occupation of Pyongyang," December 5, 1950, cited in *Du Ping Memoirs*, 131–32.

54. CPV Political Department, "Number One Political Notice," December 26, 1950, ibid., 134–35.

55. CPV Political Department, "Working Regulations Regarding Occupation of Seoul," late December 1950, ibid., 163–64.

56. CPV Political Department, "On Some Policy Issues Regarding Seoul Occupation," January 5, 1951, ibid., 164–65.

57. Gan and Li, *Kangmei Yuanchao Zhengzhi Gongzuo Zongjie*, 167–68.

58. Minutes of Hong Xuezhi–Kim Il-sung talk, September 18, 1951, cited in *Hong Xuezhi Memoirs*, 204–10.

59. Gan and Li, *Kangmei Yuanchao Zhengzhi Gongzuo Zongjie*, 169–74.

60. *Kangmei Yuanchao Zhanzheng*, 364 and 482.

61. Ibid., 512–13, 569, and 571; see also Gan and Li, *Kangmei Yuanchao Zhengzhi Gongzuo Zongjie*, 174–75.

62. *Du Ping Memoirs*, 127 and 129.

63. CPV Political Department, "Instructions on Mass Work in Korea," January 1951, CPV Political Department, *Zhiyuanjun Zhengzhi Gongzuo Zongjie*, app. 3, 358–59.

64. *Du Ping Memoirs*, 248–49; *Hong Xuezhi Memoirs*, 166–67; and Xu Yan, *Diyici Jiaoliang*, 94.

65. Xu Yan, *Diyici Jiaoliang*, 241; also Gan and Li, *Kangmei Yuanchao Zhengzhi Gongzuo Zongjie*, 168.

66. *Du Ping Memoirs*, 295.

67. Telegram, the CMC to the CPV Command, September 10, 1951, ibid., 290; minutes of CPV internal security meeting, September 22, 1951, ibid., 295–96.

68. Minutes of Peng–Du Ping talk, September 20, 1951, ibid., 292.

69. Ibid., 295–97.

70. CPV battlefield newspaper, *Shengli* [Triumph], no. 555, September 16, 1952, 2;

Shipping Advice Files, no. 2018, box 2,115, Washington National Records Center, Suitland, Md.

71. Peng Dehuai's speech on opposing corruption, waste, and bureaucracy at the CPV headquarters staff meeting, January 1, 1952, *Peng Dehuai Junshi Wenxuan*, 431–34.

72. Ibid., 432–33.

73. Gan and Li, *Kangmei Yuanchao Zhengzhi Gongzuo Zongjie*, 159–60.

74. Ibid., 161–62; *Shengli*, September 16, 1952, 2.

75. Donald Knox, *The Korean War: Oral History, Pusan to Chosin* (New York: Harcourt Brace Jovanovich, 1985), 419.

76. Roy E. Appleman, *Disaster in Korea: The Chinese Confront MacArthur* (College Station: Texas A&M University Press, 1989), 14–19.

77. Gerald Segal, *Defending China* (New York: Oxford University Press, 1985), 103.

CHAPTER 9. NEGOTIATING WHILE FIGHTING

1. Ba Jin, "Our Conversation with Comrade Peng Dehuai," *Renmin Ribao* [People's daily], April 9, 1952, 1; see also *Kangmei Yuanchao Zhanzheng*, 226.

2. *Kangmei Yuanchao Zhanzheng*, 224–26; Chinese Academy of Military Sciences, *Zhongguo Renmin Zhiyuanjun Kangmei Yuanchao Zhan Shi*, [The war history of the Chinese People's Volunteers in the War to Resist U.S. Aggression and Aid Korea] (Beijing: Military Sciences Press, 1988), 210–11.

3. *Yang Dezhi Memoirs*, 107–8; *Hong Xuezhi Memoirs*, 242–43. Peng went back to Beijing partly to receive medical treatment. Since the spring of 1952, Peng had suffered from a tumor on his forehead. Suspecting that the tumor might be cancerous, several of Peng's deputy commanders asked him to undergo surgery in Beijing. Peng bluntly rejected their appeal. On March 19, 1953, the deputy commanders twice wired the CMC, requesting that Peng receive medical treatment in Beijing. Worried about Peng's health, Mao signed a personal order to Peng on April 2: "Peng must come back to Beijing for medical treatment immediately. Peng must leave for Beijing before mid-April." China Today series, *Peng Dehuai Zhuan* [The biography of Peng Dehuai] (Beijing: Dangdai Zhongguo Press, 1993), 478–79.

4. Telegram, Mao to Peng, December 4, 1950, cited in *Zhongguo Renmin Zhiyuanjun Kamgmei Yuanchao Zhan Shi*, 76–77. Chen Jian, however, argues that Beijing's war objective went through apparent changes in the spring of 1951—from restoring the status quo to "driving the enemy into the sea" and back to maintaining control of the 38th parallel. See Chen, "China's Changing Aims During the Korean War," *Journal of American–East Asian Relations* 1 (Spring 1992): 8–41. There is some truth in Chen's assertion, but my sense is that the aspiration for seizing the whole peninsula was short-lived and never represented a consensus among the top CCP leaders.

5. *Nie Rongzhen Memoirs*, 741–42.

6. *Chai Chengwen Memoirs*, 125. Also see Qi Dexue, *Chaoxian Zhanzheng Juece Neimu* [Inside stories of decision makings in the Korean War] (Shenyang: Liaoning University Press, 1991), 177.

7. Telegram, Peng to Li Kenong and Mao, July 16, 1951, Peng Dehuai, *Peng Dehuai Junshi Wenxuan* [Selected military writings of Peng Dehuai] (Beijing: Central Archives and Manuscripts Press, 1988), 413–14.

8. Editorial, June 25, 1951, *Renmin Ribao* [People's daily], 1; instruction, the CCP Central Committee, "On Issues Related to Korean Armistice Negotiation," July 3, 1951, cited in Qi Dexue, *Chaoxian Zhanzheng Juece Neimu*, 188. The Soviet proposal was made to the public by Jacob Malik, Soviet representative to the United Nations, when he spoke on a U.N. weekly radio program, "The Price of Peace," on June 23, 1951. "As a first step"

toward settling the Korean conflict, Malik proposed, "discussions should be started between the belligerents for a cease-fire and an armistice providing for the mutual withdrawal of forces from the 38th parallel." *New York Times*, June 24, 1951, 1, 4, and 5. It is interesting that Malik omitted Beijing's demands for the withdrawal of the U.S. Seventh Fleet from the Taiwan Strait, the withdrawal of foreign forces from Korea, and a seat for China in the United Nations. This was probably done with the CCP leaders' consent. New materials are needed to clarify this issue.

9. Mao to Peng and Kim Il-sung, June 25, 1951, in Qi Dexue, *Chaoxian Zhanzheng Juece Neimu*, 187; Mao to Peng and Kim Il-sung, July 2, 1951, *Mao's Manuscripts*, 2:379–80.

10. *Chai Chengwen Memoirs*, 129–30.

11. Telegrams, Mao to Li Kenong, July 9, 1951, *Mao's Manuscripts*, 2:390–91; Mao to Li Kenong, July 12, 1951, ibid., 405; to Li Kenong, 1:45 A.M., July 14, 1951, ibid., 409; Mao to Li Kenong, 10:00 A.M., July 14, 1951, ibid., 412–13; Mao to Li Kenong, 11:00 A.M., July 14, 1951, ibid., 414; and Mao to Li Kenong, 6:00 P.M., July 14, 1951, ibid., 415.

12. Telegram, Mao to Li Kenong, 7:00 P.M., July 11, 1951, ibid., 392; Mao to Li Kenong, July 17, 1951, ibid., 422; to Mao to Li Kenong, 1:00 P.M., July 14, 1951, ibid., 415.

13. Telegram, Mao to Peng, July 26, 1951, ibid., 426. For U.S. policy toward the truce talks at Kaesong from July 10 to October 25, 1951, see Burton I. Kaufman, *The Korean War: Changes in Crisis, Credibility, and Command* (New York: Alfred Knopf, 1986), 183–209.

14. Telegram, the CMC instruction, November 14, 1951, cited in Xu Yan, *Diyici Jiaoliang: Kangmei Yuanchao Zhanzheng de Lishi Huigi yu Fansi* [The first encounter: Historical retrospection and review of the War to Resist U.S. Aggression and Aid Korea] (Beijing: Chinese Radio and Television Press, 1990), 277.

15. Telegram, Mao to Li Kenong, December 28, 1951, *Mao's Manuscripts*, 2:642–43.

16. Telegrams, Mao to Li Kenong, July 14, 1952, Xu Yan, *Diyici Jiaoliang*, 285; Li Kenong, Deng Hua, and Xie Fang to Mao, August [undated] 1952, cited in Qi Dexue, *Chaoxian Zhanzheng Juece Neimu*, 217; Li, Deng, and Xie to Mao, August 22, 1952, ibid., 217–18; Mao to the Chinese delegation at Panmunjom, February 6, 1953, ibid., 288.

17. Peng's speech at the enlarged CPV Command meeting, June 25, 1951, *Peng Dehuai Junshi Wenxuan*, 404–10; telegram, Peng to Mao, July 16, 1951, ibid., 414.

18. Mao, "Unite and Clearly Draw the Line between the Enemy and Ourselves," speech at the thirty-eighth meeting of the standing committee of the First National Committee of the CPPCC, August 4, 1952, Michael Y.M. Kau and John K. Leung, *The Writings of Mao Zedong, 1949–1976* (Armonk, N.Y.: M. E. Sharpe, 1986), 274–77.

19. Ibid., 275–76.

20. Xu Xiangqian, *Lishi de Huigu* [Remember the history] (Beijing: PLA Press, 1987), 2:797–805 (hereafter *Xu Xiangqian Memoirs*); *Nie Rongzhen Memoirs*, 757–58.

21. China Today series, *Dangdai Zhongguo Haijun* [China today: The People's Navy] (Beijing: Chinese Social Sciences Press, 1987), 70–71.

22. Mao, "Unite and Clearly Draw the Line Between the Enemy and Ourselves," 274–75. For a good study in English of the Chinese domestic situation, see Lawrence S. Weiss, "Storm Around the Cradle: The Korean War and the Early Years of the People's Republic of China, 1949–1953," Ph.D. diss., Columbia University, 1981.

23. "Footnotes of the Selected Works of Chen Yun: 1949–1956," *Wenxian yu Yanjiu* 2 (February 1982): 11.

24. Mao, "Unite and Clearly Draw the Line Between the Enemy and Ourselves," 275.

25. Mao's instructions on conducting the "three-antis" campaign on a grand scale, December 8, 1951, *Mao's Manuscripts*, 2:548–49.

26. Mao's instructions concerning the "three-antis" and "five-antis," ibid.

27. Editors' note, ibid., 3:693. The First Five-Year Plan was supposed to start in 1953, but political instability and inexperience in planning and managing economic production

subjected it to delay and constant revision. When the plan was finally put into practice in February 1955—some two years after its official beginning—it was in effect for only two-and-a-half years.

28. Telegrams, Deng Hua to CMC's General Officers Department (Zong Ganbu Ju), April 16, 1951, cited in Qi Dexue, *Chaoxian Zhanzheng Juece Neimu*, 291; PLA General Staff Department's decision, May 16, 1952, ibid., 292–93; Deng Hua to Peng, July 22, 1952, ibid., 293; Su Yu to Mao, Zhou, and Peng, August 6, 1952, ibid., 293–94; Nie Rongzhen to Deng Hua and Yang Dezhi, September 10, 1952, Nie Rongzhen, *Nie Rongzhen Junshi Wenxuan* [Selected military writings of Nie Rongzhen] (Beijing: Central Archives, 1992), 374–75.

29. Kau and Leung, *The Writings of Mao Zedong*, 275; Mao's note on the General Staff Department's report, August 16, 1951, *Mao's Manuscripts*, 3:408–9.

30. Deng Hua's speech at the CPV high-ranking commanders meeting, June 6 and 9, 1952, Deng Hua, *Lun Kangmei Yuanchao Zhanzheng Zuozhan Zhidao* [On combat organization and operations in the War to Resist U.S. Aggression and Aid Korea], internal ed. (Beijing: Military Sciences Press, 1989), 38–47; also see *Zhongguo Renmin Zhiyuanjun Kangmei Yuanchao Zhan Shi*, 216–17,

31. *Zhongguo Renmin Zhiyuanjun Kangmei Yuanchao Zhan Shi*, 217–19. See also Qi Dexue, *Chaoxian Zhanzheng Juece Neimu*, 259–60.

32. Intelligence summary of the CPV intelligence department, August 1952, cited in *Yang Dezhi Memoirs*, 123; see also *Kangmei Yuanchao Zhanzheng*, 242–43.

33. Telegram, the CMC to each army commander, August 28, 1952, *Kangmei Yuanchao Zhanzheng*, 243–44; the CPV Command, "Instruction on Closely Watching Changes of the Enemy Situation," late August 1952, cited in *Yang Dezhi Memoirs*, 123–24.

34. Intelligence summary of the CPV intelligence department, mid-September 1952, *Yang Dezhi Memoirs*, 129.

35. Telegram, Deng Hua, Yang Dezhi, and Gan Siqi (CPV's deputy political commissar) to the CMC, September 10, 1952, ibid., 129–30.

36. Telegrams, the CMC to the CPV Command, 5:00 P.M., September 12, 1952, ibid., 130; the CPV Command to the commanders of the 12th, 39th, and 68th armies, 6:00 P.M., September 12, 1952, ibid.

37. Telegram, the CPV Command to each army commander, 11:20 P.M., September 14, 1952, ibid., 130–31; see also *Zhongguo Renmin Zhiyuanjun Kangmei Yuanchao Zhan Shi*, 228–29.

38. *Yang Dezhi Memoirs*, 130–31.

39. *Zhongguo Renmin Zhiyuanjun Kangmei Yuanchao Zhan Shi*, 229–30; see also *Kangmei Yuanchao Zhanzheng*, 247.

40. *Yang Dezhi Memoirs*, 132.

41. *Zhongguo Renmin Zhiyuanjun Kangmei Yuanchao Zhan Shi*, 230–31.

42. Telegram, the CPV Command to each army command, October 3, 1952, cited in *Kangmei Yuanchao Zhanzheng*, 248.

43. *Zhongguo Renmin Zhiyuanjun Kangmei Yuanchao Zhan Shi*, 233; see also Xu Yan, *Diyici Jiaoliang*, 131.

44. Zheng Weishan's report, late 1952, Xu Yan, *Diyici Jiaoliang*, 131.

45. *Yang Dezhi Memoirs*, 134–36; *Hong Xuezhi Memoirs*, 251.

46. *Yang Dezhi Memoirs*, 134–36; *Du Ping Memoirs*, 548 and 552.

47. Deng Hua's telephone instruction to the 15th Army commander, October 21, 1952, cited in *Kangmei Yuanchao Zhanzheng*, 261.

48. Minutes of the 15th Army's command meeting, October 25, 1952, cited in *Zhongguo Renmin Zhiyuanjun Kangmei Yuanchao Zhan Shi*, 243; the 3d Army Corps Command to the 15th Army Command, October 27, 1952, Qi Dexue, *Chaoxian Zhanzheng Juece Neimu*, 273–74.

49. *Zhongguo Renmin Zhiyuanjun Kangmei Yuanchao Zhan Shi*, 243–45; also see *Kangmei Yuanchao Zhanzheng*, 265–68. Also see Nie Jifeng, "The Bloody Battle at Mount Shanggan," *Junshi Shilin* [Studies of military history] 2 (1994): 17–20. Nie was the 45th Division's political commissar.

50. Telegram, the 3d Army Corps Command to the CPV headquarters, November 5, 1952, cited in *Yang Dezhi Memoirs*, 150–51.

51. Telegrams, the CMC to the CPV Command, November 4 and 7, 1952, Qi Dexue, *Chaoxian Zhanzheng Juece Neimu*, 274–76; see also *Zhongguo Renmin Zhiyuanjun Kangmei Yuanchao Zhan Shi*, 245.

52. *Zhongguo Renmin Zhiyuanjun Kangmei Yuanchao Zhan Shi*, 246; *Kangmei Yuanchao Zhanzheng*, 269.

53. *Yang Dezhi Memoirs*, 153.

54. Deng Hua, "On Some Tactical Issues Concerning Active Defense," November 30, 1952, *Lun Kangmei Yuanchao Zhanzheng Zuozhan Zhidao*, 48–89.

55. Telegrams, Mao to the CPV Command, December 24, 1952, *Mao's Manuscripts*, 3:596–97; Mao to all the commanders of major military zone and special forces, November 8, 1952, cited in Qi Dexue, *Chaoxian Zhanzheng Juece Neimu*, 276.

56. Telegram, Mao to the CPV Command, "The Korean War Situation and Our Strategy," December 16, 1952, cited in *Zhongguo Renmin Zhiyuanjun Kangmei Yuanchao Zhan Shi*, 256–57.

57. Wang Bingnan, then director of the administrative office, Ministry of Foreign Affairs, remembered Zhou's instructions on watching Eisenhower's attitude toward the Korean War when I interviewed him in October of 1988 in Beijing. Also see *Remin Ribao* [People's daily] editorial, "Eisenhower Is Lying to the American People," November 11, 1952, reprinted in *Xinhua Yuebao* [New China's monthly] 12 (1952): 104–5.

58. Ibid., 105; also see intelligence summary of the CPV intelligence department, December 1952, *Yang Dezhi Memoirs*, 175–76.

59. Memorandum, Nie Rongzhen to Zhou Enlai, February 28, 1952, *Nie Rongzhen Junshi Wenxuan*, 366. Mao read Nie's report and passed it on to Zhu De, Liu Shaoqi, and Lin Biao. Also see Xue Qi, "An Important Strategic Decision of the CPV Command," *Dangshi Yanjiu* [Studies of CCP history] 5 (1985): 60–61; Qi Dexue, *Chaoxian Zhanzheng Juece Neimu*, 310 and 314. Western scholars have extensively debated the role of a U.S. nuclear threat in the Korean armistice. For a good summary of the debate, see Mark A. Ryan, *Chinese Attitude Toward Nuclear Weapons: China and the United States During the Korean War* (New York: M. E. Sharpe, 1989), 152–56.

60. Deng Hua, "Possible Development of the Korean War Situation and Our Task for 1953," December 4, 1952, *Lun Kangmei Yuanchao Zhanzheng Zuozhan Zhidao*, 94–102; also noted in *Mao's Manuscripts*, 3:639 n. 1.

61. *Yang Dezhi Memoirs*, 173.

62. Intelligence summary of the CPV intelligence department, December 1952, cited in *Zhongguo Renmin Zhiyuanjun Kangmei Yuanchao Zhan Shi*, 256.

63. Telegram, Mao to Deng Hua, December 9, 1952, *Mao's Manuscripts*, 3:632.

64. Mao's notes on Deng Hua's report of December 4, 1952, December [undated] 1952, ibid., 638–39; CMC directive (drafted by Zhou Enlai), December 16, 1952, cited in Qi Dexue, *Chaoxian Zhanzheng Juece Neimu*, 313–14.

65. *Zhongguo Renmin Zhiyuanjun Kangmei Yuanchao Zhan Shi*, 257; *Yang Dezhi Memoirs*, 176–77.

66. The CMC instruction, December 16, 1952, *Zhongguo Renmin Zhiyuanjun Kangmei Yuanchao Zhan Shi*, 257.

67. The CCP Central Committee document, December 20, 1952, *Mao's Manuscripts*, 3:656–58.

68. Deng Hua's speech at the CPV Command meeting, "Our Task of Preparing for the Anti-amphibious Campaign," December [undated] 1952, *Lun Kangmei Yuanchao Zhanzheng Zuozhan Zhidao*, 113–15; minutes of the CPV Command meeting, December 17–21, 1952, cited in *Zhongguo Renmin Zhiyuanjun Kangmei Yuanchao Zhan Shi*, 259–60; the CPV Command to each army command, December 23, 1952, ibid., 260.

69. Memorandum, Nie Rongzhen to Zhou Enlai, February 29, 1952, *Nie Rongzhen Junshi Wenxuan*, 366.

70. *Zongguo Renmin Zhiyuanjun Kangmei Yuanchao Zhan Shi*, 263–65; Deng Hua's speech at the West Coast Command meeting, February 9, 1953, *Lun Kangmei Yuanchao Zhanzheng Zuozhan Zhidao*, 126–40. See also Ryan, *Chinese Attitude Toward Nuclear Weapons*, 129–31. Ryan argues that the strengthening of the tunnel system was part of CPV defense against tactical use of nuclear weapons by the United States in Korea. An instruction of the CPV headquarters in November 1952 suggests Chinese concern about U.S. atomic attack on the front. There is evidence that Eisenhower was keenly interested in the possibility of using tactical nuclear weapons in Korea, but his military advisers doubted that such an action alone would be sufficient to alter the present balance in Korea. See, for example, U.S. Department of State, *Foreign Relations of the United States, 1952–1954*, Vol. 15, *Korea* (Washington, D.C., 1988), 826–27, 1014.

71. Mao's instruction on political mobilization for the anti-amphibious campaign, January 16, 1953, cited in *Zhongguo Renmin Zhiyuanjun Kangmei Yuanchao Zhan Shi*, 260–61.

72. "Chairman Mao's Speech at the CPPCC," *Renmin Ribao* [People's daily], February 8, 1953, 1. Eisenhower's "unleashing Chiang" policy was contained in his 1953 State of the Union address, when he announced that the U.S. Seventh Fleet would no longer shield Communist China from Nationalist attack; *Public Papers of the Presidents of the United States; Dwight D. Eisenhower,:1953–1961* (Washington, D.C.: Government Printing Office, 1960–1961), 12–34.

73. Telegram, Mao to Ding Guoyu, March 23, 1953, *Mao's Manuscripts*, 4:148–49. In December 1952 the League of Red Cross Societies, meeting in Geneva, had urged both the United Nations and the Communists, as a "goodwill gesture" toward peace, to consider exchanging sick and wounded POWs first. In Tokyo, Mark Clark then made a proposal for such an exchange on February 22, 1953. He did so merely because, as he told Washington, such a move would make a favorable impact on world opinion. Joseph C. Goulden, *Korea: The Untold Story of the War* (New York: Times Books, 1982), 629–30; Kaufman, *Korean War*, 305–6.

74. *Zhongguo Renmin Zhiyuanjun Kangmei Yuanchao Zhan Shi*, 265; *Kangmei Yuanchao Zhanzheng*, 49.

75. Telegrams, Deng Hua to the CPV headquarters, April 20, 1953, *Lun Kangmei Yuanchao Zhanzheng Zuozhan Zhidao*, 140–45; Mao to Ding Guoyu, March 23, 1953, *Mao's Manuscripts*, 4:149; *Yang Dezhi Memoirs*, 194.

76. Mao–Du Ping and Peng–Du Ping talks, March 1953, *Du Ping Memoirs*, 573–79; telegram, Deng Hua to the CPV headquarters, April 20, 1953, *Mao's Manuscripts*, 4:201–2 n. 3. It is important to point out that the Eisenhower administration was in fact considering a US/UN advance to the narrow neck of the Korean peninsula in the spring of 1953. Eisenhower finally gave up such a military venture because of several concerns, including (1) the significant cost of the buildup of forces on the peninsula and even the use of nuclear weapons against China; (2) seemingly shaky public opinion on expending more human and material resources in Korea; (3) increasingly strong allied—especially British—opposition to further escalation of the conflict. For key documents in this regard, see *Foreign Relations of the United States*, 15:815, 817–18, 825–27, 838–57, 892–95, 908–10, 945–46, 975–77, 1012–17.

77. Telegrams, Yang Dezhi to the CMC, April 1, 1953, and Peng Dehuai to Yang Dezhi, April 3, 1953, cited in *Yang Dezhi Memoirs*, 197–99; Mao to Peng, April 23, 1953, *Mao's Manuscripts*, 4:201.

78. The CPV Command instruction, May 5, 1953, cited in Qi Dexue, *Chaoxian Zhanzheng Juece Neimu*, 331–32; also see Deng Hua, "Supplementary Instructions on Preparing for the Summer Counteroffensive," May 5, 1953, *Lun Kangmei Yuanchao Zhanzheng Zuozhan Zhidao*, 146–51.

79. *Yang Dezhi Memoirs*, 202.

80. The CPV Command's instruction, May 5, 1953, *Kangmei Yuanchao Zhanzheng*, 290–91.

81. Ibid., 292; see also *Zhongguo Renmin Zhiyuanjun Kangmei Yuanchao Zhan Shi*, 273.

82. *Yang Dezhi Memoirs*, 205–6. General William K. Harrison, Jr., who had replaced Admiral C. Turner Joy as the UN's chief negotiator at Panmunjom at the end of May 1952, proposed a four-day recess so that the Eisenhower administration could develop a final negotiating position that would win both U.S. allies' and Rhee's support; *Foreign Relations of the United States*, 15:1053. However, since it was accompanied by a stepped-up U.S. air attack on North Korea's irrigation dams, which were crucial to the CPV food supply, Harrison's insistence on a recess was interpreted by the Chinese as part of new American scheme to escalate the conflict.

83. Telegram, the CMC to the CPV Command, May 16, 1953, cited in Qi Dexue, *Chaoxian Zhanzheng Juece Neimu*, 334–35; also see *Kangmei Yuanchao Zhanzheng*, 294–95.

84. *Zhongguo Renmin Zhiyuanjun Kangmei Yuanchao Zhan Shi*, 277. Washington's concession, which was presented by the US/UN representative at the May 25 meeting at Panmunjom, consisted of four points: (1) North Korean nonrepatriates were not to be released immediately following the armistice but were to be treated in the same manner as the Chinese nonrepatriates; (2) the custodial commission would hold nonrepatriate POWs in detention for ninety days; (3) commission decisions on individual prisoners would be made by simple majority vote; and (4) prisoners not repatriated by the end of the ninety-day period would be referred to a political conference; if after an additional thirty days any prisoners remained, they either would be released on the spot or have their fate passed on to the UN General Assembly. *Foreign Relations of the United States*, 15:1082–86. Unhappy with the new US/UN proposal, Rhee ordered an immediate boycott of the negotiations at Panmunjom, claiming that the ROK forces would fight to the Yalu alone; see *New York Times*, May 26, 1953, 4.

85. *Yang Dezhi Memoirs*, 209; telegram, the CPV Command to each army command, June 1, 1953, cited in *Zhongguo Renmin Zhiyuanjun Kangmei Yuanchao Zhan Shi*, 277–78.

86. *Kangmei Yuanchao Zhanzheng*, 298–305.

87. Telegram, Mao to the CPV Command, June 19, 1953, ibid., 307. Also see *Yang Dezhi Memoirs*, 218–19. The South Korean government "orchestrated the mass breakout of more than 25,000 [not 27,000 as North Korea claimed] North Korean POWs from four major prison camps" on the morning of June 18, 1953. Despite his awareness that Rhee might free the Korean nonrepatriates, Clark was shocked by the actual move. Kaufman, *Korean War*, 327. Also see Mark W. Clark, *From the Danube to the Yalu* (New York: Harper and Brothers, 1954), 279–80; *Foreign Relations of the United States*, 15:1196–1200.

88. *Yang Dezhi Memoirs*, 307–8; also see Wei Daizong, "Three Important Suggestions During the War to Resist U.S. Aggression and Aid Korea," *Junshi Lishi* [Military history] 3 (1994): 27–29.

89. *Zhongguo Renmin Zhiyuanjun Kangmei Yuanchao Zhan Shi*, 283–291; Clark, *From the Danube to the Yalu*, 291.

90. On July 20, Beijing broadcast a statement by the North Korean representative to the negotiations, Nam Il, which referred to a number of promises that Harrison had made, including an assurance that the United States would not support the ROK army in cases where it violated the armistice and that the South Korean government would abide by the terms of the armistice indefinitely, Kaufman, *Korean War*, 325–26. In effect, Washington had been putting pressure on the Rhee regime. Clark accused Rhee's actions

as "a unilateral abrogation" of his "personal commitment" to assign "command authority over all [ROK] land, sea, and air forces" to the US/UN command and of Rhee's reassurances in recent weeks that he "would not take unilateral action . . . untill full discussion with me." Eisenhower explicitly warned that "unless you are prepared immediately and unequivocally to accept the authority of the U.N. Command to conduct the present hostilities and bring them to a close, it will be necessary to effect another arrangement." U.S. Department of State, *Bulletin* (Washington, D.C., 1945–1954), 28:907 (June 29, 1953); *Foreign Relations of the United States*, 15:1200; see also Dwight D. Eisenhower, *The White House Years*, vol. 1, *Mandate for Change, 1953–1956* (Garden City, N.Y.: Doubleday, 1963), 185–86.

91. *Kangmei Yuanchao Zhanzheng*, 327–30.

92. *Shi Zhe Memoirs*, 506–7.

93. In English literature, however, Western scholars see the Chinese as first to make concessions on the POW issue. Some argue that China backed down because of U.S. nuclear threat. See, for example, David Rees, *Korea: The Limited War* (New York: St. Martin's, 1964), 402–7, 416–20, and Goulden, *Korea: Untold Story of the War*, xxvi. Others believe that Moscow might have pressured China and North Korea to end the war after Stalin died, or that the Chinese might have wanted to end the conflict soon because of political and economic problems at home. See, in particular, Kaufman, *Korean War*, 306, and Callum A. MacDonald, *Korea: The War Before Vietnam* (New York: Free Press, 1986), 182. See also Edward Friedman, "Nuclear Blackmail and the End of the Korean War," *Modern China* 1 (January 1975): 75–98; John Gittings, "Talks, Bomb, and Germs: Another Look at the Korean War," *Journal of Contemporary Asia* 26 (November 1975): 205–17; Rosemary Foot, "Nuclear Coercion and the Ending of the Korean Conflict," *International Security* 13, no. 3 (Winter 1988/89): 92–112. A balanced account of the truce talks using American, Chinese, Soviet, and Korean materials has yet to be written.

CHAPTER 10. CONCLUSION

1. Burton I. Kaufman, *The Korean War: Changes in Crisis, Credibility, and Command* (New York: Alfred Knopf, 1986), 337–38; *Kangmei Yuanchao Zhanzheng*, 329–32.

2. *Kangmei Yuanchao Zhanzheng*, 332–33; China Today series, *Dangdai Zhongguo Jundui de Junshi Gongzuo* [China today: The military affairs of the Chinese army] (Beijing: Chinese Social Sciences Press, 1989), 1:512; and Xu Yan, *Diyici Jiaoliang: Kangmei Yuanchao Zhanzheng de Lishi Huigu yu Fansi* [The first encounter: Historical retrospection and review of the War to Resist U.S. Aggression and Aid Korea] (Beijing: Chinese Radio and Television Press, 1990), 322–23.

3. Mao's speech at the Twenty-fourth Session of the CPGC, September 12, 1953, *SW*, 5:115.

4. Peng's report, September 12, 1953, Peng Dehuai, *Peng Dehuai Junshi Wenxuan* [Selected military writings of Peng Dehuai] (Beijing: Central Archives and Manuscripts Press, 1988), 440–61.

5. Mao's address to the CPGC, September 12, 1953, *SW*, 5:117. Indeed, fifty years after the war was ended, the Chinese still maintain that Chinese intervention was "absolutely necessary and accomplished a great deal." See, Meng Zhaohui, "Mao Zedong's Strategic Decisions [on the Korean War] Show Great Foresight," *Junshi Lishi* [Military history] 6 (1933): 3–7.

6. Peng Dehuai's speech at the Twenty-fourth Session of the CPGC, September 12, 1950, *Peng Dehuai Junshi Wenxuan*, 446–47.

7. Mao's address at the Twenty-fourth Session of the CPGC, *SW*, 5:117; also see Mao's outline of his speech for the meeting, *Mao's Manuscripts*, 4:330.

8. Peng's speech at the Twenty-fourth Session of the CPGC, *Peng Dehuai Junshi Wenxuan*, 445.

9. Yao Xu, "A Wise Decision Making in the War to Resist the US and Assist Korea," *Dangshi Yanjiu* [Studies of CCP history] 5 (1980): 13; also see Xu Yan, *Diyici Jiaoliang*, 318 and 320. As a view from a Western scholar, Jonathan Pollack argues that the Chinese intervention was a "risky but ultimately successful action" because "the Korea gamble" paid off. Pollack, "The Korean War and Sino-American Relations," in *Sino-American Relations, 1945–1955: A Joint Reassessment of a Critical Decade*, ed. Harry Harding and Yuan Ming (Wilmington, Del.: Scholarly Resources, 1989), 230–31.

10. Telegram, Mao to the Soviet government, September 15, 1953, *Mao's Manuscripts*, 4:331–32. For a brief discussion of the Sino-Soviet relations in the post–Korean War period, see John Gittings, *The Role of the Chinese Army* (New York: Oxford University Press, 1967), 119–31.

11. "News Release of the Korean-Chinese Negotiations," November 23, 1953, *Renmin Ribao* [People's daily], 1.

12. "Agreement of Korean-Chinese Economic and Cultural Cooperation," November 23, 1953, ibid. As for the process of the CPV's withdrawal in 1958, see Li Hui and Jian Shihua, "A Short Story About CPV's Withdrawal from Korea in 1958," *Junshi Lishi* [Military history] 2 (1994): 52–53.

13. Peng Dehuai's speech at the Twenty-fourth Session of the CPGC, *Peng Dehuai Junshi Wenxuan*, 445.

14. *Dangdai Zhongguo Jundui de Junshi Gongzuo*, 2:529–34.

15. Giap's recollections about Dienbienphu are cited in ibid., 534.

16. Mao's speech at the Twenty-fourth Session of the CPGC, *SW*, 5:117; see also Mao's outline of speech to the CPGC, *Mao's Manuscripts*, 4:330.

17. Zhou Enlai's speech at the ceremony to welcome the Korean War veterans, October 29, 1958, cited in *Kangmei Yuanchao Zhanzheng*, 411; Liao Chengzhi's speech at the ceremony to welcome the CPV veterans, October 27, 1958, ibid., 407; Xu Yan, *Diyici Jiaoliang*, 319–20.

18. The statistics are cited in *Bo Yibo Memoirs*, 295–96. For discussions of the "economic miracles" after the Korean War, see Ruan Jiaxin, "The War to Resist U.S. Aggression and Aid Korea and the Rise of the New China," *Junshi Shilin* [Studies of military history] 6 (1993): 13–19.

19. Mao Zedong's speech at the Thirtieth Session of the CPGC, June 14, 1954, *Mao's Manuscripts*, 4:505–6.

20. Excerpts of Mao's speeches in March and October 1955 and August 1956 are cited in Huang Xiangbing, "How the Policy of 'Overtaking Britain and Catching Up with US' Was Formed in Late 1950s," *Dangshi Yanjiu Ziliao* [Studies and materials of the party history] 4 (1988): 22.

21. Ibid., 22. See also Bo Yibo, *Ruogan Zhongda Juece yu Shijian de Huigu* [My recollections of decision making on several important policies and events], vol. 2 (Beijing: CCP Central Party Institute Press, 1993), 691–92.

22. Ibid., 692–98.

23. Immanuel C. Y. Hsu, *The Rise of Modern China*, 4th ed. (New York: Oxford University Press, 1990), 655–57.

24. Mao's address to the CPGC, September 12, 1953, *SW*, 5:117.

25. Mao's outline of his speech before the Twenty-fourth Session of the CPGC, September [undated] 1953, *Mao's Manuscripts*, 4:330.

26. Peng Dehuai's speech at the Twenty-fourth Session of the CPGC, September 12, 1953, *Peng Dehuai Junshi Wenxuan*, 446–47.

27. Peng Dehuai's speech at the meeting of high-ranking PLA commanders, December 2, 1953, ibid., 466–67.

28. Deng Hua's speech at the meeting of high-ranking military commanders, January [undated] 1954, Deng Hua, *Lun Kangmei Yuanchao Zhanzheng de Zuozhan Zhidao* [On combat organization and operations in the War to Resist U.S. Aggression and Aid Korea], internal ed. (Beijing: Military Sciences Press, 1989), 189.

29. Ibid., 190–91.

30. CPV Political Department, *Zhongguo Renmin Zhiyuanjun Kangmei Yuanchao Zhanzheng Zhengzhi Gongzuo Zongjie* [A summary of the CPV political work in the War to Resist U.S. Aggression and Aid Korea] (Beijing: PLA Press, 1989; orig. publ. for internal circulation, 1955), 308; Gan Siqi and Li Zhimin, eds., *Zhongguo Renmin Zhiyuanjun Kangmei Yuanchao Zhanzheng Zhengzhi Gongzuo Zongjie* [A summary of the CPV political work in the War to Resist U.S. Aggression and Aid Korea] (Beijing: PLA Press, 1985), 244–45 (emphasis added).

31. China Today series, *Dangdai Zhongguo Kongjun* [China today: The air force] (Beijing: Chinese Social Sciences Press, 1989), 203–11.

32. Stuart Schram, *Mao Tse-tung* (Baltimore: Penguin Books, 1972), 16.

33. Li Ke and Hao Shengzhang, *Wenhua Dageming Zhong de Renmin Jiefangjun* [The PLA during the Cultural Revolution] (Beijing: CCP Historical Materials Press, 1989), 408–9.

34. Cited in John G. Stoessinger, *Nations in the Darkness: China, Russia, and America*, 4th ed. (New York: Random House, 1986), 27.

35. Stuart Schram, *The Thought of Mao Tse-tung* (New York: Cambridge University Press, 1989), 317.

36. See, for example, instruction, the CCP Central Committee, drafted by Mao Zedong, "On Our Diplomatic Policies," January 19, 149, *Wenjian Xuanji* 14:514–18; instruction, the CCP Central Committee, "Our Foreign Trade Policy," February 26, 1949, ibid., 14:559; Mao Zedong, "Report to the Second Plenary Session of the Seventh Central Committee of the CCP," March 5, 1949, *SW*, 4:370–71.

37. Mao, "On Tactics Against Japanese Imperialists," December 27, 1935, *SW*, 1:170.

38. Mao, "Talk with the American Correspondent Anna Louise Strong," August 1946, *SW*, 4:100.

39. Philip West, "Confronting the West: China as David and Goliath in the Korean War," *Journal of American–East Asian Relations* 2 (Spring 1993): 6–7.

40. Mao, "On Protracted War," *SMW*, 228.

41. Ken Booth, *Strategy and Ethnocentrism* (New York: Holmes and Meier, 1979), 26–27.

42. John J. Mearshemier, *Conventional Deterrence* (Ithaca: Cornell University Press, 1983), 203–12. It is interesting that some Chinese military historians still insist that the Korean War offered a good lesson on how a weak army could survive in a positional defense. See Li Hui, "Some Lessons from the CPV Defensive Battles during the War to Resist U.S. Aggression and Aid Korea," *Junshi Lishi* [Military history] 3 (1994): 15–17. Li is listed as a member of the battle tactics division of the Chinese Academy of Military Sciences.

43. Peng Dehuai, *Peng Dehuai Zishu* [Personal recollections of Peng Dehuai] (Beijing: PLA Press, 1981), 264.

44. Andrei A. Gromyko, *Memoirs*, trans. Harold Shukman, 1st ed. (New York: Doubleday, 1989), 251–52.

45. *Bo Yibo Memoirs*, 291, 161–78.

46. Xu Yan, *Diyici Jiaoliang*, 340–43; *Zhongguo Renmin Zhiyuanjun Kangmei Yuanchao Zhanzheng Zhengzhi Gongzuo Zongjie*, 307–8.

47. *Dangdai Zhongguo Jundui de Junshi Gongzuo*, 1:45–51.

48. Shang Jinsuo, *Luelun yi Lie Sheng You* [On how a weak nation can defeat a strong enemy] (Beijing: PLA Press, 1990), 1–235. Also see Zhang Jing and Yao Yanjin, *Jiji*

Fangyu Zhanglue Qian Shuo (An introduction to an active defense strategy] (Beijing: PLA Press, 1985); Lin Boye, *Junshi Bianzhengfa Sixiang Shi* [History of theoretic development of military dialectics] (Beijing: PLA Press, 1989); and Huang Yuzhang, ed., *Ju Bu Zhanzheng de Zuotian Jintian Mingtian* [Limited wars: Past, present, and future] (Beijing: National Defense University Press, 1988).

49. Jonathan D. Pollack, *Security, Strategy, and the Logic of Chinese Foreign Policy* (Berkeley, Calif.: Institute of East Asian Studies, 1981), 66.

50. Zhang Shu Guang, *Deterrence and Strategic Culture: Chinese-American Confrontations, 1949–1958* (Ithaca: Cornell University Press, 1992), 85, 101–6.

51. Cited in Robert Leckie, *Conflict* (New York: Avon, 1963), 161.

52. Joseph C. Goulden, *Korea: The Untold Story of the War* (New York: Times Books, 1982), 291 (emphasis added).

53. Gene Z. Hanrahan and Edward L. Katzenbach, Jr., "The Revolutionary Strategy of Mao Tse-tung," in Franklin Mark Osanka, ed., *Modern Guerrilla Warfare* (New York: Free Press of Glencoe, 1969), 177–84. This originally appeared in *Political Science Quarterly* in 1955.

54. Akira Iriye, "Introduction: The Korean War in the Domestic Context," *Journal of American–East Asian Relations* 2 (Spring 1993): 1–3.

SELECTED BIBLIOGRAPHY

Appleman, Roy E. *Disaster in Korea: The Chinese Confront MacArthur*. College Station: Texas A&M University Press, 1989.

———. *East of Chosin: Entrapment and Breakout in Korea, 1950*. College Station: Texas A&M University Press, 1987.

———. *Escaping the Trap: The U.S. Army X Corps in Northeast Korea*. College Station: Texas A&M University Press, 1990.

———. *Ridgway Duels for Korea*. College Station: Texas A&M University Press, 1990.

Avakian, Bob. *Mao Tsetung's Immortal Contributions*. Chicago: RCP Publications, 1979.

Ba Jin. "Our Conversation with Comrade Peng Dehuai." *Renmin Ribao* [People's daily], April 9, 1952.

Bao Mingrong. "When Was the Strategy of Mobile Warfare in Korea Made." *Dangshi Yanjiu Ziliao* [Studies and materials of the party history] 7 (1988): 26–28.

Baritz, Loren. "God's Country and American Know-How." In *The American Experience in Vietnam: A Reader*, edited by Grace Sevy. Norman: University Press of Oklahoma, 1989.

Betts, Richard K. *Nuclear Blackmail and Nuclear Balance*. Washington, D.C.: Brookings, 1987.

Blum, Robert M. *Drawing the Line: The Origin of the American Containment Policy in East Asia*. New York: Columbia University Press, 1982.

Booth, Ken. *Strategy and Ethnocentrism*. New York: Holmes and Meier, 1979.

Borg, Dorothy, and Waldo Heinrichs, eds. *Uncertain Years: Chinese-American Relations, 1947–1950*. New York: Columbia University Press, 1980.

Bo Yibo. *Ruogan Zhongda Juece yu Shijian de Huigu* [My recollections of decision making on several important policies and events]. Vol. 1. Beijing: CCP Central Archives Press, 1991.

———. *Ruogan Zhongda Juece yu Shijian de Huigu* [My recollections of decision making on several important policies and events]. Vol. 2. Beijing: CCP Central Party Insititute Press, 1993.

Buhite, Russell D. *Soviet-American Relations in Asia, 1945–1954*. Norman: University Press of Oklahoma, 1981.

Cai Tianfu. "Major Lessons of the Fifth-Phase Offensive in the War to Resist U.S. Aggression and Aid Korea." *Junshi Lishi* [Military history] 5 (1990): 30–31.

Chai Chengwen. *Banmendian Tanpan* [The Panmunjom negotiations]. Beijing: PLA Press, 1989.

Chang, Gordon H. *Friends and Enemies: The United States, China, and the Soviet Union, 1948–1972*. Stanford: University Press, 1990.

Chen Geng. *Chen Geng Riji (Xu)* [Chen Geng's diary (continued)]. Beijing: PLA Soldiers' Press, 1984.

Cheng Zihua. *Cheng Zihua Huiyilu* [Memoir of Chen Zihua]. Beijing: PLA Press, 1987.

Chen Jian. *China's Road to the Korean War: The Making of the Sino-American Confrontation*. New York: Columbia University Press, 1994.

———. "China's Changing Aims During the Korean War." *Journal of American–East Asian Relations* 1 (Spring 1992): 8–41.

Chen Yun. *Chen Yun Wenxuan: 1926–1949* [Selected works of Chen Yun: 1926–1949]. Beijing: People's Press, 1984.

———. *Chen Yun Wenxuan: 1949–1956* [Selected works of Chen Yun: 1949–1956]. Jiangsu: People's Press, 1984.

Chen Zhongnong, ed. *Zhongguo Renmin Zhiyuanjun Ren Wu Zhi* [Chronicles of the Chinese People's Volunteers]. Vol. 1. Nanjing: Jiangsu People's Press, 1990.

China Today series. *Dangdai Zhongguo Haijun* [China today: The People's Navy]. Beijing: Chinese Social Sciences Press, 1987.

———. *Dangdai Zhongguo Hegongye* [China today: Nuclear industry]. Beijing: Chinese Social Sciences Press, 1987.

———. *Dangdai Zhongguo Jundui de Junshi Gongzuo* [China today: The military affairs of the Chinese army]. 2 vols. Beijing: Chinese Social Sciences Press, 1989.

———. *Dangdai Zhongguo Jundui de Qunzhong Gongzuo* [China today: Mass work of the military]. Beijing: Chinese Academy of Social Sciences Press, 1988.

———. *Dangdai Zhongguo Kongjun* [China today: The air force]. Beijing: Chinese Social Sciences Press, 1989.

———. *Dangdai Zhongguo Waijiao* [China today: Diplomacy]. Beijing: Chinese Social Sciences Press, 1987.

———. *Kangmei Yuanchao Zhanzheng* [China today: The War to Resist U.S. Aggression and Aid Korea]. Beijing: Chinese Social Sciences Press, 1990.

———. *Peng Dehuai Zhuan* [The biography of Peng Dehuai]. Beijing: Dangdai Zhongguo Press, 1993.

Chinese Academy of Military Sciences. *Sun Zi Bingfai Xinzhu* [A new interpretation of Sun Tzu's *Arts of War*]. Beijing: China's Books, 1977.

———. *Zhongguo Renmin Jiefangjun Liushinian Dashiji: 1927–1987* [Records of important events of the People's Liberation Army from 1927 to 1987]. Beijing: Military Sciences Press, 1988.

———. *Zhongguo Renmin Jiefangjun Zhan Shi* [The war history of the People's Liberation Army]. Vol. 3. Beijing: Military Sciences Press, 1987.

———. *Zhongguo Renmin Zhiyuanjun Kangmei Yuanchao Zhan Shi* [The war history of the Chinese People's Volunteers in the War to Resist U.S. Aggression and Aid Korea]. Beijing: Military Sciences Press, 1988.

CCP Central Archives. *Zhonggong Zhongyang Wenjian Xuanji* [Selected documents of the CCP Central Committee]. 18 vols. Beijing: CCP Central Archives, 1989–1992.

CPV Political Department. *Zhongguo Renmin Zhiyuanjun Kangmei Yuanchao Zhanzheng Zhengzhi Gongzuo Zongjie* [A summary of the CPV political work in the War to Resist U.S. Aggression and Aid Korea]. Beijing: PLA Press, 1989. Orig. publ. for internal circulation, 1955.

Christensen, Thomas. "Threats, Assurances, and the last Chance for Peace: The Lessons of Mao's Korean War Telegrams." *International Security* 17 (Summer 1992): 122–54.

Clark, Mark W. *From the Danube to the Yalu*. New York: Harper and Brothers, 1954.

Cohen, Eliota A. "'Only Half the Battle': American Intelligence and the Chinese Intervention in Korea, 1950." *Intelligence and National Security* 5, no. 1 (January 1990): 129–49.

Cohen, Warren I. "Conversations with Chinese Friends: Zhou Enlai's Associates Reflect on Chinese-American Relations in the 1940s and the Korean War." *Diplomatic History* 11 (Summer 1987): 283–89.

Collins, J. Lawton. *War in Peacetime: The History and Lessons of Korea*. Boston: Houghton Mifflin, 1969.

Cui Lun. "Recall the Days Working as Chief Peng's Communication Officer in the Initial Stage of the War to Resist U.S. Aggression and Aid Korea," *Junshi Lishi* [Military history] 4 (1989): 42–44.

Cumings, Bruce. *The Origins of the Korean War*. Vol. 1, *Liberation and the Emergence of Separate Regimes, 1945–1947*. Princeton: Princeton University Press, 1981.

———. *The Origins of the Korean War*. Vol. 2, *The Roaring of the Cataract, 1947–1950*. Princeton: Princeton University Press, 1990.

Cumings, Bruce, ed. *Child of Conflict: The Korean-American Relations, 1943–1953*. Seattle: University of Washington Press, 1983.

Da Wan. "Miraculous Forces From the Sky: The First Battle After Chief Peng Entered Korea." *Ren Wu* [Biographical studies] 5 (1990): 5–22.

Deng Chao. *Meidi Junshi Shang de Ruodian* [Military and strategic weakness of U.S. imperialism]. Beijing: World Knowledge Press, 1950.

Deng Hua. *Lun Kangmei Yuanchao Zhanzheng Zuozhan Zhidao* [On combat organization and operations in the War to Resist U.S. Aggression and Aid Korea]. Internal edition. Beijing: Military Sciences Press, 1989.

Deng Hua, Li Zhimin, and Hong Xuezhi. "We Remember Comrade Peng Dehuai's Brilliant Leadership of the CPV." In *Hengdao Lima Peng Jiangjun* [Senior general Peng is on the battle steed], 123–24. Beijing: People's Press, 1979.

Dingman, Roger. "Atomic Diplomacy During the Korean War." *International Security* 13, no. 3 (Winter 1988/89): 50–91.

Division of Central Archives and Manuscripts. *Song Qingling Nianpu* [The chronicle of Song Qingling]. Beijing: Central Archives and Manuscripts Press, 1986.

———. *Zhonggong Dangshi Fengyun Lu* [Records of the winds and clouds of the CCP history]. Beijing: People's Press, 1990.

———. *Zhou Enlai Nianpu: 1898–1949* [The chronicle of Zhou Enlai: 1898–1949]. Beijing: Central Archives and Manuscripts Press, 1989.

———. *Zhou Enlai Zhuan* [Biography of Zhou Enlai]. Beijing: People's Press, 1988.

———. *Zhu De Nianpu* [The chronicle of Zhu De]. Beijing: Renmin Press, 1986.

Division of Diplomatic History, Ministry of Foreign Affairs. *Xinzhongguo Waijiao Fengyun* [Winds and clouds of New China's diplomacy]. Beijing: World Knowledge Press, 1990.

"Documentation." *Cold War International History Bulletin*, Woodrow Wilson International Center for Scholars, no. 4 (Fall 1994): 61.

Dobbs, Charles M. *The Unwanted Symbol: American Foreign Policy, the Cold War, and Korea, 1945–1950*. Kent, Ohio: Kent State University Press, 1981.

Domes, Jurgen. *Peng Te-huai: The Man and the Image*. Stanford: Stanford University Press, 1985.

Dong Qiwu. *Rongma Chunqiu* [Years of my military career]. Beijing: Central Literature and History Press, 1986.

Du Ping. *Zai Zhiyuanjun Zhongbu* [My years at the CPV headquarters]. Nanjing: PLA Press, 1989.

Eisenhower, Dwight D. *The White House Years*: Vol. 1, *Mandate for Change, 1953–1956*. Garden City, N.Y.: Doubleday, 1963.

Farrar-Hockley, Anthony. "A Reminiscence of the Chinese People's Volunteers in the Korean War." *China Quarterly* 98 (June 1984): 287–304.

Feng Jinhui. *Chaozhong Zhanfu Qianfan Neimu* [Inside story of the repatriation of CPV and NKPA POWs]. Beijing: Huayi Press, 1990.

Fleming, Denna F. *The Cold War and Its Origins, 1917–1960*. Garden City, N.Y.: Doubleday, 1961.

Foot, Rosemary. "Making Known the Unknown War: Policy Analysis of the Korean Conflict in the Last Decade." *Diplomatic History* (Summer 1991): 411–31.

———. "Nuclear Coercion and the Ending of the Korean Conflict." *International Security* 13 no. 3 (Winter 1988/89): 92–112.

———. *A Substitute for Victory: The Politics of Peacemaking at the Korean Armistice Talks.* Ithaca: Cornell University Press, 1990.

———. *The Wrong War: American Policy and the Dimensions of the Korean Conflict, 1950–1953.* Ithaca: Cornell University Press, 1985.

Friedman, Edward. "Nuclear Blackmail and the End of the Korean War." *Modern China* 1 (January 1975): 75–98.

Futrell, Robert F. *The United States Air Forces in Korea, 1950–1953.* New York: Duell, Sloan and Pearce, 1961.

Gaddis, John Lewis. *The Long Peace: Inquiries into the History of the Cold War.* New York: Oxford University Press, 1987.

———. *Strategies of Containment: A Critical Appraisal of Postwar American National Security Policy.* New York: Oxford University Press, 1982.

Gan Siqi and Li Zhimin, eds. *Zhongguo Renmin Zhiyianjun Kangmei Yuanchao Zhanzheng Zhengzhi Gongzuo Zongjie* [A summary of the CPV political work in the War to Resist U.S. Aggression and Aid Korea]. Beijing: PLA Press, 1985.

George, Alexander L. *The Chinese Communist Army in Action: The Korean War and Its Aftermath.* New York: Columbia University Press, 1967.

George, Alexander L., and Richard Smoke. *Deterrence in American Foreign Policy: Theory and Practice.* New York: Columbia University Press, 1974.

Giangreco, D. M. *War in Korea: 1950–1953.* Novato, Calif.: Presidio, 1990.

Gittings, John. *China Changes Faces: The Road from Revolution, 1949–1989.* New York: Harper and Row, 1989.

———. *The Role of the Chinese Army.* New York: Oxford University Press, 1967.

———. "Talks, Bombs, and Germs: Another Look at the Korean War." *Journal of Contemporary Asia* 26 (November 1975): 205–17.

Goldstein, Steven M., and He Di. "New Chinese Sources on the History of the Cold War." *Cold War International History Bulletin,* Woodrow Wilson International Center for Scholars, no. 1 (Spring 1992): 4–6.

Goncharov, Sergei N., John W. Lewis, and Xue Litai. *Uncertain Partners: Stalin, Mao, and the Korean War.* Stanford: Stanford University Press, 1993.

Goodman, Allen E., ed. *Negotiating While Fighting: The Diary of Admiral C. Turner Joy at the Korean Armistice Conference.* Stanford: Stanford University Press, 1978.

Gordenker, Leon. *The United States and the Peaceful Unification of Korea: The Politics of Field Operation.* The Hague: Nijhoff, 1959.

Goulden, Joseph C. *Korea: The Untold Story of the War.* New York: Times Books, 1982.

Gromyko, Andrei A. *Memoirs.* Translated by Harold Shukman. 1st ed. New York: Doubleday, 1989.

Guo Fuwen. "China's Sun." *Zuoping yu Zhengming* [Literature and commentary] 2 (1988): 2–3.

Guo Huaruo, ed. *Sun Zi Jinyi* [A new interpretation of Sun Tzu's *Arts of War*]. Shanghai: People's Press, 1977.

Gurtov, Melvin, and Byong-Moo Huang. *China Under Threat: The Politics of Strategy and Diplomacy.* Baltimore: Johns Hopkins University Press, 1980.

Hackworth, David H. *About Face.* New York: Simon and Schuster, 1989.

Han Qiufeng and Li Qinyang. "Mao Zedong Inherited and Developed the Traditional Strategists' Thoughts on Military Spirit." *Mao Zedong Sixiang Yanjiu* [Study of Mao Zedong thought] 4 (1989): 73–74.

Hanrahan, Gene Z., and Edward L. Katzenbach, Jr. "The Revolutionary Strategy of Mao

Tse-tung." In *Modern Guerrilla Warfare*, edited by Franklin Mark Osanka, 177–84. New York: Free Press of Glencoe, 1969.

Hao Yufan and Zhai Zhihai. "China's Decision to Enter the Korean War: History Revisited," *China Quarterly* 121 (March 1990): 94–115.

Harding, Harry, and Yuan Ming, eds. *Sino-American Relations, 1945–1955: A Joint Reassessment of a Critical Decade*. Wilmington, Del.: Scholarly Resources, 1989.

Hastings, Max. *The Korean War*. New York: Simon and Schuster, 1987.

He Di. "The Evolution of the CCP's Policy Toward the United States, 1945–1949." *Lishi Yanjiu* [Historical studies] 3 (1987): 15–33.

He Linzhong. "Unforgettable Events." *Remin Ribao–Haiwaiban* [People's daily—overseas edition], February 18, 1986.

Herring, George C. *America's Longest War: The United States and Vietnam, 1950–1975*. 2d ed. New York: Alfred Knopf, 1986.

Hoang Van Hoan. *Changhai Yishu: Huang Wenhuan Geming Huiyilu* [A drop in the ocean: Hoang Van Hoan's revolutionary reminiscences]. Beijing: PLA Press, 1987.

Holliday, Jon. "Air Operations in Korea: The Soviet Side of the Story." In *A Revolutionary War: Korea and the Transformation of the Postwar World*, edited by William J. Williams. Chicago: Imprint, 1993.

Hong Xuezhi. *Kangmei Yuanchao Zhanzheng Huiyi* [Recollection of the War to Resist U.S. Aggression and Aid Korea]. Beijing: PLA Art Press, 1990.

Hsu, Immanuel C. Y. *The Rise of Modern China*. 4th ed. New York: Oxford University Press, 1990.

Hua Shan. *Chaoxian Zhanchang Ri Ji* [Diary on the Korean battlefield]. Chongqing: New China Press, 1986.

Huang Daoxia, ed. *Zhonghua Renmin Gongheguo Sishi Nian Dashi Ji: 1949–1989* [The chronicle of important events in PRC's forty-year history: 1949–1969]. Beijing: Guangming Ribao Press, 1989.

Huang Xiangbing. "How the Policy of 'Overtaking Britain and Catching Up with US' Was Formed in the Late 1950s." *Dangshi Yanjiu Ziliao* [Studies and materials of the party history] 4 (1988): 21–26.

Huang Yi. "Major Lessons and Problems Concerning the CPV Logistics Work in the Stage of Mobile Warfare in the War to Resist U.S. Aggression and Aid Korea." *Junshi Shilin* [Studies of military history] 5 (1990): 2–8.

Huang Yuzhang, ed. *Ju Bu Zhanzheng de Zuotian Jintian Mingtian* [Limited wars: Past, present, and future]. Beijing National Defense University Press, 1988.

Huang Zheng. *Ho Chi Minh yu Zhongguo* [Ho Chi Minh and China]. Beijing: PLA Press, 1987.

Hu Changshui. "The Formation of the Concept That Imperialism Is Paper Tiger." *Dangshi Yanjiu Ziliao* [Studies and materials of the party history] 7 (1988): 16–18.

Hughes, Emmett John. *The Ordeal of Power: A Political Memoir of the Eisenhower Years*. New York: Atheneum, 1963.

Hu Guangzheng. "On the Decision to Send Troops Participating in the War to Resist America and Aid Korea." *Dangshi Yanjiu* [Studies of CCP history] 1 (1983): 33–38.

Hu Guangzheng and Bao Mingrong. "Corrections of Some Historical Facts in 'On the Decision to Send Troops Participating in the War to Resist U.S. Aggression and Aid Korea.'" *Dangshi Yanjiu* [Studies of CCP history] 3 (1981): 57–60.

Hu Guangzheng and Ma Shanying, eds. *Zhongguo Renmin Zhiyuanjun Xu Lie: October 1950–July 1953* [The CPV order of battles: October 1950–July 1953]. Beijing: PLA Press, 1987.

Hunt, Michael, "Beijing and the Korean Crisis, June 1950–June 1951." *Political Science Quarterly* 107 (Fall 1992): 453–78.

———. "Internationalizing U.S. Diplomatic History: A Practical Agenda." *Diplomatic History* 15, 1 (Winter 1991): 1–12.

———. "Mao Tse-tung and the Issue of Accommodation with the United States." In *Uncertain Years: Chinese American Relations, 1947–50*, edited by Dorothy Borg and Waldo Heinrichs. New York: Columbia University Press, 1980.

Hunt, Michael, and Odd Arne Westad. "The Chinese Communist Party and International Affairs: A Field Report on New Historical Sources and Old Research Problems." *China Quarterly* 122 (June 1990): 258–72.

Hu Sheng. "How Did American Imperialists Attempt to Invade China in History." *Xinhua Yuebao* [New China's monthly]. 2 (1949): 275–76.

Huston, James A. *Guns and Butter, Power and Rice: United States Army Logistics in the Korean War*. London: Associate University Press, 1989.

Iriye, Akira. "Culture and International History." In *Explaining the History of American Foreign Policy*, edited by Michael Hogan and Thomas Paterson. New York: Cambridge University Press, 1991.

———. "Introduction: The Korean War in the Domestic Context." *Journal of American–East Asian Relations* 2 (Spring 1993): 1–3.

Jackson, Robert. *Air Power over Korea*. New York: Charles Scribner's Sons, 1975.

James, D. Clayton. *The Years of MacArthur: Triumph and Diaster, 1945–1964*. Boston: Houghton Mifflin, 1985.

Jiang Siyi, ed. *Zhongguo Renmin Jiefangjun Zhengzhi Gongzuo Shi:: 1924–1950* [History of the Chinese People's Liberation Army's political work], Beijing: PLA Political Institute Press, 1984.

Jiang Yonghui. *Sanshibajun Zai Chaoxian* [The 38th Army in Korea]. Shenyang: Liaoning People's Press, 1989.

Joffe, Ellis. *Party and Army: Professionalism and Political Control in the Chinese Officer Corps, 1948–1964*. Cambridge, Mass.: Harvard University Press, 1967.

Kalicki, J. H. *The Pattern of Sino-American Crises: Political-Military Interactions in the 1950s*. New York: Cambridge University Press, 1975.

Kangmei Yuanchao Zhanzheng Houqin Jingyan Zongjie—Houqin Zhanli Xuanbian [A summary of the CPV rear service experiences in the War to Resist U.S. Aggression and Aid Korea—selected cases]. Beijing: Golden Shield Press, 1986.

Kangmei Yuanchao Zhanzheng Houqin Jingyan Zongjie—Jiben Jingyan [A summary of the CPV rear service experiences in the War to Resist U.S. Aggression and Aid Korea—basic lessons]. Beijing: Golden Shield Press, 1987.

Kangmei Yuanchao Zhanzheng Houqin Jingyan Zongjie—Zhuan Ye Qinwu [A summary of the CPV rear service experiences in the War to Resist U.S. Aggression and Aid Korea—special work]. 2 vols. Beijing: Golden Shield Press, 1987.

Kaufman, Burton I. *The Korean War: Changes in Crisis, Credibility, and Command*. New York: Alfred Knopf, 1986.

Kau, Michael Y. M., and John K. Leung, eds. *The Writings of Mao Zedong, 1949–1976*. Vol. 1: September 1949–October 1955. Armonk, N.Y.: M. E. Sharpe, 1986.

Khrushchev, Nikita S. *Khrushchev Remembers: The Last Testament*. Translated and edited by Strobe Talbott. Boston: Little, Brown, 1970.

Khrushchev, Sergei. *Khrushchev on Khrushchev: An Inside Account of the Man and His Era*. Translated and edited by William Taubman. Boston: Little, Brown, 1990.

Knox, Donald. *The Korean War: Oral History, Pusan to Chosin*. New York: Harcourt Brace Jovanovich, 1985.

Kongjun Shi [History of the People's Air Force]. Beijing: PLA Press, 1987.

Korean War Enemy Materials Series. *Chaoxian Zhanzheng: Zhonggongjun Canzhan ji Lianhejun Congxin Fangong* [The Korean War: Intervention of the Chinese Communist forces and counteroffensive of the US/UN forces]. Vol. 1. Internal edition. Henongjiang: Korean Minority Press, n.d.

———. *Chaoxian Zhanzheng: Zhanxian Dongdang Shi Qi* [The Korean War: The turbulent period]. Vol. 2. Internal edition. Henongjiang: Korean Minority Press, n.d.

———. *Chaoxian Zhanzheng: Duishi Chu Qi* [The Korean War: The initial stage of the stalemated war]. Vol. 3. Internal edition. Henongjiang: Korean Minority Press, n.d.

———. *Chaoxian Zhanzheng: Duishi Zhong Qi* [The Korean War: The middle stage of the stalemated war]. Vol. 4. Internal edition. Henongjiang: Korean Minority Press, n.d.

———. *Chaoxian Zhanzheng: Duishi Hou Qi* [The Korean War: The last stage of the war]. Vol. 5. Internal edition. Henongjiang: Korean Minority Press, n.d.

LaFeber, Walter. "Crossing the 38th: The Cold War in Microcosm." In *Reflections on the Cold War: A Quarter Century of American Foreign Policy*, edited by Lynn H. Miller and Ronald W. Pruessen. Philadephia: Temple University Press, 1974.

Larson, Deborah Welch. *Origins of Containment: A Psychological Explanation*. Princeton: Princeton University Press, 1985.

Lauterback, Richard E. *Danger from the East*. New York: Harper and Brothers, 1947.

Lebow, Richard Ned. *Between Peace and War: The Nature of International Crisis*. Baltimore: Johns Hopkins University Press, 1981.

Leckie, Robert. *Conflict*. New York: Avon, 1963.

Lei Yingfu. "My Recollection of the Decision Making on Several Crucial Issues During the War to Resist U.S. Aggression and Aid Korea." *Dang de Wenxian* [The party's archives and materials] 6 (1993): 76–80.

Lewis, John Wilson, and Xue Litai. *China Builds the Bomb*, Stanford: Stanford University Press, 1988.

Li Hui. "Some Lessons from the CPV Defensive Battles During the War to Resist U.S. Aggression and Aid Korea." *Junshi Lishi* [Military history] 3 (1994): 15–17.

Li Hui and Jian Shihua. "A Short Story About CPV's Withdrawal from Korea in 1958." *Junshi Lishi* [Military history] 2 (1994): 52–53.

Li Jukui. *Li Jukui Huiyilu* [Memoirs of Li Jukui[. Beijing: PLA Press, 1986.

Li Ke. "The Chinese Military Advisory Group in the Struggle of Aiding Vietnam and Resisting France." *Junshi Lishi* 3 (1989): 28–29.

Li Ke and Hao Shengzhang. *Wenhua Dageming Zhong de Renmin Jiefangjun* [The PLA during the Cultural Revolution]. Beijing: CCP Historical Materials Press, 1989.

Lin Boye. *Junshi Bianzhengfa Sixiang Shi* [History of theoretic development of military dialectics]. Beijing: PLA Press, 1989.

———. *Xuexi Mao Zedong Junshi Zhuzuo Zhong de Zhexue Sixiang* [The philosophical points contained in Mao Zedong's military writings]. Tianjin: People's Press, 1982.

Liu Bocheng. *Liu Bocheng Huiyilu* [Memoirs of Liu Bocheng]. Vol. 3. Shanghai: People's Press, 1988.

Liu Hongxuan. "A Summary of the Theoretical Symposium on the Fortieth Anniversary of the War to Resist U.S. Aggression and Aid Korea." *Junshi Shilin* [Studies of military history] 6 (1990): 61–62.

Liu Huajing and Shan Xufa. *Mao Zedong Junshi Bianzhengfa Yanjiu* [A study of Mao Zedong's military dialectics]. Wuhan: Hubei People's Press, 1984.

Liu Liyun. "China's Mountains." *Xinhua Wenzhai* [Abstracts of New China's literature] 8 (1987): 136–39.

Liu Shaoqi. *On Internationalism and Nationalism*. Peking: Foreign Languages Press, 1949.

———. *Liu Shaoqi Xuanji* [Selected works of Liu Shaoqi]. Vol. 2. Beijing: People's Press, 1985.

Liu Zhenghua and Ying Zheng. "To Hunt the Deer in South China Sea." *Renmin Ribao* [People's daily], September 29, 1988.

Liu Zhiquan. *Zhidaoyuan Gongzuo Yishu* [The art of political work of company political instructors]. Beijing: PLA Press, 1990.

Li Weihan. *Huiyi yu Yanjiu* [Recollections and analyses]. Vol. 2. Beijing: CCP Historical Materials Press, 1986.

Li Xiannian. *Li Xiannian Wenxuan: 1935–1988* [Selected works of Xi Xiannian: 1935–1988]. Beijing: People's Press, 1989.

Li Zhimin, ed. *Zhadan yu Xianhua* [Bombs and flowers]. Beijing: PLA Press, 1985.

Lowe, Peter. *The Origins of the Korean War*. New York: Longman, 1986.

Lu Liping. *Tongtian Zhilu* [The path to the sky]. Beijing: PLA Press, 1989.

Luo Yinwen. "Realistically Putting Forward New Ideas: Two or Three Facts About General Deng Hua." *Ren Wu* [Biographical studies] 5 (1985): 61–63.

Lu Zhengcao. *Lu Zhengcao Huiyilu* [Memoirs of Lu Zhengcao]. Beijing: PLA Press, 1988.

Lu Zhikong. *Waijiao Ju Bo* [A great authority in diplomacy]. Henan: People's Press, 1989.

MacArthur, Douglas. *Reminiscences*. New York: McGraw-Hill, 1983.

MacDonald, Callum A. *Korea: The War Before Vietnam*. New York: Free Press, 1986.

Mao Zedong. *Jianguo Yilai Mao Zedong Wengao* [Mao Zedong's manuscripts since the foundation of the PRC]. Vols. 1–4. Beijing: Central Archives and Manuscripts Press, 1987–1990.

———. *Mao Zedong Junshi Wenxuan—neibuban* [Selected military works of Mao Zedong—internal edition]. Beijing: PLA Soldiers' Press, 1981.

———. *Mao Zedong Xuanji* [Selected works of Mao Zedong]. Vol. 5. Beijing: People's Press, 1978.

———. *Quotations from Chairman Mao Tsetung*. Peking: Foreign Languages Press, 1966.

———. *Selected Military Writings of Mao Tsetung*. Peking: Foreign Languages Press, 1967.

———. *Selected Works of Mao Tsetung*. 5 vols. Peking: Foreign Languages Press, 1963–1978.

Marshall, S. L. A. *The River and the Gauntlet: The Defeat of the Eighth Army by the Chinese Communist Forces*. New York: William Morrow, 1953.

Mearsheimer, John J. *Conventional Deterrence*. Ithaca: Cornell University Press, 1983.

Meng Zhaohui. "The Application and Development of Mao Zedong's Military Thought in the War to Resist U.S. Aggression and Aid Korea." *Junshi Lishi* [Military history] 1 (1991): 3–8.

———. "Mao Zedong's Strategic Decisions [on the Korean War] Show Great Foresight." *Junshi Lishi* [Military history] 6 (1993): 3–7.

Miao Changqing. "A Reappraisal of the Gao-Rao Affairs." *Lilun Xuekan* [Theoretical Bulletin] 6 (1990): 50–51.

Moraes, Frank. *Report on Mao's China*. New York: Macmillan, 1954.

Mueller, John. *Retreat from Doomsday: The Obsolescence of Major War*. New York: Basic Books, 1980.

Museum of Chinese People's Military Revolutions. *Ming Jiang Su Yu* [Su Yu: A famous senior general]. Beijing: New China Press, 1986.

———. *Peng Dehuai Yuanshuai Fengbei Yongcun* [The remarkable achievement of Marshall Peng Dehuai will be remembered forever]. Shanghai: People's Press, 1985.

Mu Xin. *Chen Geng Dajiang* [Senior general Chen Geng]. Beijing: New China Press, 1985.

Nakajima, Mineo. "The Sino-Soviet Confrontation: Its Roots in the International Background of the Korean War." *Australian Journal of Chinese Affairs* 1 (January 1979): 19–47.

Nie Jifeng. "The Bloody Battle at Mount Shanggan." *Junshi Shilin* [Studies of military history] 2 (1994): 17–20.

Nie Rongzhen. *Nie Rongzhen Huiyilu* [Nie Rongzhen memoirs]. Vol. 2. Beijing: PLA Press, 1984.

———. *Nie Rongzhen Junshi Wenxuan* [Selected military writings of Nie Rongzhen]. Beijing: CCP Central Archives, 1992.

Oliver, Robert T. *Why War Came in Korea*. New York: Fordham University Press, 1950.

Pak Toufu. *Zhonggong Canjia Hanzhan Yuanying Zhi Yanjiu* [An examination of why the CCP decided to participate in the Korean War]. Taipei: Numin Cultural Service, 1975.

Panikkar, K. M. *In Two Chinas: Memoirs of a Diplomat*. London: Allen and Unwin, 1955.

Pan Jijiong. *Meidi Yuanzi Waijiao de Pochan* [The failures of nuclear diplomacy of U.S. imperialism]. Shanghai: New Knowledge Press, 1950.

———. *Yuanzineng Wenti Shang de Liangtiao Daolu* [The two lines concerning the issue of nuclear energy]. Shanghai: New Knowledge Press, 1955.

Peng Dehuai. *Memoirs of a Chinese Marshall: The Autobiographical Notes of Peng Dehuai, 1898–1974*. Translated by Zheng Longpu. Beijing: Foreign Languages Press, 1984.

———. *Peng Dehuai Junshi Wenxuan* [Selected military writings of Peng Dehuai]. Beijing: Central Archives and Manuscripts Press, 1988.

———. *Peng Dehuai Zishu* [Personal recollections of Peng Dehuai]. Beijing: PLA Press, 1981.

Pollack, Jonathan D. "Into the Vortex: China, the Sino-Soviet Alliance, and the Korean War." Rand Corporation, R-3910-RC, Stanford, 1990.

———. "The Korean War and Sino-American Relations." In *Sino-American Relations, 1945–1955: A Joint Reassessment of a Critical Decade*, edited by Harry Harding and Yuan Ming, 213–37. Wilmington, Del.: Scholarly Resources, 1989.

———. *Security, Strategy, and the Logic of Chinese Foreign Policy*. Berkeley, Calif.: Institute of East Asian Studies, 1981.

Public Papers of the Presidents of the United States: Dwight D. Eisenhower, 1953–1961. Washington, D.C.: Government Printing Office, 1960–1961.

Quan Yanchi. *Hongqiang Nei Wai: Mao Zedong Shenghuo Shi Lu* [Inside and outside of the red wall: Record of Mao Zedong's life]. Beijing: Kunlun Press, 1989.

———. *Zouxia Shengtan de Mao Zedong* [Mao Zedong off the throne]. Beijing: Chinese-Foreign Culture Press, 1989.

Qi Dexue. "An Important Decision Making of the Chinese People's Volunteers." *Dangshi Yanjiu Ziliao* [Studies and materials of the party's history] 3 (1987): 18–21.

———. *Chaoxian Zhanzheng Juece Neimu* [Inside stories of decision makings in the Korean War]. Shenyang: Liaoning University Press, 1991.

———. "On *Heixue*." *Junshi Lishi* [Military history] 6 (1989): 40.

———. "On Some Key Issues Concerning the Decision Making of Entering the Korean War." *Junshi Lishi* [Military history] 2 (1993): 51–53.

———. "Zhou Enlai's Important Contribution to the Command of the War to Resist U.S. Aggression and Aid Korea." *Junshi Lishi* [Military history] 1 (1992): 5.

Rees, David. *Korea: The Limited War*. New York: St. Martin's, 1964.

Ridgway, Matthew B. *The Korean War*. Garden City, N.Y.: Doubleday, 1967.

Ruan Jiaxin. "The War to Resist U.S. Aggression and Aid Korea and the Rise of the New China." *Junshi Shilin* [Studies of military history] 6 (1993): 13–19.

Ryan, Mark A. *Chinese Attitude Toward Nuclear Weapons: China and the United States During the Korean War*. New York: M. E. Sharpe, 1989.

Schaller, Michael. *Douglas MacArthur: The Far Eastern General*. New York: Oxford University Press, 1989.

Schram, Stuart. *Mao Tse-tung*. Baltimore: Penguin Books, 1972.

———. *The Thought of Mao Tse-tung*. New York: Cambridge University Press, 1989.

Segal, Gerald. *Defending China*. New York: Oxford University Press, 1955.

Shang Jinsuo. *Luelun yi Lie Sheng You* [On how a weak nation can defeat a strong enemy]. Beijing: PLA Press, 1990.

Shipping Advice Files [Captured CPV documents], no. 2018, box 2,115, Washington National Records Center, Suitland, Md.

Shi Zhe. "To Accompany Chairman Mao to Visit the Soviet Union." *Ren Wu* [Biographical studies] 5 (1988): 3–24.

———. *Zai Lishi Juren Shengbian: Shi Zhe Huiyilu* [Together with historical giants: Shi Zhe memoirs]. Beijing: Central Archives and Manuscripts Press, 1991.

Simmons, Robert R. *The Strained Alliance: Peking, Pyongyang, and the Politics of the Korean Civil War*. New York: Free Press, 1975.

Song Shilun. *Xuexi Mao Zedong Zhidao Zhanzheng de Weida Shijian* [Study the invaluable experience of how Mao Zedong directed wars]. Beijing: PLA Soldiers' Press, 1983.

Song Yijun. "One Challenge and One Progress: On the Cost and Benefit of the Fifth-Phase Offensive in the War to Resist U.S. Aggression and Aid Korea." *Junshi Shilin* [Study of military history] 5 (1990): 8–19.

Spence, Jonathan D. *The Search for Modern China*. New York: W. W. Norton, 1990.

Spurr, Russell. *Enter the Dragon: China's Undeclared War Against the U.S. in Korea*. New York: New Market, 1988.

Stoessinger, John G. *Nations in Darkness: China, Russia, and America*. 4th ed. New York: Random House, 1986.

Stolper, Thomas. *China, Taiwan, and the Offshore Islands*. Armonk, N.Y.: Random House, 1985.

Stueck, William Whitney, Jr. "The Korean War as International History." *Diplomatic History* 10 (Fall 1986): 285–301.

———. *The Korean War: An International History*. Princeton University Press, forthcoming.

———. *The Road to Confrontation: American Policy Toward China and Korea, 1947–1950*. Chapel Hill: University of North Carolina Press, 1981.

Sun Baoshen. "Mao Zedong Had Predicted That the US/UN Would Land at Inchon." *Junshi Shilin* [Studies of military history] 5 (1990): 13.

Sun Jingli. "Mao Anying Was Buried in Korea." *Renmin Ribao*—Haiwaiban [People's daily—overseas edition], December 17, 1990.

Sun Ke. "On the New Development of Mao Zedong's Idea of People's War in the War to Resist U.S. Aggression and Aid Korea." *Junshi Lishi* [Military history] 5 (1990) 3–7.

Sun Yaoshen. "General Xie Fang in the War to Resist U.S. Aggression and Aid Korea." *Junshi Lishi* [Military history] 4 (1990): 43–44.

Tang Qun. "The Third Plenary Session of CCP's Seventh Congress, June 6–9, 1950." *Dangshi Yanjiu Ziliao* [Studies and materials of the party's history] 3 (1982): 672.

Teiwes, Frederick C. *Politics at Mao's Court: Gao Gang and Party Factionalism in the Early 1950s*. Armonk, N.Y.: M. E. Sharpe, 1990.

Toland, John. *In Mortal Combat: Korea, 1950–1953*. New York: William Morrow, 1991.

Tsou, Tang. *America's Failure in China, 1941–1950*. Chicago: University of Chicago Press, 1963.

Tucker, Nancy Bernkopf. *Patterns in the Dust: Chinese-American Relations and the Recognition Controversy, 1949–1950*. New York: Columbia University Press, 1983.

U.S. Department of the Army. *United States Army in the Korean War*. Vol. 1. *South to the Naktong, North to the Yalu*, by Roy Appleman; Vol. 2, *Truce Tent and Fighting Front*, by Walter Hermes; Vol. 3, *Policy and Direction: The First Year*, by James F. Schnabel. Washington, D.C.: Government Printing Office, 1961–1972.

U.S. Department of State. *Bulletin*. Vols. 12–31. Washington, D.C., 1945–1954.

———. *Foreign Relations of the United States, 1949*. Vol. 7, *The Far East and Australasia*. Washington, D.C., 1974.

———. *Foreign Relations of the United States, 1950*. Vol. 6, *East Asia and the Pacific*; Vol. 7, *Korea*. Washington, D.C., 1976–1980.

———. *Foreign Relations of the United States, 1951*. Vol. 6, *Asia and the Pacific*; Vol. 7, *Korea and China*. Washington, D.C., 1977–1985.

———. *Foreign Relations of the United States, 1952–1954*. Vol. 15, *Korea*. Washington, D.C., 1988.

U.S. Joint Chiefs of Staff. *The History of the Joint Chiefs of Staff*. Vol. 3, *The Joint Chiefs of Staff and National Policy–The Korean War*, by James F. Schnabel and Robert J. Watson, Wilmington, Del.: Michael Glazier, 1979.

U.S. Office of the Secretary of Defense. *History of the Office of the Secretary of Defense*. Vol. 2, *The Test of War, 1950–1953*. Washington, D.C., 1988.

University of National Defense. *Junshi Bianzhengfa Xintan* [A new look of military dialectics[. Beijing National Defense University Press, 1987.

———. *Kangmei Yuanchao Zhanzheng Jingyan Huibian* [A collection on combat experiences in the War to Resist U.S. Aggression and Aid Korea]. Internal edition. Beijing: National Defense University Press, 1956.

———. *Zhongguo Renmin Jiefangjun Zhengzhi Gongzuo Shi* [History of the PLA's political work]. Beijing: National Defense University Press, 1989.

———. *Zhongguo Renmin Zhiyuanjun Zhanshi Jianbian* [A short military history of the Chinese People's Volunteers]. Beijing: National Defense University Press, 1986.

Wamer, Geoffrey. "The Korean War." *International Affairs*, 56 (January 1980): 91–100.

Wang Funian. "A Summary of the Negotiations on the Korean Cease-fire." *Dangshi Yanjiu Ziliao* [Studies and materials of the party history] 6 (1983): 2–12.

Wang Jiaxiang. *Wang Jiaxiang Xuan Ji* [Selected works of Wang Jiaxiang]. Beijing: People's Press, 1989.

Wang Ming. *Polveka KPK i Predatelstvo Mao Zedong* [Half a century of the CCP and the treachery of Mao Zedong]. Moscow: Politizdat [Party publishing house], 1975.

Wang Shijun and Li Shuozhi. *Wu Zi Qian Shuo* [An introduction to Wu Tzu's *Art of War*]. Beijing: PLA Press, 1986.

Wang Yazhi. "Peng Dehuai and Nie Rongzhen During the War to Resist U.S. Aggression and Aid Korea: A Recollection of a Staff Member." *Junshi Shilin* [Studies of military history] 1 (1994): 9–15.

Weathersby, Kathryn. "Soviet Aim in Korea and the Origins of the Korean War, 1949–1950: New Evidence from Russian Archives." Working Paper No. 8, Cold War International History Project, Woodrow Wilson Center for Scholars, Washington, D.C., November 1993.

Weida de Kangmei Yuanchao Yundong [The great movement of resisting America and aiding Korea]. Vol. 3. Beijing: People's Press, 1950.

Wei Daizong. "Three Important Suggestions During the War to Resist U.S. Aggression and Aid Korea." *Junshi Lishi* [Military history] 3 (1994): 27–29.

Weiss, Lawrence S. "Storm Around the Cradle: The Korean War and the Early Years of the People's Republic of China, 1949–1953." Ph.D. diss. Columbia University, 1981.

West, Philip. "Confronting the West: China as David and Goliath in the Korean War." *Journal of American–East Asian Relations* 2 (Spring 1993): 5–28.

Whiting, Allen S. *China Crosses the Yalu: The Decision to Enter the Korean War*. New York: Macmillan, 1960.

———. *The Chinese Calculus of Deterrence*. Ann Arbor: University of Michigan Press, 1975.

Whitney, Courtney. *MacArthur: His Rendezvous with History*. New York: Alfred Knopf, 1956.

Whitson, William W. *The Chinese High Command: A History of Communist Military Politics, 1927–1971*. New York: Praeger, 1973.

Wu Ruilin. "Report to Chairman Mao on the Accomplishment of the Engineering Corps [During the Korean War]." *Junshi Shilin* [Studies of military history] 6 (1993): 25–27.

Wu Xiuquan. *Huiyi yu Huainian* [Remembering and cherishing the memory]. Beijing: Central University of the Party Press, 1991.

———. *Zai Waijiaobu Banian de Jingli, January 1950–October 1958* [My eight-year experiences in the Ministry of Foreign Affairs: January 1950–October 1958]. Beijing: World Knowledge Press, 1983.

Xiao Hua. *Jianku Suiyue* [Those difficult years]. Shanghai: PLA Art Press, 1983.

Xiao Jianning. "An Analysis of the U.S. Policy Toward China on the Eve of the Outbreak of the Korean War." *Dangshi Yanjiu* [Studies of CCP history] 6 (1987): 173.

Xiao Jinguang. *Xiao Jinguang Huiyilu* [Memoirs of Xiao Jinguang]. Beijing: PLA Press, 1987.

Xia Yan. "From Hong Kong to Shanghai." *Renmin Wenxue* [People's literature] 315 (1988): 46–47.

Xia Zhennan. "On the Relationship Between War and Politics." *Mao Zedong Sixiang Yanjiu* [Studies of Mao Zedong thought] 3 (1987): 48–49.

Xie Yixian. *Zhongguo Waijiao Shi:1949–1979* [Chinese diplomatic history: 1949–1979]. Zhengzhou: Henan People's Press, 1988.

Xinhuo Liaoyuan Editorial Division. *Jiefangjun Jiangling Zhuan* [The chronicle of PLA senior generals]. Vol. 1. Beijing: PLA Press, 1984.

———. *Jiefangjun Jiangling Zhuan*. Vol. 3. Beijing: PLA Press, 1986.

———. *Jiefangjun Jiangling Zhuan*. Vol. 7. Beijing: PLA Press, 1988.

Xiong Huayuan. "Zhou Enlai's Secret Visit to the Soviet Union Right Before China's Entry in the War to Resist U.S. Aggression and Aid Korea." *Dang de Wenxian* [CCP documents and materials] 3 (1994): 83–87.

Xue Qi. "An Important Strategic Decision of the CPV Command." *Dangshi Yanjiu* [Studies of CCP history] 5 (1985): 60–61.

Xu Peilan and Zheng Pengfei. *Chen Geng Jiangjun Zhuan* [Biography of General Chen Geng]. Beijing: PLA Press, 1988.

Xu Xiangqian. *Lishi de Huigu* [Remember the history]. Vol. 2. Beijing: PLA Press, 1987.

Xu Yan. *Diyici Jiaoliang: Kangmei Yuanchao Zhanzheng de Lishi Huigu yu Fansi* [The first encounter: Historical retrospection and review of the War to Resist U.S. Aggression and Aid Korea]. Beijing: Chinese Radio and Television Press, 1990.

Yang Chaoquan. *Zhongchao Guanxi Shi Lunwen Ji* [Collection of essays on the history of Sino-Korean relations]. Beijing: World Knowledge Press, 1986.

Yang Chengwu. "A Call on Chairman Mao." *Dangshi Yanjiu yu Jiaoxue* [Study and teaching on the party's history] 5 (1990): 49–53.

———. "The Entry of the 66th Army into the Korean War." *Dangshi Yanjiu yu Jiaoxue* 2 (1990): 55–58.

———. "On the Eve and After the Tianjin Conference." *Dangshi Yanjiu yu Jiaoxue* 3 (1990): 56–60.

———. "Preparing for Going to Battle." *Dangshi Yanjiu yu Jiaoxue* 4 (1990): 45–48.

———. *Xin de Shiming* [A new mission]. Beijing: Zhuoyue Press, 1989.

Yang Dezhi. *Weile Heping* [For the sake of peace]. Beijing: Long March Press, 1987.

Yan Shixin. "A Glorious Example of Patriotism and Internationalism: New Development of Political Work in the War to Resist U.S. Aggression and Aid Korea." *Dangshi Yanjiu* [Studies of CCP history] 6 (1984): 37.

Yan Wei, ed. *Zhongguo Renmin Jiefangjun Wu Da Yezhan Budui Fazhan Shilue* [A short history of the development of PLA's five field armies]. Beijing: PLA Press, 1987.

Yao Xu. *Cong Yalujiang dao Banmendian* [From the Yalu River to Panmunjom]. Beijing: People's Press, 1985.

———. "Peng Dehuai's Contribution to the War to Resist the US and Aid Korea." *Danshi Yanjiu Ziliao* [Studies and materials of the party history] 1 (1982): 2–12.

———. "A Wise Decision Making in the War to Resist the US and Assist Korea." *Dangshi Yanjiu* [Studies of CCP history] 5 (1980): 5–14.

Ye Fei. *Ye Fei Huiyilu* [Ye Fei memoirs]. Bejing: PLA Press, 1988.

Ye Yumeng. *Heixue: Chubing Chaoxian Kangmei Yuanchao Lishi Jishi* [The black snow: Historical records of Chinese military intervention in Korea]. Beijing: Writers' Press, 1989.

———. *Hanjiang Xue* [The blood of the Han River]. Beijing: Daily Economy Press, 1990.

Yi Yun. "When Was the People's Air Force Established." *Junshi Lishi* [Military history] 1 (1990): 55.

Zaloga, Steven J. "The Russians in MIG Alley." *Air Force Magazine* 74 (February 1991): 76.

Zhai Qiang. *The Dragon, the Lion, and the Eagle: Chinese-British-American Relations, 1949–1958*. Kent, Ohio: Kent State University Press, 1994.

Zhai Zhihai and Hao Yufan. "China's Decision to Enter the Korean War: History Revisited." *China Quarterly* 121 (March 1990): 94–115.

Zhang Baijia. "Comments on the Seminar on the History of Sino-American Relations, 1945–1955." *Lishi Yanjiu* [Historical studies] 3 (1987): 34–53.

Zhang Ding and Zhang Bing. *Lingxiu Shenbian de Junshi Gaocan* [The senior staff by the leaders' side]. Chengdu: University of Electronic Science Press, 1993.

Zhang Jing and Yao Yanjin. *Jiji Fangyu Zhanglue Qian Shuo* [An introduction to an active defense strategy]. Beijing: PLA Press, 1985.

Zhang Pingkai. *Peng Dehuai Shuaishi Yuanchao* [Peng Dehuai led the troops in the War to Resist U.S. Aggression and Aid Korea]. Shenyang: Liaoning People's Press, 1989.

Zhang Shu Guang. *Deterrence and Strategic Culture: Chinese-American Confrontations, 1949–1958*. Ithaca: Cornell University Press, 1992.

Zhang Xi. *Peng Dehuai Shouming Shuaishi Kangmei Yuanchao de Qianqian Houhou* [On the eve and after Peng Dehuai's appointment to direct the war of resisting America and aiding Korea]. Beijing: CCP Historical Materials Press, 1989.

Zhang Yisheng. "The Revolutionary Friendship Between Premier Zhou and Chairman Ho [Chi Minh]." *Yindu Zhina Yanjiu* [Studies of Indochina] 3 (1981): 12–25.

Zhao Yongtian and Zhang Xi. "The Book *Heixue* Is Seriously Faulty." *Junshi Lishi* [Military history] 6 (1989): 42.

Zhiyuanjun Yingxiong Zhuan [The chronicle of the CPV heroes]. Vol. 1. Beijing: People's Literature Press, 1956.

Zhonggong Zhongyang Nanjingju [The Nanjing bureau of the CCP Central Committee]. Beijing: CCP History Press, 1990.

Zhonghua Renmin Gongheguo Duiwai Guanxi Wenjian Ji: 1949–1950 [A collection of documents of foreign relations of the PRC]. Vol. 1. Beijing: World Knowledge Press, 1957.

Zhonghua Renmin Gongheguo Duiwai Guanxi Wenjian Ji:1951–1953 [A collection of documents of foreign relations of the PRC]. Vol. 2. Beijing: World Knowledge Press, 1958.

Zhongmei Guanxi Ziliao Huibian [A collection of materials concerning Chinese-American relations]. Beijing: World Knowledge Press, 1957.

Zhou Enlai. *Zhou Enlai Tongyi Zhanxian Wenxuan* [Selected works of Zhou Enlai on the united front]. Beijing: People's Press, 1984.

———. *Zhou Enlai Shuxin Xuanji* [Selected telegrams and letters of Zhou Enlai]. Beijing: Central Archives and Manuscripts Press, 1988.

———. *Zhou Enlai Waijiao Wenxuan* [Selected diplomatic documents of Zhou Enlai]. Beijing: People's Press, 1990.

———. *Zhou Enlai Xuanji* [Selected works of Zhou Enlai]. Vol. 2. Beijing: Central Archives and Manuscripts Press, 1984.

Zhou Yizhi and Qu Aiguo. "Chen Geng and the Vietnamese Border Campaign of 1950." *Ren Wu* [Biographical studies] 3 (1993): 42–55.

Zhu De. *Zhu De Xuanji* [Selected works of Zhu De]. Anhui: People's Press, 1983.

Zhu Tunshi. "Liu Shaoqi's Visit to the Soviet Union in 1949." *Dang de Wenxian* [CCP documents and materials] 3 (1989): 65–75.

INDEX